Echoes of a Native Land

*Peasant children selling mushrooms at the
Sergiyevskoye manor*

ECHOES OF
A NATIVE LAND

Two Centuries of a Russian Village

Serge Schmemann

LITTLE, BROWN AND COMPANY

A *Little, Brown* Book

First published in the United States by
Alfred A. Knopf, 1997
First published in Great Britain by
Little, Brown and Company, 1997

A CIP catalogue record for this book
is available from the British Library.

ISBN 0 316 64138 3

Printed and bound in Great Britain
by Clays Ltd, St Ives plc

Little, Brown and Company (UK)
Brettenham House
Lancaster Place
London WC2E 7EN

To my wife and my mother,
and to the memory of my father

И, пыль веков от хартий отряхнув,
Правдивые сказанья перепишет,
Да ведают потомки православных
Земли родной минувшую судьбу.

And, shaking from the scrolls the dust of ages,
He will transcribe these truthful sayings
So that descendants of Orthodox men will know
The bygone fortunes of their native land.

Pimen's monologue from *Boris Godunov*,
by Alexander Pushkin

Contents

Echoes of a Native Land

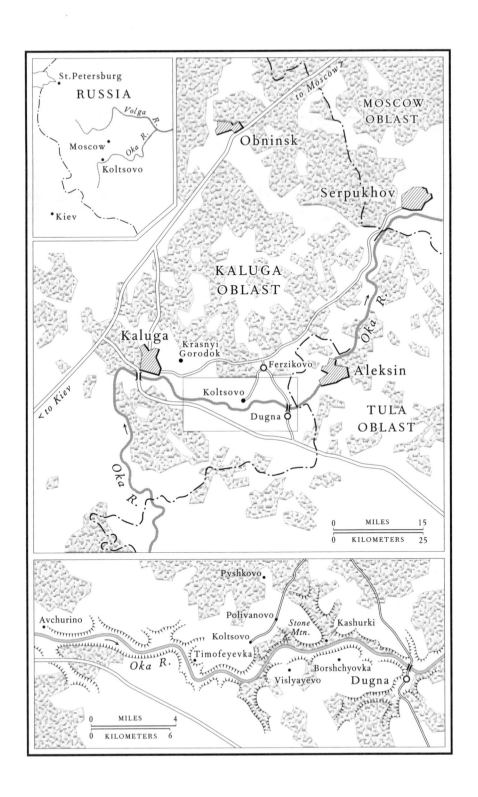

St.Petersburg

RUSSIA

Volga R.

Oka R.

Moscow

Koltsovo

Kiev

to Moscow

MOSCOW
OBLAST

Obninsk

Serpukhov

KALUGA
OBLAST

Oka R.

Kaluga

Krasnyi
Gorodok

Ferzikovo

Aleksin

Koltsovo

< to Kiev

Dugna

TULA
OBLAST

Oka R.

MILES		15
0		

KILOMETERS		25
0		

Pyshkovo

Avchurino

Polivanovo

Stone
Mtn.

Kashurki

Koltsovo

Oka R.

Timofeyevka

Borshchyovka

Vislyayevo

Dugna

MILES		4
0		

KILOMETERS		6
0		

I

A Corner of Russia

This is the story of a Russian village, known at different times over its three centuries of recorded history as Goryainovo, Karovo, Sergiyevskoye, and now Koltsovo. It lies by the Oka River in the ancient Russian heartland, 90 miles south of Moscow, near the city of Kaluga. It is a village to which I was originally drawn because before the Russian Revolution it had been part of an estate owned by my mother's family. But the Soviet government's long refusal to let me go there turned my curiosity into a mission. I finally reached Koltsovo only when Communist rule began to wane. I came to know the people; I immersed myself in the local lore; I even bought a log house there. Koltsovo became my little corner of Russia—my entry into the charm, beauty, and romance of that vast northern land, and also its backwardness, cruelty, and suffering.

I first arrived in Russia with my family in 1980, but ten years passed before I reached the village. By then the stern ideological taboos of the Soviet era were lifting, and people in the village were starting to lose their fear of talking to foreigners. Gradually, they opened up their memories and their history: how the women fooled the German occupiers who wanted to chop down the stately larches of the Alley of Love, how the old drunk Prokhor Fomichyov took the church apart after the war to trade bricks for vodka. Some went further back and remembered how in the thirties the Bolsheviks sent industrious peasants into exile and herded the rest into collectives. A retired teacher even remembered how before the revolution the peasants would stop to listen to the great "silver bell" at the church, and how village girls would gape at the bows and smocks of the young mistresses on their way to Sunday worship. The people talked about the present, too—about how youths left the village as soon as they finished school, and only the old people and the drunks stayed on; how the love child of the albino accountant was beaten to death by his son in a drunken brawl; how nobody knew what to make of the new "democracy"; how the collective farm was selling off cattle to pay its mounting debts while the director built himself a big new house.

The first person I met in the village was Lev Vasilievich Savitsky, the retired head of an orphanage that had operated there after the war, and a staunch Communist. He told me how a KGB agent had come out there a few years earlier because some foreign correspondent was trying to visit Koltsovo, claiming that his ancestors came from there. Lev Vasilievich said the agent and the village leaders concluded that the place was too rundown to show a foreign reporter, that he would only write how things had gotten worse under the Communists. And so I learned at last the real reason I had been barred so long from Koltsovo. When I told Lev Vasilievich that I was that inquisitive reporter, he fell silent, and for a while he eyed me with suspicion and unease.

Lev Vasilievich told me that the manor house had burned down in 1923, and all that remained of the old estate was a gutted bell tower, a crumbling stable, and the former parish school. The school had been a teachers' training institute after the revolution and an orphanage after the war; it was now a weekend "rest base" for workers from the giant turbine works in Kaluga, 25 miles to the west. The village and the lands were eventually formed into a *kolkhoz*, or Soviet collective farm, named Suvorov after the eighteenth-century Russian military commander. The *kolkhoz* produced milk and meat, though mostly it gobbled up government subsidies without ever turning a kopek of profit. After the Soviet Union collapsed and the collective farms were officially freed of tight government controls, the Suvorov Kolkhoz changed its name to the Koltsovo Agricultural Association and began gobbling up bank loans instead of government credits.

But on my first visit, that was not what I wanted to know. I wanted only to see beauty and romance, to walk where my ancestors had walked, to catch the echoes of a native land. It was the height of summer, I was in Russia on a brief visit, freedom was coming to the land, and the place was beautiful—a timeless Russian landscape of birches, winding rivers, log houses, and vast expanses. Lev

The gutted bell tower and the former parish school.

Vasilievich's grandson, Roma, his patched pants rolled up Tom Sawyer–style, led me to the places my own grandfather had so lovingly described: the old park planted two hundred years ago with ordered rows of linden trees; the lane of soaring larches known as the Alley of Love, which led past the Round Meadow, a low hill deliberately left wild for honeybees; the icy "Robbers' Spring," whose waters my grandfather had tapped for the house; the steep descent through the oaks and birches of the Zaraza forest, which abruptly opened onto a stunning vista of the Oka River winding through lush flood meadows, bluffs, and forests of birch.

In the evening, I sat under an apple tree outside Lev Vasilievich's house, blissfully drinking in the old stories and gossip with my hot tea. The laughter of children playing in the unpaved street mingled with the summer din of frogs, crickets, and birds. I felt I had been here before, on a glorious day just like this one, a century earlier, which my grandfather Sergei Osorgin described in his memoirs:

> In the summer, the windows all open, evening tea would be set on the terrace, and my sister Maria and I would sit on the steps, listening as Mama played my favorite nocturne of Chopin, and the evening bells would be ringing: It is already dark, only a pale-yellow streak remains in the western sky, the continuous thin trill of a small frog rises from the pond by the barn, and from the nearby village of Goryainovo wafts a peasant song, "Oh you day, this my day, finish quickly. . . ." I'm happy, totally happy, but I long for something even more wonderful . . . the sweet, romantic sadness of Chopin, what music! and how Mama plays! The watery trill sounds on, the stars of the Big Dipper grow brighter, the strong aroma of roses, sweet peas, and mignonettes, "Oh you day, this my day, finish quickly. . . ." My God, I thank You that all this was, and that it all still lives in my soul.

It was my grandfather's description of a youth spent here that first prompted me to search for this corner of Russia. When I finally gained access to it I learned that all the extraordinary resources of the world's first police state had failed to eradicate the past. It lived on behind the imposed ideological formulas and slogans, clandestine little truths cautiously stored in closed archives and in the deep recesses of people's memories.

In Koltsovo, the premier repository was Alexandra Nikitichna Trunin. In her seventies when I met her, Alexandra Nikitichna had settled in Koltsovo after the war to work in the orphanage. Her background as a history teacher soon combined with her boundless curiosity to establish her as the unchallenged authority on local lore—what the Russians call a *krayeved,* literally "knower of the region." In the 1960s, Alexandra Nikitichna set up a one-room museum in what was then the orphanage, filling it with photos, poems, and letters from local people who had made a mark in Soviet society. An ardent and honest Communist for most of her life, she earnestly rejoiced in Soviet triumphs and achievements. But there were also things that Alexandra Nikitichna kept to herself—things that could not be put in her museum.

Also in the sixties, workers dismantling a chimney of the burned-down manor house found an urn full of letters and photos, presumably concealed there by the Osorgins, my mother's family, before they were expelled. There were letters from "the boys at the front" and a postcard from one of the girls to her mother about a suitor she could not shake off. The letters circulated in the village and disappeared, Alexandra Nikitichna said. Only a few photos survived—cracked and faded snapshots of ladies in long gowns and children in a field. In the seventies, Alexandra Nikitichna's brother was secretly scanning Western shortwave radio broadcasts (a risky but common enterprise in those days) and came upon an interview with an Osorgin in Paris, talking about Sergiyevskoye. He understood that the discussion was of the former estate in Koltsovo and told his sister. In the informal seminars she held on local lore, however, Alexandra Nikitichna toed the official line, that the former landowners had been rapacious feudal exploiters.

Not all prerevolutionary history was taboo, however. If little was said about the Osorgins, everybody knew about the man who had owned these lands before them, General Kar: a certified villain of Russian history. According to the prevailing legend, Kar was a cruel Englishman in the service of Empress Catherine the Great who was banished to this estate by her for abandoning his command and fleeing before the armies of the rebellious peasant Pugachev. Alexander Pushkin, Russia's greatest poet, immortalized Kar's infamy in his history of the rebellion, and centuries of local embellishments turned the general into a truly evil figure. Exiled to his estate here, it was said, Kar used a barrel of ill-gotten gold to build himself a grand mansion modeled on an English fort. Then he had his serfs burrow a tunnel to the Oka River so he could escape if any of his many enemies came after him. All the serfs who worked on the tunnel disappeared, it was said, and when some local boys found the tunnel in the 1920s, they claimed to have seen crucified skeletons inside. According to Pushkin, Kar met an appropriate end—he was torn apart by enraged serfs. Then his devout and long-suffering widow, a princess born, built a beautiful church on the estate to expiate his sins.

Local legend did not stop there. Kar's estate was eventually inherited by his son Sergei, a sadistic wastrel who was supposed to have taken his pleasure with peasant girls and then killed them and dumped their bodies in the forest. This was why, Alexandra Nikitichna told me, the forest was called Zaraza—Contagion. Sergei went on to lose the estate in a game of cards to Mikhail Gerasimovich Osorgin, a military man who went mad on his very first visit to the property when he realized that Kar's pious mother was buried in the estate church, and so Sergei Kar had in effect gambled away his own mother! A few years ago, Alexandra Nikitichna said, workers digging on the site of the old church came upon a skeleton draped in fine black cloth, with precious rings on

*The grand mansion at Sergiyevskoye, modeled on an
English fort.*

the bones of the fingers. The rings disappeared, and local kids were caught
playing soccer with the skull.

Of course, there was a buried treasure. Sometime in the 1960s, Alexandra
Nikitichna said, a man arrived with two beautiful daughters and settled in the
abandoned stable, in the linden park. Every night he dug in the park; then one
day they were gone, leaving behind an unfilled hole. Who he was, or what he
found, nobody ever learned.

Alas, when I began to research the history of the place I often found that the
facts did not measure up to the legend. It turned out that General Kar was of
Scottish, not English, descent and he was probably less a coward than a victim
of court intrigue. The forest was named Zaraza not because of decomposing
maidens but after an archaic meaning of the word, "steep and uneven ground,"
which it certainly is. But what is truth? The facts of history? The version the
Bolsheviks imposed? Or the legends that live among people? In the Soviet
Union, "history" as science always bore the stigma of ideology, while the legends at least had the dignity of age.

* * *

What is true is that after Mikhail Gerasimovich Osorgin took over the estate, three generations of Osorgins were raised on it and formed an almost mystical bond with their Sergiyevskoye, the name by which they knew it. My grandfather Sergei Mikhailovich was the second son of the last owner of Sergiyevskoye. Born in 1888, he spent his childhood there. Many years and changes later, bent over with asthma but still full of humor and life, in a New York City apartment overlooking the George Washington Bridge, he took out his vintage Russian typewriter and began to write.

"My dear children and grandchildren, I would like to pass on to you the memories of my youth, those distant years of complete happiness." He wrote of the passing seasons and the holidays, of the harmony of a patrimonial order and the beauties of his corner of Russia: "It is a known fact that the finest stretch of our beautiful Oka River is between Kaluga and Serpukhov, where the river flows east and both banks are high, and therefore especially lovely. We lived right at that part of the Oka."

A romantic, witty, and deeply religious man, Sergei elevated the Sergiyevskoye of his childhood to a universal, spiritual home: "I believe everyone in a hidden corner of his soul has his Sergiyevskoye. For the Russians it does not have to be in Russia, or in France for the French: It is there where the soul first opened to receive God's universe and its marvels. . . . Sergiyevskoye is that lost worldly paradise for which we all yearn, believing that if only we could return, we would be happy."

I grew up with his stories. Before I was old enough to know there was a Soviet Union, I knew there was a Sergiyevskoye, where the forests were full of mushrooms, where my grandfather and his brother built a gravity pump to bring water from the Robbers' Spring, where wolves roamed hungry in the winter, and where one autumn day my grandfather shot himself in the leg with a pistol and the local doctor tried (and failed) to dig the bullet out with sewing scissors.

Of course, it is to be expected that people who have had a happy childhood will describe in loving terms the place where they grew up. But Sergiyevskoye appeared to exercise a similar spell on many others. One worldly cousin of the Osorgins, Prince Grigory Nikolayevich Trubetskoi, Tsar Nicholas II's ambassador to Serbia, came to Sergiyevskoye a few months after the 1917 revolution. The visit had a powerful emotional effect on him, perhaps because he had just completed a harrowing trip from southern Russia through areas ravaged by civil war, and found himself in an idyllic remnant of a world he knew was dying.

"All who came to them [the Osorgins] felt themselves in Sergiyevskoye as in a spiritual sanatorium," he wrote. "The Osorgins loved their Sergiyevskoye as one can only love a close and precious being, and they especially cherished its natural beauty, which indeed was marvelous."

The Bolsheviks had already taken away the Osorgins' lands and part of their house, but they stayed on, believing they would be safe among friendly and loyal peasants until the revolutionary blight passed. People from the village continued coming to them as before, for medical treatment and for counsel, and later to bring them flour, sugar, kerosene, and cloth.

Trubetskoi painted a remarkably affectionate portrait of the family—close, loving, musical, devout, generous, cultured—and of a corner of Russia that remained harmonious and good even as the rest of the country was falling apart.

One of my grandfather's four sisters, Maria Osorgin, was talented at drawing, and she recorded one of the last summers at Sergiyevskoye in a series of exquisite silhouette sketches. The cook still discusses the menu with the mistress; the girls work in the garden in their long skirts and straw hats; my grandfather, stooped by a wound he suffered on the German front, sits in a wicker chair alongside his childhood love and fiancée, Sonia Gagarin; his father, Mikhail Mikhailovich, still the *barin*—the local lord—strolls about magisterially with his patriarchal beard, his large dog, Neron, and his pants rolled up country-style.

Trubetskoi, a member of an aristocratic family prominent in the final chapter of tsarist Russia for its ardently liberal politics, found the last communion with the old order wrenching: "Will I really never see Sergiyevskoye again? I cannot accept this. Such corners of Russian life, so suffused with an Old Testament, loving, and firm spirit, must not disappear. How many simple people found in Sergiyevskoye a beacon of light for moral and material assistance! How many of their friends and acquaintances, having suffered in life's storms, found respite at the hospitable hearth of this peaceful cloister! The loss of such refuges, however few they may be—or perhaps because they are so few— would be an irreplaceable one for Russia. The only consolation is that the good seeds sowed for so many years in this fertile soil cannot perish without trace: 'their memory is from generation to generation.' "

The Osorgins' life at Sergiyevskoye came to an end in October 1918. The local Bolshevik committee came and ordered them out, giving them three days to leave. Old servants and peasants were overcome by grief and confusion. The night watchman complained that "from so much thinking I've developed a nymphozoria in my head"—a condition no one had heard of until then. The bailiff fussed about, preparing provisions and arranging for six young men to accompany the Osorgins all the way to Moscow. Arseny Georgievich Dzhu-verovich, a Serbian doctor who had worked at Sergiyevskoye throughout the war in the hospital the Osorgins had set up in their house, came out from Kaluga to say goodbye and wept like a child. The last surviving former serf, the 90-year-old laundress, stood with tears streaming down her face, making the sign of the cross over the departing masters.

One of those who watched them leave was a village girl named Ninochka. Many years later, as Nina Georgievna Semyonova, a staunch Communist and the retired administrator of the Moskva Hotel, near the Kremlin, she heard about me and wrote for me a series of poignant vignettes from her youth. One was a description of the exit of the last *barin* of Sergiyevskoye, whom she knew as "Mikhal Mikhalych." She calls the village Karovo, as it was called under General Kar and continued to be called by local people.

> The last time I saw Osorgin was when he was leaving Karovo after the confiscation of his estate and all his property and land. I remember the day of the departure. . . . He stood on one of the large carts on which their things were piled, those things they were allowed to keep. Mikhal Mikha-lych spoke briefly to those gathered around the carts. I was thirteen then, and of all the things he said, I remember only this: He pointed to every-thing around him—the central building, the wings, the linden grove—and he said, "I knew this would come to pass. Take care of all this: You can have an excellent sanatorium or health facility here. Use it, but don't destroy it." In those days manor houses were burning everywhere. Many women were crying.
>
> He bowed in all four directions and said, "Forgive me if ever I hurt or insulted any of you." The *muzhiks* [peasant men] furtively wiped away their tears. Finally the carts left. Many accompanied them to the Ferzikovo station and helped load the train.

What happened afterward to the Osorgins was a typical saga of the "for-mer people," as the Soviets branded the gentry, officials, and intelligentsia of the fallen tsarist order. The old Osorgins and three of their children moved to a Moscow suburb now called Peredelkino, where their house became a center for other relatives who had stayed on in Soviet Russia. After their youngest son, Georgy, was executed by the Bolsheviks, the Osorgins quit Russia and made their way to Paris with three of their daughters and Georgy's widow. There, in 1931, they were reunited with their three other children, including my grandfather Sergei. He had gone to southern Russia after the revolution, got married, then left for Europe with his wife when the White armies collapsed. My mother was born in Baden-Baden, Germany, in 1923.

Nina Semyonova died in 1993. I never did meet her, though I have many pages of the notes she wrote for me, in a hand that grew progressively larger as her eyesight failed, all diligently bound, signed, and dated. She came from a different universe than my grandfather, but her Koltsovo was as dear to her as his Sergiyevskoye was to him. "My motherland, Russia, is the same for us all," she wrote. "But every one of us has a small corner of this vast motherland, our own motherland, where we were born, raised, went to school, and set off on life's path. My motherland is the village of Koltsovo."

What happened to Sergiyevskoye after the revolution was also in many ways typical. In the first flush of building a brave new world, the Bolsheviks took over the big house for a farming commune, the First Workers' Agricultural Commune. On May 1, 1923, the manor house burned to the ground. The official version was that it had been destroyed by "reactionary bandits and former White Guardsmen." In fact it was torched by resentful peasants while the *kommunary,* the original settlers of the new communes, were out celebrating May Day. The peasants hated the commune for appropriating the best lands and equipment.

The subsequent history of the village was the usual one of collectivization, purges, and the steady consolidation of Communist control. Eight of the fifteen families living on the ridge around Alexandra Nikitichna's house were expelled in the 1930s, when the Bolsheviks cracked down on the *kulaks* ("fists"), the category into which they put any relatively successful or independent peasant. God knows, none of them here were rich; at most, they had an extra horse or a small grinding stone of their own. Some villagers were drawn into the apparatus of coercion. Misha Tinyakov joined the Cheka—the precursor of the KGB—and came to arrest the Osorgins after the revolution. Seryozha Golubkov joined the Cheka out of patriotism. Naïvely, he protested against the ruthless methods the "Chekisty" were using; soon after, his family was told that he had shot himself.

The last manager of the Osorgin estate, Nikolai Shutov, was run out of town by the Bolsheviks as a *kulak,* though a grandson and two granddaughters were still living in the village when I last visited. One of the granddaughters, now in her eighties, proudly described to me his end. It was during the war. He was walking down the road, an old man, when some German soldiers came by and tried to take away his carved walking stick as a souvenir. When he resisted, they smashed in his skull with his stick.

As elsewhere in the former Soviet Union, World War II is the proudest memory among the old people. Most of the men fought at the front, and the women labored in the rear. Koltsovo briefly fell under German occupation and afterward served as a base for a Red Army air reconnaissance unit. After the war, an orphanage was opened in the old parish school for the countless children left homeless by the war. Alexandra Nikitichna recalled the problems that arose when the young waifs began reaching adolescence. Not knowing how else to keep the boys and girls in line, she took the boys aside and explained that if they kissed a girl, one thing would inevitably lead to the next, and the boy would be shot. And what, I asked her, did you tell the girls? Alexandra Nikitichna hid her face in embarrassed laughter: "That if they got pregnant, *I* would be shot." Some of her former wards—foster children, really—still write her, she said.

Even in the best of times, life was never easy here. Much of what seemed quaint to me on my first visit was bondage to the villagers. The huge wood-burning stoves required endless work; drinking water had to be carried in buckets from a distant tap; the outhouse stood in ankle-deep mud; and potatoes, beets, and onions were grown not as a hobby but to survive. The road to Koltsovo was paved only after my first visit in 1990; before that, there were days when the nearest town, Ferzikovo, 8 miles away, could be reached only by tractor. The village shop was always bare, and even the most basic staple—the dark, crumbly bread—was not always available. When it was, it quickly sold out, because under the convoluted Soviet pricing system, it was cheaper to feed hogs and chickens with baked bread than with grain. Alcoholism, the most widespread Russian disease, was rampant.

This backwardness stemmed as much from Soviet policy as from tradition. Alexei Andreyevich Lagutin, Alexandra Nikitichna's gentle and hard-working neighbor, hated to see good land go to waste, so when he settled in Koltsovo he plowed some empty land by the river and planted it with melons, tomatoes, cabbage, and other fruits and vegetables, which he shared freely with the orphanage and other villagers. The *kolkhoz* director was furious: "What are you trying to do, show us up?" He made Alexei Andreyevich an electrician. Alexei Andreyevich never learned to curb his love of growing things, however. His kitchen garden was a marvel of productivity, and whenever I came I would find him experimenting with some new variety.

Once, while his wife was preparing tea, he pulled out an old concertina, ran his stubby, work-hardened fingers over the keys, and magically drew a romantic tango from the vintage bellows. In the first years after the war, he recalled, when it seemed as if their "bright future" was finally within reach, the villagers would gather in the linden park on a summer night and dance to his music. They were all gone now, he said; only he and his wife and a few others remained. Alexei Andreyevich fell ill in the spring of 1994. His wife got word to me to bring some medicine, but I arrived too late. He had been impossible in the clinic, she said, insisting that she bring fresh food for all the patients. She also said he repeatedly asked after me: "When is Sergei Alexandrovich coming? I have so much more I need to tell him."

When I arrived in Moscow with my wife, Mary, and our three children in 1980 as a correspondent for the Associated Press, I intended, when time permitted, to find the Sergiyevskoye that my grandfather had described and to rummage a bit in my roots. Nothing more. There were more pressing concerns: our arrival coincided with the Soviet invasion of Afghanistan, the exile of Andrei Sakharov to Gorky, the boycott of the Olympic games, and the physical disintegration of Brezhnev and the other old men who ruled in the Kremlin. Before the year was out, I had joined *The New York Times* and gone to New York for several months of orientation. I never expected that reaching Sergiyevskoye would prove so difficult, or that it would evolve into a mission, or that ten years would pass before I got there.

We arrived in Moscow on the overnight train from Helsinki on New Year's Day 1980. We were coming from the peak of summer in Johannesburg, my last assignment, into one of the coldest Russian winters of our stay. Because of the holiday, the train was almost empty. We had only one can of Finnish beer with which to celebrate, and we sat spellbound by the fairy-tale Russian landscape unfolding under a full moon: log cabins buried in the silver snow, birches glowing blue in the moonlight, a horizon that stretched across two continents.

Both Mary and I are of Russian descent and speak the language. The Russian Revolution was too distant from us for us to share the sense of loss of our grandparents, yet we are old enough to have been nurtured on stories of witch's huts on chicken legs, the rich harmonies of the Russian Orthodox liturgy, and the sepia-toned photographs of great-grandmothers in lacy white gowns and whiskered great-uncles in uniforms arrayed under the lilacs of a country house. Our grandparents had read *Robinson Crusoe* to us in Russian in the hayfields along Lac Labelle, in Quebec, where many Russian relatives spent their summers because the birches, mushrooms, and long summer evenings reminded them of Russia.

My parents were both born after the revolution and outside Russia, and both studied in France. But they were raised as Russians, and we spoke Russian at home. Their parents came from the two different poles of old Russia, St. Petersburg and Moscow. My father's grandfather Nikolai Schmemann was a typical senior civil servant, down to a Baltic-German heritage and a disdain for everything outside of St. Petersburg. A jurist, he rose through the ranks of the Ministry of Justice to seats on the two highest institutions of the tsarist state, the Senate and the Council of State. At the time of the revolution, he held the second-highest grade in the civil service, Actual Privy Counselor.

His service record (*formulyarnyi spisok*) in the Central State Historical Archive in St. Petersburg traces an irreproachable career until the final entry, this one in smudged ink, dated December 14, 1917: "By decree of the Provisional Government of Workers and Peasants," Nikolai Schmemann was "to be considered dismissed as of 25 October 1917, with the right to apply according to established procedures for a pension." He was 67 and would spend his last days in Paris.

I know little of Nikolai's roots, only that his father, Eduard, was a Lutheran and came from Courland (now Latvia). The law in tsarist Russia was that if one parent was Russian Orthodox, the children had to be, so Nikolai Eduardovich himself and his eight children all grew up in the Russian Church, the main instrument of assimilation in the tsarist empire. My grandfather and father both regarded themselves exclusively as Russians.

Nikolai's sixth child, born in 1893, was my grandfather, Dmitry Nikolayevich Schmemann. He was studying law at the University of St. Petersburg when the First World War intervened. Assuming, as many did at the time, that the war would be brief, he interrupted his studies to join the army. He fought as an infantry officer until the end of the war, then served with General Nikolai Yudenich's anti-Bolshevik army until it was pushed back into Estonia and disbanded in 1920. There Dmitry was joined by his wife, Anna Tikhonovna (née Shishkov), and it was there that, on September 13, 1921, she gave birth to twins, Andrei and Alexander. The latter was my father. From Estonia, the family moved first to Yugoslavia and then to France, where I was born in 1945. In June 1951, my father, a Russian Orthodox priest, theologian, and church historian, was invited to teach at an Orthodox seminary in New York City, and we crossed on the grand *Queen Mary*. I was six, and my sisters seven and three.

My mother's family, the Osorgins, were typical members of the provincial gentry whose spiritual capital was Moscow. Rooted in their rural estate, bound into a large extended family by elaborate (and embarrassingly close) intermarriage, they focused their lives on family, church, coziness, and archaic patriarchal principles. If they served the state, it was as reserve guard officers, provincial magistrates, marshals of nobility, or governors, and they held the courtiers, bureaucrats, and Germans of St. Petersburg in disdain.

Even in Paris, where my parents met and married, Petersburgers and Muscovites had their separate colonies. The Schmemanns attended the elegant Cathedral of St. Alexander Nevsky on the rue Daru, near the Arc de Triomphe, which was frequented by former imperial ministers and surviving Romanovs. The Osorgins attended a tiny wooden chapel built by their extended family in the Parisian suburb of Clamart. After my great-grandfather Mikhail Mikhailovich Osorgin left Russia in 1931, he was ordained a priest and served the family parish, where all the singers and parishioners were his relatives. Nevertheless, my two grandfathers became close friends, and after my father was ordained a priest in 1948, his first parish was the Clamart chapel.

My father's writings and broadcasts were well known to the liberal intelligentsia of the Soviet Union (a fact that played an important role in the reception I received when I arrived in Moscow as a reporter). He studied at the St. Serge Theological Institute in Paris, where the theological revival that had begun inside Russia with the Church Council of 1917 continued under instructors like Father Sergei Bulgakov, a Marxist economist who became a renowned philosopher and theologian. In the United States, my father became the dean of St. Vladimir's Orthodox Theological Seminary, located first in New York City and then just north of the city in Yonkers.

My father plunged into American life with ardor. He became the guiding spirit in forming the Orthodox Church in America out of parishes founded by nineteenth-century emigrants from Russia; he crisscrossed the country on lecture tours; he devoured American politics, literature, and hot dogs with equal zest. Though at home in Russian literature and culture, and more articulate in Russian than most Soviets I met, he was never an émigré consumed by the pursuit of a lost way of life. On the contrary; his mission as a theologian and educator was to free his church from ethnic limitations. He was a man who lived in the present, as fascinated by what was happening in Soviet Russia as he was by the Camelot of John F. Kennedy and the French literary journals that piled up in our bathroom.

At the same time, he never rejected a spiritual responsibility for Russia. His books were translated and circulated secretly as *samizdat* in Russia. The last one he wrote he dedicated to Russia. From the early 1950s until his death on December 13, 1983, he made weekly broadcasts to the Soviet Union in Russian

Alexander Schmemann.

over Radio Liberty, the main series on spiritual themes, another on culture. Radio Liberty and all other foreign broadcasts were heavily jammed in the Soviet Union, but Russians knew how to tune to the edge of the frequency, or they tape-recorded the broadcasts outside major cities, where jamming was not effective. In all, my father made more than three thousand 15-minute radio broadcasts, which, along with his writings, gave him considerable renown among the Russian intelligentsia. When Alexander Solzhenitsyn was expelled from Russia in 1972, my father was one of the first people he sought out. In one of his letters smuggled to the West before his expulsion, Solzhenitsyn had written:

> For a long time I listened with spiritual pleasure over *Svoboda* [Radio Liberty] on Sunday nights, when it was possible, to the sermons of the "doctor of philosophy, Father Alexander" (the last name was never given), and

I marveled at how genuine, contemporary, and elevated was his art: Not one note of falsehood, not a millimeter of strain, without the false tribute to mandatory form or ritual, when the listener becomes a bit embarrassed for the preacher or for himself—always a strong, profound thought and profound feeling.

Many Russians today still tell me how important the broadcasts were to them, providing reassurance that Russian culture and spirituality had not been snuffed out by Communism.

In a talk my father gave in New York in 1977, which was published in the March 1994 issue of the journal *Novyi mir* in Moscow, he described the peculiar state of his generation of Russian emigrants:

"Emigrant" presupposes that a person emigrated from somewhere, but I, for one, never emigrated from anywhere: I was already born an "emigrant." And although I have never been in Russia, I have always, since I was conscious, identified myself unequivocally as a Russian—and this despite my having lived almost thirty years in France and accepted French culture as something very close, almost my own; and in recent years, I can say without exaggeration that I not only have embraced America, but have dedicated the major part of my life's work to it.

So it was that I arrived in Russia with a claim and a reference. Dissidents usually assumed that an American reporter who spoke relatively fluent Russian had to be a spy, but they were more willing to trust the son of "Father Alexander"— though some still wondered why the authorities would allow the son of such an émigré into the country.

Moscow during the Soviet era was one of the most exciting and challenging assignments for a foreign correspondent. The constant struggle with a police state bent on controlling every strand of information made every scoop a major triumph. Add to that the James Bond–like tingle of KGB bugs and tails, the pleasure of an evening spent talking with Russian friends in a steamy kitchen, a beat that stretched across 11 time zones, and a steady appetite for Soviet stories among American readers, and it is no surprise that generations of Moscow correspondents left Russia forever marked. Nobody should regret the passing of the Communist order, no matter how ugly the sequel; but many an old Moscow hand will confess to a furtive nostalgia for the great story that was the Soviet Union.

The time may come when people will not believe that there really was such a place. The Soviet Union was about as close to a totalitarian state as I hope any nation will ever come; if the system softened in its last decades, it was from fatigue, senility, corruption, and inefficiency, not for lack of meanness and paranoia. Though the West lionized Mikhail Gorbachev as a reformer, it is important to remember that his goal was not to destroy or even humanize Communism, but to perpetuate it. The difference between him and his predecessors was that he thought he could modernize Communism without undermining it, while they had no illusions that it could be sustained by anything other than force.

By the time we came in the 1980s, what made the system appalling was no longer raw terror, which had abated after Stalin's death, or even the silly pretensions of Communist propaganda, which nobody took seriously. It was that the Soviet state had turned every normal function of a society into its antithesis: It created a politics emptied of choice, a religion devoid of faith, a culture stripped of individuality and creativity, and an economy that barred initiative. Its constitution guaranteed every conceivable right and then subordinated them all to the whim of the Party. It compelled people to shout "peace and friendship," and laced its borders with barbed wire and mines. It spouted superlatives but glorified mediocrity, crushing anyone who dared to rise above the faceless mass—even if it was only to grow fine cabbages, as Alexei Lagutin had done.

I remember watching a Soviet space launch on television. The ground controller asked the cosmonauts how they felt. The response from the heavens was pure Sovietese: "There is no deviation from the norm." That was the ideal: no deviation from the norm. The Soviet state asked not for faith—true believers were the first to be devoured in the purges—but for submission to the Soviet norm. The state imposed its control by a crude combination of brutal force and all-embracing paternalism. The state was the source of every necessity and nicety: If you acquiesced, it granted you a roof, a holiday at the Black Sea, health care in a special clinic, and monthly parcels of sausage and butter. If you were a loyal writer, it published your books in respectable numbers; if you were a cooperative scientist, it disseminated your research. And if you never deviated from the norm, it might even honor you with the ultimate perk—a trip abroad; first to a "friendly" country like Bulgaria, then perhaps to the Third World, and ultimately, if you stayed unswervingly loyal, to Paris or New York.

If, however, you resisted, the perquisites vanished, the doors closed, and friends were warned to look away. And if you persisted in your defiance, the state unsheathed the full arsenal of its vengeance: persecution, labor camps, exile, insane asylums, death.

The relatively small number of overt dissidents did not mean that everyone else supported the regime. Rather, it reflected the extraordinarily high cost of defiance, plus a habit of compromise nurtured from infancy and a longing for a measure of repose after seven decades of unremitting repression, hunger, war, and shortages.

At the inauguration of Boris Yeltsin as president of Russia in June 1991, the Patriarch of the Russian Orthodox Church, Alexiy II, spoke what I thought was an important truth:

> You have assumed responsibility for a country that is gravely ill. Three generations grew up under conditions deadly to any inclination or enthusiasm for work. At first, people were dissuaded from spiritual labor, from prayer; then they were dissuaded from thought, from the desire to discern the truth independently. And finally, deliberately or accidentally, people were dissuaded from work, diligence, and initiative.

The Russian Church was among the most prominent victims of this illness. When Communism fell, many leaders of the Church—the Patriarch among them—were charged with reaching their positions only by colluding with the state, and even of serving as agents of the KGB. Some probably did. From the outset, the Communists targeted religion as one of their major enemies, and an entire department of the KGB, the Council on Religious Affairs, existed solely to combat and control religion.

I came to know the Patriarch and interviewed him about these allegations, and I am convinced he was never an agent of the KGB. He undoubtedly had a secret code name, as any man of his prominence would. And as a bishop, he was locked in constant maneuvering and compromise with the vigilant state, since otherwise there could be no services, no ordinations—nothing. Critics will say that he and other hierarchs were seduced by the gilt and pomp of their position, that they should have opted for martyrdom. Perhaps; but the Patriarch was convinced that the Church could not go underground and remain the Church, that it was his sacred duty to preserve the essence of the faith against the atheist assault, whatever the cost.

After the incredible war that the Communists waged on religion, I believe he viewed every liturgy, every church kept open, every baptism, as a victory. And they were. The position of the state toward religion was unambiguous: It was an enemy to be destroyed. So while every compromise the Church made could be condemned, as they are by the critics, as betrayal, by the same logic, every concession the state made was a victory for the Church.

I have interjected the Patriarch and the Church here because the moral dilemma they faced was the same as that confronted by any person or institution which deviated from the Soviet norm. They had to compromise to survive, and the overwhelming majority opted to survive. I cannot sit in judgment over any of them, especially when the state often succeeded in making the alternative at least as morally dubious. What would you do if you were a bishop of the Church and were given a choice between signing a letter of loyalty to the state and having a thousand priests executed in the Gulag?

I also always bore in mind something told to me by the author and dissident Lydia Chukovskaya, daughter of Russia's favorite children's author, Kornei Chukovsky. Soon after my arrival in the Soviet Union I went to meet her at the writers' colony of Peredelkino, where she maintained her father's house as a museum (she sheltered Solzhenitsyn there in the weeks before his expulsion). It was a time when Western correspondents did a lot of reporting on dissidents and "refuseniks" (Soviet Jews who applied to emigrate and were refused), and as I prepared to take my leave, she said: "Don't neglect the dissidents, but never forget that there are two hundred and sixty-eight million other people who wake up every morning in this country who are not dissidents."

I often wondered where I would have stood if fate had not sent my grandparents abroad. I suspect I would have been among the 268 million. The essayist Ian Buruma spoke also for me when he wrote of his reaction to all the legends of heroic resistance to the Nazis that he had heard as a youth in Holland:

> I read piles of books about Dutch Maquis and silk-scarfed RAF pilots. And yet the frightened man who betrayed to save his life, who looked the other way, who grasped the wrong horn of a hideous moral dilemma, interested me more than the hero. This is no doubt partly because I fear I would be much like that frightened man myself. And partly because, to me, failure is more typical of the human condition than heroism.

Besides, eschewing active dissidence was not tantamount to moral failure. Far from it. I knew many people, and knew of thousands more, who were forever quietly defying the system in countless little ways: secretly circulating *samizdat* literature, writing poetry "for the drawer," privately baptizing their children, studying Hebrew, protecting friends. It was enough for the authorities to relax their vigilance for a moment for someone to take advantage of the opening thus provided. One of the boldest magazines in the late 1960s, to take but one obscure example, was the weekly television guide; alongside the schedule of television programs it printed over the course of several weeks some astoundingly bold literary works. The reason was that the guide fell under the responsibility of the television censors, not the periodicals watchdogs, and the former never thought to check the schedule. It was, of course, found out and closed in short order.

Whether a foreign correspondent wanted to or not, he or she was automatically thrown into the politics of dissent. On the one side was a police state that abhorred international censure; on the other were dissidents and refuseniks, whose goal was to make their plight known in the West. So we foreign reporters, and especially those of us who spoke Russian, became a lifeline to the dissidents and a bane to the state. Not a week passed without a meeting in front of the Obraztsov Puppet Theater across from our housing compound to pick up some "declaration" from a dissident who earnestly believed that its publication would be a sensation; or a meeting with Elena Bonner at 3:00 a.m., when the police quit guarding her door for a few hours; or a walk in the park with Natan Sharansky's brother Leonid; or a vigil outside a courtroom where some dissident was being found guilty; or a drive to a distant suburb, with the KGB tailing me in a tan Zhiguli, to hear another woeful tale of injustice, desperation, and anger.

Editors and journalism reviews would declare sometimes that we spent too much time on the dissidents. They were probably right. But what choice did we have? To explain to a desperate woman from Siberia that her imprisoned husband was not a "good story"? To give the KGB the satisfaction of turning away from their victims? To feign neutrality in a country that treated us as a dangerous enemy? I had no pretensions to heroism, but neither did many of the people who fell afoul of the system. Usually they simply had a conscience that finally forced them to speak out; and when they did, could we who were free to tell the rest of the world about them just turn away?

I remember how Bella Akhmadulina, a popular lyric poet, marched into the infamous Serbsky psychiatric clinic—where dissidents were "treated" for a condition the KGB called "lazy schizophrenia," whose major symptom was resistance to Soviet rule—and demanded that her friend and fellow poet Dmitry Prigov be released. Prigov, a noted eccentric, had been picked up for pasting up slips of paper with pseudo-Soviet slogans on them. Release him, Akhmadulina demanded, "or there's no telling what I will do." "What will you do?" asked an anxious KGB officer, aware of both Bella's popularity and her reputation for unorthodox behavior. "There's no telling," she repeated. She really did not know, she told me later, but the authorities recognized that she was poised at that limit beyond which she could become their public and permanent enemy. That was how many people became dissidents. The KGB released Prigov.

In those days, foreigners in Moscow spent a lot of time debating whether the Soviet state was a linear descendant of the tsarist empire or the perverse new fruit of a totalitarian ideology. Those who took the former position drew on the huge body of prerevolutionary works describing corrupt officials, dissembling peasants, chronic inefficiency, alcoholism, despotism, and all the other ills so evident in the Soviet Union. They liked to quote from the nineteenth-century Marquis de Custine, who marveled at the xenophobia, misery, and filth he encountered ("The Russians of all classes conspire with an unanimity which is extraordinary in causing duplicity to triumph among themselves"). Those in the latter camp countered by pointing to the great achievements of Russian culture, to the worldliness of the Russian elite and the spirituality and wisdom of the peasantry, and joined with Solzhenitsyn in depicting Communism as an alien ideology that had put an otherwise noble and promising nation in thrall. In this scenario, Russia was on a slow but essentially proper historical track when a brutal Bolshevik coup d'état, facilitated by disastrous wars in Japan and Europe, aborted its development.

For myself, I find it difficult to accept that a totalitarian system was the inevitable successor to Russian autocracy. With or without the revolution, the Russia of absolute monarchy, landed gentry, and a disenfranchised peasantry was rapidly drawing to a close. At the rate the old gentry landowners were selling off their lands, there would have been no large agricultural estates left by the 1920s. The monarchy was already in decline long before the First World War touched off the social and political upheavals that forced Tsar Nicholas II to abdicate. We can only speculate how things might have developed had Nicholas not brought Russia into the war, or had he stepped down earlier. As it was, no class or structures were capable of halting the slide into chaos, and it was into this vacuum that the Bolsheviks eventually stepped, gaining power far more by deceit, ruthlessness, and terror than by persuasion. Even then, the enterprising spirit that briefly flourished in the seven years of the "New Economic Policy," 1921 to 1928, when for tactical reasons the Bolsheviks briefly loosened their grip on the economy, offered a glimpse of an alternative scenario.

At the same time, it is undeniable that the Soviet Union was created by Russians, and reflected distinctly Russian illusions and flaws. The Communists would not have succeeded if their raw material had been leavened more liberally with democracy, tolerance, and understanding of the rule of law. The only authorities ever known to the Russian peasants and workers, who made up the bulk of the population, were force and religion. When the tsarist world collapsed, it was the Bolsheviks who had the strongest force and the most compelling new religion. Certainly the radical intelligentsia bears the greatest responsibility for what followed, but I believe that all Russians must ask what it was in their history, culture, and character that allowed to be created a state that inflicted so much suffering on the world and on themselves.

However obsolete, inequitable, or impractical that old world may have been, whatever we may think of the monarchy and the society that supported it, its abrupt collapse tragically severed Russians from their roots and culture and denied Russia whatever chance it might have had for normal development. It was not only an elite or an economic system that the Communists dismantled and replaced; an entire world was laid waste. Industry and initiative were shackled; religion was crushed; art was perverted; the land was raped.

The greatest blow, I believe, was to the *derevnya*—the village, the countryside. The *derevnya*, with its peasant villages, rural estates, churches, and monasteries, was the heart of Russia, the ultimate source of its culture and character. "Petersburg is our parlor, Moscow our maids' room, the countryside our study," wrote Pushkin, and, indeed, there would have been no Pushkin without his rural Mikhailovskoye, no Tolstoy without his Yasnaya Polyana, no Turgenev without his Spasskoye-Lyutovinovo. The countryside figures centrally in much of nineteenth-century Russian literature, whether as a life-giving force at Levin's estate in *Anna Karenina* or a stifling prison in *Uncle Vanya,* a writer's canvas in Turgenev's *Hunter's Sketches* or a vehicle for social commentary in Gogol's *Dead Souls* and Goncharov's *Oblomov*. This tradition was continued into the Soviet era by the so-called village writers, nationalists like Rasputin and Belov who used the devastation of the traditional village as a metaphor for the destruction of Russia.

Returning after an absence of fifty years to the place where Sergiyevskoye had once stood, to the village where she had witnessed the exit of the old landowners and dreamed of building a new world, Nina Semyonova found a wasteland:

> After many years I returned to my native village, in 1967. I could not believe my eyes, it was so run-down. The linden park was in terrible condition, almost half the trees were chopped down. Only a half-destroyed bell

tower remained of the church. The cross was broken (probably shot out)—by the way, it was not gold, as we believed in our childhood, but thick glass. The pine lane was almost gone—more exactly, the left row had ceased to exist. I couldn't recognize my native Karovo-Koltsovo. Several villages had united into the Suvorov Kolkhoz, but I didn't see one person toiling in the fields. From Ferzikovo to Koltsovo, my heart ached at what I saw. The fine paths on which we once ran barefoot were gone. The roads were also gone. The last hope rested with the Kaluga Turbine Works [successor to the old school] which took over in such horrible condition what was once one of the prettiest corners of Kaluga Province. The peasants abandoned it—mostly the children. They left for the cities. Only sick and old people stayed.

History has passed a sufficiently harsh verdict that we need not judge who of them was right and who was wrong; the Osorgins, with their archaic patrimonial world view, or Nina Semyonova, with her faith in a brave new world. In the end, they both lost their birthright, their illusions, and their bearings, as well as the spiritual and cultural heritage my grandfather called Sergiyevskoye.

2

Dreamy Syerzh

Until September 25, 1992, when President Boris Yeltsin finally opened all of Russia to travel by foreigners, huge tracts of the Soviet Union—almost a quarter of its territory—were closed to foreigners. These included 21 major cities, among them Gorky (now Nizhny Novgorod), Sverdlovsk (now Ekaterinburg), Vladivostok, Omsk, and Tomsk; all border areas; and the entire length of the rivers Yenisei and Lena. Furthermore, many open areas were effectively closed because the only access to them was via roads or airports that were off-limits. Broad rings around Moscow and Leningrad were closed except for major through highways. Driving to Sheremetievo International Airport in Moscow or the Trinity–St. Sergei Monastery at Zagorsk, for example, required transiting a closed zone in which it was forbidden to stop the car. Some cities, like Kaluga, could be reached by rail but not by car. Others were "closed" cities, where planes refueled while foreigners were herded into separate lounges.

For any travel outside Moscow, foreign reporters were required to submit a "travel notice" to the press section of the Foreign Ministry at least 24 hours before leaving Moscow. Further, we were required to buy our tickets through a special agency, the UPDK (Directorate for the Diplomatic Corps), an organization that oversaw all aspects of the lives of resident foreigners in the Soviet Union, from providing apartments and maids through arranging schools and even supplying scraggly fir trees at Christmas. It was impossible to elude these controls. Sales clerks for air and train tickets always asked for identification, and if they spotted a foreigner they would immediately call the KGB. Cars owned or used by foreigners had special license plates that the traffic police, the GAI (State Automobile Inspectorate), would check at their regular posts on every major road against lists of foreigners' cars authorized to travel that road on that day. And if the GAI was napping, there was always the KGB tail. I remember the first time we spotted him, when I pulled off the road to Vladimir for a picnic with my family. There was nowhere to hide, and we watched him sitting on the hood of his car a half mile away, watching us. We never got used to the surveillance.

The region of Koltsovo/Sergiyevskoye was technically "open," as were the two nearest cities, Kaluga and Tula. But the highway to Kaluga was closed (it went past some military industrial sites), as were large zones around Tula (for the same reason). The first time I went to Kaluga, in the spring of 1980, it was by *elektrichka*, the local electric trains that fan out from Moscow in a radius of about 60 miles. The train was packed, as usual, with people who descended on Moscow daily to scour the capital for basic goods—shoes, clothes, housewares, food. (A joke at the time went: "What is long and green and smells of sausage?" Answer: "The *elektrichka* to Kaluga.") An average of about 2 million outsiders were said to invade Moscow daily, mostly women who arrived early in the morning and left late in the evening, dead-tired and loaded down with sacks of goods. I went on a spring evening, and the fatigue was almost tangible: the five bulky women wedged around me with their heavy sacks fell instantly into a deep sleep.

On this first visit to Kaluga, my purpose was simply to get a glimpse of provincial Russia. I liked the town. Though badly bruised by neglect and ringed with shoddy Soviet-style apartment blocks, the city sits dramatically on a high bluff over the Oka River, and its old center is a lovely ensemble of eighteenth-century churches, ornate merchants' mansions, and a covered marketplace built in a style somewhere between Asiatic and Gothic.

In November 1984, when I went back to Kaluga specifically to search for Sergiyevskoye, transition was in the air. Leonid Brezhnev and Yuri Andropov had died, and Konstantin Chernenko was clearly about to, but the old guard was hanging tough. The big guessing game was whether Andropov's young protégé Mikhail Gorbachev would get in.

I had only a vague idea then where Sergiyevskoye was located. I didn't know it had been renamed Koltsovo, and Soviet maps showed no Sergiyevskoye,

Goryainovo, or Karovo, all the former names I knew. I had a general idea of its location from my grandfather's memoirs: He said it was on the river, 12 versts (1 verst is about two-thirds of a mile) from the railroad station of Ferzikovo, which was still there, as were some streams and villages he named.

I had made several formal requests to the Ministry of Foreign Affairs for permission to explore the general area, but each time they waited until the last moment and then refused me. I was told either that I had not been specific enough in my reasons for wanting to go there, or that I could not drive there, or that it was closed "temporarily," or for "technical reasons," but the answer was always no. They never elaborated, and I knew it was useless to ask. These decisions were made by the KGB, and the Foreign Ministry Press Section was merely the courier. I assumed at the time that they simply didn't want a correspondent mucking about on back roads, or didn't want me to see soldiers harvesting potatoes, or that it was simply easier to say no than to figure out what I was up to. But the more they refused me, the more my interest was piqued. I figured that if I could at least pinpoint the location, I could eliminate one excuse they had given for keeping me away.

In Kaluga, I headed first for the regional museum, a fixture of every Russian provincial city. Kaluga's was housed in a striking prerevolutionary merchant's mansion, with giant wrought-iron lanterns flanking the entrance. A sign on the door read: "Closed: Sanitary Day" (every Soviet museum usually designated one day a month for cleaning). Next I tried the library, a large modern building. A helpful librarian showed me several books from a special section on local history, but none had anything about Sergiyevskoye. In parting, she gave me a Kaluga lapel pin and a Finnish ballpoint pen.

The next morning I walked back to the museum, but it was still closed. I decided to try to see the director anyway and walked in through the service entrance, startling several people sitting in her office. I explained who I was and what I wanted, and the director, a middle-aged woman, said there was a man in Kaluga who was interested in the history of former estates. He was a city architect named Alexander Sergeyevich Dneprovsky, and, indeed, he knew where the Osorgin estate had been. He promised to take me there by riverboat in the spring; in the meantime, he offered to dig up some materials. I thanked the director and went back to Moscow. A few weeks later, Dneprovsky appeared in Moscow with a copy of an article from a 1910 issue of a periodical called *Kaluga Antiquity* (Kaluzhskaya starina). It was about the Sergiyevskoye church, and it marked my first concrete discovery about Sergiyevskoye in the Soviet Union.

To my great surprise, these first tentative attempts to locate Sergiyevskoye drew a furious reaction from the state. On March 26, 1985—two weeks after Chernenko died and Gorbachev came to power, opening the final chapter in Soviet history—the newspaper *Trud*, organ of the Soviet "trade union movement" and, with a daily run of 12 million, the largest Soviet daily, attacked me with rare malice. And to make sure the word reached anyone I had contacted or might try to, the article was reprinted in the local Kaluga and Ferzikovo newspapers.

The headline was "Warning: Diversion! DREAMY SYERZH." The Russian word for "dreamy," *dremuchiy,* is commonly used in fairy tales to describe a deep and dark forest, and "Syerzh" is a transliteration of the English/French form "Serge," as opposed to the common Russian "Sergei." The effect was to portray me as someone alien, almost unreal. The article, which carried the byline "I. Viktorov," rehashed several previous attacks on my stories and then got

The article as it appeared in Trud, *March 26, 1985.*

to the heart of the matter: "You read the screeds of the head of the *New York Times* bureau and you begin wondering: Why has this American Schmemann such a powerful nostalgia for tsarist Russia?"

What followed was rich in venom and sarcasm. It struck at my mother by name and noted that both my brothers-in-law were clergymen: "Now it will probably become clearer why the American journalist, on arriving in Moscow, began rushing among the gold cupolas, putting up candles and crawling out of his skin to be accepted as one of us." Curiously, the article made no mention of my father. Perhaps the KGB wanted to avoid giving him or his weekly broadcasts any publicity; more likely, he "belonged" to a different unit of the KGB, and the press watchdogs had no license to infringe on others' turf.

"Currently, Schmemann is in a sweat trying to locate his maternal Osorgin estate in Kaluga Oblast," the article continued. "Why? Maybe he hopes that delighted peasants will greet him with songs and bread and salt, and, bowing low, will rejoice at the return of the heir of the lands and will offer a thanksgiving service at the church in his honor?"

After a bit more in this vein, the article recalled an earlier attack on me over a story about Odessa, in which I had written of the Odessan knack for wisecracks:

> At the Privoz market in Odessa, Schmemann heard the question, "How much for your sore throat?" But he did not hear another: Syerzh, how much for your "reveries"? But then he does not conceal that his income is high, and his expenditures in the USSR are minimal. It's only that the work is a bit hard . . . and Mister Schmemann begins to complain about the vacuum that forms around him when he leaves on his regular "hunt for sensation." It probably does not enter his head that aside from a natural allergy to White-Guardist offshoots, the Soviet people have always had a hostile revulsion for those who spread ignorant drivel. Among American readers as well.

It was pretty nasty stuff. Colleagues in the Western press corps called to express solidarity, while Soviet translators of *The New York Times* watched carefully for my reaction, obviously under instructions from the KGB. My reaction was mixed. It was obviously unpleasant and worrisome to be bashed so harshly and publicly, especially when it was not entirely clear why, but such attacks were also a mark of honor in those days, a confirmation that a correspondent had scored a hit. I especially appreciated the last line about American readers, which I assumed was added by censors so that the article would not appear to acknowledge that many Russians knew of my "ignorant drivel" over the Voice of America's shortwave broadcasts, which they were not supposed to listen to. Yet I had never written about Sergiyevskoye; I had not even been there. Why such malice? Why give me such publicity?

The author of the article, I. Viktorov, died before the advent of glasnost, so I never got to ask him. In any case, it is unlikely even he knew. He was from Kaluga, and his colleagues said he was a decent man and a decent journalist, and that he probably received a direct order from the KGB, complete with the facts he was to use and the conclusions he was to draw. The embroidery was left to him. I have to acknowledge that it was pretty imaginative stuff, especially given the probability that he never actually read any of my articles, and that he had no idea who I was. Sarcasm and indignation drip from the page, and to this day some of my friends still call me *dremuchiy Syerzh*.

It was not the first time I had been attacked in the press, but I never really understood why they chose to attack the stories they did. The targets were all articles I considered sympathetic, or at worst innocuous. One was a standard little feature about Soviet names, how after the revolution it was fashionable to give children names like Melsor (for Marx-Engels-Lenin-Stalin-October-Revolution) and how Russians were now returning to traditional names like Vladimir and Oleg. Another was a rather favorable survey of new Soviet films; another, a feature on Odessa and the disappearance of its Jewish heritage.

Press attacks were not random. It was the KGB, not the newspaper itself, that decided whom to attack, when, and how. The first article assailing me appeared in *Literary Gazette* soon after I began working for *The New York Times* and was written by Iona Andronov, a notorious hatchet man for the KGB. Among other things, he wrote that he had known my parents "before they emigrated to Israel," and that they were sorely disappointed in me. I took that, among other things, as an attempt to disassociate me from my father. At about the same time, I learned that someone was going around "warning" acquaintances of mine that Father Alexander Schmemann had only two children, both daughters, and so I could not be his son.

Andronov also wrote the second attack. I was unabashedly satisfied to learn soon after that Italy had denied him a visa to attend a film festival there because of his alleged KGB links. Years later, Andronov surfaced as a successful candidate in the first multiparty elections to the Congress of Peoples' Deputies (the one Yeltsin eventually dispersed with tanks, on October 4, 1993). Andronov ran in the tourist town of Suzdal in the guise of a "democrat." (In the first elections organized by Gorbachev in which more than one candidate could run for each seat, every candidate claimed to be a "democrat," though many were in fact hardline Communists.) In the Congress, however, Andronov showed his true colors, viciously attacking Yeltsin, the real democrats, and any foreign-policy initiative that appeared conciliatory to the West. During one heated debate, Andronov turned on Sergei Kovalyov, a gentle dissident who had spent many years in prison for his firm adherence to human rights, and snarled, "I despise you." Invariably natty in a tweed jacket and aviator glasses, and fluent in English, Andronov unfortunately became a favorite commentator among American television reporters.

The *dremuchiy Syerzh* article was different from the earlier attacks in that it was considerably more personal, and it assailed me for a private and, one would think, harmless rummaging in my roots. What it had in common with the earlier attacks was that it depicted me as a hostile emigrant masquerading behind professions of sympathy and kinship. (I got that to the end—the last time from an elderly and embittered woman who, on learning that my forebears had left Russia at the time of the revolution, nodded bitterly and said, "That explains why you support Yeltsin. You want him to destroy our country.")

In the official Soviet worldview, all expatriate Russians were by definition enemies. When emigrants came to the Soviet Union as foreign diplomats, businessmen, or reporters, the Soviets made a point of not using the normal Russian spelling of their names (like calling me "Syerzh" instead of "Sergei"), and demonstratively giving them the title "Mister," which has a sarcastic ring in Russian. So to the Soviets, I was a foe not so much because I was especially bold (I was not), or because I made any dramatic revelations (alas, I had not), or because I actively tried to undermine the system (it didn't need my help), but simply because in that system it was enough to be a Western reporter with Russian roots to be perceived as an enemy. I did try to puncture whatever official lies I could, of course, and I have reason to believe that in some measure I managed to get under the skin of the state. The Soviets certainly got to me. I have a list of 13 license plate numbers of cars that followed me around Moscow only in my last years, when I became increasingly sensitive to them. It was usually the same car, a tan Zhiguli sedan, and the most common number was и-0396-мж. I'd know immediately whenever Elena Bonner, Andrei Sakharov's wife, was in town from Gorky, where he was under house arrest, because a Volga sedan (number 6145ммв) would take up the chase. The surveillance was not particularly subtle. When I walked out of our compound on the ring road, Sadovo-Samotechnaya, the policeman on duty would dart into his booth and grab the phone, and и-0396-мж, parked on the sidewalk two blocks up the street, would quickly drive up. Toward the end I started playing all sorts of silly games—making illegal U-turns, leaving and returning without going anywhere, parking the car and taking a subway—just to goad them. One time I thought I had lost them, when suddenly I saw in my rear-view mirror the tan "Zhig" racing toward me. I darted into a left-turn lane, and when it passed me I saw an antenna sticking out the window and a goon in the back seat with headphones on. They must have planted an electronic tailing device in my car. It was a horrible feeling, and when my first tour ended I left with immense relief. After we returned in 1991, I was not aware of any regular surveillance.

We used to say in those days, "Just because you're paranoid doesn't mean you're wrong." I do not claim that my case was extraordinary; I'm sure many other reporters, and foreigners generally, got the same treatment. The point is that the state placed such importance on maintaining control over the minds and souls of its people that it took the trouble to follow reporters like me, to bug our homes, to plant articles in the press. That surveillance was only a small part of a massive operation that planted inverted-umbrella jamming antennas in every city across the Soviet Union, screened every publication, isolated all foreigners in guarded compounds, controlled the use of every copying machine, bugged thousands of telephones and homes, and recruited thousands of informers.

Nevertheless, I think the Soviets had a special aversion to people like me. The scorn heaped on "this American Schmemann" and the talk of my "high income" were meant to trigger a reaction often noted by foreigners: Russians' resentment of other Russians better off than they. It was not the first time I had encountered this attitude. In fact, one of my earliest stories out of Russia for *The New York Times* was about just that. I had arrived with my family in Suzdal, a small town 3 hours' drive from Moscow with a bewildering accumulation of churches and monasteries, and after we checked into the big Intourist complex, we went to the restaurant. The place was almost empty, but a sturdy maître d' in the requisite ill-fitting suit blocked our passage rudely at the door: "No places." "But I have three hungry kids, and we've been traveling all day," I implored in Russian. He turned his back. I went off in search of the director of the complex to find out what this was about. She was horrified: "Please forgive us! I'm afraid he mistook you for a Russian!" She was apologizing because a Russian had "mistaken" me for one of his own.

I thought at the time that this must be a Soviet trait, because I had not encountered it among any of the expatriate Russians I knew. Later I was stunned to read the following comment in the memoirs of my great-grandfather Mikhail

Mikhailovich Osorgin, describing his service as a local magistrate: "Already then I was clearly aware that a peasant is civil and considerate only to someone in his bracket. But he will peck to death anyone poorer, and will be jealous of anyone richer—and if he can safely hurt him, he will not miss a chance to do so."

In the Soviet era, there was a well-worn joke about a peasant who complains that his neighbor has a cow and he does not. "So you also want a cow?" "No, I want you to take his away." I often felt that Moscow's irritation with the Solidarity movement in Poland was rooted in such feelings—the Russians saw the Poles as fellow Slavs putting on airs. Alas, these instincts have become even more glaring in post-Communist Russia, where those without money brand all the newly rich as "mafia," while those who have money flaunt it with breathtaking garishness, racing through Moscow in opulent sedans with a total contempt for pedestrians and slower-moving cars.

But even if such attitudes explain the tone of the *Trud* article, they do not explain why the article was ordered to begin with. One possible purpose was simply to scare away people who might want to help me in my search for Sergiyevskoye. Word of my visit undoubtedly spread quickly through the provincial grapevine of Kaluga—rumors spread with remarkable speed in the Soviet Union—and anyone who had read it would think twice about meeting with me.

There was something more. Soviet officials, who generally had no inkling of the world outside, tended to view foreigners in their own image. Since Soviet reporters in Washington were expected to bash away at American policies and problems, it was presumed that American reporters in the Soviet Union had been "instructed" to do the same. And so, when I wrote about politics, economic shortages, or cold-war disputes, the worst that might happen was that Tass, the official Soviet news agency, would run a halfhearted item accusing the *Times* of "raising a hullabaloo" (a favorite word), which really meant, "There goes that hopeless bourgeois press again." That was what foreign correspondents were expected to do. When, however, I ventured off the prescribed course and took a stab at Russian customs, culture, or history—or, even worse, when I intimated a shared heritage—then I was invading a jealously guarded monopoly on the soul of the people.

I don't think the Kremlin cared so much what people in New York read. The problem was that most of what American correspondents wrote, and certainly everything about the society and culture, was played back to the Soviet Union over the shortwave broadcasts of Voice of America or Radio Liberty. Huge numbers of people listened to these stations, and they had an enormous impact.

Over seven decades of Communism, Russians developed an extraordinary ear for forbidden truths, and these circulated with uncanny speed. A political joke born over breakfast in Moscow might well reach dinner tables in Vladivostok.

The irony is that in trying to counter our work, the KGB only made things worse for itself. People who might have missed the broadcast learned from their own press that there was an American "Syerzh" with roots in the Kaluga region who was worth a full page in *Trud*. I made many a new acquaintance on the strength of such publicity. When I finally met Natan Sharansky in Israel, he remembered reading an attack on me in *Pravda* while in a Soviet prison and concluding that whoever I was, I must be doing a good job to evoke such irritation.

In any case, the *Trud* article awakened me to the determination of the authorities not to let me reach Sergiyevskoye. Several years passed before I learned the true scope of that effort. In 1990, a good friend in Moscow, Kathleen Burton Murrell, an expert on old Russian architecture who spent many years in Moscow with her husband, a British Foreign Office Kremlinologist, paid a visit to the Kaluga museum and met the director. They were talking about how times had changed, and the director told Kathy how several years earlier the KGB had ordered her to close the museum while a nosy American reporter was in town.

In July 1994, on a visit to Koltsovo, I got to talking with Mikhail Ivanovich Golubkov, who for a long time had served as chairman of the village council and was now living there in retirement. The Golubkovs had deep roots in the village. Just before the revolution, Mikhail Ivanovich's grandfather, Yakov Golubkov, had been among the first peasants to attempt independent farming. Mikhail Golubkov had lived and worked all his life on the Suvorov Kolkhoz, save for service on the Romanian front during World War II. A simple and cautious man, he still felt uneasy talking to a foreigner. So he spoke of everything except what I wanted to learn: he spoke of his adventures as a veterinarian during the war, of a recent operation he had had in Kaluga for a small hernia during which the anesthesiologist had struck a nerve and left him temporarily paralyzed. I listened and sympathized (especially with the lamentably typical story of Russian medical treatment). Then I guided him back to my question: What had happened when I first applied to come to Koltsovo?

Well, yes, they had come to check the place out, he ventured. A black Volga sedan—the basic transportation of Soviet officialdom—arrived with a couple of men. They approached him as chairman of the village council and told him an American reporter who was descended from the former landowners wanted to visit. What did he think? "I told them it was better for him not to come," Golubkov confessed. "The old house had burned down, only that gutted bell tower was left of the church, the *kolkhoz* was a mess. What would he write? That we had made a mess of his grandfather's place? What's the point? They looked around for a while and left."

Later that day, I drove to Kaluga to do some digging in the library. "I know you," said the librarian, introducing herself as Lyudmilla Vladimirovna Kalashnikov. "I was the librarian when you came many years ago. It was November 1984. I know, because I had just come back from my first trip abroad, to Finland, and I gave you my Finnish ballpoint pen. Remember? It was so unfortunate, the museum being closed and all."

She had heard about my search from other people, and we chatted amicably for a while. Finally I came to the point: Why did they block me back then? Lyudmilla Vladimirovna made a pained face: "Don't hold it against us, Sergei Alexandrovich! There was nothing malicious; we had nothing against you. It was simply that the place was so run-down, they were afraid you would write about how it had deteriorated. I mean, if you invite people to your house, you don't show them the messy rooms, you try to show them the nice rooms. That's really all there was to it." Now, as if trying to make amends, she did everything she could to help me, even arranging a permanent library card free of charge. I apologized for taking her ballpoint pen, which must have been something of a luxury in Kaluga in 1984.

I ended my first tour in Moscow in 1986 without having reached Sergiyevskoye. The last months were enormously busy. I spent a few weeks in Johannesburg in the fall, preparing for what I thought would be my next assignment. While I was away a colleague, Nicholas Daniloff, of *U.S. News & World Report,* was arrested in Moscow in retaliation for the arrest of a Soviet official in New York. (He was released when charges against the Russian were dropped.) Glasnost was gathering pace. Gorbachev and Reagan held their second summit meeting in Reykjavik, after which a major dispute erupted over what was really said. I worked on a series of farewell articles.

Shortly before our departure, I described my frustrated search for Sergiyevskoye to my good friend Evgeny (Zhenya) Popov. Zhenya was a fine writer of short stories who had been one of two members thrown out of the Writers' Union in 1979, after a group of writers had tried to publish a collection of their works independently in a "literary almanac" called *Metropol.* The twenty-three participants included most of the best-known names in the literature of the "thaw": Andrei Voznesensky, Bella Akhmadulina, Andrei Bitov,

Bulat Okudzhava, Semyon Lipkin and his wife, Inna Lisnyanskaya, Fazil Iskander, and the bard Vladimir Vysotsky. Though the collection contained nothing particularly hostile or threatening to the state, the very notion of an independent journal drew a vehement response from the KGB. The homes of many of the writers were searched, materials for the journal were seized, and the participants were haled before the union, which mounted a smear campaign in the press. In the end, Popov and Viktor Erofeyev, the two youngest members, were expelled from the union. (Despite the best efforts of the KGB, *Metropol* was published in the United States by the late Carl Proffer and his Ardis Press.)

Zhenya, a radiant, bearded Siberian with a marvelous sense of humor, a remarkably compact writing style, and incontestable integrity, was one of my closest friends in Moscow. When, at my farewell party, I told him of my quest, he became intrigued and agreed to continue it. He had one great advantage: Since being thrown out of the Writers' Union, he had held the implausible job of salesman of portraits of Soviet leaders. The work allowed him to travel freely to gather material for his stories. After quickly convincing some rural Party boss that he needed a fresh set of Politburo portraits—especially since the faces were changing so rapidly in those days—he would pull out a bottle of vodka and learn everything he could.

I left Moscow with my family in December 1986. I was supposed to take up a new assignment in South Africa, but the government there closed down the *Times* bureau in Johannesburg just when we were to arrive. After several months in limbo, I was assigned to Bonn—a twist of fate that enabled me to cover the remarkable story of the fall of the Berlin Wall and the reunification of Germany, for which I was awarded a Pulitzer Prize.

In the Soviet Union, meanwhile, the revolution launched by Gorbachev quickly gained momentum. Andrei Sakharov returned from his exile in Gorky; banned books were published; legislatures were elected; taboos were punctured; political prisoners were "rehabilitated." In 1988, I heard from Zhenya Popov. Now fully restored to the Writers' Union, his membership backdated to his first published work, he wrote that he and his wife, Svetlana, had finally reached Sergiyevskoye. Moreover, they were coming to Germany. Unsure as to whether we would get to see each other there, given the explosive events I was covering, he put his feat into writing on the train. By way of explanation, a Zaporozhets was the entry-level Soviet vehicle, a tiny, sputtering machine built in Ukraine (it is a matter of some mirth among Russians these days that the pathetic little car now ranks as an "import"); "lesser motherland" is a term used by Russians to distinguish one's birthplace from the greater motherland, which is Russia.

Posnan (Poland)

Dear Seryozha!

I begin a brief story, not sad, but momentous, about how Svetlana and I visited your lesser motherland in the former village of Sergiyevskoye (Karovo, Goryainovo), now the Suvorov Kolkhoz, village of Koltsovo.

This came to pass on the 27th of June, 1988. I must note that June was rather dry, and only thanks to this were we able to reach the appointed place. Two earlier attempts failed. On the first try, I left in my Zaporozhets, and if it had not broken down right at the start of the voyage, the trip would never have ended, since I would have become mired in Karovo mud; it was autumn. Slime.

. . . And so—it was a magnificent, hot, dry Moscow–Kaluga day. We drove through Serpukhov, Tarusa, forests, hills, ravines, the Oka was glistening. Passing a plaster statue depicting deer, we stumbled into Ferzikovo, a small, godforsaken town, where we met some *kolkhoznik babas* standing in a trailer behind a tractor, singing a song of indeterminate content.

By the Ferzikovo store called "Cultural Wares," I set about consulting with the local population on the subject of locating Sergiyevskoye, "where there was a large church and a large house."

But I kept coming upon people who either moved here recently or were young. They merely shrugged their shoulders. Only two old women, hearing me through, firmly declared that this is none other than the Rassvet *kolkhoz*. "Take the road to Dugna." I went, passing another plaster statue, this one of a woman *kolkhoznik* with a harvest in her hands.

The sun warmed us merrily. "What fine asphalt roads they have here," I said, and was immediately punished as I abruptly drove onto a stretch of incredible rocks and horrifying train tracks. I came to rest in a cloud of dust before the chairman of the Rassvet *kolkhoz* with the question, "Where, finally, is Sergiyevskoye, Karovo, Goryainovo?" The chairman asked me why I might need this information, and, learning that I was a writer, and then having studied my writer's identity document, which was kindly returned to me in March 1988, when I was reinstated in the Writers' Union, incidentally with my full writer's seniority, he told me that I had come to the totally wrong place, and that he knows Karovo, that there is a livestock farm there now, that I need to return to Ferzikovo, go past the shashlik stand, and take another road.

This we did. Through the dust, past the gypsum *kolkhoznik*, but when we decided to have a bite at the shashlik stand, administered by a Caucasus cooperative, it transpired that I had left my bag with documents, money, etc., at Rassvet.

We had to drive past the *kolkhoznik* two more times. But this time the director of Rassvet met me as a dear friend and said he had been preparing to search for me "by radio."

From Ferzikovo to Koltsovo the road goes generally uphill and presents a terrible picture of mud, as described already by N. V. Gogol. But it was DRY, and we drove on, even though local "heavy-metallists," Ferzikovo fanatics of hard rock in black leather jackets, had to push their motorcycles uphill. Go ahead and ridicule the Zaporozhets after this! This is a good, this is an ADEQUATE car. A week later I took her to Seliger Lake, where we bought a house, and the roads are the same. And, as you see, we returned. . . .

Massive, centuries-old oaks suddenly appeared on the side, a descent, another steep rise, a field with compact haystacks, and suddenly a bell tower appeared in the distance.

But the way to it through the hardened mud was barred by a neat road sign, "No Through Traffic," and I stupidly went downhill to make a detour. Coming to my senses, I drove around the sign and we finally found ourselves in Karovo. At any rate, in Koltsovo, though that is the name for a group of villages.

So there it was. We arrived in the godforsaken wilderness. The manor house was gone. There remained only mounds overgrown with nettles, parts of outbuildings. Of the church, only a half-collapsed bell tower. In the cemetery, new graves, the oldest maybe fifty years old, though there are a few fallen tombstones that look older.

The old parish school survived. An addition was built onto it, and it is now a "rest base" of some large Kaluga factory. Until 1978 it was an orphanage, whose graduates recently gathered from afar for a reunion. We descended to the Oka, had a swim. We found a timetable for ships that go between Serpukhov and Kaluga. A place of wondrous beauty! Forest, sand, water. On our return we met an old man, Savitsky, Lev Vasilievich, former director of the orphanage, pensioner. He recounted that there had been a commune in the manor house, that the house had burned down in the twenties. He said the parish school at first was the Karovo teachers' vocational school . . . that when they broke up the chimney they found an urn with letters, that there is a legend that the younger Osorgin won the estate in cards, that the park remains and from a helicopter you can see paths in the initials *M M O*, that local people are certain there is a treasure buried there, but though they've dug a lot, they've found nothing.

... On the return trip, my starter failed, but a kind tractorist gave me a push and almost without further ado I drove through Kaluga to Moscow. It was growing dark when I drove up to my house, thinking of all that I had seen today.

Zhenya
the Moscow–Cologne train
12/29/88,

P.S. We made out some faded lettering in the church:
VNIDU V DOM TVOI . . .

In July 1990, I went to Moscow on a brief assignment to cover a crucial visit by the German chancellor, Helmut Kohl, during which he finally won Gorbachev's endorsement of the reunification of Germany. As soon as Kohl left I called Zhenya, and we set off for Sergiyevskoye. This time the Foreign Ministry had no objection; more than that, the official the *Times* dealt with seemed genuinely happy that I could finally go and even asked if he might someday come with me.

I will never forget those first impressions, the first glimpse of the Oka through the birches and oaks. A small tug chugged slowly upriver, and Lev Vasilievich's grandson, Roma, stood in the shallows with his tousled hair bleached by the sun, a stalk of grass between his teeth, just as my grandfather had surely stood there, and as I might have. Songbirds raised a deafening chorus in the forest behind us. Soon the riverboat pulled up, ramming prow-first into the sandy shore to let passengers off. My grandfather wrote that when he was a student in Moscow he liked to travel the last leg of his trip home by steamboat from Tarusa, about 40 miles downriver, spending the night on the ship and rising early to take coffee on the deck as he approached Sergiyevskoye.

Then Lev Vasilievich made a surprising announcement. There was a young couple in the village who had actually been to Paris and tried to find the Osorgins, but had failed. They were very interested in the history of the place. Would we like to meet them? I suspect he had deliberately delayed this announcement to prolong his monopoly on our time.

We walked back past the rest home and the park to the village, a cluster of log cabins on a steep bluff, and knocked on the door of one of them. A slight man of about thirty, with a large beard and gentle blue eyes, opened it. I introduced us, and he rushed back to get his wife, who was napping. We walked in just as she emerged from behind a partition, drowsy with sleep, and explained who we were.

"Schmemann? Osorgin? Popov?"

Yes, yes, yes.

She began slapping herself, certain she was still asleep.

Svetlana (Sveta) Trunin was a teacher in the village school, and her husband, Alexander (Sasha), did general chores at the rest base that now occupied the former orphanage, though he was a graduate in philology of Moscow University. He was the son of Alexandra Nikitichna Trunin, the keeper of local lore, who subsequently became my good friend and invaluable guide.

Sveta's stepmother had been born in France (a complicated and fascinating story in itself), and a year earlier she had arranged for Sasha and Sveta to go to Paris. There they actually found an Osorgin, a cousin of my mother, but he was rushing off to Rome and had no time to give them. In Paris they bought several

Sasha Trunin and his daughter, Anya.

books by Alexander Schmemann, and several by Evgeny Popov, who was their favorite contemporary Russian writer. In their log house, they actually had a photograph of Popov with several other writers on the wall. And now, in this godforsaken village in which the last foreigner to set foot had been a German invader, the son of Alexander Schmemann and grandson of an Osorgin suddenly shows up with Evgeny Popov in the bearded flesh!

Our amazement was no less. Here, deep in the devastation and mud of the Russian countryside, among the ruins of a home from which my grandfather had been expelled 72 years earlier, in a village with no phones and no plumbing, in a log house still heated by the sort of huge Russian stove I thought existed only in fairy tales, we found people just back from Paris who knew all about us and were curious about the history of Sergiyevskoye. Moreover, Sasha wrote poetry, and eventually Zhenya Popov helped him publish several of his poems in *Novyi mir.*

We walked through the village, pausing here and there to chat as word spread of our presence. A group of gold-toothed women wandered by: "So you've come to buy us back, is that it? And I don't even have anything to wear in Paris!" And they exploded in laughter.

It was, as the Texas-bred ambassador to Moscow, Robert Strauss, liked to say, "all a little too *Roossian,*" and that was exactly what I wanted. After so much effort to find the place, I wanted to see its beauty, not the rusted machinery; I wanted to find a quaint old Russia with *izbas* (log cabins), babushkas, and Russian stoves, not to think of the endless toil that mere survival here required. I wanted to see the gutted bell-tower as a romantic ruin, not as a monument to a dictatorship that savaged every church, melted down every bell, smashed every icon.

But Sasha had grown up here, and unlike sentimental city slickers like me, he loved the land for what it was:

> *A cloud, a stick, it's all the same*
> *on the frail motherland . . . Calves*
> *graze on the meadow, guiltily blinking,*
> *lost in thought they scratch their horns on a log*
>
> *dropped here some time ago. In the bushes*
> *geese stroll slowly and grandly*
> *with squealing goslings; there,*
> *and wherever you can see,*

lie pieces of tractors,
combines, seeders, and harvesters.
The land appears less sick,
than sad and pitiful.

Oh homeland . . . Ugliness, beauty—
immutable neighbors.
Love alone glorifies you,
unshakable, like the childhood

that we possess and guard . . .
All else is separate.

At least the collective farm was named after Alexander Suvorov, the renowned military commander of Catherine the Great's day, instead of having one of those ridiculous Bolshevik names every other *kolkhoz* in the area carried: "Red Partisan," "Path to Socialism," "Lenin's Testament," "Activist," "15th Anniversary of October," or, my favorite, "Voluntary Labor." In most other ways the *kolkhoz* was much like every other in central Russia: a ramshackle cluster of unfinished cinderblock buildings, equipment rusting where it had been abandoned, houses that looked like listing woodpiles squatting among the squawking chickens, yapping dogs, gaping children, abandoned axles, threatening geese, vegetable gardens, woodpiles, and mud. The exceptions were a row of new houses built for families that had fled from various ethnic wars, and an elementary school, whose dozen teachers were probably the only votes Boris Yeltsin ever got in Koltsovo.

The Suvorov Kolkhoz was among the poorest in the region. The population had been shrinking steadily since World War II. Only three villages remained in the collective farm, compared with twelve right after the war. Few young people remained once they finished school, and few came back from military service. The ones who did were those who wanted nothing more from life than 200 rubles a month and vodka. There were 280 households in Koltsovo; of these, 150 were part of the *kolkhoz* and 50 were the homes of retired people. Half the men I met were drunk, and most of the others looked as if they would be if they had the wherewithal. The bus that linked Koltsovo to Ferzikovo was actually a 10-ton military truck with a cab welded onto the bed. The only public phone in the village was out of order.

Ah, but things were changing for the better now, I declared with a knowing smile to Lev Vasilievich. Having been away from the Soviet Union for several years, I shared the naïve Western conviction that everyone was happy with the spread of political and economic freedom, that people would soon get back the land, and that pride of ownership coupled with the natural force of free enterprise would make Russia prosperous and happy.

"Not a single peasant here would take land," Lev Vasilievich snarled dismissively. Back in the 1920s, when the Bolsheviks permitted that brief bloom of free enterprise known as the New Economic Policy, "each farmer had a horse and worked from dawn to dusk," he continued. "Such peasants don't exist any more. Now you'd destroy everything if you took away the *kolkhoz*. These people don't even know how to grow anything. On payday they get drunk for three days and then stay sick for two."

"Before, we produced everything we needed—barley, hemp, flax," said Lev Vasilievich's wife, Tatiana Tikhonovna. A native of Koltsovo, she recalled the now-distant time before collectivization, when everyone, young and old, worked in the fields through the summer, and the men spent the winter in Tula working in the arms factories. Despite her recent bout of pneumonia, her house was impeccable and the storerooms were filled with preserves for the winter.

"My father put whatever he earned into equipment; he never spent on himself. We had a small mill for our grain; we had two cows, two horses. Needless to say, in the thirties they wanted to *razkulachit* him." The word means literally to "de-*kulak*-ize," and refers to the brutal repression of the more industrious farmers during the collectivization campaign of the 1930s.

"They took everything. But at least we managed to convince them that we did not charge others for the use of the mill"—which the Bolsheviks condemned as economic exploitation—"so my father was not shipped off to Kazakhstan. I know only one person exiled there who survived."

The memories flowed on, now a litany of destruction. The church was the pride of the village until the Communists ordered it taken apart in the 1950s, purportedly because the brick was needed for a new barn. The only reason the bell tower still stood, with its rusted cross and weeds sprouting from between the cracked bricks, was because when Prokhor Fomichyov finally finished taking the church apart brick by brick, the old people threatened to take him apart if he touched the tower. Fomichyov swapped the brick for vodka, a hundred bricks for a liter, and drank himself to death in his house on the hill. He lay dead for several days, his head slumped among the empty bottles and his body frozen, before anyone bothered to bury him.

The Communists also ordered the *kolkhoz* to dismantle the ingenious gravity pump that my grandfather and his brothers had built to bring water to the house. Why? Because others don't have one, was their explanation. Villagers used to cut the grass around buildings and on the edges of fields as hay for their own cows, but the Communists banned that, too. Thereafter, the peasants had no choice but to steal hay from the *kolkhoz*, while shrubs and weeds grew out of control around buildings and along roads.

Naïvely, I felt compelled to challenge the villagers' sense of resignation, to argue against the belief that no change was possible. Why not take the offered land and give it a try? Why not gather that year's bountiful apple crop, which was falling and rotting on the ground, and take it to Kaluga or Moscow, where the fruit would fetch good money? Why not fix the phone line, whose tattered ends dangled from a pole?

Raising such questions, I fell into a long line of outsiders—foreign travelers, landowners, novelists, conquerors—who have alternately taken delight in Russia's rural idyll and railed at its squalor and resistance to change. Under the Communists, so-called village writers bemoaned the erosion of the "real Russian values" that the village purportedly sustained, while Marxist ideologues condemned the village as a breeding ground of superstition and reaction that was best bulldozed to make way for an agriculture organized along military lines, with brigades of workers and specialists housed in barrackslike apartment blocks waging campaigns of sowing and harvesting.

In all these great debates, the only people never consulted were the peasants, who accounted for 86 percent of the population at the time of the revolution. They were left in their squalid huts, the women toiling in the fields, the men working in the cities or serving in the army, all eking out a bare existence and concealing what they could from the rapacious landlords and bureaucrats. The emancipation of the serfs in 1861 freed the peasants from formal bondage to the land but did little to improve their lot. Half the arable land was given to landowners as their private property, the other half to communes for allocation among village families. The peasants remained official second-class citizens, with different taxation, military obligations, and laws. Whether viewed patronizingly as "little brother" or coldly as raw labor, the peasant was not an individual but a piece of a faceless *narod*, or people, which formed an adjunct of the Russian land.

One hundred thirty years before I came there, a pioneering Russian agronomist named V. Deilidovich undertook the first serious study of agriculture in

Sergiyevskoye peasants, early twentieth century.

Kaluga. It was 1861, and Alexander II had just issued his manifesto emancipating the serfs. But Deilidovich found nothing to be optimistic about: "They look on land cultivation here not as an enterprise from which they could make a decent living, but as an unavoidable consequence of having land," he wrote of the peasants. "It is hard to find an enterprise where there is so much 'what if,' 'maybe,' or 'good enough' as agriculture," he continued. The problem lay, he felt, in a vicious circle of poverty, struggle, indifference, and laziness: "Already the fact that the majority of men leave to find work elsewhere, leaving women, old people, and children to do the field work, testifies to a lack of respect for farm work and for agriculture in general.

"But then, it is true that the Kaluga *muzhik* cannot limit himself to tilling the soil, because often it cannot meet all his needs," he continued. "The land is poor and gives little reward for labor, because it receives little fertilizer, and there is little fertilizer because there is little cattle, and there is little cattle because there are few meadows, and those are inferior, and there is competition from the southern, more productive provinces. All this dampens enthusiasm for land cultivation and its improvement and forces men to seek other work in the province and far beyond."

And if the peasant did improve the yield of his land, Deilidovich might have added, most of it would go to the landowner or the state. You tilled the land because you had no choice; if you had enterprise, energy, and time, they were better invested in paid labor. So things continued to be done as they always had. The time to sow and the time to harvest were determined by signs and holidays: Oats were sowed when the frogs began to croak or the hickory began to bloom; haying began on Saint Peter's Day. Grain was harvested by hand right up to the revolution, and fields were rotated in three-year cycles—winter wheat, spring grains, fallow. To Deilidovich, this was the most glaring example of all that was wrong with Russian agriculture: "Our three-field system, in its simplicity, in its ability to produce adequately without undue effort or worry, has so fused with our Russian laziness that it can be changed only as a result of a hard and palpable blow of necessity.

"But then, we've had no one to comprehend these things until now. Landowners, regarding land cultivation as a lowly occupation, left it totally in the hands of peasants; and the peasants worked without deliberation, as long as things got done."

When they came to power, the Soviets proclaimed the emancipation of the peasants. But in the end the regime proved to be only the most brutal and callous of the peasants' masters, condemning as *kulaks* those who dared try to rise above the herd, making it easier to steal than to buy, destroying religion and custom and giving little more than empty promises in return.

In the fall of 1991 I talked to Alexei Fedoseyevich Pronin, chairman of the regional *soviet*, or council, in Ferzikovo, about why private farmers were meeting so much resistance from the collective farms.

"This business will be born in suffering," said Pronin, a small, chunky man who, like most of his comrades in rural administration, had been the local Communist Party secretary and stayed in the same office, changing only his title, after Soviet rule crumbled. Getting land was not the problem, he said. "There's a resistance, a psychology built up over seventy years. The *kolkhozniks* won't take a risk. Every time they tried to work for themselves they were crushed. In the sixties, their tiny private plots fed half the country, but then Khrushchev took all their animals away."

These things cannot be explained in pat phrases, nor can they be understood in a single visit. It takes time to peel away the layers of suspiciousness and dissembling, to begin to appreciate the survival instincts and the distrust of change evolved over centuries of serfdom, in constant struggles against stingy soil and a hard climate, in an endless progression of wars, uprisings, fires, and plagues.

Out here, the great causes and reforms that have swept over their land—Holy Russia, dictatorship of the proletariat, emancipation, collectivization, privatization—have rarely meant more than added grief and confusion. Survival has meant ensuring that you plow your own small plot of land in time and produce enough, but not so much that anyone would notice; that you stay on the right side of the *kolkhoz* director and that he stay on the right side of the local authorities.

The reward is those rare and precious moments of peace and security, that evening on a bench with a neighbor as the sun sinks behind the distant birches, a glass of vodka on a festive occasion, an old romantic ballad and an oft-repeated war story to bring back the glory of the front.

3

Exotic Aliens and Serfs

A bankrupt *kolkhoz*, an overgrown mound where a big house had once stood, a crumbling bell tower with a rusted cross, some pretty scenery. Was that all?

No, there was also the past: rich layers of memory, history, and legend that the Communists had tried to bury, and which were now breaking out through the cracks of the disintegrating Soviet state in the many old archives that were becoming again accessible.

When I returned with my family for a second tour in Moscow, in February 1991, I began traveling more frequently to Koltsovo. I spent many a long evening with Alexandra Nikitichna Trunin. I wrote about Sergiyevskoye in *The New York Times* and made some appearances on Russian television and in the press, and people began seeking me out—people who had grown up in Koltsovo, or whose parents came from there, and who wanted to share some memories or photographs, or to ask questions. Everywhere I encountered the same fascination, the same longing to reclaim the past.

I discovered information that I never thought still existed—archives filled with documents, records, letters, memoirs, photos, all filed in cardboard folios, tied with little ribbons, sorted in boxes, and tucked away in former churches, institutes, universities, or libraries, maintained through long years of disuse by a loyal caste of archivists. Russians have always had a propensity to squirrel away every piece of paper, but I had never suspected the Communists would bother to maintain so much that so completely contradicted their deliberate suppression and revision of the past. To these prerevolutionary papers the Soviets added millions of their own, leaving behind a mammoth trove of documents that will keep historians busy for generations.

With the coming of glasnost, the hidden caches of memory came back to life. Most of the ones I saw were in remarkably good shape. The Russian state took record-keeping seriously: official records were fastidiously copied, stamped, notarized, cross-referenced, and filed, and the bureaucracy prescribed the quality of paper for each level of communication. Important documents—deeds, grants of arms, appeals to the sovereign—were on stock that even now feels new.

Nothing was too personal to preserve, it seemed. At the Central State Historical Archive in St. Petersburg, an archivist found letters that my grandfather Dmitry Schmemann had written from the trenches of World War I to the wife of the Agriculture minister. There was also a telegram sent by his father, Senator Nikolai Schmemann, to the State Council, regretting that he would miss the opening session because he was in Sevastopol at the side of his son Sergei, a naval lieutenant: "4 February 1916. My son's condition is grave. Both legs amputated. Cannot return for start of session. Request month leave." With it is a telegram signed by the chairman of the council, dated February 15, 1916, expressing condolences from the entire council on the death of Nikolai's son.

In the manuscript section of the Lenin Library in Moscow (now the Russian State Library) I found the complete, voluminous handwritten memoir of my great-grandfather Mikhail Mikhailovich Osorgin, which he began writing after the revolution, and which he left behind, along with other family documents, when he quit Russia in 1931. Juliana Samarin, a granddaughter of Mikhail Mikhailovich living in Paris who has a wealth of family archives, spent two years deciphering his handwriting; her typewritten manuscript eventually reached two thousand pages.

A charming young archivist couple in Tula, Dmitry and Irina Antonov, invited me to visit the Tula State Historical Archive, where I sat absorbed by Mikhail Mikhailovich Osorgin's confidential communications when as governor of Tula he tried nobly but unsuccessfully to cope with the revolution of 1905. In the morning of October 21, 1905, a day that would end with dreadful bloodshed at the main intersection of the city, he sent an encoded telegram to the Interior minister in St. Petersburg: "Situation in Tula growing more alarming daily. Passions among groupings of various leanings so hot that can be strife any minute. Have no means to prevent. Believe cannot use troops: result would be general discontent. Demonstrations in the streets occur daily."

At the State Archive in Kaluga, a local history teacher found Maria Kar's 1806 letter to the bishop of Kaluga proposing to build a new church on her estate. At the Military Historical Archive in Moscow, in the palace built by Peter the Great's Swiss favorite, François Lefort, I leafed through the military records of Cornet Sergei Mikhailovich Osorgin and Staff Captain Dmitry Nikolayevich Schmemann, my grandfathers. I also read a faded order dissolving the Semyonovsky Life Guards, one of the two oldest regiments of tsarist Russia, signed in big letters by the last regimental adjutant: "Schmemann." In the Central State Archive of Literature and Art, in a peeling old building off the Leningrad Prospekt, I read in the intimate diaries of my great-grandmother's sister, Olga Trubetskoi, about adolescent reveries and an amateur play that proved vitally important in eventually bringing me into the world. Even in Ferzikovo, the local newspaper editor opened for me the bulky files he had painstakingly copied out of old Communist records—including the nasty attack in *Trud* in 1985, which he had duly reprinted.

I became entranced by these archives. Each visit was a magic journey: In some obscure old building, sitting at a battered wooden table under an old brass lamp, I would untie a musty cardboard folio and enter into a world of great-uncles and great-grandparents, listening to their worries and joys, sharing their tragedies, coming to know them. Often I had companions on my journey—a young historian probing the long-restricted history of the First World War, a graduate student rediscovering the gentry, an archivist fascinated to share the research of an émigré descendant.

Finally, 11 years after I first came to Russia, I was finding my past, my Sergiyevskoye.

The more I visited Sergiyevskoye, the more it enchanted me. The mud was treacherous, the winters pitiless, the backwardness and inefficiency appalling, but the landscape was that timeless collage of birches, meadows, log cabins, and rivers of which Pushkin wrote, "It smells of Russia here." The lyrical landscape painter Vasily Polenov was only one of many who celebrated the unassuming beauty of the Oka and its environs, and many a poet found inspiration in the profound Russianness of the lands around Kaluga. Tolstoy's Yasnaya Polyana was not far off; Chekhov spent the summer of 1891 a few miles from Sergiyevskoye; Pushkin often stayed on the nearby estate of his in-laws, the

Goncharovs. Gorodnya, another nearby estate, was home in the early nineteenth century to Princess Natalia Petrovna Golitsyn, a *grande dame* and ardent card player known (behind her back) as the "mustachioed princess." She had played with the likes of King George III and Marie Antoinette, and it was said she never lost. It was she whom Pushkin used as the model for his *Queen of Spades.*

The ancient town of Tarusa, about 40 miles downriver from Sergiyevskoye, was the home of the poet Marina Tsvetaeva and a magnet for writers and artists in both Russian and Soviet times. "There is probably no place near Moscow that is so typical and touching in its scenery," wrote one frequent visitor, the writer Konstantin Paustovsky. Great monasteries dotted the land—there were 28 at one time or another in the province of Kaluga, including the monastery of Optina Pustyn, whose renowned *startsy*—monks venerated for their spiritual insight—drew pilgrims from far and wide. The best-known of the *startsy*, Amvrosy, was probably the model for Dostoevsky's Zosima in *The Brothers Karamazov*, and there is a theory that Tolstoy was on his way to Optina Pustyn when he died at the train station of Astapovo.

Two heroes of Russian legend, the monk-warriors Alexander Peresvet and Rodion Oslyabya, came from these parts. They were dispatched by the revered national saint Sergei of Radonezh, abbot of the Trinity monastery, north of Moscow, to fight alongside Prince Dmitry Donskoi in the Battle of Kulikovo in 1380, when the Russians first challenged the Mongol occupiers. The battle opened with single combat between Peresvet and the Mongol warrior Chelubei, in which both were felled. The *ataman* Kudeyar, a pitiless bandit chief whose conversion to pious monk is recounted in a ballad every Russian child knows by heart, prowled the nearby forests of Dugna. And it was in Kaluga that a pretender to the Russian throne, the "False Dmitry," and his Polish princess held out until he was hunted down in 1610.

The Kaluga region drifts into Russian history in about the tenth century, when Slavs were already using the Oka River to reach the Volga at Nizhny Novgorod, while the pagan Viatichi tribes still wandered the deep forests and swamps of the Oka's upper reaches. It was the Viatichi who evidently gave the river its name, from *ioki,* their word for water.

Early histories record the usual succession of feudal wars, Tatar raids, and other horrors. The Black Plague swept through in 1352, then the right bank of the Oka was seized by Lithuanian princes. Chronicles tell of a battle fought in 1372 near Lyubetsk, 8 miles downriver from Sergiyevskoye: "They met near the city of Lyubutska and the Muscovites chased the Lithuanian regiment and

Prince Olgerd ran." After that, Prince Dmitry Donskoi of Moscow and "the wily and stern" Prince Olgerd of Lithuania agreed that there be "no wars among us, and princes must not meddle in each other's affairs." All that remains today of Lyubetsk is the overgrown mounds of its earthen fortifications. Kaluga itself is first mentioned in the chronicles in 1389, as a village in the principality that Dmitry Donskoi bestowed on his third son, Andrei.

On the eve of the eighteenth century, the region was so ravaged by famine, plague, bandits, and successive invasions by Poles, Cossacks, and Crimean Tatars that the local prince was unable even to raise a military force. A survey at the time described a devastated land, with many abandoned or decimated villages. A survey of Kaluga after a fire in 1626 listed 171 surviving households and only 207 people (though by 1681 it had 1,045 households, 20 churches, and a wooden fort). Eighty-five percent of the surrounding lands was wilderness, and the rest was speckled with tiny hamlets.

In the first mention of what would become Sergiyevskoye, the village of Goryainovo (a part of Koltsovo is still called by that name) is listed in seventeenth-century records as having five persons living in three houses, and six vacant houses. The survey said that the hamlet had been moved from another, more ancient site and was land held partly in tenure (*pomestie*) and partly as property (*votchina*) by the Begichev family. There are records of a parish church standing near the village in 1730 on land donated by the Begichevs. Of other villages that would become part of Sergiyevskoye, Koshorkina (later Kashurki) is listed as inhabited, while Shakhovo and Pyshkovo are listed as vacant. An issue of the journal *Kaluga Antiquity* dedicated to the centenary of the Sergiyevskoye church in 1910 noted that in various places around the estate there were earthen mounds—remainders of Tatar and Lithuanian fortifications. The journal also reported that a peasant girl in Polivanovo, a village near Goryainovo, had found the remains of a pitcher with ancient silver coins in her garden.

Local history gathers speed in the eighteenth century. With the rapid expansion of his empire, Peter the Great launched a search for a place deep in central Russia to set up a foundry that would be safe from invaders. In 1702, the Tula industrialist Nikita Demidov received a patent to build an ironworks in Dugna, 8 miles downriver from Sergiyevskoye, with the responsibility of supplying cannon, cannonballs, and iron to the state.

Communist histories depict the Dugna works—no doubt accurately—as a typical hellhole of early Russian industrialization. The government sent serfs from Smolensk to provide what was essentially slave labor for the primitive smelting operations. Routine punishments included whipping and putting salt in the open wounds, binding workers in chains and throwing them in deep holes, burning them with white-hot brands, and tying logs to their legs. The first rebellion on record occurred in 1741, for which two serfs were hanged, two exiled, and about two hundred beaten with knouts. The next uprising, in 1752, lasted two and a half months. It was in Dugna that Communism first gained a foothold in the region, in 1905, when a young Communist schoolteacher named Vyacheslav Mikhailovich Brilliantov began agitating among workers and peasants. The ironworks still stand, a rusted tangle of winches, buildings, refuse, and foul streams.

In the eighteenth century Kaluga's merchants grew prosperous, selling local lambskins, leather, and wax as far abroad as Danzig, Berlin, and Leipzig, and bringing back wool, silk, paper, and cotton. Kaluga reached its zenith in 1800, when it was made a diocesan center; it then listed 120 factories, including five sail manufacturers employing a total of 1,400 workers. Its last great moment—before it was thrust out of the economic mainstream by the coming of the railroads—was in the war against Napoleon, when Kaluga served as a major distribution and mobilization center for the Russian armies. Kaluga Province was initially ordered to raise "two soldiers per one hundred souls" (serfs) for the war, and the force it mustered eventually amounted to 13,680 infantrymen and 1,320 cavalrymen in six regiments and a local militia. Casualties, as in all of Russia's wars, were enormous: of 1,105 men sent to the war by the town of Tarusa, only 85 returned. After the Battle of Borodino in 1812, many feared that Napoleon would turn toward Kaluga, and the city was evacuated. Napoleon marched on Moscow instead. The town of Kaluga was spared again when Napoleon retreated, but the surrounding province was not, and many cities and villages were devastated. At Goryainovo, villagers moved their livestock into caves by the river to hide them from the invader.

Records show that in 1775, Major General Vasily Alexeyevich Kar bought at auction a large estate on the Oka between Kaluga and Aleksin, with a manor in the village of Goryainovo. According to a general survey at the time, this consisted of an old wooden house with a fruit orchard, two ponds, and stables with horses "of German and Russian breeds."

Kar's forebears had been military men going back to Thomas Car, one of three brothers who left Scotland in 1618 to seek their fortune in the service of the first Romanov tsar, Mikhail Fyodorovich. A letter survives from King

James of England and Scotland, dated April 20, 1618, addressed to "the righte highe, righte excellente and right mightie Prince The Lorde Emperour and greate Duke Michaell Phederwitch of all Russia," commending the Car brothers "to your favorable consideration." The letter concludes with a request for what would today be called a multiple-entry visa: "If at anie time they have desire to return and see theire frinds in theire owne Countries, We praie that when they shall suite it at your hands, yee will graunte the same."

Vasily Alexeyevich was a fifth-generation Russian Kar and seems to have been thoroughly Russified. His mother was a lady-in-waiting at the imperial court, and Kar himself served as a court page and married a lady-in-waiting to Catherine the Great, a Princess Khovansky. Before his disgrace, Kar had a solid reputation. He saw extensive action in the Russian army, as well as in the armies of France and Austria, and was promoted to major general in 1770, at the age of 40. Kar's heritage was hardly unusual in Russia at the time. From the time of Ivan the Terrible in the sixteenth century, tens of thousands of foreigners came to seek their fortune in Russia, many Scotsmen among them.

In Russian histories, Kar figures invariably as a villain. His downfall began when an armed uprising broke out in the Ural region led by a fugitive Cossack named Emelian Pugachev, who claimed to be Tsar Peter III, Catherine's husband, who had been overthrown and murdered in 1762. In 1773 Catherine assigned Kar, who had distinguished himself in crushing a Polish uprising, to destroy Pugachev. Kar set out expecting a quick victory over what he (and Catherine) thought of as a routine peasant uprising. Instead, he found himself confronted by a massive insurgent force that held sway over a great territory in the Urals and Siberia, and was threatening to move on European Russia.

In the very first clashes with Pugachev, Kar's forces were badly mauled. He dispatched messages to St. Petersburg and, leaving his troops in a secure position under the command of his deputy, set out for the capital, presumably to describe the true state of affairs. He advised the president of the Military Collegium, Count Zahar Chernyshev, of his decision in a dispatch dated November 11, 1773, noting that in any case, no action was possible until he received artillery and reinforcements. A week later Kar sent another message saying that he had been seized by a terrible fever and a fistula, and was heading to Moscow for treatment. Evidently aware that his actions entailed political risk, he concluded the dispatch with a request to Chernyshev to confirm his decision, "to avoid great damage in the case that my enemies might try to give a different interpretation."

Kar's first message did not reach St. Petersburg until November 25, whereupon

Chernyshev promptly gave it "a different interpretation," and fired off a furious dispatch to Kar accusing him of relinquishing his command without permission and ordering him to return immediately to the Urals, "even if you are on the outskirts of St. Petersburg." Chernyshev sent a copy of this dispatch to the military commander in Moscow, Prince Mikhail Nikitich Volkonsky, just in case Kar showed up there.

A few days later, on November 30, Catherine removed Kar from his command and "banished him from both capitals"—the state capital of St. Petersburg and the spiritual capital of Moscow. In an angry *ukaz* relayed by the Military Collegium, she declared that Kar's oath and his duty required him not to spare even his own life, "while you, talking of an onset of illness, left a post whose importance was known to you; and in such weakness of spirit in a person of your rank, whose duty it is to serve as an example for his subordinates, Her Imperial Majesty does not find firmness in you for Her service, and hereby orders the Military Collegium to release you from the same and to discharge you." Soon after, Kar purchased the estate on the Oka River that would come to be known as Sergiyevskoye, with the old wooden house, fruit orchard, ponds, and stables.

Sixty years later, Kar's purported cowardice was fixed in history by Pushkin's popular histories of the Pugachev rebellion. Pushkin pored over records of the uprising and produced the story *The Captain's Daughter* and *History of the Pugachev Rebellion*. In Pushkin's account, Kar

> totally lost heart and no longer thought of victory over the despised rebel, but only of his own safety.
>
> He reported everything to the Military Collegium, unilaterally surrendered his command claiming sickness, issued some "wise" advice about how to deal with Pugachev, and, leaving his forces to [his deputy, Major General] Freiman, left for Moscow, where his appearance created a general stir. The Empress issued a stern decree dismissing him from the service. From that time he lived in his village, where he died in the beginning of the reign of Alexander I.

In a separate volume of annotations, Pushkin was even more damning:

> Before this, Kar had been utilized in matters requiring sternness, even cruelty (which does not yet presume courage, as Kar proved). Beaten by two rebels, he fled under the pretext of delirium, bone fracture, fistula, and fever. Arriving in Moscow, he sought an audience with Prince Volkonsky

to explain, but the latter refused to receive him. Kar went to the Assembly of Nobility, but his appearance created such a commotion and such outcries that he was compelled to leave hastily. In these days, public opinion, if it exists at all, is considerably more nonchalant than it was in olden times. This man, who sacrificed honor for his personal safety, nonetheless came to a violent death: He was killed by his peasants, driven beyond patience by his cruelty.

One of Prince Volkonsky's adjutants at this time was Colonel Gerasim Grigorievich Osorgin, a hereditary military man from the Volga region. Among the Osorgin family papers in the Russian State Library in Moscow is a letter of commendation from Volkonsky for Colonel "Asorgin": "While assigned to me, he performed every duty given him, including important secret missions during the Pugachev outrage, with zeal and diligence." There is no indication what Osorgin's secret missions were, but they may well have related to the Kar affair.

Seventy years later, Colonel Osorgin's son, Mikhail Gerasimovich Osorgin, would buy Kar's estate from the disgraced general's son, Sergei Vasilievich Kar.

Pushkin's *History* appeared in 1834, twenty-nine years after General Kar died. His version of the cowardly general took root in local legend and grew. By 1910, *Kaluga Antiquity* reported that according to popular lore, Kar "used barrels of gold he brought back from the Pugachev campaign to build himself a great house, resembling a castle, which is still the ornament of the village." Further, the journal reported that he was indifferent to religion and did not look kindly on the religious devotion of his wife, and sometimes left her to walk alone the 2 versts to the nearest church, which was old and small.

In the Soviet era, the Ferzikovo *Red Banner* dropped the allegations of religious indifference, which under militant atheism had become a virtue, but branded Kar a "typical English pedant." The paper reported that Kar separated out shiftless peasants from hard-working ones and settled them in a village called Lenilovka, from the word *len'*, lazy. A part of Koltsovo is still called that. This segregation, continued the *Red Banner*, was evidence that "Kar was stern and legalistic to the level of pedantry, like a real Englishman."

In a modern guidebook to the region, Koltsovo is listed as the former estate of the infamous Kar, "who, having been sent against Pugachev, feigned illness and, grabbing a barrel of gold, fled from his troops. Catherine exiled him to his village, but here too he left an evil memory: He was extremely cruel to his peasants, and was helped in this by English overseers."

In the stories I heard in the village, Kar was a dastardly, greedy, godless, and cowardly Englishman (or German) who took out his frustration over his aborted military career in sadistic behavior and lived in constant fear of retribution for his many misdeeds—which was why he had an escape tunnel dug from his fortresslike house to the banks of the Oka.

I was told that in the 1920s, a local boy, Filip Golubkov, found an entrance to the tunnel under the bell tower and inside saw crucified skeletons. I eventually met Golubkov, a retired artist then in his eighties, and he confirmed the finding of the entrance to the tunnel—but from the river, not the bell tower, and, alas, without skeletons. "We always used to hear about the tunnels, and we found a cave that seemed to lead somewhere," he said. "We made torches and went in, but after a hundred meters we got scared and left. I was thirteen." Yet Golubkov had also heard the story of a tunnel by the bell tower with skeletons, so maybe it was true. I looked for a tunnel, both by the bell tower and by the Oka, but never found one.

The legends also said that the construction of Kar's house was managed by Englishmen who routinely beat the worker-serfs and threw them off the upper floors for the smallest infraction. Kar was also said to have had a German estate manager who beat a peasant woman to death with a stick for popping a berry into her mouth while picking strawberries for the lord. The legends concluded with moral justice: The peasants killed the English construction foreman and cemented his body into the wall of the house. In the end, they tore the despised Kar to pieces.

Kar's progeny were appropriately bad. We have already met his second son, Sergei, who purportedly raped and killed peasant lasses and disposed of their bodies in the forest, and who lost the estate in a game of cards. Kar's firstborn, Alexei, was disinherited by his father at age 17 for his "dissolute and frivolous life." In 1805, less than a year before his death, General Kar published a public notice warning that "henceforth no one and in no way" should extend Alexei any credit or trust. Kar willed his estate and the bulk of his other properties to Sergei, then 13, leaving lesser legacies to two daughters. What it was that turned Kar against his older son is not known. But Alexei, a handsome and heroic artillery officer who lost a leg in the wars with Napoleon and retired with honor, did not die a pauper. General Kar's childless younger brother, Filip Kar, liberated the serfs on his estate near Rostov-Velikiy and in return obligated them to pay 10,000 rubles a year to Alexei and his heirs.

Kar might have remained a dastardly foreigner in history and legend forever had it not been for Kathleen Cook, an Englishwoman who had long lived in the

Soviet Union and was not about to let the Russians get away with what she saw as calumny against a fellow Brit.

Kate Cook is one of those rare foreigners who became enchanted by Russia at some point in life and managed to settle there despite the formidable obstacles posed by the Soviet system. She was a student at Oxford when Khrushchev opened the Iron Curtain a crack and created new interest in the Soviet Union, and the "thaw" inspired her to switch her studies from German to Russian. In 1966 she won a scholarship for a year's study at Moscow University, and there she found work with Progress Publishers, which specializes in translations of Soviet works into Western languages. In 1971 she married a Russian and settled in Moscow.

Nonetheless, she remained English, with all the diligence and respect for fair play that entails; in fact, she confessed, "the older I get, the more English I feel." In her travels around Russia, she read the self-same Kaluga guidebook that I saw, with its reference to the "English" general of evil memory who once had an estate in those parts. "I discovered this was Pushkin's Kar and became quite interested," she told me. "I began looking for traces, and I found there were lots. I found quite a bit in the Lenin Library. I discovered various reference works. Noble families are easier to trace; they were fairly accurately recorded up to the revolution.

"If one looks at it psychologically, I felt sorry for him. (For God's sake, don't write it down.) There are times I have felt very lonely here, and I felt that if he had been unfairly accused, I could set it right. He was always referred to as an *Anglichanin*, an Englishman."

Kate, I'm sorry; I did write it down. I couldn't help it; I, too, am an outsider among my people and have known the longing to set the record straight.

I met Kate through Kathy Burton Murrell, our friend and neighbor who in her many years in Moscow as the wife of a British diplomat became probably the leading expert on Moscow's architectural history. Kate was her old acquaintance, and Kathy realized that Kate and I were interested in the same place, Sergiyevskoye—Kate through the Kars, I the Osorgins. By then, Kate had amassed a considerable volume of material on Kar, much of it in conflict with the legends.

She discovered that his banishment was lifted by Catherine's son and successor, Paul I, and that the next tsar, Alexander I, returned the old general to full imperial favor and rank. Furthermore, she found that the records of the Church of Sts. Peter and Paul on Novaya Basmannaya Street in Moscow show that Major General Vasily Alexeyevich Kar "died in a Christian manner"—that is, of natural causes—in his own house on February 25, 1806, at the ripe old age of 78, and that the vicar bishop of Moscow officiated at his funeral two days later. So much for official disgrace and being torn asunder by enraged peasants.

And his cowardly flight? That idea came into question as early as 1862, less than 30 years after Pushkin's *History*. Kate found a book from that year by a historian named Ya. K. Grot, who pored over the archives and concluded that Pushkin had seen only part of the record. Grot allowed himself a deferential wag of the finger at the immortal bard:

> The behavior of Kar in the first period of the Pugachev uprising is known to us only from the short story of Pushkin and the decree firing this general that he included in his story. But the more definitive the judgment passed on him by the empress and condemning him for posterity, the more it is vital to know all the factors for his actions. His unilateral departure from the army at the most critical moment was undoubtedly at the least extremely careless and unwise, but whether it was done out of cowardice—from "weakness of spirit," in the language of the decree—is a question that can be resolved only on the basis of original documents.

Grot's documents show, for example, that before returning to St. Petersburg, Kar arranged his force in a secure position and sent several demands for artillery and reinforcements at a time when the military was strained for men—it was a period of recruitment, and many troops were tied up either fighting Turkey or assisting in combating the aftereffects of a recent plague. Kar's reports and letters betray no cowardice; there are corroborating messages from other officers confirming the gravity of his illness, which left him semiconscious at times. In any case, he never had a chance to give his side of the story.

It is also noteworthy that Kar's successor in command against Pugachev, General Alexander Ilyich Bibikov, was appointed even before Kar had been relieved of his post, and proceeded to do exactly what Kar proposed: He spent two months gathering a force sufficient to tackle the uprising. Four months after taking command, Bibikov died of fever—evidently the same disease that brought Kar down.

Overall, the documents suggest that Kar fell victim not to cowardice but to court intrigue and Catherine's frustration. It appears likely that the generals in the high command urgently needed a scapegoat to present to the angry empress for their failure to properly assess and address the Pugachev uprising; Count Chernyshev certainly seemed determined not to let Kar into either St. Petersburg or Moscow, where he might have described the true state of affairs.

Furthermore, the records raise some question as to whether Catherine ever saw Kar's reports describing the scope of the rebellion: Her *ukaz* dismissing him accuses him of leaving his troops because of illness, without noting that he originally left in order to confer with the high command and fell ill only later, while en route to the capital. In any case, the documents do not support Pushkin's brutal indictment. But Grot's research faded into obscurity, while Pushkin's became mandatory reading for every Russian schoolchild.

Pugachev was finally defeated and captured in August 1774. In November of that year he was brought to Moscow and shackled to a wall of the State Mint, where he was put on display daily for two months. Contemporary accounts say women fainted before his fiery gaze and fierce voice. On January 16, 1775, Pugachev was taken by cart to Bolotnaya (now Repin) Square, shouting along the way: "Forgive me, Orthodox people, if I did you wrong." After he was decapitated and quartered, his severed parts were displayed for several days around Moscow, then incinerated, and the ashes scattered.

Kar, meanwhile, settled on his estate, which he named Karovo, and set about improving his new property. He ordered the construction of a vast new house with two broad wings that ended in round towers, as well as several new outbuildings. He never completed the house, and neither would the Osorgins; much of the second floor and the entire third floor were never finished or used. Beyond the courtyard, Kar laid out a well-ordered grove of linden trees, the "park" that today still cools the spring air with its sweet fragrance.

It was the dawn of the golden age of the Russian nobility. The reigns of Peter III (1762) and Catherine (1762–96)—his widow, successor, and probable murderer—saw the final separation of the nobility's privileges from mandatory state service, and the confirmation of the gentry's unconditional ownership of land and the people on it.

In the original scheme of things, which was institutionalized when Ivan III threw off the Mongol yoke in 1480 and adopted the title "tsar" (Caesar), the nobles (*dvoriane*) were military and civil servitors who were assigned specified lands (*pomestiye*) to sustain them while they served the tsar. With time, the lands turned increasingly into hereditary properties (*votchiny*), though every male *dvorianin* was still required to perform service for the state.

Peasants were initially considered independent workers of the land, with obligations to support a *dvorianin* and to provide specified numbers of men for military service. Until the late sixteenth century, they were allowed to choose

A model of the Sergiyevskoye manor house.

where to live—though they could move only once a year, in the week before and the week after Saint Yury's Day, November 26, presumably because the harvesting chores and the preparations for winter were concluded by then. The problem was that peasants began increasingly to flock to rich landowners, leaving lesser *dvoriane* without the men or means to fulfill their military obligations. So in 1580, Boris Godunov, the power behind the sickly Tsar Fyodor Ivanovich and a future tsar in his own right, issued a decree that henceforth peasants must remain wherever his *ukaz* caught them. Thus began three hundred years of serfdom.

The nobility gained its rights about as arbitrarily as the peasants lost theirs. Tsar Peter III—who far preferred being Karl Peter Ulrich, Duke of Holstein-Gottorp, and spent much of his seven-month reign drilling troops, trying to make Russia as Prussian as possible, and playing with dolls—issued his "Manifesto on the Freedom of the Nobility" largely to make the Russian *dvorianstvo* more Western. Catherine (a German princess by birth who, unlike her husband, preferred being a Russian ruler) became convinced after the Pugachev rebellion of the need to strengthen landowners as the first echelon of state control over the rapidly expanding empire, and she further increased the privileges of the *dvorianstvo*. The empress, who corresponded with Jean-Jacques Rousseau and kept abreast of the latest in European liberal thought, granted the *dvoriane* a state-of-the-art "Charter on the Rights, Freedoms, and Privileges of the Russian Nobility." It guaranteed the inviolability of the "honor, life, and property" of the *dvorianin* and confirmed "for all times the freedom and liberty of the hereditary Russian nobility."

The result was that whatever residual rights the serfs had enjoyed disappeared, and they effectively became the property of landowners, who could exile them to Siberia, sentence them to hard labor, or send them into lifelong military service. "The peasant is dead in the law," declared the revolutionary writer Alexander Radishchev. Thus the original rationale for serfdom—so the peasant could serve the warrior, and the warrior the tsar—fell away, and Russia became divided into two separate and egregiously unequal worlds.

The fact that Russia's *dvorianstvo* gained its privileges and lands solely at the pleasure of autocratic monarchs distinguished it from the European feudal nobility, which by and large amassed its powers and riches first and then struck a compact with the monarch. Ivan Turgenev, a writer born to the serf-owning gentry who spent much of his life in Europe, was one of the first Russians to muse publicly on what this difference implied. The Russian *dvorianstvo*, he wrote, "had no inherent rights. Its rights were granted, and that not so long ago. It had no fortified castles in any sense—neither physical nor moral. It had no power; it only served power." The Russian landowner came by his lands and serfs not by conquest or compact but by the will of the tsar, Turgenev continued. "The Russian *dvorianin* served and serves, and in this is his strength and significance—not in the ownership of peasants, which is a chance development that came about not of necessity but through incompetence and misunderstanding, and that was legalized by chance."

On the land, it was certainly not a partnership that made for productive or innovative agriculture. The landowners never became "gentlemen farmers" in the manner of English squires or plantation owners in the American South. The Russian landowners had no interest in agriculture; for most of them, the *imeniye* (property) was a source of income and provisions, and maybe a pleasant summer home. They usually left cultivation of the land largely to the peasants and took no interest in agronomy.

But that "chance development" of "ownership" of the peasant by the landowner, however unjust or unproductive, also contributed to creating what the world today knows as Russian culture. "However strange this may seem to the reader, it should be noted that serfdom had its positive sides for Russian culture as a whole," wrote the late Soviet cultural historian Yuri Mikhailovich Lotman. "It was on this basis, however distorted, that the nobility had a measure of independence from tsarist authority—an independence without which there can be no culture." And the great Russian culture of the eighteenth and nineteenth centuries was the culture of the *dvorianstvo*. "This cannot be erased from history," he wrote.

The *pomeshchiki*, as landowners continued to be known, began using their newfound leisure and power to transform their isolated lands into country seats. Thousands of such estates sprouted across central Russia, with their forested parks and their churches, their creaky manor houses wreathed in lilac, their libraries, grand pianos, and provincial languor, their patriarchal order and stern codes of family and honor. In the cities, too, the ponderous houses of seventeenth-century boyars (noblemen), with their peaked roofs and tiny windows, gave way to imported neoclassical, baroque, and neo-Gothic forms, adapted to varying degrees of success by serf architects and craftsmen in plaster, brick, and wood.

Finding themselves financially independent, young gentlemen took to putting in two or three years in a fashionable Guards regiment before "retiring" with a handsome uniform and a respectable rank to a comfortable squire's life, spending winters in St. Petersburg or Moscow—depending on social tastes and means—and summers at the country estate, the *imeniye*. For the unambitious and indolent, it was a perfectly satisfactory life. But for the ambitious or talented, it could be stultifying. Turgenev coined the term "superfluous men" to describe an entire breed of young men who vented their frustrated energies in desperate gambling, carousing, dueling, and cruelty, or else sank into inertia. The country estate could be a refined and cozy "gentry nest," but it could also be the stifling cage of Chekhov's *Three Sisters*.

"Russian petty tyranny, the main motor of our culture and its biggest brake, was expressed most brightly in the lifestyle of landowning Russia," mused Baron Nikolai Wrangel, secretary of the Society for the Protection and Preservation of Memorials of Art and Antiquity, writing in the early years of this century. "The distinctive poesy of estate culture—a pungent blend of European refinement and purely Asiatic despotism—was feasible only in an epoch of slavery."

Much as Peter the Great compelled his courtiers to build him a European city in the swampy delta of the Neva, so the nobility compelled their serfs to become musicians, actors, painters, embroiderers, and jesters. "The unrestrained fantasy of these homegrown Maecenases created amusing, grotesque ventures, often silly parodies, but sometimes charming, original, and surprising magic," wrote Wrangel. There were serf artists who became famous, like Andrei Nikiforovich Voronikhin, who was put through the Academy of Arts by his master—and probable father—Count Alexander Stroganov, himself descended from a serf. Voronikhin designed the Kazan Cathedral in St. Petersburg in loose imitation of St. Peter's in Rome, as well as the Gorodnya manor of the Princes Golitsyn, near Sergiyevskoye. But there are also many accounts of cruelty and arbitrariness: Count Alexei Arakcheyev, the all-powerful minister under Alexander I, beat his serf architect mercilessly for the smallest mistake, while at Otrada, the regal estate of Count Vladimir Orlov, some serfs would toil all day in the forge and then have to perform onstage in the evening.

Of course, the splendor of the manors varied as widely as the wealth and ambition of their lords. Some rivaled the brilliance of imperial palaces: the Otrada of the Orlovs, the Ostankino of the Sheremetyevs, the Bogoroditsk of the Bobrinskys, the Arkhangelskoye of the Golitsyns (and later the Yusupovs). At the other end were wooden houses barely more luxurious than a peasant hut. The large majority were somewhere in between—sprawling wooden mansions in a neoclassical style with enough rooms for estate offices and all the cousins. Most reflected a greater emphasis on coziness than splendor. Their walls were papered in warm designs and hung with carpets and paintings (often the work of a serf)—family portraits, urban scenes, and exotic landscapes were favorites. Rich leather bindings lined glass-covered bookcases ("On the shelf, alongside the pistols, Baron Brambeus and Rousseau"). Perhaps because of the brevity of the northern summer, most landowners preferred half-wild, wooded "parks," with their choirs of songbirds, mushrooms, and wild strawberries, to formal gardens, and flowering meadows and orchards to lawns.

Not many of the old manors still stand, and those that do are usually in deplorable condition. However, some have survived as museums, sanatoriums, or hospitals—Tyutchev's Muranovo, Pushkin's Mikhailovskoye, Turgenev's Spasskoye-Lyutovinovo, Tolstoy's Yasnaya Polyana, the Trubetskois' Uzkoye, the Gagarins' Nikolskoye-Gagarino—and these still exude the warm feel of a sprawling family home rather than the formal splendor of a French château.

The age of the *dvorianstvo* was a relatively brief one, already well on its way to oblivion when the Bolsheviks drew the final curtain. Already in 1910, Wrangel had written:

This culture, this lifestyle, this whole past, so close in time, now seems to retreat several centuries back with every passing year. Just as their great-grandfathers in the time of [Tsar] Alexei Mikhailovich seemed alien and inexplicable to people of the age of Catherine, so the 150-year life of serf-owning Russia has disappeared forever from us. And it is for this reason, perhaps, that we feel enticed and caressed by an old tale of exotic aliens and serfs, of redwood furniture and houses with columns on the banks of sunny ponds.

4

Cards and Madness

Kar was certainly an "exotic alien." Yet among his neighbors in his day it was less his disgrace and foreign roots than his agricultural methods that attracted attention. A quarterly journal named *Urania,* founded in 1804 by a school-teacher in order to "multiply means of disseminating generally useful knowledge on moral and natural subjects," published in its fourth (and, alas, last) issue a ringing paean to Kar's estate, under the title "Ceres' Feast, or the Festival of Landworkers." (The journal also listed Kar among its prominent subscribers.)

"Common sense and firmness of spirit—attributes associated with prosperity—often lead to useful actions worthy of emulation," counseled the journal. Among the "useful actions" attributed to Kar it noted that he had introduced a new method of fertilization, "entirely different from other workers of the land," by mixing manure, rotted wood, and ash from burnt straw in a hole.

But the innovation that most impressed *Urania* was the major feast that Kar would organize on the completion of the harvest. "The ancient Greeks, more specifically the Athenians, would hold celebrations twice a year in honor of Ceres of Eleusis, the patron of agriculture," reported the journal (though the goddess of agriculture worshipped in the Eleusinian mysteries was probably Demeter rather than her Roman equivalent, Ceres). "Master Kar likewise in his bucolic estates organizes a festive celebration for the peasants responsible for the rural abundance, discussing with them the successes of land cultivation and treating them to the fruits of his wisdom and concern."

Fifty-six years later, in the first major study of agriculture in Kaluga, V. Deilidovich still held Kar up as a model farmer, though he was more skeptical about the exiled general's motives: "An energetic man, businesslike, with a strong will and still very young, he undertook agriculture on his estate from nothing to do, from boredom."

Kar began by culling out the lazy peasants and settling them in a separate village. Their children were taken away and taught crafts; upon coming of age they were married into undersized families. Kar compiled his own code of laws, which he followed "almost pedantically." Contemporary reports have it that while he trusted and even liked his manager, Fyodor Ivanovich Turchaninov, he reprimanded and punished him for the smallest infractions (in local myth, his name evolved into "Turchonok," or "Turk," and he became "a cruel Turk").

Kar increased the number of cattle on his estate in part to increase the yield of manure for fertilizer, and for this he switched from the venerable three-field rotation system to the more productive four-field system used in England. He introduced plows drawn by two horses, which became known by his name; they were "rather light and unstable but quite good for the time." He had drainage canals dug in low-lying fields, and contemporaries marveled that even in the

Peasant dances.

rainiest summers his grain was never damp. The yield from his fields was large and constant.

A graduate student in Kaluga who researched old estates in the region concluded from such evidence that "with the excellent system of farming, with well-developed cattle-raising and strict observance of established procedures, Kar's estate was truly a showcase."

But then, Kar was a rare bird. Very few landowners stayed on their estates year-round and undertook "agronomy," and Kar himself was not a farmer by choice. More often than not, those who did try to improve the land ended up frustrated. After my first article on Sergiyevskoye was published in the *Times*, Richard Nixon wrote to me that he had begun to understand Russia when he read Tolstoy, and especially Levin's frustrations with his peasants in *Anna Karenina:* ". . . he saw clearly now that his present farming methods were based on a harsh and bitter struggle between him and his hired laborers, a struggle in which on the one side—on his side—there was a continuous and strenuous effort to remodel everything in accordance with what he thought to be a better method, and on the other side, the natural order of things."

The only landowner to approach Kar in agricultural achievement at the time was his upriver neighbor Dmitry Markovich Poltoratsky, the owner of the estate Avchurino. Poltoratsky founded the Moscow Agricultural Society, replaced wooden plows with iron ones, studied English, German, and Swiss methods of agriculture, and in 1792 settled permanently at Avchurino to apply his knowledge. There, with his English estate managers (apparently a common breed at the time, though I suspect many were really Germans or Poles), he introduced novelties such as carrots, turnips, beets, potatoes, and beans into the crop rotation. But since these vegetables were largely unknown in Russia at the time, most ended up as feed for pigs—except the potatoes, which the serfs refused to harvest at all out of some religious prejudice. Indeed, efforts by the government to forcibly introduce the cultivation of potatoes led to some of the most violent serf revolts of the nineteenth century, the so-called "Potato Uprisings" of 1840 to 1844. Today, potatoes are the staple of rural Russia.

Besides, Deilidovich noted, Poltoratsky's agricultural system was "purely English," but his management was "purely Russian"—that is, sloppy—and, "as a result, there were frequent failures." Poltoratsky's experiments lost huge amounts of money even as they gained considerable renown: Avchurino was visited by Tsar Alexander I in 1816 and the future Alexander II in 1837. The first royal visit was a disaster: the peasants hitched the wrong pair of horses to the plow and, having no idea what was expected of them, they balked. The tsar, who had come to promote greater involvement by gentry landowners in agriculture, left in a huff.

The fact is that in Kar's day it was not at all fashionable for landowners to dabble in land management. Writing in 1861, the year of emancipation, Deilidovich noted that "it is only very recently, and then very cautiously, that it has become possible to talk in our salons about grain cultivation and its inescapable adjunct, fertilizer [then predominantly manure]. Until then it was never mentioned in the drawing room; it smelled bad, it was said, so how could this be a proper task for a gentleman?

"Then how was it in their day with Kar and Poltoratsky?" continued Deilidovich. "Contemporaries looked on these two mavericks with horror and bewilderment, they looked on them not only with hostility but laughed behind their backs and only waited for a chance to laugh in their faces. Echoes of those days are heard even today. But Kar barricaded himself behind his English reserve." (Again that *Anglichanin*.)

I don't doubt that the grandees in Petersburg turned up their noses at manure and raised their eyebrows at Kar and Poltoratsky, but there is evidence that Kar's neighbors, at least, actually liked and admired the fallen general. One of the best-known chronicles of that era, *Grandmother's Stories*, described Kar as "an exemplary manager, generous host, hospitable and gracious." The "grandmother" whose accounts were compiled in the book was Elizaveta Petrovna Yankov, and her father, Pyotr Mikhailovich Rimsky-Korsakov, had an estate near Kar's. This was how Elizaveta Petrovna heard the Kar story as a girl:

> He served in the military as a general and was, it appears, in very good standing with the Empress, because when the Pugachev rebellion flared up, the sovereign wrote him in her own hand that he should go against the renegade. He rushed to fulfill the command and went there; but then the rumor spread that Kar had fled to his estate. How so? The rumor reached my father: "What nonsense, how can this be?" He would not believe it. Afterward the rumors were confirmed: They said that for some reason he suddenly gave over his command to another and himself left without permission. Everyone condemned this, and for a long time many feared to visit him. Father, however, did visit him: "What matter to me that he is in disgrace? I am visiting an acquaintance, and if he has had a falling out in his service, then the law should judge him, not I."
>
> He lived in his village, occupied himself with agriculture, and was a very good manager and an enthusiastic builder: He built his manor "to

glory." He was rich, lived in great prosperity, and never hinted that he had been severed from the service. When the Empress died, he was summoned to St. Petersburg. Everyone thought, "Trouble." Not at all: His case was reexamined, and he was allowed to live freely wherever he wanted. He was a very considerate and kind person. We visited him more than once when he settled in Kaluga.

But if his honor was restored by the tsar, if he was renowned in the region for his agricultural prowess, if he threw great Eleusinian mysteries for his peasants and was not such a bad guy after all, how did Kar go down in local lore as such a villain? There is no conclusive evidence, of course, that he did not turn tail in the Urals. Furthermore, emulating the ancient Greeks and being civil with fellow noblemen does not necessarily preclude cruelty to serfs, and his treatment of lazy peasants indicates at the least that he was a demanding master (though I suspect many a landowner who tried his hand at estate management must have considered far more forceful measures against the legendary sloth of the Russian peasant). There was also his harsh treatment of his older son, and reports (unconfirmed) that his younger son and heir, Sergei, ran away from home at an early age.

In the end, I suspect that Kar's legacy was shaped less by what he did than by his foreign roots. However Russified he might have been, none of his chroniclers, Pushkin included, ever seemed to forget that he was a foreigner, an *Anglichanin*, a *nemets*. (*Nemets* today means German, but in Pushkin's time it was used for all northern Europeans, and sometimes foreigners in general. The word derives from *nemoi*, which means "mute"—apparently in the sense of not speaking Russian.) In a footnote to his history of Pugachev, Pushkin offers an assessment of foreigners who fought against Pugachev: "All the *nemtsy* in the middle ranks acquitted themselves honorably: Michaelson, Muffel, Mellin, Dietz, Demovin, Duve, etc. But all those who were in brigadier and general rank acted poorly, hesitantly, without spirit: Reinsdorp, Brandt, Kar, Freiman, Korff, Wallenstern, Bilow, Decalong, etc., etc." It should be noted, however, that in tsarist Russia xenophobic tendencies were significantly qualified by pride of lineage of whatever national origin (Pushkin himself was enormously proud of an Ethiopian great-grandfather, from whom he inherited distinctly African features), and within the nobility a foreign heritage was often more a distinction than a blot.

Foreigners were active in the Muscovite state long before Peter the Great began importing Europeans wholesale to modernize his empire, and thereafter they became a conspicuous component in the bureaucracy and military. The 1897 census reported that 35,000 positions in the civil service alone were filled by German-speakers, a category that did not even include the numerous Russified Germans. That inevitably fueled resentment among Russians, especially outside cosmopolitan St. Petersburg. In a place like Kaluga, someone of foreign descent would be conspicuous in any case, since traditional landowners were by and large Russians.

I was amused to note that the smearing of Kar as "an English pedant" carried over to Osorgin. One of the few Soviet references to Mikhail Mikhailovich Osorgin describes him as a "senator and Anglophile." He was never the former, and certainly not the latter.

Kar and his wife both died before Pushkin's *History of Pugachev* was published, in 1834—he in 1806, she in 1833. So it was their progeny who had to face the ensuing disgrace. Was that why Sergei Kar began signing himself "Karo" or "Karro"? Is that why the disinherited Alexei Kar fell into undisclosed but serious trouble—probably a duel—narrowly avoiding a court-martial?

After Kar's death, his devout widow, Maria Sergeyevna, took charge of Sergiyevskoye as trustee for her 14-year-old son Sergei, and soon she petitioned the bishop of Kaluga for permission to build a "stone church" (meaning non-wooden, in this case brick) on the manor. An architect named Ivanov was engaged, and over the next four years an imposing church in the "Catherine" style of Russian baroque rose between the house and the river, its belfry soaring above the tallest pines.

Describing the church a hundred years later, *Kaluga Antiquity* declared it the pride of the province: "Many individuals possessed of esthetic taste who have been in the churches of both capitals were delighted on seeing the Sergiyevskoye church with its beauty, and acknowledged that this church belongs not in a village but in a capital, noting that they had seen many churches in the capitals that were more richly decorated than this one, but that they rarely found churches whose decorations united so much taste and refinement."

The church was brightly lit from 33 windows and decorated with fine and precious icons, many covered with gilded silver and embedded with precious stones. Especially esteemed was an icon to the "Mother of God, the Consolation of All Who Sorrow," covered in heavy gilded silver, which parishioners donated in 1848 in gratitude for their deliverance from a terrible flood. On August 1, 1900, a cross of thick glass was mounted on the belfry, whose refracted

The Sergiyevskoye church.

light could be seen from a great distance. There were ten bells, "artfully selected so that when they were rung they made fine music." The largest, cast in Moscow and brought from the Ferzikovo railroad station with great effort and ceremony, weighed 156 *poody* (two and a half tons) and was known as the "silver" bell (a measure of silver added to the bronze was believed to clarify the ring). It was rung only on Easter and other great feasts.

The church's favorable location on the high wooded bank of the Oka, said *Kaluga Antiquity,* "probably gave rise to the popular belief that the spot had been indicated by the Mother of God herself, whose icon in honor of the Intercession appeared twice on the self-same spot."

The church was completed in September 1810, and on the first of October,

Bishop Evlampiy of Kaluga presided over the festive consecration. The central altar was dedicated to the Protection of the Holy Mother of God; the two side chapels to the patron saints of Vasily Kar and his son Sergei. According to *Kaluga Antiquity,* Bishop Evlampiy preached at the dedication on a verse from the Fifth Psalm: "I will come into Your house in the multitude of Your mercy; in fear of You I will worship toward Your holy temple." Evlampiy warmly lauded the widow Kar, and "in conclusion of his word, the bishop appealed in a prayer to the Lord that He would watch over this divine temple and all praying in it."

Soon after the church was finished, the devout widow took the veil at a convent in Kaluga as Mother Evpraxia—to pray away the evil doings of her husband, some said. When she died, the bishop (now Nikanor) honored her request to be buried in her Sergiyevskoye church. A stone in the right-side chapel, surrounded by an iron railing, marked her tomb: "With the blessing of the Most Blessed Nikanor, bishop of Kaluga and Borovsk, here lies the body of the builder of this holy temple, Madame Major General Maria Sergeyevna Karr, born princess Khovansky. She passed away at the Kaluga women's monastery the 22nd of September, 1833, a tonsured nun. A funeral was held on the 24th, and her body was placed in this holy temple, that with the help of God she established, on September 25 of this 1833rd year. The years of her life were 77."

By now her second son, Rotmister Sergei Vasilievich Kar (*rotmister* was a cavalry rank equivalent to captain), was the master of the estate. He changed its name to Sergiyevskoye, after himself. Why he did so is not known, but it is possible he may have been trying to distance himself from the opprobrium brought on his father's name by Pushkin. Local people, however, continued to call the village Karovo.

Sergei Kar showed little interest in his lands. He never married, and according to the few accounts that remain, he lived a rather wanton life—even if he did not throw any local maidens into the Zaraza forest. According to a story passed down by the Osorgins, Sergei Kar ran away from home in his youth and wandered through foreign lands, including several years reportedly spent in America.

In any case, sometime in 1843 he was playing cards at the English Club, the most exclusive gentlemen's club in Moscow (members would place their sons on the waiting list at birth). Whether because he was losing, winning, or simply bored, Kar raised his voice above the general hubbub in the playing room and declared: "My Kaluga estate is for sale for 600,000 rubles. How happy I would be if a buyer showed up and freed me of it!" From another table, a voice shot back,

"I buy it!" It was an enormous sum in those days. The voice belonged to Mikhail Gerasimovich Osorgin, a wealthy Muscovite enjoying good cards that day.

Mikhail Gerasimovich was the son of Gerasim Grigorievich Osorgin, the colonel who had served Prince Mikhail Volkonsky as adjutant during the Pugachev rebellion. Gerasim Grigorievich amassed a tidy estate through two lucrative marriages. He died when his son was 17, but because Mikhail Gerasimovich suffered bouts of madness, the inheritance remained in trusteeship until he was 24.

Despite his affliction, Mikhail Gerasimovich launched into a promising career as a magistrate and married the daughter of a wealthy Smolensk landowner, Varvara Andreyevna Lykoshin. A spate of deaths in her family (her two brothers and two sisters and all their children) greatly expanded the Osorgins' wealth and properties. But Mikhail Gerasimovich never escaped the curse of his madness: even during periods of lucidity he was moody, impulsive, and difficult, and he spent many nights reveling or gambling.

And so it came to pass that he heard Kar's exclamation at the English Club that day and made his offer, evidently on a whim. His grandson, my great-grandfather Mikhail Mikhailovich Osorgin, picks up the story:

> My grandfather knew nothing of this estate. He had a minor property in the same Kaluga *uyezd* of about 75 souls, which carried the family name, Osorgino, but nobody ever lived there, and I don't think there was even a house there. Nobody ever learned what it was that prompted my grandfather to intervene in the conversation he overheard; it was as if some fate pushed him to it. He said afterward that he thought this gentleman, who turned out to be Sergei Vasilievich Kar, was jesting, and since he [Osorgin] was in a cheerful spirit, thanks to felicitous cards, he, to his own surprise, and also in jest, replied, "I buy it." S. V. Kar rose, bowed to Grandfather, announced his name, and courteously declared, "The estate is yours whenever you please to conclude the sale." Mikhail Gerasimovich never retreated from his word—this was his unwavering rule, even in minor things, and all the more so in as serious a matter as this—so right then and there they settled on a time to conclude the sale and on the terms of payment.

And that was how Sergiyevskoye passed to the Osorgins.

It was a large and imposing estate. Records show that in 1841, two years before the sale, Sergiyevskoye was ranked among the largest and richest estates in Kaluga Province. It had more than 600 "souls" (serfs), covered 3,084 *desiatin*

(8,327 acres), and comprised eight villages. The largest, Goryainovo, had 140 households; others were Kashurki with 86, Polivanovo with 64, Pyshkovo with 58, Shakhovo with 33, Alfierovo with 28, and Dmitrovka and Zinovo with 23 each. Four streams ran through it—the Ozhzhyonka, Semga, Pakhabna, and Kamola—and there were several large forests—Korki, Kholodki, Andreyevsky, and the Zaraza forest, which covered the steep descent from the manor to the river.

The old house was massive, rising solid and imposing on a hill, with a lookout on the roof from which on a clear day the gilded cupolas of Kaluga could be glimpsed. "They say the architect who built this house was an Englishman, and he gave it a stern, impressive, respectful look, not sparing materials," wrote Mikhail Mikhailovich. The white-painted walls were more than three feet thick, made of brick baked from clay that had been mashed smooth by bare feet. One of the walls hid a secret stairway from the basement to the attic, and a labyrinth of cellars stretched the length of the house, from which the infamous tunnel purportedly ran to the Rock Mountain. The garden walls and the tall bell tower nearby often led passersby to mistake the estate for a monastery.

For all the talk of an English architect and English stolidity, the house was utterly Russian in its innumerable anomalies. Much of the second floor and the entire third floor of the main block, intended as the main residence floors, were never finished, and everyone and everything—family, manager, servants, offices, and services—were spread out along the long, low-ceilinged ground floor. Still, even without the upper floors, the house was spacious—the family quarters alone stretched for a hundred yards. In the central part were the main hall, the reception room, the billiards room, a study, and other "formal" rooms. From there, curving hallways led to two wings, one for the adults and the other for the children and their governesses and nannies. Each room had a name that stuck long after its origins were forgotten: "chocolate room," "bishop's room," "cornflower room," "general's room," "round room," "green room," "classroom." The furniture was the usual mishmash of a country house; an ornate redwood end table from a onetime lodging in St. Petersburg or Moscow might stand alongside a ponderous homemade divan of painted wood. The wings ended in large round towers, but they did not match. After one burned down in 1876, the first Mikhail Mikhailovich rebuilt it in a different style, intending someday to rebuild the other. One of the towers was still standing as late as 1977—a huge, crumbling turret rising from a tangle of brush.

THE
SERGIYEVSKOYE
ESTATE

From a plan prepared by
I. Yu. Yarova 1991

A   Site of church, destroyed 1952;
    the bell tower still stands

B   Site of the manor house, destroyed 1923

C   Grass circle at center of formal driveway

D   Linden garden

E   Site of gazebo, with view of Oka

F   School, now a weekend retreat of the
    Kaluga Turbine Works

GG Alley of Love

H   Site of vodka distillery

I   Site of greenhouse

J   Site of cattle yard

K   Site of poultry barn

L   Site of bull barn

M   Apple orchards

N   Site of barn

O   Site of stables

P   Site of workshop

Q   Site of threshing barn

R   Round Meadow

S   Robbers' Spring

T   Leveled field for bonfires

U   Former path to Oka

V   Zaraza Forest

x   New houses and roads

   Buildings of the old estate

```
0            METERS            200
|----|----|----|----|----|----|

0            MILE              1/8
```

Koltsovo
Village

Ozhzhyonka Stream

H   I

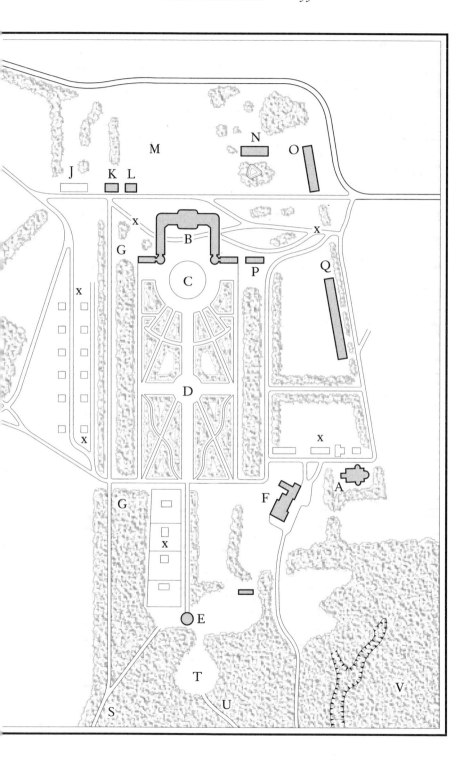

Like all old houses, Sergiyevskoye was haunted, and strange knocks and groans would be heard at times. The first Mikhail Mikhailovich and his wife ordered a religious service every month and sprinkled the rooms with holy water to chase out the demons.

The house and its wings embraced a courtyard, which carriages entered through opposing gates in the wings. White acacias covered the wings; black Crimean roses, bluebells, and jasmine edged the driveway, and tall poplars and spruces bordered the house from the outside. The courtyard opened through an ornate iron gate to the linden park, also walled in, beyond which a birch-lined alley led to the gazebo on the bluff over the Oka.

People in Koltsovo then and now firmly believe that the linden park forms the initials *M M O*, for Mikhail Mikhailovich Osorgin. Those who have seen the estate from the air insist this is so, and one old man there has written a poem on this theme. I never quite saw how the linden trees formed *M M O*, and if they did it was not deliberate, since they were planted by General Kar. But the later groves of firs and spruces were planted by the first Mikhail Mikhailovich and his Saxon forester, Oskar ("Karl Ivanovich") Menges, and these might well form *M M O*.

To the side of the park was the church, and behind the manor house stood the farm buildings, which eventually came to include a cattle barn, a poultry coop, stables, workshops, a hay shed, a granary so large it could easily hold half the grain harvest of the county, a long threshing barn with a steam-powered mill, a large greenhouse, and a distillery (distilling vodka was permitted on large estates and brought healthy profits, but the second Mikhail Mikhailovich dismantled the one at Sergiyevskoye out of principle when he took over). A steep hill descending to the Ozhzhyonka stream was planted with apple trees, which in spring still cover the hillside with blossoms.

When the deed was signed, Mikhail Gerasimovich went out to look over his new lands. In accordance with the custom of the time, he was accompanied by a full entourage, including a butler and his assistants, several coachmen, cooks, and other servants. But as any Russian would anticipate in a venture that had begun with a game of chance, fate would never allow so easy a conclusion. It was the butler who subsequently compiled a report on what happened for Mikhail Gerasimovich's wife. In the style of the time, he referred to his master in the plural:

We arrived safely, and we were met correctly. The *barin* went around the whole house, the entire manor. They were pleased to be satisfied with everything. The *barin* gave instructions that the last room by the gates be prepared for him, where none of the Masters Kar had ever lived. They found this corner to their liking and said it would be their office. While I unpacked, and the cook prepared lunch, Mikhail Gerasimovich went to the church, which is very close to the house; you need only walk diagonally across the recently planted French garden [the linden park]. They were not there too long, and returned in a mood blacker than a cloud. I did not understand—I see that matters are not well; I wonder, could it be that the clergy greeted our *barin* with insufficient respect, or something else? But I dared not ask. Our father-*barin* sits there, not himself, not so much angry as pensive. After lunch we lay down to rest. I stayed behind the door to keep an eye out, and I hear them constantly sighing and muttering something to themselves. All I could make out was that they constantly mention the mother's grave, saying, "Lord, to sell the grave of one's mother, what a sin." They arose downhearted, refused tea, and at night, when they went to bed, they turned and groaned in their sleep. In the morning they began saying totally mixed-up things. I was terribly frightened. I tell the rest of our people, "What's happened with Mikhail Gerasimovich? Could it be that someone put the evil eye on them?" At one moment they order a carriage to go to the club, at another they command that we dispatch someone to Iversk to have a memorial service held for his mother, though for some reason he calls the late lady Maria, not Ekaterina, apparently forgetting her name. Here I understand that things are very bad. We are in an unfamiliar place, there is no one around, so I dared disturb You, and dispatched this report.

On receiving the dispatch, Mikhail Gerasimovich's wife, Varvara Andreyevna, immediately came out with a doctor. They found her husband severely agitated, and transferred him to Moscow. On the basis of the butler's story, the family concluded that his derangement was due to his discovery that Sergei Kar had sold the estate where his mother was buried.

Mikhail Gerasimovich remained incoherent for about six months, until he abruptly came to one morning. Varvara Andreyevna was in deep prayer before the family icon, Our Lady of Jerusalem, when suddenly Mikhail Gerasimovich addressed her in his normal voice: "Varenka, why are you crying and praying? I am totally well." The respite lasted a year, during which he set his affairs in order. Convinced that Maria Kar's fate awaited all Osorgins if Sergiyevskoye remained in the family, he wrote a will ordering that the estate be sold and the money distributed as dowries for his three daughters. After a year he again lost his mind, and never recovered it again.

Varvara Andreyevna found a way around his will. Upon his death in 1850, she arranged for the daughters to cede Sergiyevskoye to their only brother, Mikhail, which they did on his marriage in 1857. In exchange, Varvara Andreyevna gave the daughters other estates and her Moscow house.

But Mikhail Gerasimovich's premonition was realized: no Osorgin thereafter lay undisturbed in Russia. He and Varvara Andreyevna were both buried at Ostrovnya, their estate near Moscow, and the property was sold in the early 1880s by their son. When their grandson tried to find their graves some years later, a priest led him to an overgrown and unfenced churchyard in the forest, with several identical, cracked, and almost indecipherable tombstones of black marble. These were his ancestors, among them Mikhail Gerasimovich and Varvara Andreyevna.

Their son, the first Mikhail Mikhailovich, was buried side-by-side with his wife, Maria Alexeyevna, at the Novodevichy monastery in Moscow under a black granite tombstone he designed. The women's monastery still stands, a beautiful walled ensemble popular with tourists and Muscovites. Adjacent to it is a cemetery with two sections, one prerevolutionary and one Soviet. It is here that Nikita Khrushchev is buried, and here, too, lies Nadezhda Alliluyeva, Stalin's second wife, who killed herself; she was the mother of Svetlana Alliluyeva. But most of the tombs inside the monastery proper, where the Osorgins were buried, were leveled in Soviet times.

By chance, a survey of the cemetery was completed in 1926, two years before the tombs were razed. It shows that Mikhail Mikhailovich and his wife were buried behind the Uspensky Church, and that a tombstone of black granite with a cross and icon marked their graves. The Novodevichy monastery has been beautifully restored in recent years. I went there with my wife on a lovely spring day in 1994 and put flowers behind the former church, which is now an art gallery.

The next Mikhail Mikhailovich Osorgin and his wife were already buried abroad, in Clamart, France. My grandfather is buried with my grandmother in Roslyn, New York. They, I hope, will rest in peace.

As for Maria Sergeyevna Kar, Mother Evpraxia: on one visit to Sergiyevskoye I met Anastasia Nikolayevna Iokhin, who was born in 1918 and who remembered that when the church was still open the first thing people did on entering was to walk over to the tomb of the founder and place a candle before it. The rest I have described—how her tomb was broken into and her bones became playthings.

All that remained of her beautiful church, whose taste and refinement were the glory of the province, was the gutted tower with its faded letters. These, I realized, were an inscription from the same Fifth Psalm on which Bishop Evlampiy had based his homily on that festive October day in 1810 when he appealed to the Lord to watch over the church: "*Vnidu v dom Tvoi i poklonyusya ko khramu sviatomu tvoemu* . . ."—"I will come into Your house in the multitude of Your mercy; in fear of You I will worship toward Your holy temple."

5

A Spiritual Cradle

The Osorgins were masters of Sergiyevskoye for only 75 years, but those years spanned from serfdom to revolution. (The next stage of Russian history, the Soviet Union, also lasted 75 years, and marked an even more dramatic passage—from revolution back to serfdom.)

Mikhail Gerasimovich Osorgin's son, the first Mikhail Mikhailovich, began life as the master of serfs and lived to see them sit in the first Duma, the ill-fated legislative assembly elected in 1906. The second Mikhail Mikhailovich, born two months after the emancipation of the serfs but still raised in the baroque world of Swiss nannies, consumptive tutors, and clubby Guards regiments, lived to see his universe consumed by revolution, and ended his days abroad. Six of his seven children would finish their lives in emigration. But to the end of their days they would all regard Russia as their motherland and Sergiyevskoye as their spiritual cradle. One son, Georgy, did not have the chance to leave Russia; in 1929 he was executed by the Bolsheviks on the Solovetsky Islands, the first labor camp of the infamous Gulag.

The Osorgins were not always at Sergiyevskoye, of course. Many winters were spent in St. Petersburg, Moscow, or abroad. The entire family moved to St. Petersburg for the years the second Mikhail Mikhailovich spent at the school of the Corps of Pages and in the Chevalier Guards (1876–83); and when he served successively as vice governor of Kharkov and governor of Grodno and Tula (1898–1905), that was where the family lived. But Sergiyevskoye was always their home and their haven.

My grandfather Sergei Osorgin, born in 1888, spent his childhood and youth at Sergiyevskoye, and his memoirs evoke a mystical never-never land in which the seasons, feasts, labors, peasants, and *barins* blended in an immutable harmony:

> Sergiyevskoye was a spiritual and physical cradle for us. Of course, when I say Sergiyevskoye I presuppose that setting and that moral air which surrounded us when our parents taught us to talk, to pray, and to think. This air so suffused our upbringing that it is hard to say where the one ended and the other began.
>
> . . . When I write at the start of these memoirs of a "dear place" where I hope to find eternal rest, I am thinking precisely of that spiritual heritage which Sergiyevskoye left me. My "dear place" lives: When, after the revolution, I ripped my soul out of the past in blood and agony, its many roots retained much of that dear soil in which I was reared, my beloved, priceless Sergiyevskoye—enough remained to support me through life, to keep me from wasting away and becoming a homeless, restless wanderer. You too, my children, and you, my grandchildren, you are not foreign, you have your rightful, personal place by my side, on that same dear Sergiyevskoye soil, which will nourish you and give you life, if only you do not turn away from it. So listen to your father and grandfather. I will try, as I can, to show you our sacred, unforgettable Sergiyevskoye.

When Varvara Andreyevna Osorgin became mistress of Sergiyevskoye in 1843, the Russian empire was at its zenith. Russia had chased Napoleon back to Paris and was rapidly expanding to the far corners of the Eurasian expanse. The St. Petersburg court was among the most splendid in Europe. The arts flourished: Pushkin's vibrant language opened an extraordinary century of literature; Italian opera and French theater played in St. Petersburg and Moscow. Prosperous Russians took the waters at German spas, lost fortunes at Monte Carlo, spent winters in the "capitals" and summers on their ever grander estates, financed and lavishly maintained by legions of serfs and hosts of servants.

But it is the fate of empires that their moment of greatest glory is also the beginning of their decline. The victory over Napoleon introduced young Russian officers to the republican stirrings of Europe, and in 1825 they mounted the pathetic rebellion against the absolute monarchy known as the Decembrist uprising. Thereafter the monarchy turned ever more defensive and absolute; the tsarist bureaucracy became increasingly intolerant of dissent, and a new secret police plunged into a bloody game of cat-and-mouse with a radical and ever more violent revolutionary intelligentsia.

Born in the last years of the eighteenth century, Varvara Andreyevna Osorgin was of a generation of Russian gentry that spoke and thought exclusively in French. In those days, younger children addressed older ones with the formal *vous,* and added "brother" or "sister" after their name (as in "Mikhail-brother" or "Varya-sister"). Older ones called younger ones only by their names and used the informal *tu.*

Varvara Andreyevna spent her winters in St. Petersburg or Moscow and her summers at Sergiyevskoye. Her life was strictly ordered. Morning tea was a ritual to which she admitted only her son and daughter-in-law. She would invariably have her personal mix of herbal and green teas, and biscuits freshly baked that morning, served by her own butler.

After her husband lost his mind, Varvara Andreyevna thought it best not to educate her son at home, as was the custom of the time, and she enrolled him first in a boarding school for young noblemen in Moscow (in what is now the Pashkov House, across from the Kremlin), and then in the military academy in St. Petersburg. At age 16 he was commissioned in the Hussar Life Guards regiment.

Every summer, Varvara Andreyevna would visit her three married daughters on their estates, taking with her a sizable retinue. Her conveyance was an elaborate *dormeuse,* a sleeping carriage drawn by six horses with places inside for six persons—plus a bookcase, a medicine cabinet, and a folding iron table with two chairs. The right rear cushion raised to uncover a water closet. Through special windows, passengers could talk to the butler ensconced in a leather seat next to the coachman, or a maid sitting in a separate compartment attached high to the rear (the maid had to double as brakeman). Large compartments in various nooks of the carriage held ample luggage. Varvara Andreyevna did not like to sleep in the *dormeuse,* and servants and cooks were sent ahead with wagonloads of furniture, carpets, and provisions to set up lodgings at suitable inns. Varvara Andreyevna had even larger carriages built for her son and her eldest daughter, Maria Benckendorff.

Varvara Andreyevna was remembered among peasants as crusty and tough. Sergei Osorgin, who never knew his great-grandmother, was shamed by a story he heard from a very old peasant. In his youth, while serving as night watchman at Varvara Andreyevna's house in Moscow, he fell asleep. "People in our neighborhood were brazen," he told young Sergei. "They got into the storehouse and cleared it out. And I'm asleep! In the morning the *barynia* was informed, and she ordered that I be taken to the precinct and lashed forty times. After that I never slept on duty again. The *barynia* was disciplined herself and gave no breaks."

When her son neared the age of 25, Varvara Andreyevna set about arranging his marriage. One of her acquaintances in Moscow, Prince Alexei Dmitrievich Volkonsky, had a daughter on whom he doted, and everyone agreed that the wealthy hussar and the young princess made a sterling match—everyone, that is, except the couple in question, who showed no interest in each other. So on Mikhail Mikhailovich's twenty-fifth birthday, April 13, 1857, Varvara Andreyevna got busy: She arranged a family outing to the Trinity–St. Sergei monastery in Sergiev Posad (called Zagorsk under the Soviets), to which she invited the Volkonskys.

Varvara Andreyevna had a reputation as a tasteful and refined hostess, though in this more sedate era we may not appreciate what followed as an example of restraint or subtlety. She took several rooms in the monastery hotel and filled them with fine furniture, rich wall coverings, and luxurious carpets from her house in Moscow. After church, she served her guests an exquisite supper. "Though not given to the opulent Russian feasts of the Volkonskys," recounted her grandson, the second Mikhail Mikhailovich, "she nevertheless never served fewer than six courses of fine French cuisine, where different sauces, condiments, and legumes played major roles." In case this was not enough, a boudoir of sorts was set up where it was arranged for the targeted couple to find themselves alone.

Still, nothing happened. So the next day, Varvara Andreyevna went for broke. She sent her son-in-law, Semyon Okhliabinin, to her son with the message that Maria Volkonskaya was in love with him, and that he was obliged to make known his intentions. At the same time, another courier informed Prince Volkonsky that young Osorgin was in love with his daughter but was reluctant to speak out for fear of a refusal. The stratagem worked. The next day intermediaries once again went forth from the Osorgin house on Bolshaya Basmannaya to prepare the way, and on April 16, Varvara Andreyevna finally made a formal proposal to Prince Alexei Dmitrievich on behalf of her son for the hand of his daughter. On the very next day—it was Holy Saturday, the day before Easter—"all Moscow" was invited to the betrothal.

On the day after that, Varvara Andreyevna added a postscript in her own broad hand to the instructions she dispatched regularly to her foreman at

Sergiyevskoye: "On the receipt of this, announce to all our good and true servants that God has willed to grant me a great joy: Mikhail Mikhailovich is engaged and was yesterday betrothed to Princess Maria Alexeyevna Volkonsky, for which I ask a service of thanksgiving with the singing of 'Many Years' to the affianced groom and bride."

"Of their engagement they told little," wrote their son, the second Mikhail Mikhailovich, "but my mother always stressed that once she gave her consent and received her parents' blessing, she fell in love with her fiancé with all her soul and maintained that love to the end of her life." For the rest of their lives, the couple would exchange special glances during Holy Saturday services, the anniversary of their engagement. They were married in the evening on May 31, 1857, in their parish church, the Church of the Great Martyr Nikita, and spent their honeymoon at Ostavnya, their estate in Zvenigorod, where the manor was decorated and illumined for them, and the ancient St. Savva Monastery glowed across the Moscow River under a full moon.

Varvara Andreyevna died three years later. Her son was on a visit to a family property near Nizhny Novgorod when he saw in a dream that his mother was dying. He rushed home but arrived too late.

The first Mikhail Mikhailovich Osorgin was largely typical of his generation in that he never found a true outlet for his wealth, talent, or energies. He considered a military career in his youth and, indeed, made a brilliant hussar. Tall and slim, he was a fine horseman, a superb hunter, and a keen billiards player. His regimental comrades included many a rising star—Iosif Gurko, later a celebrated field marshal in the Russo-Turkish wars; Count Mikhail Loris-Melikov, later chief minister to Tsar Alexander II; and his brothers-in-law Dmitry Zhemchuzhnikov and Prince Alexei Alexeyevich Volkonsky, the latter a notorious playboy. As a young cavalry officer, Osorgin served as aide-de-camp to Grand Duke Mikhail Pavlovich and participated in the Hungarian campaign of 1849, though he saw no action. But on marrying, he resigned his commission and settled into a life divided among Sergiyevskoye, the capitals, and an annual trip to take the waters at a German spa. He broke the routine only briefly, when he served as a provincial magistrate in Kaluga.

To the end of his days, Osorgin remained a *barin* of the old school, utterly devoted to tsar and family, disdainful of commerce, bound by rigid codes of chivalry and honor. His archaic formality was sometimes a source of amusement to younger generations. One grand-niece, after singing a song, was taken aback when Mikhail Mikhailovich kissed her hand and lavished praise upon her talent in courtly French; all he lacked, she whispered to a friend, "was a pow-

The first Mikhail Mikhailovich Osorgin in his study.

dered wig and sword." Aloof with servants and peasants, he commanded a deference verging on reverence, even when simply writing a letter. "He wrote rarely, but when he did, it was an event," recalled his son. "Mama protected his peace, people walked down the corridor on tiptoes—'the old *barin* is writing'—lunch was delayed until he finished, and the letter itself was entrusted with special instructions to the mail carrier for delivery to the post office."

Osorgin's son, the second Mikhail Mikhailovich, was never close to his father. A fussy, pedantic, and sensitive man who far preferred Italian opera to hunting, the son at times chafed under his tough father. It was old Osorgin's grandsons who learned from him to love hunting and riding, and two of them, Sergei and Georgy, served with distinction as cavalrymen in the First World War.

Raised in considerable wealth and the expansive lifestyle of a serf-owning *barin*, old Osorgin never really adapted to reduced means. When the younger Mikhail Mikhailovich was compelled to resign his commission in the Chevalier Guards and return to Sergiyevskoye to save the estate from bankruptcy, he was dismayed to discover what his father considered a modest lifestyle: "Nobody ever visited, but in the kitchen there was a chef with a helper, who prepared as many as ten dishes per dinner. Nobody drank, but wines were always placed on the table. Servants were cut back, but there were at least a steward, a butler, a waiter, four maids, two laundresses, and a bookkeeper."

"Grandfather was not at all a snob, but his times could not but leave their imprint on his character," wrote his grandson Sergei.

> Wherever he lived, whether in Sergiyevskoye or Petersburg, he remained the same aloof *barin*, following the lives of his peasants and servants from on high—though attentively and with scrupulous fairness. . . . One has to understand that Grandfather had to live through emancipation, the start of the revolutionary movement after the Japanese war, and finally the Manifesto of the 17th of October [1905] and the duma. What a break in way of life! What a re-evaluation of ancient values he had to undergo! Rarely, very rarely, I would hear Grandfather talking of the old days with old men like himself, but there was never a note of bitterness or protest— "Of course, everything's different now, but . . ."

Old Osorgin's wife, Maria Alexeyevna, had none of his aloofness. Small and plump, she always wore a black embroidered cap (a white one on church days) over hair severely drawn back, and she delved into every detail of the household and the peasants' lives, even after the management of the household formally passed to her daughter-in-law. Her grandson Sergei painted a delightful portrait of his fussy, devout "babushka":

> Babushka followed the lives of her people with her whole heart and took a warm part in their joys and tragedies. . . . She had many godsons and goddaughters in the village. Once, sitting on the terrace, Babushka saw a soldier on leave walking through the courtyard. At that time one of her godsons was doing his military service. Babushka peered through her lorgnette—"Vasya, come over here, Vasya!" The soldier came over and drew himself to attention. "Hello, Vasya." "I wish you health, Maria Alexeyevna!" he replied in the military manner. "You are Vasya, aren't you?" "Yes ma'am, Maria Alexeyevna!" But Babushka's doubts deepened—"No, you're not Vasya at all." "No ma'am, Maria Alexeyevna!" "Well, go on, go on."
>
> Babushka did not immediately surrender the entire household to my mother, especially the bookkeeping, the dairy farm, and the icehouse, and resolutely watched over them, attending the milking of the cows in the early morning and the evening. For this an armchair and a table were

placed by the icehouse with a mountain of different prayer books. The morning prayers and the appropriate devotional hymns had to be read, but there was no time for this, so it all had to be done at the same time. On a bench at Babushka's feet sat the bookkeeper, Anastasia Maximovna, and next to her the tub into which the milkmaids poured their milk, reporting the name of the cow as they did: "Khitrushka, Malinka . . ." Babushka affectionately wagged her head, whispering, "Oh sweetest Jesus, have mercy on us . . ." as she watched from the corner of her eye how much milk was being given: "Anastasia Maximovna, why has Malinka fallen behind?" "I don't know, Maria Alexeyevna. Perhaps you'd better ask the herdsman." The herdsman, waiting in the field with his whip coiled on his shoulder, comes over to be questioned, and the matter is soon made clear—Malinka was lonely yesterday but now seems happy and fine, and Babushka, with a contented sigh, resumes her whispers, "Rejoice, O Mother of Life, rejoice, O Unwedded Bride. . . ."

Once, by chance, our neighbor, Sofia Emmanuilovna M., came upon this scene and could not believe it: "No, this is phe-no-me-nal! It's charming! It's eighteenth-century!"

Despite the radical changes in the world around them, the old Osorgins lived out their lives in full harmony and love. She died first, after 49 years of marriage, and at her funeral her husband stood over her open casket for a long time, wagging his long gray beard and talking to her in gentle tones, his face awash in tears. Now and then, walking over to his children's old Swiss nanny, he would say, "*Nyunichka, venez la voir, de plus en plus jolie*" ("Nyunichka, come see her, prettier and prettier"). He died in 1910. Sensing the approach of the end, he said to his son: "Misha, read the prayer." "Which?" "The parting. . . ." At that moment he died, and a nightingale that had long finished singing suddenly burst anew into loud song.

Maria Alexeyevna's father, Prince Volkonsky, was one of those eccentrics that provincial life—with its isolation, enforced leisure, and abundance of cheap labor—seemed to churn out in profusion. Legends about him were legion, and they all painted an impossible but lovable *barin* who would be utterly at home in Gogol's *Dead Souls* or Tolstoy's *War and Peace* (whose crusty old Prince "Bolkonsky" he in fact vaguely resembled). Born to an illustrious name, he knew everyone in St. Petersburg and Moscow, and was not abashed to barge into their reception rooms to demand justice or a favor for a friend. He had no sense of money and was always near bankruptcy, which he finally achieved, and he was forever involved in hopeless schemes. His table was renowned for its abundance of Russian fare; he never set it for fewer than ten, and usually fed many more. Neither bankruptcy nor blindness in his last years altered his ways, and he was dearly loved by all who knew him.

On his estate, Volkonsky maintained a huge retinue, including a peasant theater and orchestra, liveried servants, and forty horses. But the horses were old and lame, the servants' tunics were worn through at the elbow and heavily patched with different fabrics, the floor of the theater was rotted through, the orchestra played mercilessly off-key, and its director was always drunk. Before mounting the carriage, the ancient coachman had to evict roosting hens.

When his Osorgin grandchildren and great-grandchildren came to visit, Volkonsky would bend over backward to amuse them. That usually meant cranking up the fountain he once had installed in the flower bed: The contraption was fed from a large, rusty tank mounted on posts directly by the terrace, blocking the view, which leaked faster than it could be filled. "All it took was for the children to notice it, and Great-Grandfather would get all excited," wrote Sergei Osorgin. " 'Hey, Petka! Vanka! Senka! . . .' After lots of hard work, an ancient, rusted pump would be brought into motion, and after a while a bit of water would spurt pathetically from a pipe. But Great-Grandfather was happy."

Volkonsky's affairs were in a perpetual mess, and his cattle, seed, money, and lumber were pilfered mercilessly. One time, Volkonsky bought a new sowing machine, a novelty at the time, which he proudly sent his grandson to inspect. Young Osorgin could not find it anywhere, until Volkonsky himself recognized a piece of the machine that the cook was in the process of chopping into kindling. "Dedushka didn't even get angry. He broke into a good-natured laugh and immediately set about tasting the dishes and ordering something new," marveled the grandson.

After lunch, Volkonsky would lie down, and somebody—his daughter or a grandchild, if they were visiting—would read to him and rub his feet. He always had the same book read to him, *The History of 1812*, by Bogdanovich; when he finished, he would start again from the beginning. On rising he had a glass of tea, which he would send back if it was not scalding hot, barking, "I didn't ask for ice." With the tea he exchanged his pipe for a Marilan Doux cigarette, very long and sweet, which he kept in a silver case engraved with a view of the Bolshoi Theater. If he had not yet completed his morning prayers he would do so now, sending an aerial kiss to every icon by turn.

*Four generations of Osorgins. From left: Sergei, Liza,
the second Mikhail Mikhailovich, Mikhail, Maria
Alexeyevna, her mother Princess Maria Volkonsky,
the first Mikhail Mikhailovich.*

Maria Alexeyevna's mother was Volkonsky's second wife. The first had died young and left him with two small children, and after ten years of widowhood, during which he acquired a reputation as something of a Don Juan, he decided that his children needed a mother. One day a broken carriage forced him to spend the night at the house of a poor, widowed landowner with a large family, one Dmitry Kutuzov (a cousin of the field marshal who led Russian troops against Napoleon). With his typical impetuousness, Volkonsky decided that Kutuzov's eldest daughter, already over thirty, was perfect for his needs and made an immediate proposal, insisting that the marriage take place then and there. Three days later he came home with a new *barynia*. She proved a poor stepmother; after giving birth to a daughter, Maria, she drove his first two children away.

Princess Volkonsky developed elephantiasis and swelled to enormous proportions in her old age, becoming virtually immobile. After Volkonsky's death

she asked to live in Sergiyevskoye, but moving her proved to be a major operation. Because of her size, she could not fit into a normal passenger wagon, so
Baron Derviz, the chairman of the Ryazan Railway and a friend, put a special
car at her disposal, into which she and her custom-made divan were loaded
from the freight platform. Her old coachman, Sidor, was sent ahead with her
specially built carriage, in which she finally arrived in Sergiyevskoye. She spent
her remaining years there, mostly in prayer or reading spiritual literature. Her
walls were hung solid with icons, and when she made her daily devotions she
had a maid turn her ponderous sofa toward each image in turn. On her death
she left a request to be buried alongside her husband at the Novodevichy
monastery in Moscow. This proved to be a whole operation in itself, and her
grandson went to considerable trouble to prepare a casket of appropriate size
and to arrange transport.

With Russia's vast distances, and with the roads virtually impassable in spring
and autumn, the village was often an isolated, self-contained colony. At
Sergiyevskoye, the four generations of Osorgins and their army of servants,
nannies, and tutors were usually supplemented by relatives and a changing
array of hangers-on. In 1870, for example, Mikhail Mikhailovich records that
two of his sisters moved in with their husbands and children. Another entry in
his memoirs reads: "On July 30 all the Gagarins and Lermontovs arrived. The
Lermontovs came for two weeks, the others stayed until the end of November."
    In this insular world, servitors often grew into family. Anne Tomi, a Swiss
governess everyone called Nyunichka, came when the second Mikhail
Mikhailovich was born and stayed until her death 37 years later, presiding over
the samovar, the mail, the preparation of jams and fruit liqueurs, the purchase
of mushrooms and berries from village children, Christmas tree decorations,
and many other important matters. Tall, gaunt, prominent of nose, tempera-
mental, and not too bright, she almost always dressed in black and wore a black
medallion on her breast with a portrait of her late fiancé, and she never let it be
forgotten that in an earlier incarnation, while in the service of a Countess
Donau in Prussia, she had once held the infant Kaiser Wilhelm II in her arms.
She grew fully into the family, serving as confidante, comforter, chaperone, and
friend to three generations of Osorgins. Even as a governor, the second Mikhail
Mikhailovich, when overcome by the burdens of office, would seek refuge in
old Nyunichka's room. "I would lie down on her couch, and in her calm, level
voice, her spectacles perched on the end of her nose, darning something for my

parents, she would talk about the past, about my childhood or adolescence, when there were no worries." At such times even his wife knew not to interrupt.

When the first Mikhail Mikhailovich died, in 1910, Nyunichka seemed to conclude that her life's work was done. She sorted out her trunks, sat back in her armchair, and began to withdraw. The doctor found nothing wrong, but he recognized what was happening: "Her candle has burned to the end; she will not rise," he said. She died soon after, leaving behind a note to the second Mikhail Mikhailovich and his wife: "*Mes chers adorés, Lise et Michel.*" She thanked them for all the happiness, concern, and love she had found at Sergiyevskoye and concluded: "*En rejoignant mes chers Monsieur et Madame, je vous bénis tous et prie Dieu de vous avoir en Sa Sainte et très Haute Garde, vous deux et vos enfants. Adieu, mes chéris*" ("Rejoining my dear Monsieur and Madame, I bless all of you and pray to God to keep you under His Holy and Almighty Protection, the two of you and your children. Goodbye, my dears").

Then there was Tagochka, a Swiss governess who came for the next generation of children and married the tutor, Isidor Grigorievich Blonstein, who taught Russian, arithmetic, history, and geography; there was Mademoiselle Catherine Picard, the Swiss housekeeper; and a large supporting cast of visiting tutors (dance, piano, drawing), plus an ever-changing cast of relatives and neighbors. The latter included the Poltoratskys from neighboring Avchurino and Alexander Semyonovich Raevsky from Timofeyevka, a tall, handsome bachelor whose nearby estate was full of peasant children who distinctly resembled him, and who traveled only on horseback, was a celebrated connoisseur of songbirds, and grew delicious cherries.

And, of course, there was Platon Evgrafovich Evgrafov. His permanent presence at Sergiyevskoye is something of an enigma, largely because whenever he is mentioned in memoirs or letters the authors never deem it necessary to explain who he is or why he is there. It is simply taken for granted that he belongs there, entertaining the children with his stories, undertaking important missions ("Platon Evgrafovich was sent ahead to prepare our arrival . . ."), setting off the celebrated fireworks without which no family celebration was complete, keeping score at billiards. All Osorgin children knew Platon Evgrafovich's life story, which the second Mikhail Mikhailovich retold in his memoirs. In its passage from the steppes of Asia to a Russian manor, from a slave to a life companion, his is a saga of the young Russian empire—its wild frontiers, rich mélange of cultures, and unpredictable fates.

Platon Evgrafovich began life as Dzhasaul, the son of a poor Kirghiz nomad named Kapsyk in the Kirghiz-Kaisatsk Horde in the Central Asian steppes.

Unable to feed the boy, Kapsyk left him in the yurt of a rich man named Makai-Tamishi-Ka-Kak. The latter sent little Dzhasaul out to help tend his flocks, for which the boy was given one cup of goat's milk a day. He was always hungry; once he stole the tail of a newly slaughtered cow and gnawed at it all day. One day, while Makai-Tamishi-Ka-Kak was in the fields, an itinerant Cossack peddler showed up and sold Makai-Tamishi-Ka-Kak's wives a heap of finery. They had no money, so they gave him Dzhasaul. The Cossack was happy, since he could sell the boy in Siberia (in those days a Kirghiz "prisoner" could legally be bound in serfdom for 25 years). The second Mikhail Mikhailovich recorded Platon Evgrafovich's words as the latter continued his story:

> He sat me, a small boy, on his saddle, and to tame me he gave me a crust of bread. I had never tasted anything finer, *batyushka-otets* [literally "little-father-father," an endearment Platon Evgrafovich sprinkled liberally in his speech], and I immediately liked my Cossack. Night fell. We stopped for the night, tethered the horses, built a campfire, when suddenly we hear the sound of hoofbeats, and two sons of Makai-Tamishi-Ka-Kak gallop up to us; they said their father had returned and screamed at his wives— how could they sell me to the infidel Russians? They ordered that the wares be paid for in money and that I be brought back. The Cossack refused, and I stood there shaking, thinking of the delicious bread he gave me. If I return I'll starve again, plus I'll be beaten. They argued and yelled a long time, they nearly fell to fighting, and at last the Cossack says, "Let him decide himself whether to go with you or with me." Of course, I wanted to stay with the Cossack. The Kirghizes got angry and spat at me, "Let your soul perish," and left. Thus I remained with my new master.
>
> . . . We traveled on a long time with the Cossack and finally reached Kiakhty. There he sold me to the head of the customs service. It was bitter for me to part with my Cossack, but what's there to do? You live not as you want, but as God wills. Soon after I settled in with my new master they summoned a priest to baptize me. I didn't know what a priest was, *batyushka-otets*. I look, some long-haired types bring in some kind of tea, put on golden clothes, and suddenly say to me, "Undress." I trembled all over, thinking something bad is coming, and when they lifted me and dunked me in this tea, I began bellowing at the top of my lungs, broke away from them, and ran away naked into the street, so they barely caught me. From then on they began calling me Platoshka [the diminutive for Platon] and would say, "Look here, you're a Christian now, not a Mus-

lim." But I understood nothing, I was young, stupid. What I understood was that I was beaten at Makai-Talishi-Ka-Kak's and I'm beaten here, except that here I'm fed as much as I want. Sometimes I ran off to my godfather, the Cossack Evgraf, my former master [from whom Platon had gotten his patronymic, Evgrafovich], or to the priest; they taught me how to pray.

I began coming of age; how old I was, God knows. One thing I do remember, *batyushka-otets,* is that young women began appealing to me about the time Napoleon came, especially those with long braids. At times I'd cast a glance at them and get a whack: "Go fetch a pipe for the *barin.*" The *barin* was stern and lived richly; no goods passed his customs post without something from the merchant. The house was a full cup.

Platon Evgrafovich moved with his new master first to St. Petersburg and then to Moscow, where he was eventually set free. A talented craftsman, he soon gained a reputation as a tuner of musical instruments, fiddler, and jack-of-all-trades. Prince Volkonsky was an especial admirer of his music and his fireworks, and one day he impulsively asked Platon Evgrafovich to come live on his estate, offering to put at his disposal a pair of horses and a coachman of his own. Platon Evgrafovich agreed, and before long he embraced this coachman, Nikifor, as the family he had never had. He found him a wife, baptized and tutored his daughter, married her off, brought her husband into his house, and stood godfather to her first son, named Platon.

His strongest attachment, however, was to Volkonsky's daughter Maria, who was about four when he moved in, and to whom he remained loyal to the end of his days. When she fell ill with typhoid fever at the age of twelve, he stayed constantly at her side, sleeping on the floor by her door until she recovered. When she married Osorgin, he moved with her to Sergiyevskoye and became as much a fixture at the Osorgins as he had been at the Volkonskys, staying with them whether they were in Sergiyevskoye, Moscow, or St. Petersburg.

Platon Evgrafovich's idiosyncrasies were legion. When they were in St. Petersburg he addressed all of Mikhail Mikhailovich's friends as "chairman," and cawed like a crow at the top of his lungs whenever he saw one of them in the street. He was also a repository of family legends and a storyteller par excellence. When he went to confession, Platon Evgrafovich recited his sins so loudly that the entire church was intimately familiar with his failings. Then, when the service ended and he was walking out of church, he would invariably exclaim, "*Batyushka-otets,* how weary I am of these priests!"

His most important role at Sergiyevskoye was on name days. After the church service, the traditional *krendel* (a pretzel-shaped cake), and the festive dinner, Platon Evgrafovich, resplendent in an old-fashioned frock coat, would formally present to the person whose day it was the program of the evening's fireworks. At twilight everyone would move into the garden, where benches were set under multicolored lanterns, and the first signal rocket would rise. The fireworks would often fail, and Platon Evgrafovich's voice would be heard out of a cloud of smoke: "This damned one, *batyushka-otets*, was last year's." The last number would be Platon Evgrafovich's pièce de résistance: A massive owl would appear high in a tree, with flapping wings and a fountain of sparks spewing from its beak. Few ever actually saw the fantastic bird through the thick smoke, but the effect was memorable.

This was the Sergiyevskoye where my grandfather was raised, and which he sanctified in his memoirs. For Sergei Osorgin was a hopeless romantic, elevating the routine of daily life to grand heights of chivalry, drama, and passion. When the First World War broke out, he rushed to join the "Immortal Hussars"—a regiment renowned for plunging passionately into the bloodiest battle—dreaming of leading cavalry charges and returning grievously wounded to Sergiyevskoye to be nursed by his beloved Sonia (all of which actually came to pass). Sergei also had an artist's eye for detail and a keen sense of humor, and his vignettes vividly capture the sounds and smells and little dramas of country life.

His Sergiyevskoye is, of course, idealized; the real one had its share of misery, inequity, and inefficiency—which will also be described. But I believe it is no coincidence that after the revolution, the village produced a remarkable number of honest, believing Communists, like Nina Semyonova, Nikolai Shmanenkov, and Alexandra Trunina, who really did try to build a better world. I believe they were nourished by the same "moral air" as my grandfather, the same harmony and faith.

. . . But why go to all this length to justify a bit of romance? Why not just enter awhile into my grandfather's sweet, enchanting Sergiyevskoye:

> In the evening, from the door of our playroom, we could see the other wing of the house, the "old half." The acacias under the windows were almost covered by snow, and smoke colored pink by the twilight rose in straight columns from every chimney against a backdrop of old birches, blue-gray with frost.

Sergei Osorgin in New York City.

Wolves, which were very numerous then, were so emboldened by cold and hunger that they came right up to the house, and one morning our nanny told us that during the night wolves had torn apart the mean yard dog, Venerka. Taking a walk that day, we actually saw some clumps of red fur near the servants' wing, all that was left of Venerka. Often at the table we heard talk that last night in some village, most often the forest village of Pyshkovo, wolves had dug through the roof of a shed and killed three or four sheep or a calf.

I remember one sunny, freezing morning we were walking with our governess Didite and not far from the barn we saw a big, unfamiliar dog sitting in the snow. We paid no attention until a passing *muzhik* anxiously sat us in his sleigh and brought us home. "Didn't you see the wolf? You have to be careful, mistress, they're desperate now." A couple of times late in the evening, already lying in bed, in the total silence of a winter night, I heard the howl of the wolf, rising slowly, tragically, eerily. You did not have to know much to recognize it: so wild a cry, a sound of deathly grief, a threat.

And it was curious: Through it I sensed all the more our children's room, so warm, so cozy, so safe from any threat. The vigil light burns with a steady red glow, Nanny knits by candlelight, her needles click, the clock pendulum slowly, calmly tick-tocks. Lord, how good it is!

Among the most delightful pages in my grandfather's memoirs are his celebrations of nature. So absorbed was he in the drama of the seasons that he and his mother took to writing regular reports for the "Spring Bulletin" column in the Moscow newspaper *Novoye vremya*—which birds had returned, which flowers were blooming, which butterflies had appeared—many of which were published.

In fact Sergei intended to make natural studies his life's work, and before the First World War interrupted his studies, he was a promising student of zoology at Moscow University, headed for a professorship. He writes here of that mystical moment in these northern lands when the long siege of winter is finally broken:

At last the evening would come when the sky clouded over, the temperature warmed, and a thick fog arose, and that night the last battle would be joined between spring and the departing winter. In the morning, Nanny would announce, "The ice is moving." For this my mother herself came with us. The whole road to the Oka, the entire forest rang with the sound of water, which burbled, hummed, or thundered as it rushed to the river. On the clearing in front of the ferryman's hut there were always some logs and overturned boats, and we would sit on them and look at the Oka. The ice moved in a solid sheet—very slowly, almost imperceptibly, but irresistibly. In that slowness there was a sense of unbelievable, elemental power.

Loud cracks and rumblings would come from the steep turns in the river in front of the Rock mountain and up past Borshchyovka [a neighboring manor]: The ice is breaking, climbing onto the shore or rising upright before heavily sinking back. Past us flows a tree, a bush ripped from the bank somewhere, a forgotten rick of hay, a fisherman's lean-to. . . . The next day, our gentle Oka is unrecognizable. The whole flood meadow is underwater, the opposite bank is also covered, so you can't see the bend in the river. Gulls dive into the water, and if they catch too large a fish, they fly to shore to eat it, accompanied by the jealous squawks of the others. The ferryman, Anfimy, reports that the first gaggles of geese and cranes have flown over, while along the path in the forest we hear the first timid peal of the chaffinch.

The Osorgins were a very musical family, and Sergei's Sergiyevskoye is always alive with music.

Mama began early to teach us children's songs—"I'll Sit Me by the Window," "Dusk Fell, a Babushka Sat"—which we sang along with her, trying to harmonize, and from there music flowed into us in a wide stream: We heard my mother play the piano alone or four-hands with my father; we heard the village choral songs, so melodious and harmonious; we heard the bells ringing in church, each peal so fitting to the service for which it is intended—the slow, mournful peal of the Easter Lent, the funereal tolling of the "minor second," as we called it, which began when the casket first left a village *izba* for the church, the festive Sunday summons to church, and the "triple peal"; we heard the lark, the oriole, and the nightingale; we heard the wind in the forest, which resonates like a violin string through the pines and spruces. Afterward, we moved on to the great piano and symphonic works on our own, and learned all there was to learn.

It was not only Sergei who remembered the music. Old people from the village told me how they would sneak up to the house to listen through the open windows to "the girls" play, and stop what they were doing when they heard the festive tolling of the great "silver" bell.

This bell was the pride of the village. It was ordered after an earlier bell had cracked and began making a terrible buzz. "They're laughing at us beyond the river," muttered the embarrassed villagers. So the damaged bell and another one that was rarely rung were sent off to Moscow to be melted down into a new bell. One Sunday the priest announced that the bell was ready. A massive cart was specially built to transport it from the Ferzikovo railroad station. A huge throng met it there and accompanied it the 8 miles to Sergiyevskoye, all the men taking turns, 40 at a time, pulling the cart. At the church, the two-and-a-half-ton bell was blessed, and then, with great effort and suspense, hoisted aloft. When it was finally in place, the covering was taken off and the 360-pound tongue was attached. The shiny new brass glittered from the high tower. Dmitry Evseyev, the assistant church warden, climbed up for the first ring. He was highly agitated. Sergei Osorgin recalled the moment:

> "Pray, mates!" Evseyev shouted, and people began crossing themselves, some falling to their knees. Evseyev began swinging the tongue back and forth, faster, harder, and then it struck. . . . I awaited that first ring with indescribable worry. Will the tone be unfamiliar, alien, or, God forbid, bad? But the ring was marvelous, full, mighty. What followed! Old *babas* sobbed, tears welled in the eyes of the *muzhiks*, everyone began to talk, though the comments were not always pious: "Now at last they in Vislyayevo [a village across the river] will scratch themselves!" "Why?" "Ours is a hundred and fifty *poody*, theirs only eighty."

My grandfather's longing for the lost world of his youth has been echoed among innumerable expatriates and exiles the world over. But can there have been another emigration that has felt so profound a sense of loss and longing— what the Russians call *toska*—for their native land? Perhaps this is because so many of them left with their souls "ripped out in blood and agony." Yet they at least remained free to remember, and to record what they remembered. Within Russia, the past was forcibly locked away and replaced with a concocted Soviet version of history.

On my last visit to Kaluga before leaving Russia, I noticed people snapping up a book from a sidewalk stand. It was a reprint of a prerevolutionary tourist guide to Kaluga. Leafing through it, I was struck by the preface, in which the editor explained why he was reissuing the old guidebook:

> The time has come to look back and speak honestly about what we, Russians, were, and what we became. History—here it is, just reach out your hand; but how long did they have to close our eyes, distort history, falsify it, conceal it, to turn us into Ivans who don't know our kin and dance on our forefathers' graves? Thank God, we are starting to part without regret with all that propaganda debris that seeped like the finest dust into every pore of our existence. Tear it out, shake it off, and with wonder you will see the noble glitter of the old—a living light that warms the soul.

Russians to whom I have given my grandfather's manuscript to read have invariably been deeply moved by his celebration of life, by the "living light" of his Sergiyevskoye. A veteran local reporter in Ferzikovo, Alexander Viktorovich Kandidov, who had delved deeply into the history of the region but had only a vague notion of the former landowners at Koltsovo, read my grandfather's memoirs one night and on the next day kept repeating, "All this we lost. All this we threw away."

6

Real Country People

A history of the Osorgin family published in 1900 by the Russian Genealogical Society puts considerable emphasis on the many things they were not: "The ancient line of Osorgins, or, in the more correct old form, Osor'ins, do not belong in the first ranks of the illustrious families of the Muscovite state. . . . Among members of this family we will not find boyars, *okolnichi* [the top two ranks of courtiers], major statesmen, or military leaders who decided the outcome of battles."

It continues in this vein for a while. However, the writer's purpose is not to belittle the family, which in the course of centuries honorably supplied warriors and officials to Muscovite princes and tsars in the regions of Murom and Vladimir, but to cast all the greater glory on the Osorgins' one illustrious figure. "The Osorgin line is dear to us not by the military feats of its members, not by holders of high state office; it is dear to the whole Russian nobility by the fact that this surname was borne by Saint Juliana of Lazarevskoye (Iuliania Lazarevskaya)."

Juliana lived in what was arguably the most tempestuous stretch of Russia's tempestuous history, those decades in the late sixteenth and early seventeenth centuries that embraced the reigns of Ivan the Terrible and Boris Godunov, and the "Time of Troubles" that followed, when Russia was brutalized by political terror, Polish and Swedish invasions, civil wars, peasant uprisings, poverty, famine, pestilence, and roaming bands of brigands.

The daughter of a high official in Nizhny Novgorod, Juliana was married to one Georgiy Osor'in, "a husband of good birth and prosperous," who spent most of his time away at war. She came to be revered for her devotion, modesty, and charity as she dutifully managed her household in the chaotic conditions of the time and bore thirteen children, of whom seven died in infancy, one was killed by a servant, and one was slain in battle. Her hagiography says she bore all her hardships in humility and prayer; during a famine in 1600 she shared her last grain with the hungry and set free those servants who thought they could survive better on their own. She died in 1605, and her grave in the village of Lazarevskoye, near Murom, soon became a focus of veneration.

The chronicle of Juliana's life written by her son Kalistrat "Druzhina" Osor'in is regarded as a classic of Russian hagiography. Druzhina pleads with readers not to dismiss his chronicle as simply an idealization of his mother by a doting son: "You, my brothers and fathers! Do not hold against me that I wrote this being crude and imperfect. And do not think that this is all untruth, done for maternal ties. The all-seeing eye of the Lord Christ, our God, sees that I do not lie."

The canonization of Juliana in the reign of the first Romanov tsar, Mikhail Fyodorovich (1613–45), not only recognized her devotion and charity but also marked an effort by the Church and the state to restore a measure of order to the ravaged nation by demonstrating that sanctity could be achieved through domestic life and normal devotion, and not only through the "egotistical monastic salvation" in which so many people sought refuge in the "Time of Troubles."

Their sainted ancestor was greatly venerated by the Osorgins. A Brotherhood of Saint Juliana was established at Sergiyevskoye in 1894 to assist needy parishioners, and a fragment of her relics was brought to Sergiyevskoye amid great ceremony on October 6, 1913, and mounted in an ornate icon in the church.

The remains of Saint Juliana were kept until 1917 in the church in Lazarevskoye. After the revolution, her relics and those of many other saints were seized by the Bolsheviks. Ancient reliquaries were broken open amid revelry and hooliganism to demonstrate that saintly remains were just ordinary bones. Propaganda films survive of these riots of desecration, but often the effect was the opposite of that intended. Word spread among the people that God had deliberately turned the holy relics into old bones so they would not fall to the godless Communists. The Bolsheviks quietly abandoned the campaign—

Drawing of the icon of Saint Juliana.

which was to have culminated in a massive exhibition of relics at the Kazan cathedral, in Leningrad, converted by the Soviets into a museum of atheism—and hid the confiscated relics safely away.

When relations between the state and the Orthodox Church improved under perestroika, many surviving relics were returned to the Church. We heard on our return to Moscow in 1991 that Saint Juliana's reliquary had been located in the cellar of the provincial museum in Murom and had been restored. When my mother, named Juliana after her ancestor, came for a visit in March 1992, we drove to Murom, a battered old city on the Oka River to the east of Moscow. There, in the newly reopened Church of the Annunciation, we stood before the beautifully restored reliquary of Saint Juliana, my mother's patron saint and great-great-great-great-great-great-great-great-great-grandmother.

Saint Juliana was a fitting patron for a family that sanctified duty, devotion, family ties, and service.

In 1903, as governor of the province of Grodno (now divided between

Poland and Belarus), the second Mikhail Mikhailovich made a speech to newly appointed land captains in which he set out the guiding principles of his service and his caste.

The land captain, *zemsky nachalnik*, was an office instituted by Alexander III as an extension of imperial control in the provinces. Appointed by the government, usually from among the local landowning gentry, the land captain had broad administrative and judicial authority over peasants of a specified area, typically between fifty and a hundred settlements. Liberals frowned on the office for the arbitrary authority it represented, but to a staunch monarchist like the second Mikhail Mikhailovich, who began his civil service as a land captain, it was the embodiment of the sacred duty of a *dvorianin* in his station between the autocrat anointed of God and the childlike "people."

All the notables of the province, resplendent in their full-dress uniforms, sat hushed in the ceremonial armorial hall of the governor's residence as Osorgin addressed the new land captains, while his family huddled behind the doors to listen. Among them was the 15-year-old Sergei:

> "Remember, gentlemen," Papa said in conclusion, "you have been honored with the highest confidence, you are preparing to serve the motherland, which is served first by the tsar, as her first son and first defender! Our people are simple and guileless, they are simpler and lower than you, and they love their tsar with a selfless love, as children love their father. You, representatives of the sovereign, are placed closest of all to the people, you personify for them imperial authority. Beware of betraying their trust. Beware of disturbing the people's soul, their childlike faith, and their love for their Tsar! May God help you, gentlemen."

So moved was my grandfather just recalling these words that, writing about it some fifty years later, he became effusive: "If all Russian officialdom had been composed of people like Papa, Russia would even now be living in peace and power, 'to our glory, to the fear of our foes!' " If, he might have added, the other 85 percent of the population was as guileless and devoted as his father presupposed.

Setting aside this fairly substantial "if," the Grodno speech was an expression of the ideal model of autocratic rule, and it was issued by a man who was the model of a fair, conscientious, and incorruptible viceroy. Tsar, motherland, and the Orthodox faith were not variables in his worldview, not a political system but absolutes.

His reverence for the tsar was unfeigned. Mikhail Mikhailovich described the rapture of his first contact with the tsar, when Alexander II visited his school in St. Petersburg. The Gosudar, or "master," as the tsar was commonly addressed, had only to utter "Hello, children," for Osorgin to be overcome with ardor: "I think I was not alone in feeling such a rush of devotion to him that I was ready to fulfill any command and to do the impossible."

His son Sergei, raised with revolution already in the air, wrote in his memoirs that his entire upbringing instilled in him feelings of "unlimited loyalty and love—precisely love—for the Throne, for tsarist rule, so inextricably bound to Russia, to the motherland." These feelings of devotion to the monarchy and implacable hostility to Communism survived long into emigration.

There is no denying that the Osorgins were more provincial, naive, patriarchal, religious, and simply old-fashioned than many of their peers, but this was precisely why, I believe, they personified much of what was good and decent in old Russia. Labels of "liberal" or "conservative" are misleading when applied to this caste. They were conservative to the marrow in their adherence to the privileges of the landed gentry, monarchism, and traditional religion, but their intimate familiarity with rural life and their paternalistic sense of responsibility for "their people" often put them in conflict with the bureaucrats in St. Petersburg and on the side of political reform.

The profoundly patriarchal Mikhail Mikhailovich was pegged as a "liberal" on the prerevolutionary political scale for his old-fashioned insistence on justice and fairness as a governor. But when he spoke of "reform," it was only in the context of autocracy; when he spoke of "the people," it was as a stern but caring parent; and whenever he uttered the word "revolution," it was always with utter disgust.

The peasants of Sergiyevskoye were obviously not as guileless and simple as the Osorgins would have us believe. But they responded to the paternalism of their *bariny* with a loyalty and respect that continued long after the Osorgins were stripped of their lands and status. When the Bolsheviks evicted the Osorgins from Sergiyevskoye, local people wept and organized an escort to protect them all the way to Moscow. And long after that, into the hungry 1920s, the villagers supplied them with wagonloads of provisions, asking nothing in exchange.

The Osorgins regarded themselves as real country people, intimate with nature and "the people," unlike their Trubetskoi cousins, whom they dismissed as patricians for treating the countryside only as a place to relax. Conversely,

Grigory Trubetskoi, the second Mikhail Mikhailovich's favorite brother-in-law, liked to poke fun at his sister's fussy and principle-riddled husband, whom he called "Mishanchik," for his patriarchal and pedantic approach to country living.

The visiting Trubetskois loved to spend long summer evenings with their Osorgin cousins in the gazebo at the edge of the steep bluff overlooking the Oka. But Grigory recalled with amusement that "old 'Mishanchik' did not like 'kowtowing' to nature and usually hurried everyone home. He acknowledged walks only through the fields and only with a purpose, and he thought it shameful to stroll about for no reason, like us city dwellers, who were accustomed to treating the countryside as a place of leisure."

For Trubetskoi, those days in the countryside were bliss: "In the evening, in the spring, filled with the song of nightingales, we would return home to the dining room, where the samovar was hissing. After tea the whole family played cards, and the parents would get as excited as the children. We retired early, country style, to rise early."

Life at Sergiyevskoye was, indeed, "country style." During the school year, children were awakened at seven-thirty, morning lessons were from nine to noon, the children took a walk from noon to two, then lunch, then evening classes until seven. Next came evening tea and games (or dances, if there were visiting cousins) until nine, then prayers and bed.

The children had lessons in Russian, French, German, arithmetic, history, geography, catechism, art and drawing, music and dancing. The second Mikhail Mikhailovich complained in later life that his mother taught music only to his sister, considering it a useless pursuit for a boy, but both sexes were taught dancing, which was regarded as an indispensable social skill. Young people entering society were expected to have sufficient mastery of the waltz to be able to make refined conversation as they swirled around the ballroom floor, while the dashing mazurka was an opportunity for a young man to strut his macho stuff.

The "facts of life" were not taught. On the contrary, Mikhail Mikhailovich's mother blacked out whole sections of the Bible that she deemed too explicit for adolescents. Mikhail eventually looked them up in an intact Bible, but his sister refused to read what he found. The same puritanical approach extended to the farmyard. When Mikhail once asked the coachman what a gelding was, his father quickly cut off the answer. Of course, the coachman later filled him in. Mikhail Mikhailovich noted that one of the early pleasures of marriage was reading all the "serious literature" that until then had been forbidden him.

Even young Mikhail acknowledged that country life could be awfully

Mikhail (left) and Sergei Osorgin playing hoops.

tedious. After his sister Varya married and moved out in 1882, when he was 21, the second Mikhail Mikhailovich spent each evening reading to his grandmother and then playing cards with her and his parents. "I had nothing else to do. I confess it was difficult; I would soon get drowsy, and for this reason I started taking opium, which in large doses provided several hours of stimulation before it put one to sleep. I took ever larger doses, reaching 115 drops, which would have been poisonous had I not been accustomed to it, but at least I could read without breaks, and I read many things to the old ones." He was probably talking of morphine, an opium derivative readily available at the time in various preparations; in any case, there is no further mention of opium or other narcotics in his memoirs, and I never heard anyone else mention it.

Social obligations could be equally stultifying. It was customary to call on neighboring landowners during their parish feasts, and that meant an annual call on the Raevskys every August 30 at their neighboring Timofeyevka. "At old Madame Raevsky's end of the table the talk was always of preparing preserves and jams; at Raevsky's end they talked only of hunting, and people like Dzhunkovsky and Ilchenko always lied shamelessly. They always sat too long at table, and moving to the living room for coffee and fruit (which we always brought) was a relief."

The major winter diversions were music and amateur theatricals. The mistresses of Sergiyevskoye were all accomplished pianists, and Varya, who had a fine alto voice, gave recitals both at Sergiyevskoye and in St. Petersburg. Though never particularly close to his sister, and a touch jealous of her successes, Mikhail Mikhailovich conceded her talent: "What can I say; she was exceptionally talented, and her rich, velvet voice was even richer due to her great dramatic talent. Anton Grigorievich Rubinstein himself, accompanying her in his romance 'Open for Me the Dungeon,' was effusive in his gratitude for her marvelous interpretation of his musical idea."

The performances at home seem to have been a bit better than the concerts in Kaluga, a provincial capital whose social and cultural life was then, as now, exceedingly dull. A local historian before the revolution, Dmitry Malinin, spared no image to drive home the point: "Public life in Kaluga never spouted like a fountain, and in the nineteenth century it died entirely," he wrote. He listed a few brief spells of social animation, usually generated by a new governor, after which "the beating of the pulse of social interests again weakened and gradually returned to its previous lethargy." That, Malinin noted in passing, made Kaluga eminently suitable as a place of "internal exile," an instrument for controlling political adversaries that the tsars used occasionally and the commissars unrestrainedly. Under the Soviets, inmates who survived their term in the Gulag were barred from living within 100 kilometers of Moscow, and Kaluga was favored as a place of residence by former *zeks* (political prisoners) because the *elektrichkas*—the electric commuter trains—made it possible to visit Moscow regularly.

The second Mikhail Mikhailovich described a concert at the Assembly of Nobility in which his mother, Maria Alexeyevna Osorgin, was to play four-hands with a local luminary, Count Alexander Golovin. It became plain after the first number that the count was drunk, and after the intermission Maria Alexeyevna refused to go on playing with him, especially as their final number was technically demanding. Sensing disgrace, Golovin threatened to challenge

Osorgin to a duel, so Maria Alexeyevna agreed to go on. The performance was brilliant, and only Maria Alexeyevna's family noticed that she played both parts while Golovin sat nodding uselessly. Golovin later came to Sergiyevskoye to apologize and wept in shame in Osorgin's study.

The younger Mikhail Mikhailovich's wife was even more talented at the piano than her mother-in-law. Her father, Prince Nikolai Petrovich Trubetskoi, was a noted patron of music, co-founder of the Russian Musical Society in Moscow and friend of the brothers Anton and Nikolai Rubinstein, as well as other celebrated musicians of the day. In fact, it was through music that the young Mikhail Mikhailovich met his "Liza," Elizaveta Nikolayevna Trubetskoi. After her father ran into financial difficulties and was compelled to sell Akhtyrka, the Trubetskoi estate outside Moscow, he took a position as vice gov-

Family and friends playing cards at Sergiyevskoye.
Mikhail Mikhailovich (2nd) is second from left,
his father Mikhail Mikhailovich (1st) is seventh from
left, Maria Alexeyevna Osorgin is tenth from left,
Liza Osorgin is fifth.

ernor of Kaluga, where his home became a social and musical center. Before long, Varya Osorgin's singing came to the attention of the Trubetskois, and she brought her brother into their large fold.

Liza Trubetskoi visited Sergiyevskoye for the first time in the summer of 1885, to rehearse one of the plays the Osorgins and their neighbors occasionally staged. These were serious productions: talented relatives were summoned from distant estates to play key roles, elaborate scenery was built in the dining room, music was rehearsed. Liza's elder brother, Sergei Nikolayevich Trubetskoi—who was to gain renown as a philosopher and the first elected rector of Moscow University—later acknowledged that when he first came out to Sergiyevskoye, he had an excuse prepared in case boredom compelled him to beat a retreat.

Instead, the next summer it was he who wrote a libretto for a musical play, and it was a smash hit (Sergei Trubetskoi was acknowledged as the master of the family stage, and his charades and spectacles were celebrated among his relatives and friends). The play was performed on June 23, 1886, with Mikhail Mikhailovich in the lead and Liza in a minor role. Mikhail Mikhailovich emerged from the experience hopelessly in love. Following a brief but frenzied courtship, he and Liza were betrothed on July 8 and married August 27 in the Church of the Resurrection in Kaluga. After a honeymoon curtailed by homesickness, the young couple returned to Sergiyevskoye as its new master and mistress, greeted by villagers with gifts of eggs, chickens, and embroidered cloths, and by choral singing late into the night.

By coincidence—or destiny—my parents also met through that same musical play, when it was staged 54 years later in the Paris suburb of Clamart, where the large house of the Trubetskois, on the rue de la Forêt, was a social center for their many relatives and friends. My mother recently unearthed a copy of the libretto. It really is quite clever, and remarkably current. Called *The Last Word in Science,* it is about a dull and impotent Spanish king who is told by a devious prime minister and a "liberal" parliament that if he fails to produce an heir within three weeks, he must marry the daughter of an evil intriguer. The king appeals for help to an alchemist, who manages to create the requisite son out of a passing bacterium. In the Kaluga production, King Kumunduros the All-Wise was played by Mikhail Mikhailovich Osorgin. In Clamart, he was played by Sasha (Alexander) Schmemann, while the lovely and lovesick Eulalia was acted by Liana (Juliana) Osorgin. It was the winter of 1940–41; my father was 19, my mother 17. They soon became engaged and were married two years later, on January 23, 1943.

As for Mikhail Mikhailovich and his bride, they soon settled into the routine of country life. "We divided time among work, walks, music, and daily reading. . . . In the evenings, my wife, a serious musician, played many things and introduced me to music which before that had been terra incognita for me. We played four-hands, though I was not in her league. I, for my part, introduced her to opera, which she knew but little—and little liked."

For the most part, the agricultural innovations attempted by Kar were abandoned under the Osorgins, and the peasants largely resumed doing things the way they had learned "from our fathers and grandfathers." In his 1861 study of Kaluga agriculture, Deilidovich noted that General Kar's successors "were unable to sustain the mechanisms of the agricultural organization, and it went downhill: The cultivation of the land has been neglected, the crop rotation has fallen back to the usual three-field system, cattle have fallen off, and with it grain yields, so that by the end of the first half of the current century there remain only a few traces of the former organization of the rich estate of V. Kar." Then he added, "They say that the current owners of Goryainovo [Sergiyevskoye] seek again to raise the property to that high level of organization it had under Kar, but the degree to which their goal has been achieved is not known."

Actually, the first Mikhail Mikhailovich did try. He hired a professional German agronomist, Leopold von Krause, and the two of them built a steam mill, introduced clover into the crop rotation, and made a number of other changes. Osorgin even linked his office to the manager's with a telegraph salvaged by old Prince Volkonsky, but it was never used. (A telephone was installed at Sergiyevskoye in 1887, but superstitious older servants refused to answer it.)

The second Mikhail Mikhailovich disapproved of Krause. "He was very young, knew a lot of theory, but knew absolutely nothing about the conditions of central Russia, and managed the estate with difficulty," he wrote. "Nyunichka [the Swiss governess] took an instant dislike to Leopold Karlovich, but my father, always making plans for some kind of new scientific management, much patronized him."

How often I heard that in my years in Moscow—that a modern agricultural technique, or Western democracy, or some other Western practice was not applicable to Russia. I suspect Krause's real problem was not "the conditions of central Russia" but the mindset of the Russians.

One year Krause used weather conditions to determine when the oats should be sown, rather than the customary saint's day. The suspense was palpable. The first Mikhail Mikhailovich constantly went out to inspect the fields, and on Holy Saturday he actually forgot to attend church as he stood gazing with joy and relief at the first shoots. Another time, Osorgin and his manager decided to brand numbers on the horns of the cattle. The peasants grumbled, and when the winter proved so severe that all the straw on the roofs of farm buildings had to be used as fodder, and a fifth of the cattle died of hunger, they muttered that this was God's revenge for despoiling the cows' horns.

In the village, the cycles of nature and religion were one. Farm work was ordained by saints' days, the seasons were measured in church feasts, the passages of life were marked by sacraments, and no undertaking was ever begun without the priest and a *molieben*, a service of prayer.

The winter was formally declared at an end on Yegor's Day (Saint George, April 23), when the priest went into the barns and stables to bless the cows and horses before they were released to pasture for the first time. Peasant women did the same in their sheds, sprinkling their cows with holy water and driving them outdoors. Then the clergy would move on to the fields, where the priest would sprinkle holy water in every direction. Tradition called for the deacon, in full vestments, to lie down on the ground and be rolled along until he was almost unconscious, but the deacon in the time of my grandfather categorically refused to do his part.

From then on, it was a furious race against time. Frost could still strike on an early May morning, so peasants kept vigil, and if temperatures dropped they rushed out to build smoky fires and to wrap the apple blossoms in a protective pall. Everything else had to be sown and fertilized before haying began, on Peter's Day (June 29). Soon the wild strawberries ripened, peering out from under the forest flowers—Night Beauties, Ivan-da-Maria, Mother-of-God Teardrops, Ivan-Tea. Village children brought the berries to sell on plates wrapped in kerchiefs. Nyunichka was the designated buyer, bargaining in her fantastic Russian, and limitless strawberries were served at breakfast, lunch, and evening tea.

Harvesting began on the feast of the Kazan Icon of the Mother of God (July 8). August was divided into the "three Saviors": the "honey Savior" (Feast of the Life-Giving Cross, August 1), when honey and beehives were blessed and summer began drawing to a close; the "apple Savior" (Transfiguration, August 6), when fruits were blessed; and the Feast of the Savior Not-Made-by-Hands (August 16), when the seed for winter rye was blessed.

On the day after the third Savior, a sowing machine was towed into freshly plowed and harrowed fields. A wooden cup of blessed seed was put on the machine, and Mikhail Glebov, the village foreman, led the peasants in prayer, facing by turn in each direction of the compass. Then he would crumble holy bread into the seed and, walking hatless into the field, would cast it with a broad, timeless sweep. Autumn had begun.

Nina Semyonova, a village girl of 11 at the time of the revolution, recalled those days in one of the sketches she sent me:

> One fine day, men would begin cutting hay with scythes in the early morning. Women would appear in the fields at midday in festive dress, so they looked like flowers stacking the rows of hay. There were more people in the field than you could count, and not a single machine. By Pokrov [Feast of the Protection of the Virgin Mary, October 1], the harvest was all in—except the cabbage, which was gathered after Pokrov.

Sergei Osorgin described the threshing that followed:

> In the village the smell of smoke grows stronger from the drying sheds, where the sheaves of rye are drying, and from the threshing barns comes the clear, precise sound of flailing—hard, demanding work! If there are three or four flails, it's simply "trap-tap-tap" or "trap-tap-tap-tap," but if there are five or six flails, then each must skip one out of four or two out of five strikes, only swinging the flail, so as not to strike a neighbor's. Approaching the workers, it is obligatory to say, "God be your help," to which they, not missing a beat, reply "Our thanks," and again "trap-tap-tap."

Soon came the first frosts, and the forests gradually fell silent. The last birds to head south were the rooks. It was said that they left on the eve of Pokrov, the parish feast at Sergiyevskoye, between the evening vigil and the morning liturgy. The weather worsened, the mud rendered the roads impassable, windows were caulked with moss, and storm windows were installed, with containers of coarse salt placed between the windows to absorb the moisture.

> And then one morning you awake and there is an unusual light through the shutters, not yellow sunlight, but bright and white. Nanny opens the blinds and opens the shutters, Good Lord! Snow! The whole yard, the acacias, our front garden, all are covered with snow. Large airy balls of snow already hang in the fir trees. We watch in excitement from the window: A *muzhik* goes by, still in regular boots, but with snow in his beard; the ever-

Haying.

frisky sparrows in the acacias shake off the snow and for some reason tangle briefly in a fight. Suddenly a joyous shriek from the children's room: "Sleigh, sleigh, the first sleigh!"—it's the yardman bringing firewood behind the blind mare, Zhelannyi.

Winter reached its apex on Saint Spiridon's Day (December 12), when, according to peasant lore, "the sun turns to summer, winter to the frost." By then preparations were well underway for Christmas. Children made all the decorations for the tree, guided by the German governess.

At last came Christmas—"the church service in the overflowing, overheated winter church, the festive singing, the smell of rough lambskin coats, the screams of babies who were being diapered in the dark over by the huge stove at the entrance before Communion." In the evening the children were secluded in the study until, at last, the gay march from *The Little Humpbacked Horse* sounded and the doors to the living room were opened. "The Christmas tree! How many of them I remember, in all ages, in different decorations, in different rooms, houses, cities, countries—this was the final chord, the zenith of the entire winter!"

The Feast of the Baptism (Epiphany, January 6), when the frost was cruelest, was the day on which water was blessed. Rooks returned on the day of Saint Gerasim "of-the-rooks" (March 6), and the thaw would start on the day of Saint Alexei "Snowmelt-from-the-Hills" (March 17). Soon it was Annunciation (March 25), when by custom all the songbirds that had been kept through the winter in a large cage in the dining room—siskins, goldfinches, robins, bullfinches, and crossbills—were set free.

On Forgiveness Sunday, the beginning of the 40-day Easter Lent, servants would come by during evening tea—Yegor the steward, Yevmeniy the second steward, Filip the cook, the pantry steward, the stove-tender, the kitchen boy—and, walking up to each *barin*, adult and child, they would bow low and say, "Forgive me where I have sinned," and would plant a kiss on the master's shoulder. To this the masters would reply, "God will forgive you; forgive you me," and would kiss the servant on the head.

Finally it was spring, Easter. This was the greatest feast, the celebration of resurrection and rebirth after the deep winter and strict Lenten fast. The entire week before Easter, Holy Week, was given over to church services and preparations. The coachman spent all his time gathering the ingredients and the cook nabbed volunteers to help prepare enough *kulichi* (cylindrical cakes) and *paskha* (a rich concoction of cottage cheese, cream, eggs, and sugar molded in a pyramid) for the festal table, and as gifts for the whole staff, and everyone spent all Thursday between church services dyeing eggs. On Holy Saturday all these foods were blessed, and after the midnight procession and Easter service they were distributed.

After the midnight services came the great Easter binge, *rozgoveniye,* at which all the foods forbidden throughout Lent were avidly devoured. The Osorgins would prepare three festal tables—in addition to the one for the family, there were an "upper table" in the children's room for household staff and a "lower table" in the laundry for the rest of the workers and anybody else who might appear in church—about a hundred in all. In Soviet times, Russians forgot everything about Easter except the feast. It became traditional to stop by a church for a minute or two at midnight and then to have at it.

On the Monday after Easter, after the liturgy at the church, village men visited the clergy and were treated to pie and vodka. On succeeding days, village councils would visit Mikhail Mikhailovich to exchange the traditional three kisses and to present him with Easter eggs, in exchange for which they were treated to vodka in the manager's office.

Many other special days were scattered through the year. Prayers were always held at the manor house on the day of Cassian the Roman, benefactor in business, and on the Feast of the Burning Bush, as protection against fire. The Kaluga Icon of the Mother of God, a specially revered image to which miraculous powers were attributed, was brought to Sergiyevskoye once a year, and when it was carried from house to house in every village, peasants would lie on the ground for the image to be carried over them.

A uniquely local tradition was the veneration of the grave of one Parfeny, a local *yurodivyi* (a simpleton whose condition was believed to reflect special grace) who was buried in an old cemetery near Popovka. The peasants believed that Parfeny's relics would one day be hallowed and their village thus glorified, and on his saint's day they took home pinches of soil from his grave.

There was no real distinction in the village between the secular and the religious, between tradition and cathechism. The Savior, his Mother, the saints, and the icons were as inherent a part of this universe as the seasons, the harvests, and the floods, the births and the deaths. The *krasnyi ugolok* ("beautiful corner") in every peasant hut, with its red votive light and its icons draped in embroidered cloth, was as indispensable as the massive Russian stove that occupied a third of the house and spread its life-sustaining warmth through the deep winter. A cherished icon of a saint was a confidant, protector, judge, and talisman, ever gazing directly into your eyes and knowing your every misdeed.

Long after the Soviets had closed the village church and stamped out the feasts, the old traditions lingered. Villagers who never saw the inside of a church visited the graves of their family on Easter, and Pentecost remained a day of festivity even for the Young Communists, who would gather in the linden grove to sing and dance. And in a world where wresting bread from the unyielding soil and the momentary summer was a perpetual miracle, it was natural to bless the cow and to say a prayer before casting the seed.

Unlike the Western parish priest, the Russian *pop* lived only marginally better than his peasant flock. Little educated, not averse to vodka, he supplemented his meager income with produce from his own lands and food or money received as compensation for performing weddings, funerals, baptisms, and the many *moliebens* that accompanied important events. His social standing was not particularly high in the village, as reflected in folk sayings such as: "When the *pop* comes, hide the bread."

As a rule, the cleric owed his position less to vocation than to birth. The clergy was effectively a caste; priests were commonly married to daughters of priests, and their children attended provincial seminaries to become clergymen or parish-school teachers. Many common Russian surnames derive from clerical clans—Popov, Diakonov, Ponomaryov, Voznesensky, Arkhangelsky, Rozhdestvensky.

The Sergiyevskoye church, like most village parishes, had four paid clergymen—priest, deacon, *diachok* (subdeacon, or reader), and *ponomar'* (sexton). The priestly dynasty at Sergiyevskoye was venerable. A clerical family named Begichev, which took its name from the original landowners, served parish churches in the area in one capacity or another for 180 years. The second-to-last priest, Father Dmitry Izvekov, effectively inherited the parish by marrying a Begichev, while Father Sergei Vatolin, the last pastor, married Izvekov's daughter. Vatolin's son remained after the revolution as a teacher in the local school, and his offspring still own a house near the demolished church.

Since the entire Russian Orthodox liturgy was chanted, there was a premium on priests, deacons, and subdeacons with fine voices. For her generosity in building the Sergiyevskoye church, the bishop of Kaluga paid Maria Sergeyevna Kar the honor of assigning priests with good voices to her parish. The first, Father Pyotr Grigoriev, had been dean at the Kaluga cathedral; the second, Father Ivan Beliayev, had such a lovely tenor that he was ordained a deacon at age 17, in violation of all the rules. The last subdeacon at Sergiyevskoye, Ilya Pokrovsky, "was of huge height and sang an octave lower than the deacon, but cruelly off tune, and he read rather badly." On the other hand, he was married to the granddaughter of the senior deacon in Kaluga, "and he had an angelic personality. Everything was forgiven him and everybody liked him."

Initially, Maria Sergeyevna Kar made unusually generous arrangements for the clergy. She built each of the four clerics a house, which she undertook to heat and repair, and she let them keep their cattle in her barn. Furthermore, she established generous salaries of 300 rubles a year for the priest, 150 for the deacon, and 75 each for the subdeacon and sexton—a tidy sum at the time, which the clergy could expect to almost double with the other special services they performed—plus four pails of rye flour to be shared in the same proportions. She also assigned the priest a servant and a carriage. In exchange, Maria

Sergeyevna exacted a pledge that the clergymen would keep their houses clean and would be careful with fire, and that they would dress decently—that they would not wear an *armiak*, the heavy peasant coat of crude cloth, or *lapti*, the peasant footwear of birch bark.

This comfortable arrangement did not survive Madame Kar's demise. Her son Sergei made the clerics heat and fix their own houses, took away the priest's servant and carriage, and drove the clerical cattle out of his barn. Things improved somewhat for the clergy under the Osorgins—at least until 1908, when Mikhail Mikhailovich sold most of his land to peasants and parceled out 130 acres to the churchmen. "Thus instead of their calm former life, members of the clergy now must worry about acquiring all the implements needed for land cultivation, and to procure bread by the sweat of their brow," lamented *Kaluga Antiquity*.

The Osorgins were very devout. The second Mikhail Mikhailovich described how he would rise before dawn to pray before the icon of the Kaluga Mother of God when it was on its annual visit to Sergiyevskoye: "I especially liked to come in the early morning on the day of parting, when there was nobody in church except the watchman stoking the stove; it was still dark, and the only lights were the votive candles before the wonder-working icon, the relics of Saint Juliana, and the Savior Not-Made-by-Hands, and you could pour out your soul, and it felt so sweet." Mikhail Mikhailovich was drawn to the priesthood as a youth, a vocation he realized only after he quit Russia; at the age of 70, he was ordained to the priesthood and assigned to serve a small family parish outside Paris. His son, the third Mikhail Mikhailovich, helped to found the St. Serge Theological Institute in Paris and taught liturgical music there; his brothers both directed choirs; all the girls sang; and the youngest, Antonina, took monastic vows in France.

In contrast to his father, Sergei Osorgin confessed that wonder-working icons and relics and other such things posed "prickly questions" for him. "But the *muzhiks* believed so firmly and unquestioningly, they prayed so ardently as they crawled on all fours under the icon, the old women held three fingers so firmly to their white headscarves and so convincingly whispered, 'Our Lady, help us,' that such liberal doubts quieted of themselves," he wrote.

I, too, experience many a "prickly question" as the Church now seeks to revive itself after seventy years of militant atheism, bringing back not only genuine devotion but also xenophobia, intolerance, anti-Semitism, and superstition. But Russia was never a secular society, and much of Russia's turmoil today is not only political and economic disorientation but the loss of a guiding faith. Where it finds one—and whether it comes freely or through the knout of a new despot—will do much to determine where Russia goes from here.

In our secular world it is difficult to appreciate the importance of religion in societies such as Russia's—all the more so because Western histories have usually treated the Russian Orthodox Church solely as the ideological and ceremonial arm of the throne. That it was, to be sure. Russian Orthodoxy was the official state religion, and the Church was the institution responsible for elementary education, censorship, and the promulgation of the official ideology of Tsar, Motherland, and Orthodox Faith. The tsar was "the anointed of God," and during his coronation he assumed the attributes of a priest, entering the sanctuary through the Royal Doors and taking Communion wine directly from the chalice, as only priests did. His consort was required to adopt the Orthodox faith (at which time she also acquired the patronymic "Fyodorovna," in honor of Fyodor Romanov, father of the first Romanov tsar, Mikhail Fyodorovich, and thus the progenitor of the Romanov dynasty). A subject's denomination was a central factor in defining nationality: a Russian was Russian Orthodox, a German was Lutheran, a Pole was Catholic, a Tatar was Moslem, a Jew was a practitioner of Judaism. Conversion to Orthodoxy lifted most ethnic barriers to advancement in the tsarist service. If either parent was Orthodox, a child had to be baptized into the Orthodox Church.

But the Church was not only an ornament and prop of the monarchy. The concept of "Holy Russia" as the heir to Rome and Byzantium, the myth of the Russians as a people imbued with a special spirituality, was central to the culture, and religion permeated every aspect of daily life. Churches and monasteries dotted the landscape in bewildering profusion. The Kaluga diocese alone had 650 churches (350 of brick and 300 of wood) and nine monasteries. The whole of Russia at the turn of the century had more than 40,000 parish churches, served by 63,000 priests and three times that many full-time deacons, subdeacons, and sextons, plus more than 1,000 monasteries with about 85,000 monks and nuns.

The Bolsheviks understood well the power of religion. In attacking it, their goal was not simply to neutralize a reactionary institution, but to rip religion out by its roots and replace it with their own ideology. The Bolsheviks made no distinction among faiths: Jews, Moslems, Baptists, Catholics, and sectarians were persecuted with the same zeal as Orthodox Christians.

Perhaps Russia cannot move forward until it has rebuilt what was destroyed. In any event, restoring severed links is a powerful compulsion. A nation's history is its soul, and it was history, first of all, that the Communists tried to destroy. Alas, today's young priests and believers—along with all the businessmen, politicians, intellectuals, workers, and peasants whose development was stunted by the Soviet illusion—must reinvent the wheel before they can roll on. But they are doing it, and at a remarkable rate. It may not be pretty; but, then, healing wounds never are. In the end, I find myself in agreement with my grandfather. There is a powerful force in the remarkable rebirth of countless parishes across the land, a healing force that I believe outweighs the inevitable distortions of a religion held captive so long.

Immediately after Easter, negotiations began with the peasants. After their emancipation from serfdom, the villagers contracted to do specified work for the landowner in exchange for the use of his fields and other perquisites. The peasants worked as a village; each had a "society," headed by an "elder," which negotiated with the landowner and distributed common lands for use among the peasants. At Sergiyevskoye, paid workers did the plowing and haying, while the villages undertook to do all other field work, including the maintenance of roads and fences, in exchange for the use of pastures and hayfields and the right to gather mushrooms, nuts, and berries, plus supplies of ropes and brooms.

The estate of Sergiyevskoye comprised eight villages, four large and four small, and the contracts were arranged so that half were renewed each year. Negotiations were concluded on Saint Thomas Sunday, a week after Easter, "to chase the hangover of Easter week with the vodka that was always given out on the conclusion of negotiations."

Vodka was as central to peasant life then as it is now. Mikhail Mikhailovich accused Krause's Polish successor as estate manager of being too generous with vodka—"every discussion with a society, every undertaking, ended with vodka, and there were even specified amounts established by custom for each village," he wrote. Extraordinary amounts were thus consumed, though the steward quietly added water to the barrels.

Osorgin noted a curious phenomenon that persists in Russia to this day: "Men would not agree to perform any work outside the contract for any sum of money, but only for vodka, even if the vodka was worth less than the money offered." Today, village men often agree to take on tasks such as chopping firewood, spreading manure, or cutting hay only in exchange for vodka, and a Muscovite who has a country house routinely takes a case along. The vodka is often consumed on the spot.

A stern moralist, Mikhail Mikhailovich tried hard to combat drinking. He eventually restricted the distribution of vodka to those days when the workload was really severe. But with the elimination of vodka, he admitted, Sergiyevskoye also lost those happy evenings when peasants would come over for their ration and would fill the house with choral singing.

Of course, it was not all singing and vodka. The first record I have of any disquiet among Sergiyevskoye peasants is precisely over these contracts. On July 12, 1905, the land captain of the local *uyezd* (district) filed a report to the governor in Kaluga: "The unrest among peasants of six villages in the Osorgin estate is based on the small size of the holdings. The elder of the village Kashurki, Ivan Demichev, is the presumed instigator. Propose to fire and arrest."

Eight days later, he sent another report:

> Unrest persists among peasants temporarily obligated to Osorgin (villages of Sergiyevskoye, Zenovo, Dmitrievka, Shakhovo, Kashurki). The problem began two years ago because the peasants received fewer allotments than surrounding villages, and they need land. They annually contract to do haying and fattening for Osorgin, and they also do labor for him for the right to gather mushrooms, nuts, and berries in his forests. . . . Then they started asking peasants in Kashurki to pay not in labor but in money, and in 1904 the village was given no fields at all. The peasants cut hay on some meadows anyway, and all were fined. This added to the dissatisfaction.

I don't know how the issue was resolved. But peasant life in central Russia always tottered on the brink of survival, and every mushroom and hayfield was precious. In one of her letters to me, Nina Semyonova described what she remembered of life in the village:

> Peasants made their clothes and shoes with their own hands, and the poor walked about in *lapti*. A beauty might have *lapti* looking like crystal slippers, so skillfully did they know how to make them. Through the long winter nights, I marveled with my child's eyes how their golden hands spun flax into large balls of thread from which they weaved linen. The things they purchased were sugar, kerosene, herring, and a few other things. Girls wore cotton frocks to church, while men wore only what they made themselves. The households in Karovo and the surrounding villages

were about the same—a horse, a cow, five sheep, some pigs, and fowl—chickens, geese, ducks. Money was hard to come by, and surplus production was sold. Some *muzhiks* left in the winter to work in the city.

Disease stalked the village and manor alike; a late spring or early frost could spell famine; roads were impassable for many weeks at a stretch; vodka took its toll.

Fire was a special danger to houses built of pine logs and roofed with wood shingles or straw. A fire could mean instant impoverishment for both a peasant and a *barin*. Special services against fire were held on the Feast of the Burning Bush, with a procession around the entire estate, and candles lit in church on Epiphany were saved for the rest of the year and lit at home during thunderstorms to protect against lightning.

Whatever heavenly protection that offered, however, was offset by another tradition, which held that a fire started by lightning was a divine act and so could not be put out. Sergei Osorgin recalled coming upon one such blaze:

> In the nearby village of Polivanovo, lightning struck a solitary house, and people stood about staring while the subdeacon threw an old Easter egg into the fire—the only action permitted in such cases. My father flew at the crowd like a hawk. "Why are you standing about with mouths agape? Water! Now! Bring buckets!" "But Mikhal Mikhalych, it was started by a thunderbolt. . . ." "I'll give you such a bolt. . . . Nikolai, get these idiots moving!" He did, and the house was saved.

One great fire destroyed the huge drying barn, along with the entire harvest of oats and clover. The barn, 80 yards long and 10 yards wide, had a roof of straw; it burned for three days with a blaze so bright that people at the train station in Ferzikovo, 8 miles away, reportedly could read at night by its light. Enough brick was salvaged from the barn to build a two-room elementary parish boarding school in 1887, which stands to this day, and for repairs on the entire estate for the next 15 years.

Nina Semyonova described another such disaster:

> Nothing foretold a disaster on that clear Palm Sunday in April. People with bouquets of pussy willows stood at the service in church. Suddenly someone rushed into the vestibule of the church, yelling, "The *barin's* barn is burning!"
>
> The people poured out of church. A huge pillar of smoke was rising from the back buildings of the estate, and the roof of the last building in

the long yard of the barn was burning. Burning straw, the roof covering, flew noisily with the eastward wind directly at Karovo. All this we saw running up with the people. Mikhal Mikhalych, out in front in white trousers, rushed right into the mud at the entrance, trying to undo the latch, but inside, the animals, crazed with fear, were pressing too hard against the gate. Finally two *muzhiks* got in from the other side and pushed the latch, and Mikhal Mikhalych, mired in mud, pulled it out, barely managing to leap aside as the panicked animals rushed out with a terrible bellow and scattered in all directions. The *muzhiks* tried to catch them, but Mikhal Mikhalych shouted, "Everyone home, save your roofs!"

We returned home scared. My father was sitting on the roof, and my mother was handing him water. We began helping, carrying water from our stream. It was the same all around—*muzhiks* were sitting on the roofs of their houses and members of their family were handing them water. Our roof was metal, but other buildings were in danger.

The *barin*'s barn burned down. And Mikhal Mikhalych's white trousers covered with manure stayed in my memory a long time. This was probably 1914, because in that same year we saw my uncle off to the war. Soon my father also left for the war.

Travel could be treacherous. Carriages were forever toppling over or breaking down on the rutted roads. One visiting bishop arrived in Sergiyevskoye without the rear compartment of his elaborate carriage; it was located several miles back, with a seriously injured archdeacon still inside. Maria Alexeyevna Osorgin developed a fear of carriages after two accidents. The second, in the summer of 1874, happened when a drunken coachman began whipping the horses as they were negotiating the steep descent to the river. The troika bolted, throwing everyone from the carriage; Maria Alexeyevna landed face-first on a sharp rock and smashed her teeth and face. Thereafter she rode only if there was no alternative, and then would get out and walk down steep hills.

Her phobia had a curious consequence. When a son was coming home to Sergiyevskoye, she would not go to the station for fear of the carriage ride, and she would not let anyone else meet him, because she wanted to be the first. So the son would hitch a ride, and a servant would be posted in the lookout atop the house to alert the mistress to his approach.

About the only medical treatment peasants received in those days was from village folk healers or from well-meaning landowners, who often dispensed more charity than healing. The second Mikhail Mikhailovich became engrossed at one point in the medical theories of one Count Mattei and started treating peasants with grains and "electric liquids." "I think that however you treat the people, they'll still turn to you if only you're caring and prepared to listen patiently," Osorgin discovered. "At least that's how it was with me; despite the total ineffectiveness of my treatments, patients were plentiful, and I even had to make house calls."

Some came for as little as a dollop of sympathy. Liza Osorgin once returned from a walk and saw a frequent patient waiting for her. "Hello, you've come for me?" "For you, Lizaveta Nikolavna, for you." "Just wait here, I'll be right out." "Oh, it won't be necessary, Lizaveta Nikolavna. I've already had a chat with Nanny."

Liza acquired such experience as a healer that the family doctor admiringly called her his "colleague." Once, a *muzhik* from a distant village brought his wife: "What's happened, Lizaveta Nikolavna, is that a worm crawled into her head during haying. In the winter, nothing, but in the summer it turns into a frog and jumps around, driving the *baba* out of herself." The poor *baba* really did go out of her mind from terrible migraine headaches, and Liza helped her. Another old woman complained that "a goat gnawed her in the side"; it turned out to be a hernia.

To be fair, medical treatment was not much better for the *bariny* on their isolated estates (or, later, for the workers on the Soviet collective farm), or even in the capitals. As a young officer, Mikhail Mikhailovich once had to hold a candle while three doctors chiseled at the skull of his comrade Pyotr Norov to get at what they had diagnosed as "a boil under his skull." "It's hard to believe now how this operation was done, without any antiseptic preparations," Osorgin recalled. "The surgeons didn't even put on smocks, but simply started to operate on him on his bed. One chloroformed him, another held the scalp apart, and the surgeon chiseled away at the skull with what looked like a simple chisel and hammer. . . . They found no pus, the operation was in vain, and Petya died without regaining consciousness."

At Sergiyevskoye, after young Sergei accidentally shot himself in the leg with a pistol, the only doctor who could be found in Kaluga was their old *accoucheur*. Lacking any surgical tools or anesthetic, he tried to cut to the bullet with a pair of sewing scissors while Sergei stoically chain-smoked cigarettes. The governess passed out at the sound of tearing flesh, and in the end the poor doctor gave up. The bullet remained in my grandfather's leg to the end of his days, and when retelling the story he would roll up his pants leg and let us feel it, though I don't think I ever did.

While Sergei was recuperating, his Osorgin grandmother, Maria Alexeyevna, began to vomit with increasing frequency. She was transferred to Moscow, where doctors diagnosed stomach cancer. Approaching death, she asked for ice cream. Mikhail Mikhailovich recalled that all Moscow was draped in festive bunting and everything was closed that day, which had been declared a national holiday for the baptism of Nicholas II's son and heir apparent, the tsarevich Alexei. Osorgin rushed about madly trying to find ice cream. When he finally did and returned, his mother was dead.

A terrible tragedy struck Mikhail Gerasimovich Osorgin's youngest daughter, Sofia. She and her husband, Dmitry Appolonovich Zhemchuzhnikov, had invited a cousin, one Kolokoltsev, to a hunt at Ierusalimskoye, their estate near Smolensk. Over lunch Kolokoltsev got worked up about some political argument, but no one thought anything more of it, and everyone went to change for the hunt. Zhemchuzhnikov came out first and sat down on a stoop to wait. His son Polya, looking out his window, suddenly saw Kolokoltsev walk out and fire a shotgun directly at his father. Polya leaped out of the window and ran up to his writhing parent, yelling to Kolokoltsev, "Why did you kill Papa?" The latter emptied his second barrel point-blank into the youth and ran off, laughing madly.

Sofia behaved nobly. She saved Kolokoltsev from peasants who had seized him and were about to maul him. She dressed her husband's wounds—a deep gash in his side and a shattered right hand. She sent for a priest to perform the last rites for her son and held him in her arms until he died, in terrible agony, seven hours later. Soon after, the Zhemchuzhnikovs quit Ierusalimskoye. Dmitry served as regional postmaster in Oryol for a while, and then inherited another estate from a distant relative and settled on it, immersing himself in raising horses. Ierusalimskoye passed to a niece, Liza Benckendorff, who sold it.

Death was a regular visitor. The first Mikhail Mikhailovich's first son, Alexei ("Lyolya"), born in 1860, died in the winter of that same year of scarlet fever. His father carried his small casket himself to a grave hewn in the frozen ground near the altar of the church. It was one of the coldest winters in memory; people saw jackdaws freeze on the wing.

Sergei Osorgin described an encounter his grandmother had:

"I remember once one of Babushka's favorites, Vladimir the second coachman, was bringing in the mail and Babushka saw that a procession was heading toward the church with a small child's casket. 'Vladimir, who are they burying?' 'My daughter, my daughter, Maria Alexeyevna, my daughter.' 'How did this happen?' 'Her tongue was tied, the tongue was, and the *babka* cut it.' 'With what?' 'A sickle, Maria Alexeyevna, a sickle.' 'Go on to church, poor Vladimir. Why didn't you say anything earlier?' 'Never mind, Maria Alexeyevna, never mind, they'll bury her without me, without me.' "

Vladimir was the brother of Mikhail Glebov, the village foreman. During Lent, their other brother, Zinovy, fell ill. He developed pneumonia and steadily declined, despite efforts by the second Mikhail Mikhailovich:

> He was brought home to his father, and I visited him twice a day. The neighboring medic was summoned, and he showed me what to do. In the evening I sat for quite a long time in his *izba*. In the icon corner stood a clean table with a lamp covered by a lamp shade, a rarity in a peasant house, and the old father, Gleb Makarov, told me of the old days, when their village of five houses, called Lenilovka, stood where the trench is now. He wept that God was taking not him but his son, still full of strength, and, indeed, Zinovy soon died.

Lenilovka was the village that General Kar had set up for lazy peasants. So Mikhail Glebov, the universally respected village foreman, was descended from serfs who had been segregated for their laziness a century earlier!

7

A Leave-taking of Past Greatness

The emancipation of the serfs in 1861 was a blow for landowners, but not necessarily a boon for the supposedly liberated peasants, who remained largely without rights and effectively bound to the *barin* and the land, now by backbreaking debts, dues, and taxes. The more serious economic blow to landowners was the rise of transatlantic shipping and the spread of railroads in Russia, which brought amber waves of cheaper grain from the New World and the Black Earth regions of southern Russia. The gentry estates of central Russia were never at any time particularly profitable or efficient, so when grain prices dropped by half between 1876 and 1896, landowners were driven to mortgage their estates and to sell off lumber and land.

The numbers of landowners who could derive a living off their lands dropped precipitously at the close of the nineteenth century. As marshal of Moscow nobility, Prince Pyotr Nikolayevich Trubetskoi estimated that by 1890, 60 percent of the nobility was unable to support a family on earnings from land alone, and by the turn of the century the figure was at 80 percent and climbing. Long before the 1917 Revolution formally banned the private ownership of land, the gentry estate of central Russia was effectively extinct, and most of the *dvoriane* were quite successfully adapting—even prospering—without their hereditary privileges.

A nineteenth-century view of the village of Koltsovo,
with the manor in the background.

church bells pealed. When the luminary arrived, the flustered village priest forgot all protocol and reached out to shake hands, and a peasant ran across the
field dragging along his grandson and yelling, "Your Highness, Prince, wait!
Let me look at you, or I might die and never see a tsar!" The grand duke, a liberal and tolerant man, suffered it all with good humor, entreating the Osorgins
"for heaven's sake" to change into everyday clothes, and giving the peasant lad
a pat and a silver coin. K.R. did not buy Sergiyevskoye.

It was not originally intended for young Mikhail Mikhailovich to enter the military. Rather, he was to attend a classical Gymnasium and enter the university.
A wave of student unrest at Moscow University in 1875, however, so alarmed
his mother that she shifted her son to the military track.

That took some doing. The Osorgins were not of sufficiently prominent
birth or rank to automatically qualify for the most prestigious military schools
or regiments. The school of the Corps of Pages (Pazhesky Korpus), for example, admitted only the sons or grandsons of officials who held top ranks in the

military or state service, while regiments of the Imperial Guards, especially the Chevalier Guards (Kavalergard), put a premium on lineage and fortune. But the aristocratic maternal grandfather, Prince Volkonsky, pulled some strings and got young Mikhail Mikhailovich accepted into the Corps of Pages.

The Corps was unabashedly elitist. Its graduates formed something of an old-boy network in the Guards regiments, the court, and the government. Since the school was formally a military academy, the best students in the senior class also served as pages in the imperial court. Mikhail Osorgin, always a good student, was one of those selected from his class to be a page; he and "Mimka" Neidgardt were assigned to serve the empress, Maria Alexandrovna. Normally this was a plum assignment, because the empress traditionally gave her pages a gold watch with her monogram on their graduation. In this case it proved a major disappointment, for the empress was sick almost the entire winter, and the first time Osorgin and Neidgardt saw her was at her funeral. Moreover, when the minister of the Court sent up the usual request for gold watches to Alexander II, the tsar sent it back with the note, "Don't bother; wife was always sick." The pages were consoled by friends who told them that the slight was not aimed at them but at the unfortunate empress, whom the tsar had never liked. Indeed, soon after her death, Alexander II married his mistress of long standing, Princess Ekaterina Dolgoruky, who was years his junior and had already moved into the palace, with her children by the tsar, before the empress died.

Service at the court was not easy. Under his gold-embroidered black tunic a page had to wear white chamois breeches so tight, it took several friends to pull them on. Once on, they were moistened so that they would cling tautly. Before heading off to the palace, every page was shaved by an old barber named Gullert (Alexander II sternly banned beards in the military and the civil service, and most officers and officials tried to emulate his luxurious side-whiskers), and then had their hair plastered down with sugar water, with a forelock on the right side. All this was accompanied by repeated inspections from the company commander. Finally, under the command of the school adjutant, Staff Captain Argamakov, the pages piled into a court carriage and headed off to the Winter Palace. There they dropped their capes off at the Commandant's Entry and went to the entrance used by their imperial charge. On major occasions, the pages gathered in a hall near the Gold Drawing Room, where Osorgin and Neidgardt usually stayed idle for the rest of the day. Bored with the long wait, they once went into the Gold Drawing Room and stretched out on a couch, until they suddenly heard the ailing empress coughing next door, whereupon they quickly scrambled back to their hall.

The large number of both entrances and Highnesses inevitably led to mishaps. Osorgin was once assigned to a grand duchess who had married a German prince and was returning to St. Petersburg for the first time in many years. None of the palace staff recalled what she looked like, but the veteran doorman thought he knew every other Romanov, and promised to give Osorgin a wink when an unfamiliar one rolled up. Soon a carriage pulled up, but Osorgin could not tell whether the coachman was wearing his three-cornered hat fore-and-aft, which meant "Romanov on board." He thought he saw the doorman wink and dutifully fell in behind the elderly lady who disembarked. At the top of the grand stairway, the woman turned around and whispered, "You've made a mistake. I'm not a grand duchess." Osorgin bowed and dashed back down, where another grand duchess (not his) was just pulling up. But "Kotya" Obolensky, the page assigned to this one, was mistakenly waiting at another entrance, so Osorgin ran up and took her cloak and train. Following her into the rotunda, Osorgin spotted Obolensky behind an unfamiliar grande dame. "This one's yours," Obolensky whispered, and while the women exchanged grand-ducal kisses, the pages quickly swapped their cloaks and charges.

Maria Fyodorovna, the wife of the future Alexander III, was the favorite of the pages for her small attentions. Once, during a state dinner, a page spilled some hot soup on her décolleté'd shoulder and then grabbed her napkin in horror and started vigorously rubbing her bare skin. Maria Fyodorovna quietly asked him to stop, then smiled and put a finger to her lips, signaling to other guests that her stern father-in-law, the emperor, was not to learn what had happened.

Virtually every graduate of the pages' school entered a Guards regiment. The Guards were the quintessence of upper-class machismo. "This privileged nucleus of the army, which gave Russia theoreticians, thinkers and drunken profligates, quickly evolved into something between a band of brigands and a cultural avant-garde," wrote the cultural historian Yuri Lotman. "Those same Guardsmen who went drinking in pubs and never knew how to pay off their debts, on becoming counts and princes and inheriting huge estates, became rather famous people in Russian history."

Formally an elite military force to defend the tsar, the Guards were in the vanguard of all Russia's wars and graduated many of tsarist Russia's most prominent figures. Two empresses, Elizabeth and Catherine, were put on the throne by Guardsmen, and at many other junctures in Russian history the Guards were in the thick of things, either because of their proximity to the tsar or through the old-boy network of former Guardsmen. Nicholas II was never as happy as he was in the officers' mess of a Guards regiment, immersed in the secure world of military order, glittering uniforms, and manly talk of horses, wine, gypsies, and duels. The four top regiments—Chevalier Guards, Horse Guards, Hussar Life Guards, and the Preobrazhensky infantry regiment—defined snobbery; acceptance required impeccable pedigree, high connections, and independent wealth.

Gentlemanly profligacy was taken for granted, but within the fine bounds of proper *façon*. Getting drunk on vodka, for example, was *mauvais ton*, but getting sloshed on champagne was laudable—so long as it was dry. ("Believe me, prince," Prince Urusov instructed Prince Trubetskoi on the morning after the latter's induction into his Guards regiment. "Any demi-sec is first of all emetic, and secondly as insolent as separate cuffs or traveling in second class.") There were limits to womanizing, too—the wives of regimental comrades were strictly off limits. Tsar Nicholas II's own brother, Grand Duke Mikhail Alexandrovich, was compelled to quit the Cuirassier Life Guards regiment—of which his mother, the dowager empress Maria Fyodorovna, was honorary chief—after he struck up a romance with the wife of a fellow Cuirassier. Even though she subsequently got a divorce and married the grand duke (and became the Countess Brasova), "that woman" was deemed to have so tarnished regimental honor that a junior officer who was spotted in her loge at the opera was summarily drummed out of the regiment. Grand Duke Mikhail's morganatic marriage also temporarily lost him his slot in the succession and forced him into exile—but that's another story.

On March 1, 1881, the young Mikhail Mikhailovich Osorgin, newly commissioned a cornet in the Chevalier Guards, participated in a ceremonial inspection by Alexander II. He had often seen the tsar before as a page at court, and he noted that on this day the Gosudar appeared troubled and pensive. Osorgin had just returned to his quarters with a friend when they heard what sounded like a cannon shot. Osorgin mechanically glanced at his watch, because a cannon was fired daily at noon from the Fortress of Sts. Peter and Paul (it still is). It was already after one. Then another thud sounded from the same direction. Soon after, Osorgin's servant, Semyon, rushed in, shaking, and announced: "They say the tsar's been killed."

Osorgin and his friend leapt into a cab. Driving past the Kazan Cathedral, they saw to their right a huge crowd on the Ekaterinsky (now Griboyedov) Canal. People were weeping and crossing themselves and shouting, "He's

Mikhail Mikhailovich Osorgin in his army uniform.

killed! He's killed!" The entire square in front of the Winter Palace was packed, and as Osorgin made his way toward the palace in his Guards uniform, people cleared the way, some shouting, "Go, go defend him!"

The first bomb had left Alexander II unscathed, but instead of fleeing, he stepped from his sleigh to inspect the damage. The second bomb mortally wounded him and the assassin, Ignaty Grinevitsky, a member of the terrorist organization known as the People's Will. The Guards regiments were put on full alert. Back at the barracks, Osorgin met an officer, "Bazya" Gendrikov, who had rushed to the site of the explosions:

> Gendrikov was riding in the court *manège*, located across the canal from the site of the incident. The first explosion shattered the windows in the *manège* and Gendrikov fell. He ran out and nearly fell from the shock of the second explosion. When he reached the place where the Gosudar was lying, people were already trying to raise him and lay him in his sleigh. The lower half of the Gosudar's body was a formless, bloody mass, his head was bare, and blood was seeping down his sheet-white face. Grand

Duke Mikhail Nikolayevich ordered that the Gosudar be taken to the nearby palace of Grand Duchess Yekaterina Mikhailovna, but Alexander whispered, "home." Gendrikov mounted the running board, put his regimental cap on the Gosudar, and held his head to the very palace. They went at a walking pace, surrounded by a unit of infantry that by chance had been marching past.

Alexander II died soon after, and with him the moderate cause. That was the intent of the People's Will: the "Tsar-Liberator" was on the eve of taking the first step toward a constitution, and for the zealous revolutionaries that would only have delayed the social cataclysm that they ardently believed in. The regicide was an enormous shock. Nobody who lived through that day ever forgot it. A multidomed church in the fanciful style of St. Basil's Cathedral in Moscow was raised over the spot of the assassination. Formally the Church of the Resurrection, it came to be known as the Savior-on-the-Blood.

Regicide was hardly new in Russia's history. Alexander II's grandfather Paul I and his great-grandfather Peter III had both been assassinated. But there was a difference: Peter and Paul fell in palace coups intended to rid Russia of weak monarchs, and their successors conspired with their aristocratic assassins to conceal the murders from a populace that still believed in the "Father Tsar" and would have been enraged to learn of their true fate. Alexander II died instead at the hand of an assassin acting in the name of that populace to rid Russia of monarchy. The autocracy and the nation were parting ways.

The shock of the assassination was offset in conservative circles by tacit relief that the "Tsar-Liberator" who freed the serfs, compelled officers to shave their beards, and was about to undermine the autocracy with a constitution was being succeeded by a solid, Russophile conservative, the richly bearded Alexander III. Osorgin, newly inducted into a regiment that personified the establishment, echoed that satisfaction: "They say that when the new Gosudar was told that it would be too dangerous for him to participate in the transfer of [his father's] body to the Sts. Peter and Paul Cathedral, he smashed his fist on the table and said that if anyone dared interfere with his final duty to his father, he would not leave stone standing on stone in St. Petersburg. Immediately there was a sense of such will and energy that everyone rallied and liberals fell silent."

Before long, Count Mikhail Loris-Melikov, the minister of the Interior and effective head of the government in Alexander II's last years, was pushed aside by Konstantin Pobedonostsev, the arch-reactionary Procurator of the Holy Synod of the Russian Orthodox Church. With Loris-Melikov went the projected constitution and his belief that stern suppression of terrorism had to be coupled with political concessions. Dry, humorless, and unyielding, Pobedonostsev was the prototype of future Communist ideologues.

At the government session called a week after the assassination to determine the fate of Loris-Melikov's reforms, Pobedonostsev made a speech that was interrupted twice by approving applause from the new tsar: "There are those who want to introduce a constitution in Russia, if not immediately, then at least to take a first step. But what is a constitution? The answer to this question is given by Western Europe. The constitution that exists there is a tool of every lie, the source of every sort of intrigue." From there, Pobedonostsev lashed out at all of the assassinated tsar's reforms, down to the emancipation of the serfs. "The peasants are given freedom, but no strong authority is imposed on them, without which a mass of dark people cannot function."

The change was felt immediately. Within days, Osorgin reported, officers and officials were walking around with stubble on their chins, sprouting the beards that the Westernizing Alexander II had banned and the Russophile Alexander III now favored. Pobedonostsev was appointed tutor to the new heir apparent, the future Nicholas II.

Soon after the assassination, Osorgin was invited by a fellow Chevalier Guards officer whom he idolized, Count Alexander Vasilievich Adlerberg, to his quarters. Sasha Adlerberg was well connected: his uncle, Count Alexander Vladimirovich Adlerberg, was the minister of the Imperial Court under Alexander II. After conspiratorially checking behind the doors and locking them, Adlerberg asked Osorgin to swear that he would never disclose anything of what followed. He then told him of the Sacred Brotherhood (Svyataya Druzhina), whose creation the new tsar purportedly endorsed, and whose members were sworn to safeguard the monarch and the monarchy. Overwhelmed by the trust of his comrade and his own feelings for the monarch, Osorgin declared himself ready to give his all.

The Sacred Brotherhood was apparently a creature of Pobedonostsev, who regarded terror and conspiracy as the surest weapon against terror and conspiracy. Osorgin dutifully did not probe into the origins of the secret organization, and as a junior member he was in any case not in a position to know. The brotherhood had elaborate rites of secrecy. Every "brother" had a number and a code name (Osorgin was number 27, code name Hurrah), and was required to recruit five new members. Each brother, moreover, knew only the one who had recruited him and the ones he recruited. If members had to meet, they signaled their brotherhood by passing their right hand before their knee.

Soon after, Osorgin was sent by Adlerberg to another officer, "Chernomor" Panchulidzev, who led him into a library concealed behind a false panel of his apartment and appointed him archivist. Thereafter, Osorgin spent many of his evenings and all his Saturdays collating intelligence and filing papers. The Sacred Brotherhood received several major donations from rich merchants and maintained an external intelligence service in Paris as well as internal security services in Moscow and St. Petersburg. Panchulidzev told Osorgin that the brotherhood had actually succeeded in foiling two terrorist attacks. Through intelligence from Europe, they seized a young woman purportedly preparing to assassinate the Interior minister, Count Nikolai Ignatiev, and they learned of plans to attack the tsar and the Kaiser when they met in Poland. The monarchs changed their plans and met instead aboard a ship in the Baltic Sea.

Osorgin never confirmed these claims. But once, poring through a pile of underground publications received from Europe, he and Panchulidzev came across a radical underground newspaper published in Geneva with a complete list of the brotherhood's members and functions—including their own names and code names and the exact location of their archive. That contributed to serious misgivings Osorgin was already beginning to feel about the organization. One of its activities was to assign young Guards officers to take up positions along the route the tsar was to take through St. Petersburg. The route was supposed to be a secret, but the appearance of officers in uniform along certain streets served only to disclose it. When Osorgin once directed a policeman's attention to a suspicious character, he turned out to be the chief of security from the Interior Ministry.

When the archconservative Count Dmitry Tolstoy was appointed minister of the Interior in 1882, he ordered the Sacred Brotherhood disbanded and took over its archives. Osorgin subsequently spotted signs that led him to believe a new secret organization was operating; but if it was, he was not invited to join.

I would not be surprised if there were more than one secret organization on the right, but I doubt they were any more competent or useful than the Sacred Brotherhood. Russians are notoriously given to conspiracy theories, when incompetence offers a far more plausible explanation for a debacle.

In any case, the tsarist secret police were hardly the finely tuned machine that its Soviet successors became. As governor of Tula, Osorgin discovered that one of the local marshals of nobility, a man of ultraconservative views and limited intelligence, was under secret police surveillance. It turned out that this marshal had been in St. Petersburg when Interior Minister Vyacheslav Konstantinovich von Plehve was assassinated, an event that happened to coincide with the name day of the Tula governor. Wishing both to congratulate the governor and to advise him of the assassination, the marshal cabled the governor: "Congratulations. Plehve killed." The police read the telegram and duly put the man under surveillance. But when real revolutionaries went into the streets of Tula during the 1905 revolution, the police admitted to Osorgin that it recognized none of the leaders, and that none of the people they had under surveillance played any role.

After Alexander II's assassination, revolutionary ferment shifted from the basements of radical intellectuals to factories and villages. An economic depression, a series of crop failures, the spread of education, and the proliferation of leftist propaganda all contributed to the growth of unrest. Two conservative ministers of the Interior, the most powerful office in the government, were assassinated in quick succession (Dmitry Sipyagin and Plehve). As vice governor and then governor between 1898 and 1905, Osorgin grappled daily with assassinations, strikes, and demonstrations, especially in the western provinces of Kharkov and Grodno, with their volatile stew of nationalities and religions—Jews, Catholics, Russian Orthodox, Poles, Lithuanians, Latvians, Belorussians, Ukrainians, Russians.

The Osorgins achieved their social goals in St. Petersburg. Varya married a rising military officer, Yakov ("Yasha") Zhilinsky, and young Mikhail was accepted into the Chevalier Guards regiment. Ironically, it was the financial strain of these achievements that compelled Mikhail to resign from his regiment after less than two years of service, at 22, and to return to Sergiyevskoye to cope with his family's imminent bankruptcy. Money was so tight that at one point the entire family moved into one small wing of the house and made do with one coachman and one cook.

But even with such economies and hands-on management, the estate could no longer sustain a growing family. So young Mikhail Mikhailovich did what an increasing number of landowners were doing, and secured a position in the civil service. Many new local offices and institutions were being created or revised at that time, and Osorgin worked first in the education system, than as a local magistrate, then, as of February 1890, as a local land captain.

Energetic, methodical, and businesslike by nature, Osorgin plunged into administrative work with fervor, quickly developing a reputation for fairness and conscientiousness. Soon he was elected local marshal of nobility, and on May 2, 1898, at the age of 37, he was appointed vice governor of Kharkov Province.

*Mikhail Mikhailovich Osorgin in his first civil service
job, as a land captain, flanked by peasant officials.*

The governor was an influential figure in a Russian province, not so much because of his formal powers, which were vaguely defined, but because all other institutions of local authority were underdeveloped and in constant flux. As a personal representative of the tsar, the governor was firmly identified as *nachalnik*, "chief," and it was to him that people turned with problems and complaints. The system survived into Soviet times, when an *oblast* Party Committee secretary was something of a local viceroy. In the tsarist province as in the Soviet *oblast*, the local administration depended in great degree on the style, personality, competence, and connections of the governor.

Osorgin's seven years of service as vice governor and governor were marked above all by quickening revolution, with which governors were often left to cope with their own limited resources. Already when he was appointed to Kharkov, anything could spark a demonstration.

Sergei Osorgin, who was nine when his father arrived in Kharkov and thirteen when the family left, recalled one summer when a group of political prisoners was to be transported out of the city. A crowd of three or four thousand gathered, singing revolutionary hymns and waving red flags. His father, the acting governor, arrived with a company of infantry, but that only riled the mob further, and a confrontation seemed inevitable. "Suddenly there was a hubbub in the back rows of the demonstrators and somebody shouted, 'Cossacks!' In one minute there was no crowd, no flags, no shouts. Everyone disappeared, and Papa, not believing his eyes, watched a lone Cossack cross the railroad bridge on a cart at the bottom of the hill, evidently delivering packages. That was the reputation of the Cossacks!"

The story has its element of adolescent bravado, but it also reflects the limitations of a governor against increasingly aggressive crowds. In these conditions, it was those governors who were prepared to bend the rules who won the day.

In late March and early April 1902, a massive uprising of peasants erupted in Poltava Province and spread into neighboring Kharkov. Osorgin was in his fifth year as vice governor, and a new governor, Prince Ivan Obolensky, reputed to be a firm disciplinarian, had just taken office. The size of the insurrection was unprecedented for the time: 38,000 people from 174 villages took part, and 105 estates were destroyed. Osorgin took an instant dislike to the swaggering Obolensky (a relative of his wife's), but he acknowledged a grudging respect for the way he handled the crisis.

The outbreak of the insurrection coincided with the assassination of Dmitry Sipyagin, the Interior minister, and Osorgin learned of both events on his return from a trip to St. Petersburg. He was met at the station by a police official who reported, "Everything is in order, but the minister of the Interior has been killed, and uprisings have broken out in Kharkov Province. Peasants have rebelled in Valki *uyezd*, and the governor has gone there." A curious definition of "everything is in order."

When the mob of peasants first began looting and burning estates in Poltava Province, the governor there, Alexander Karlovich Belgard, went by the book and asked the provincial military commandant for troops. The latter dispatched a battalion of infantry, and all Belgard could do was chase after the mob from estate to estate, invariably arriving after the estate was in flames and the looters had fled. When the peasants crossed into Kharkov Province near Valki, Obolensky also demanded troops. But when the Kharkov commandant assigned him a battalion of infantry, Obolensky dismissed them and ordered a hundred Cossacks to come with him to Valki—an order for which he had no authority. Before moving on, Obolensky took his personal train back to Kharkov to attend an *opéra bouffe* whose prima donna he particularly fancied. Osorgin was indignant but grudgingly acknowledged that this shameless diversion proved useful in reassuring the nervous population that everything was under control.

After the opera, Obolensky took his train back to Valki. The moon was full, and by its light he led his Cossacks into a village whose peasants that day had destroyed an estate and pillaged a sugar factory. Obolensky set the Cossacks loose; within minutes, all the peasants were rounded up and the Cossacks unleashed their brutal whips. Word spread quickly, and the next day peasants everywhere were rushing to return stolen goods. Local police, emboldened by the retreat, embarked on what Osorgin called "a bacchanalia of beatings." Soon peace was restored, not only in Kharkov but in Poltava.

Though Obolensky had exceeded his authority at every turn, he was singled out for praise by the newly appointed minister of the Interior, the reactionary Vyacheslav Plehve, who came to Kharkov and publicly said to Obolensky, "I have come to learn from you how to stop peasant uprisings." Governor Belgard of Poltava, who had tried to go by the book, was fired.

The official endorsement of violent and unauthorized methods, as long as they were effective, deeply troubled Osorgin. His moral quandary was intensified when Obolensky became the target of an unsuccessful assassination attempt. The attacker was a confirmed revolutionary named Kochura, and his arrest confronted Osorgin with a conflict between his official duties and a deep religious opposition to the death penalty. The conflict would resurface at several fateful junctures of his career.

He encountered the sentiment first on the night before the conspirators in the assassination of Alexander II were to be hanged, when he suffered as if it were he or his child who was about to die. "At that moment all other thoughts were deafened by the feeling of endless pity for those who were at the end of their existence; I suffered with them the animal fear of the impending and inescapable; I was tormented by the sense of helpless grief that their families must be experiencing; I understood and endured with them that protest that they must be feeling. I was ready to scream, to weep, and I understood the depth of the Christian teaching: Love thy neighbor as thyself."

One of the condemned conspirators was pregnant, and her execution was delayed until she gave birth. The others were hanged; one of them broke the rope twice and was hanged only on the third attempt, violating a tradition by which a breaking rope was regarded as a divine sign to spare the condemned. Listening in horror to the account of someone who witnessed the executions, Osorgin was reminded of an old woman named Kashkin he had known in Kaluga, whose son was among the 21 intellectuals (Dostoevsky was another) sentenced to die in 1849 for their participation in the Petrashevsky circle, a group that met regularly in St. Petersburg to discuss socialist ideas. Madame

Kashkin traveled to St. Petersburg for the execution and watched the firing squad take its position in front of her son, when it was announced that the sentences had been commuted. For the rest of her life, the woman's head shook uncontrollably.

Executions were actually a relative rarity at the turn of the century. The first governor Osorgin served under in Kharkov, German Tobizen, repeatedly had to postpone the execution of a band of murderers because he could not find a competent executioner. At one point, reading in a newspaper about an execution in the Caucasus, he cabled authorities there to lend him their executioner. They flatly refused. Tobizen then seized on the extraordinary scheme of offering an imprisoned criminal parole if he would serve as hangman. The plan was blocked by a prison official who declared that if the prisoner was prepared to kill, he was by definition ineligible for parole. In the end, Tobizen was left with no choice but to commute the death sentences, to Osorgin's relief.

As for Kochura, Obolensky's attacker, Alexei Lopukhin, head of the Police Department in St. Petersburg (and another cousin of Osorgin's wife), tried to resolve the dilemma for Osorgin by transferring the trial to Kiev. But before long, probably at Obolensky's initiative, Osorgin was dismissed, and it was half a year before he received his next assignment, as governor of Grodno Province. He was assigned there at the request of Prince Pyotr Sviatopolk-Mirsky, the moderate governor-general of the Western Provinces.

Osorgin began his service as governor of Grodno in February 1903. The territory of this province is now divided between Poland and Belarus, and before Osorgin arrived it was considered a backwater; under four previous governors, only one political arrest had been made. "Alas, under me it was not that way," he lamented. "There was vigorous revolutionary propaganda; the Jewish Bund [the General Union of Jewish Workers in Russia and Poland] was strong in the city of Grodno and in the province, Belostok and Krynki were hotbeds of struggle against factory owners." So hot was Belostok, in fact, that Osorgin installed a special telephone line from the city to his office in Grodno, which sounded a siren rather than a ring.

The tensions were not only between workers and employers but also between Jewish and Polish workers. Assassination attempts were constant, including shots fired at Osorgin. The gunmen were rarely caught in Belostok; most would disappear into the labyrinth of the narrow streets in the workers' neighborhoods. One victim was the local police chief, Yelchin, whom Osorgin had known as a boy at Sergiyevskoye. Yelchin was shot trying to disperse a march of striking workers. Osorgin attended his funeral and tried to bolster the morale

Mikhail Mikhailovich Osorgin at his desk as governor
of Grodno.

of the local officials: "Every police officer thought that his turn would come soon, and attitudes toward me changed. Before that, the industrialist Mors would always lend me his carriage when I came to Belostok; now he refused under various pretexts, fearing for his carriage if someone threw a bomb. I myself did not take anyone with me in my carriage, not wishing to endanger anyone else."

Osorgin and other provincial governors in this period often found St. Petersburg frustratingly deaf to their appeals. In 1904, Osorgin was confronted with a volatile situation at a glass factory at Cherniany Rudy. It had been confiscated from a Pole and purchased at an auction by owners who halted production in anticipation of selling off the property piecemeal. As a result, five hundred workers, many of them Belgians, were receiving no pay. Visiting the workers' homes, Osorgin found conditions so desperate that he was reminded of Zola's *Germinal*. Workers were starving, and in one house a baby girl had been lying dead for four days because no one had the strength or the money to bury her. He bombarded Vilnius, the regional capital of the Western Provinces, and St. Petersburg with messages, demanding that the owners be found and emergency funds freed.

Receiving no reply, he went by train to the new governor general in Vilnius, Alexander Freze, who sent him to the chief of the Police Department in St. Petersburg, Alexei Lopukhin, who sent him to Sviatopolk-Mirsky, now minister of the Interior, who sent him to the minister of Finance, Count Vladimir Kokovtsev, who accused Osorgin of "exceeding his authority" in freezing the assets of the factory. Here poor Osorgin lost his composure. His voice trembling, he threatened that if the owners were allowed to get away with their actions, he would take Kokovtsev to court. "I don't know what worked on Kokovtsev, my logic or my emotion, but he gave in immediately," Osorgin wrote. Osorgin's only reward was the knowledge that one small crisis was averted. It is notable that all the officials except Kokovtsev—Freze, Lopukhin, and Mirsky—were Osorgin's acquaintances or relatives.

Another of Osorgin's duties was in sharp contrast to these incessant crises. His province was the site of the tsar's favorite hunting preserve, the Belovezh forest, a magnificent wilderness that re-entered history on December 8, 1991, when the leaders of the Soviet republics of Russia, Ukraine, and Belarus—Boris Yeltsin, Leonid Kravchuk, and Stanislav Shushkevich—met there and declared the Soviet Union formally dissolved.

Though a monarchist to the marrow, even Osorgin was taken aback by the opulence of the imperial hunt. "I think he [the tsar] did not know himself what the price of his hunt in Belovezh amounted to in worry, labor, and expenditures," he wrote.

The preserve had begun as a 540-acre forest in which Alexander II built a modest, ten-room lodge; Alexander III expanded the lodge into a vast palace, and Nicholas II added a twenty-room guest house and huge wings, and had every room faced with paneling made from trees found in the Belovezh forest. By Nicholas's time the preserve covered 621,000 acres in three *uyezds,* and Alexander II's original fenced-in plot was just a shelter for sick animals.

In late August 1903, with war clouds gathering over the Far East, Nicholas came to hunt, accompanied by, among many others, his brother the Grand Duke Mikhail; his cousin the Grand Duke Nikolai Nikolayevich, and his uncle the Grand Duke Vladimir. The entire forest was divided into parcels of about a square kilometer each, outlined by clearings that were planted with grass so that the imperial carriages could move silently. On the eve of each hunting expedition—there were two a day—beaters would drive animals into two neighboring quadrants and seal them off with nets. When the tsar and his party arrived, a battalion of infantry drove the game toward the shooters, who would shoot first into one quadrant, then turn around and shoot into the other. A sharpshooter was always posted alongside Nicholas lest a wounded animal charge, but the tsar was a fine shot and never required help. Two or three dozen animals were killed each day. In the evening, by the light of torches, the hunters held the traditional "streek"—the game was laid out in front of the palace and something akin to taps was played on hunting horns.

One day, over dinner, the empress expressed her delight at the way the carriages rolled silently through the forest, noting that they were audible only when they crossed an occasional wooden bridge. This was meant as a compliment, but Prince Vyazemsky, the manager of imperial domains, ordered that each bridge be covered with turf by morning. They were, prompting Osorgin to ponder, "Poor Gosudar! He doesn't even know what goes into fulfilling his wishes." Indeed, the tsar deported himself with almost naïve simplicity, seemingly unaware of the fuss he caused. In church, noted Osorgin, the imperial family stood surrounded by a throng of peasants, who would push past them unceremoniously to light a candle.

Osorgin did not permit himself to criticize the Gosudar, but he did betray the distaste of the old Muscovite nobility for the haughty St. Petersburg courtiers, and especially the many Germans among them—a presence that he, like many Russians, held against the dour, unsociable empress, Alexandra Fyodorovna, a German granddaughter of Queen Victoria of England. "In general," he wrote, "the total ignorance of the Russian language in the tsar's court always made a sad impression on me; between themselves, the sovereigns always spoke English, and with their entourage, down to the riding master, German; indeed, the dominance of the German element at the court was considerable."

That the foreign element was substantial, in the court as in the military and the civil service, is indisputable. Of the 215 men appointed to the Council of State, the highest institution of the state, in the reign of Nicholas II, 48 were of German origin. But 28 of these (including Senator Nikolai Eduardovich

Schmemann) were baptized in the Russian Orthodox faith, the main indicator of assimilation, and considered themselves Russian. As for language, I'd like to have reminded Osorgin that his own grandmother, Varvara Andreyevna, spoke only French, and would scold any grandson who dared lapse into "vulgar" Russian. But then, that's just the pique of an offshoot of that "German element."

September 5 was the regimental holiday of the Chevalier Guards, and Osorgin and other members of the regiment hosted the imperial couple at a formal dinner. The dinner passed in total silence save for two mandatory toasts, to the regiment and to the tsar, and immediately after dessert the tsar rose and left. Osorgin later learned that the tsar had received alarming reports from the Far East that day.

Nicholas's diary entries for those days suggest no concern over the Far East, or over much of anything save the weather and the hunt. But then, his diaries hardly ever touched on state affairs; if they were the sole record of his life, he would now be remembered, if at all, as a prosperous and dull country squire, perfectly happy to spend his days hunting, shooting billiards, and taking tea with his beloved wife. Only the occasional reference to the inspection of a regiment or to a few hours spent "reading my papers" suggests his monarchical status.

The entry for September 5, for example, makes no mention of the Far East, or of the silent regimental dinner. On the other hand, the tsar meticulously noted and underlined the game he bagged, as he always did:

> The day was much cooler than previous days, but still glorious. We left for the hunt by railroad to the Starinskoye estate. Recognized some enclosures. Saw much game, but got to shoot only once at a boar. Altogether, there were killed: 31 animals. We returned home at 5¼ by carriage along the new road from Zverints. Read intensively until dinner and in the evening.

The two-week stay in Belovezh ended September 10:

> For the last time, we rode out to the hunt with Prince Golitsyn and Grünwald. Misha [the Tsar's brother, Grand Duke Mikhail] was in the forest from the night before. A gray morning turned into a wonderful, clear day. In the end I had bad luck—I <u>killed</u> only a <u>boar</u> and a <u>fox</u>. Today there were 23 kills. The <u>total result</u> for the entire stay—12 bison, 6 moose, 69 deer, 36 Daniel deer, 201 goats, 83 boars and 41 foxes. Altogether 448 kills. Of this, I killed: <u>2 bison, 1 deer, 4 Daniel deer, 10 goats, 6 boar, 5 foxes</u> and a <u>grouse—29 kills</u>. Packed. Returned home at 5¼. Dined as always. The last streek was

very beautiful. At 11½ said goodbye to all the foresters, hunters, troops and residents of Belovezh. Sadly bid farewell to this lovely, peaceful place.

Nicholas II would have few more such peaceful hunts. The war against Japan opened the final chapter of the tsarist empire. A mammoth blunder, the war was encouraged by Plehve as "a little victorious war to stop the revolutionary tide." Such sentiments were bolstered by the notion prevalent at the time (and still lurking 40 years later in Washington, when the Japanese were preparing their attack on Pearl Harbor) that Japan was just an insular little nation, and that Orientals could never win a war against Europeans. In St. Petersburg, Osorgin overheard someone say, "Why cancel court balls when this is not even a war, but just a small punitive expedition against the conceited Japs?"

The war began in January 1904 with a surprise Japanese attack on Port Arthur, and at the start it roused a wave of patriotism in Russia. The sinking of the cruiser *Varyag* and the gunboat *Koreyets* by their own crews, so they would not fall in enemy hands, was fashioned back in Russia into legend and song. But from the very outset there were also voices of caution. Osorgin's brother-in-law, General Yakov Zhilinsky, was chief of the General Staff, and in private conversations he confessed his misgivings about plunging into a war so far away, and with a divided military leadership. Characteristically, the tsar evaded a hard choice in choosing between two rivals by appointing both as military commanders. The popular favorite, General Alexei Kuropatkin, was named commander of the Army, while the tsar's own favorite, Admiral Evgeny Alexeyev, regent of the Far East and a hardliner on Japan, was named commander in chief. It was left to Zhilinsky to sort out their totally differing strategies.

Sergei Osorgin was 15 when the war broke out, and he recalled a classmate at the Grodno Gymnasium who was so seized with patriotism that he organized marches and demonstrations and even interrupted a theater performance to demand that the audience sing "God Save the Tsar." The classmate, Fedya Aliabiev, finally ran off to join the Siberian Rifles regiment. For a while he wrote breathless letters to his old classmates, but then they stopped. "Subsequently it turned out that he fell into a revolutionary circle, where he was turned around and became a passionate revolutionary," Osorgin wrote.

Aliabiev was not alone. As the war dragged on and the setbacks came one after another, soldiers from the Far East began coming back disillusioned and angry. The image of an all-powerful empire was beginning to crumble.

The second Mikhail Mikhailovich was in St. Petersburg on the day in April 1904 when word came that the flagship of the Russian Pacific fleet, *Petropavlovsk*, had struck a mine and sunk at Port Arthur, taking many lives, including that of the fleet commander, the celebrated explorer Admiral Stepan Makarov.

> I was staying at the Anglia Hotel, overlooking St. Isaac's Cathedral. I'll never forget the horrible, oppressive sensation of the ringing of the cathedral bell for a state memorial service for the sailors who had perished. I remember how I stood for a long time at the window, listening to that mournful, measured tolling and watching the arrival of the military, civil, and court personages.
>
> Since I am writing this many years later, I can be suspected of ascribing feelings to myself in the knowledge of what came to pass, but I give my word that this is a totally objective account of what I felt then. This glittering convocation of the imperial family and the whole civil, military, and court world to the sound of the funeral bell seemed to me a leave-taking of Russia's past greatness. For a long time I could not shake this impression.

Fourteen months later, the humiliations culminated when the Russian Baltic fleet, after steaming for months all the way around Europe and Asia, finally arrived in the Far East, only to be routed by the Japanese on May 27, 1905, off the island of Tsushima. By this time strikes, terror, and peasant unrest were raging across the land.

"It became clear to all that the war was lost, disgracefully lost, and the former greatness of Russia, the faith in her might, had been irretrievably undermined," wrote Osorgin.

Without faith and without might, the monarchy had little hold over Russia. There were no developed institutions of state, no political consensus, and the social chasm in the nation was growing ever broader. Perhaps, just perhaps, if there had been a strong and enlightened tsar at the helm, that faith might not have collapsed. But there was only the kindly, indecisive Nicholas and his neurotic German wife, and later the diabolical Rasputin, incessantly changing ministers, advisers, and direction. It is almost painful to read the pleas and warnings of those who saw what was looming, and to feel the anguish of their frustration and despair as the monarchy lurched toward doom.

At this time Osorgin was honored by being appointed a chamberlain of the court (not for his dedicated service as a governor, but in recognition of his organization of the Belovezh hunt). When he came to receive his appointment from the tsar, the monarch was no longer the demigod who had sent him into ecstasy as a youth: "Seeing him for the first time since Belovezh, I was especially struck by the slovenliness of his dress. He was dressed, as in Belovezh, in a military jacket, although it was winter, but where the jacket had been snow-white in Belovezh, it now seemed somehow dirty, and the Gosudar himself seemed gray and careworn."

The devoted monarchist would not say more, but he was well aware of the weakness at the helm. He first encountered it in a conversation in St. Petersburg with his superior, patron, and friend Prince Pyotr Sviatopolk-Mirsky, who as governor general of the Western Provinces had appointed Osorgin to serve in Grodno. After the assassinations in quick succession of two iron-handed ministers of the Interior, the tsar changed course and offered the post—at that time by far the most powerful in the realm—to the moderately liberal Sviatopolk-Mirsky. Nicholas assured the old man that he fully shared his principle of "confidence in the public" and his support for representative institutions. Sviatopolk-Mirsky was reluctant, but the tsar's mother, the dowager empress Maria Fyodorovna (probably the real instigator of his appointment), pleaded with him. "You must fulfill my son's wish; if you do, I will give you a kiss," she told the embarrassed prince. He accepted the post, but Nicholas quickly and typically cooled to him. At about this time, Osorgin called on Sviatopolk-Mirsky:

> After completing our business we stayed in his cabinet, awaiting the usual summons from the princess to lunch. Here, recalling our close relations, he became somehow morally unbuttoned. A person who never criticized his Sovereign, he told me that his situation was becoming intolerable. The Sovereign had even canceled his regular audiences under various pretenses, demanding that he make his reports in writing. Sviatopolk-Mirsky felt that he had lost the Sovereign's confidence, and he believed that a personal clarification was necessary, but the Sovereign would not even reply to this request.
>
> "I have totally ceased to understand the Sovereign," Sviatopolk-Mirsky said.

It was a cry from the heart that must have shocked Osorgin. But soon the storm clouds grew even darker. On January 9, 1905, workers marching to present a petition to the tsar were fired on, and about one hundred fifty people were killed. Several days after the disaster, Sviatopolk-Mirsky stepped down and was succeeded by Alexander Grigorievich Bulygin, a former governor of Kaluga. Bulygin was the sixth minister of the Interior under Nicholas, and there would be seven more. Svyatopolk-Mirsky held the office less than half a year.

The slaughter on Palace Square, which came to be known as "Bloody Sunday," was the opening shot of the 1905 revolution. Disenchantment over the war merged with spreading political discontent. Strikes swept the land. Manors burned in Kursk, Oryol, and Chernigov. The tsar's brother-in-law, Grand Duke Sergei Alexandrovich, governor general of Moscow, was blown to bits by a terrorist bomb. Nicholas's response was to appoint the brutal General Dmitry Trepov as governor general of St. Petersburg with dictatorial powers.

As the crisis deepened, the cries to the tsar grew more anguished and desperate. Among the most fervent of those who still believed that the chasm between monarch and people could be bridged were Osorgin's Trubetskoi in-laws, who had become prominent political liberals.

Prince Sergei Nikolayevich Trubetskoi, a popular and respected professor of philosophy, who was soon to become the first elected rector of Moscow University, was co-opted by leaders of the *zemstvos*, the organs of limited self-rule set up in the 1860s, to present to the tsar their urgent appeal for a representative assembly and fundamental social reforms. Until then the tsar had steadfastly refused to meet gentry opposition leaders, but the *zemstvo* congress that met in May 1905 hoped that Trubetskoi's august name and moderate views would serve to impress on Nicholas the gravity of the gathering storm.

The audience, on June 6, 1905, established Trubetskoi as a national figure. When Nicholas entered the hall at 12:40, he struck those present by his timidity and aloofness. Perhaps because of this, Trubetskoi turned professorial, pacing the room and speaking with ardor and eloquence as he tried to convince the Gosudar that the *zemstvos* and the people were still loyal to him, but that they felt lost and betrayed when the government balked at granting promised reforms. Trubetskoi spoke without notes. The tsar followed his every word, nodding occasionally; several members of the delegation were on the verge of tears.

Relentless and harsh hatred, encrusted by ages of constrictions and outrages, sharpened by need and sorrow, lawlessness and the difficult economic conditions, rises and grows and it is even more dangerous, more contagious, more prone to inflame the masses in that it, at first, robes itself in patriotic forms. That is the terrible danger, Gosudar, which we, living in the land, have fully experienced and which we consider our duty to report to your Imperial Majesty. We are not lying, Gosudar! The only solution to these internal needs lies in the path you have shown, Gosudar, in calling together representatives of the people.

. . . It is essential that all your subjects, equally and with no distinctions, consider themselves Russian citizens, that parts of the population and various civic groups not be excluded from the national representation and thus become enemies of the renewed system; it is essential that there be none outside the law and no unfortunates. . . . As the Russian tsar is not the tsar of the nobility, not the tsar of the peasants or of the merchants, not the tsar of classes, but the Tsar of all Rus', so also the elected people from the whole population, called to work with you on the affairs of state, should serve general and not class interests.

Nicholas solemnly agreed. "From this day on, I see in you my helpers," he told the heartened delegates. But two weeks later, he received a delegation led by the reactionary Count Vladimir Bobrinsky, who directly attacked Trubetskoi's position, impressing on Nicholas that he was "the first among the nobility of Russia." Now Nicholas agreed with him.

Sergei Trubetskoi's older half-brother, Prince Pyotr Nikolayevich Trubetskoi, the marshal of nobility in Moscow, followed Sergei's lead on June 18 as the spokesman for a conference of provincial marshals. Though normally more deferential than Sergei, he now abandoned all decorum and assailed the monarch directly: "Here, today, you have the kindness to receive us and to agree with us, but tomorrow you will receive Dorrer and you will agree with him!" Such wavering was rapidly eroding public confidence, Trubetskoi raged on, to which the pale Nicholas could only stammer, "I have already heard this." Two days later, just as Trubetskoi knew he would, Nicholas received the archreactionary Count V. F. Dorrer, marshal of nobility in Kursk Province, and endorsed all his demands.

8

"We Will Renounce the Old World"

Even as the tsars' domains expanded in the nineteenth century through the Caucasus and Central Asia and across Siberia to the distant Pacific, their capacity to rule stretched thinner and thinner, until war and revolution punctured it and sent the monarchy into a fatal tailspin. The Soviet Union repeated the pattern, reconquering and expanding the empire deep into East Europe, only to collapse once the center could no longer hold. What is it that has made this great nation so incapable of steady rule? "Russia," said one wise observer, "is not underdeveloped. It is misdeveloped."

All through its history, Russia's rulers—autocrats, dictators, reformers, and reactionaries—have wrung enormous sacrifices from their people to achieve the power and respect that they believed to be Russia's due. The country's vastness, natural wealth, and history convinced each ruler in turn that it was destined to greatness, to be the Third Rome, Holy Russia, the vanguard of a brave new world. But just when he seemed to be on the verge of realizing Russia's greatness and might, the ruler would find that somewhere along the line he had lost his exhausted, battered, and alienated people.

Yegor Gaidar, the architect of the first post-Communist reforms in Russia, described the vicious circle in *Izvestia* shortly after being ousted from Yeltsin's government: "Russia's race for a place in the civilized world recalls Achilles' chase after the tortoise—through superhuman effort, Russia would manage to 'catch up and overtake,' especially in military technology. Yet the world would 'unnoticeably' but steadily move on, and again after disgraceful and torturous setbacks the country would 'regroup for a leap' and make another lurch, and everything would be repeated."

It was to feed the military might of the state that peasants were originally bound to the land as serfs. It was toward this same end that Peter the Great shaved the beards off his boyars and sought to "hew a window into Europe" by building his new capital on the swamps of the Neva delta. It was in the name of an all-powerful state that Stalin slaughtered 10 million of his own and brutally regimented the rest.

The results *were* awesome: the greatest land empire in history, the largest army, the most megatons, the biggest spaceships, the most Olympic medals. The problem was that in their frenzy to achieve might, Moscow's rulers ended up at war with their own people. Battered and wrung out, the people would turn away and make a mockery of their rulers' ambitions. The last years of tsarist rule, when revolutionary assassins relentlessly stalked government ministers, and the degenerate religious charlatan Rasputin manipulated "the anointed of God" through his neurotic wife, were a parody of a Holy Russia. In the same way, the last years of Communist rule, when a succession of walking corpses and a dead ideology were artificially sustained in the Kremlin only by a massive political-police apparatus and a ravenous military machine, mocked the pretensions of the "workers' paradise."

What Russia's regimes learned too late was that a state based on a coercive central force cannot survive without it. Once Nicholas abdicated, the tsarist state collapsed in anarchy; once Gorbachev diluted Communist control, the entire Soviet universe of political machinery, industrial relationships, police controls, and imperial bonds fell helplessly apart.

It was Gaidar's hope that the vicious circle could be broken, that it was possible to prevent a tyrannical center from re-forming, and the first steps of the scaled-down Russian Federation were in that direction. But Russia's continued political floundering since the collapse of Communism, and the uncontrolled spread of corruption and lawlessness, make the eventual revival of a domineering center seem ever more probable.

On the same day that the Russian fleet was trounced at Tsushima, Osorgin was appointed governor of Tula Province, to the south of Moscow and to the east of Kaluga Province. There, in a few stormy months, he suffered firsthand the fallout of Russia's crumbling greatness.

"Let this story show how the provinces suffered through this troubled time, how provincial administrations were not kept informed by the central administration about affairs of state, why many governors, me among them, must admit in full conscience that they were not in control of the situation," he wrote.

The capital of the province, the city of Tula, was an old arms-manufacturing center rich in the kinds of provincial oddballs described by Gogol in *Dead Souls*—like Batashov, the owner of a famed samovar factory, who ordered that his amputated leg be buried under a marble tombstone with the inscription: "Here lies, until that joyous morning, the leg of Hereditary Citizen and Merchant of the First Guild Batashov." Among the city's traditions was to hold fistfights on the frozen river during Lent. The finest boxer was Ivan Parmenych Kolokolin, a big, mean reactionary who owned several bakeries, and who never missed a chance to send his "boys" to beat up leftist demonstrators.

At least Sergiyevskoye was near, and many of the landowners in the province were Osorgin relatives. The latter was not necessarily a boon, however, because the gentry was as polarized as the rest of society, and Tula landowners, including the Osorgins' kin, numbered among them some of the most ardent figures from both sides of the divide.

Osorgin's predecessor as governor, Vladimir Karlovich de Schlippe, had been a fierce conservative. The most prominent conservative landowners in Tula were the Samarins, Slavophiles whose "Samarin Circle" became a center of opposition to the notion of constitutional monarchy. The leader, Fyodor Dmitrievich Samarin, was married to one of Liza Osorgin's sisters; his younger brother, Sergei Dmitrievich, would marry the Osorgins' daughter Juliana.

When Osorgin arrived in Tula the liberal camp was led by Count Vladimir Alexeyevich Bobrinsky, master of Bogoroditsk, one of the most splendid estates in Russia. But after one of Bobrinsky's erstwhile disciples led an uprising in one of his villages, Bobrinsky abruptly metamorphosed into a fervid reactionary; he subsequently organized the Tula Union for Tsar and Order, a gentry-based law-and-order group (the rebellious disciple was shot dead leading a prison uprising in Tula). Osorgin's vice governor, Alexei Nikolayevich Khvostov, a member of an influential family of Tula landowners, was politically neutral at the outset but later became an archconservative and the second-to-last minister of the Interior under Nicholas II.

The most avid liberal and *zemstvo* activist in the province (after Bobrinsky's conversion) was Prince Georgy Yevgeniyevich Lvov, who would briefly serve as the first head of the Provisional Government formed after the abdication of Nicholas II. One of Lvov's most dedicated aides in the *zemstvo* administration was Nikolai Sergeyevich Lopukhin, Liza Osorgin's cousin, who subsequently married another Osorgin daughter, Sofia (the only Osorgin to marry at Sergiyevskoye).

Osorgin himself, despite his ardent monarchism and innate conservatism, developed a reputation as a liberal in Kharkov and Grodno because of his tolerance, honesty, respect for law, and principled opposition to the death penalty. His wife's four Trubetskoi brothers were by then among the most influential moderate-liberal politicians in Russia.

Sergei Trubetskoi was the most remarkable of that remarkable family. Historian of philosophy, Christian thinker, Slavophile, and liberal politician, he gained widespread popularity after his appeal to the tsar was published. Two months later, in August 1905, he persuaded Nicholas to grant autonomy to Moscow University, and on September 2 he crowned that achievement by being chosen as the university's first freely elected rector.

But student demonstrations and mass meetings persisted at the university, and on September 21, Trubetskoi ordered it closed to avoid violence. It was a measure of his popularity that when he announced the decision to an auditorium full of boisterous students, they neither jeered nor protested. During the confrontation, Trubetskoi, physically and morally exhausted, became faint and had to finish sitting down. He traveled to St. Petersburg several days later to deliver petitions from his students to the minister of Education, General Vladimir Glazov. In the evening of September 29, 1905, Trubetskoi collapsed, and several hours later he died, aged 43. His last words were, "Now they will calm down." "Who?" he was asked. "My boys."

They did not. Funeral services for the popular rector in St. Petersburg and Moscow turned into massive and sometimes violent left-wing demonstrations. Osorgin could not leave Tula for the funeral because of unrest there, but his wife and eldest son went. A procession with the body from the hospital to the railway station in St. Petersburg grew so vast that when Trubetskoi's sister Olga fell, she would have been crushed had the young Mikhail Osorgin not stood over her on all fours, bellowing for attention. For the first time since the funeral of the writer Turgenev in 1883, the government permitted memorial wreaths to be carried in the procession, and Trubetskoi's widow had to make a major effort to ensure that a wreath of white orchids and laurels from the tsar was carried along with the others, many of which bore inscriptions hailing Trubetskoi as a fallen "freedom fighter."

The scene was repeated in Moscow, where tens of thousands of people from all walks of life accompanied the body from the station to the university chapel, where services were held, then to his home, and from there, in a vast, candlelit procession, to the Donskoi Monastery, where Trubetskoi was buried. In one of many eulogies, a representative of Moscow University students declared: "The death of Trubetskoi proves again that in Russia, great, free men can only die." Another student, Lutsky, read a poem he had composed to the memory of Trubetskoi:

> *He inflamed us by the mighty word*
> *And blessed us for the fight to the death.*

In reality, Trubetskoi had battled bouts of deep despair, and it was to avert the violence that he foresaw with painful clarity that he threw himself into the political fray. But his death turned the philosopher, aristocrat, monarchist, and reluctant politician into a martyr of the revolution and a champion of "the fight to the death." Osorgin wrote:

> The size of the crowd for Seryozha's funeral was totally unusual: It was a tally of the forces of revolution. The only church singing was at the grave; otherwise the crowd sang revolutionary songs—"You have fallen victim in the momentous struggle" and others.
> . . . With my wife's return from the funeral, a more or less normal life came to an end. The revolutionary mood began to gather not by the day but by the hour, until it poured over into a general strike.

The history of the revolutions of 1905 and 1917 was written in St. Petersburg and Moscow, but it is in the chaos and anguish of the province that the human tragedy and the horror of those upheavals stand out most starkly.

The second Mikhail Mikhailovich was a principled and religious man devoted to order and monarchy, and he recognized from the outset that he was not the one to lead Tula through this time of revolutionary tumult. In the first days of October, all the bread bakeries in Tula went on strike, except for two that were kept open by the military. Supporters and opponents of the strikers repeatedly formed mobs in various places throughout the city. Osorgin recalled his attempt to disperse one such mob:

> Once I grabbed a bunch of Cossacks and went to disperse a crowd so large that it could have halted work even in those bakeries protected by soldiers. The mob was breaking into private homes, pouring kerosene into the wheat bins of those they suspected of selling bread. When we caught up

to this crowd, not far from Sennaya Square, I ordered the Cossacks to disperse them; then immediately I made a mistake. When I saw the vicious faces of the Cossacks (they had had it up to here with these strikes) as they lifted their whips and moved on the crowd, and when I saw the crowd, most of them adolescents, bolting with shrieks and screams, my heart sank and I screamed in a hysterical voice, "Back! Don't!"

The Cossacks angrily backed off from the taunts of the youths, and Osorgin realized that he would fail.

From this moment I understood that I would never succeed in crushing the unrest—not because of cowardice, but because of a sense of humanity that was entirely out of place here. I lost the ground under my feet, and my faith in myself. All my feelings were ambivalent. I understood that the future would be even more terrible; the bakers' strike was only the prologue, though it struck at the basic needs of the population.

Tula was a tinderbox. Its large weapons industry, railroad depots, samovar factories, and sugar refineries were a breeding ground of revolution. At the same time, small merchants and workers in the armaments factories formed a solid arch-conservative core. The old worker neighborhood of Chulkovo was a stronghold of conservatism. Since the time of Peter the Great, preference in employment at the weapons and ammunition factories was given to the sons of workers, and these hereditary employees valued their free apartments and high wages. The fiercest right-winger was Kolokolin, the boxer and bakery owner, who rode around the city threatening to restore order with his "boys." Against this, the governor had a totally demoralized police force, a regiment of infantry reservists, a company of Cossacks, and the guards at the armaments factories.

On the ninth day after Sergei Trubetskoi's death, Osorgin's father, the first Mikhail Mikhailovich, went to Moscow for a memorial service (in Russian tradition, services are held on the ninth and the fortieth days after a death). Old Osorgin returned to Tula on the last train before a general strike halted rail traffic. The strike began October 8, and by the end of the month the entire Russian railway system was almost at a standstill. The first *soviet* (council) of workers' deputies was formed in St. Petersburg; another was formed in Moscow. There were peasant uprisings in many regions.

"I felt as if I were the head of a besieged city," wrote Osorgin. The strike was St. Petersburg's problem; the governor's was to keep Tula calm and find lodging and food for thousands of passengers stranded there. What exasperated

Osorgin was that neither he nor any other governor received any advance notice or guidance from Interior Minister Alexander Bulygin or his ruthless deputy, Dmitry Trepov, by then the real power in the government as head of the martial-law regime in St. Petersburg.

In fact, the only official communication Osorgin received was a request from Grand Duke Nikolai Nikolayevich, who was hunting on his estate near Sergiyevskoye, to send him a cipher clerk. The grand duke had received a coded message from his cousin the tsar, which turned out to be an order to get back to the imperial residence at Peterhof at once. As governor, Osorgin had to find a secure way of getting him there: "The demand of the grand duke was categorical, and an order of the Gosudar was not open to debate," he wrote. So Osorgin devised a plan to get the grand duke out in the guise of a hunter accompanied by several Cossacks and policemen dressed as hunters. They got that way to Serpukhov, where a darkened locomotive took the grand duke through the night to Moscow, where another darkened locomotive waited to smuggle him to St. Petersburg. There, the tsar appointed his cousin commander of the Imperial Guard and of the St. Petersburg military district.

On October 18, 1905, Osorgin was surprised to learn that on the previous day the tsar had issued a manifesto promising civil liberties and representative institutions, which came to be known as the Manifesto of the 17th of October. The provincial governors received no advance notice of this explosive document. Osorgin was having breakfast with several officials when the head of the telegraph office called to say that a service message had just come over with the "Highest Manifest." "What manifest?" the governor asked. "How should I put it," stammered the confused official, "it looks like a constitution."

Intended to still the revolution, the Manifesto of the 17th of October only added fuel to the fire. Leftist radicals seized on it as a concession to their strikes and redoubled their efforts; reactionaries felt betrayed and began organizing in earnest; peasants sensed a weakening of authority and took to torching estates. In Tula, jubilant leftists poured into the streets with red flags to celebrate, prompting a horrified Osorgin to offer his resignation to the newly appointed prime minister, Sergei Witte: "I cannot in the blink of an eye be so reborn as to consider yesterday's criminal, now proclaiming his misguided views even louder, as a citizen equal to myself." There was no reply.

The chaos continued to mount, and on October 21 it broke into bloodshed. The day was a national holiday, marking the eleventh anniversary of the tsar's accession to the throne. A vast right-wing throng gathered at the cathedral in the Kremlin (a term for the walled center of all old Russian cities, not just

Moscow) with a large portrait of the tsar. Parade troops were pushed totally off to the side. Osorgin seized on the idea that a prayer service would calm the reactionary mob, but the bishop, Lavrenty, a tiny, bent old man who deliberately surrounded himself with similarly short clergy, was lost in the crowd. As a result, nobody saw or heard the service, and the mob howled even louder.

After a while the crowd seemed to thin, and Osorgin went home. But no sooner had he doffed his uniform than he was informed that the mob was headed toward his residence. There was no carriage standing by, so Osorgin went out on foot to confront the throng. He saw that they were dragging a woman, decently dressed but disheveled. When they saw Osorgin, they yelled that they had the "culprit" and were bringing her to him for punishment. Osorgin took the woman and thrust her into the vestibule of his house, where his wife and the household were huddling in fear. He began trying to calm the mob, saying that if they wanted to please the tsar, "it could only be through labor and calm." But passions continued to mount. One man, a fat merchant with many medals, threw himself trembling at Osorgin's feet and began kissing the hem of his coat and, echoing the rampant anti-Semitism of the far-right, screamed hysterically: "Your Excellency, we will disperse only when you swear that not one Yid will remain in the city."

Osorgin tried another tack, leading the crowd back down the street and saying that he wanted to telegraph their greetings to the tsar. That at least saved the poor woman. She was a teacher named Evdokiya Shishorina, who had come to the assistance of one of her students; the unfortunate youth, Alexander Blazhenkov, had failed to remove his cap when the mob filed past with the portrait of the tsar, and he was being thrashed when Shishorina intervened. The boy escaped, but she was seized instead.

Now, fearing that the Cossacks would eventually take the law into their own hands, Osorgin decided to order them moved from billets in the middle of the city to the outskirts.

Then came word that a new mob was moving toward the governor's house, this one with red flags and singing, "We will renounce the old world. . . ." Again the governor went out, and this time he was met by several youths in leather jackets carrying Browning automatics. Osorgin calmly asked them what they wanted. The spokesman for the group said he was authorized by "revolutionary and liberal forces" in the city to assure him that they were fully satisfied with his correct and loyal behavior toward them. ("My humble thanks for the compliment!" Osorgin noted ironically.) But now, the spokesman continued, they were compelled to demand two things: that he move the Cossacks out of the city, and that he turn the security of the city over to their "people's militia."

Osorgin answered with all the calm he could muster that he had already ordered the Cossacks moved, but not in response to their demand, and that he was not authorized to create a militia. The leftists appeared satisfied.

Five minutes had not passed when the phone rang. A "black hundreds" mob (as the right-wing reactionaries came to be known) of workers from the arms and ammunition factories, armed with hunting rifles, swords, and axes, was moving toward the Red crowd. Osorgin ordered his carriage, but it was still not hitched. Then came another call: "Shots on Kiev Street!" The governor rushed off on foot, and on his way to the center he was picked up by the military commander, who had also heard the shots. Moments later they galloped into Kiev Street, a broad, badly paved street that ran the length of the city; Osorgin estimated that less than ten minutes had passed since the first call.

The street was empty and dark. Isolated shots could be heard, but it was impossible to determine where they were coming from. A bullet whistled past. Bodies lay here and there, most of them at the intersection of Kiev and Posolskaya streets. Osorgin and the commander drove to a nearby barracks and summoned

Posolskaya Street in Tula, where a bloody clash took place on October 21, 1905.

a company of soldiers. Suddenly they heard galloping horses. Osorgin thought the Cossacks had come in on their own, and shouted: "Halt! Dismount!" He heard something flop to the ground, and at that moment the electric street lights flickered on. Before him stood about thirty peasants with staves, holding their panting workhorses. "We were told our people were being beaten," one of them said. Osorgin ordered them home.

He sent for firemen to collect the bodies and, accompanied by the soldiers, set off down the street on foot. Clusters of people stood here and there. Sporadically the lights would go off, throwing everything into darkness. Osorgin approached each group, quietly ordering them off the streets. He walked the length of Kiev Street, encountering no resistance. When he reached the police station, he asked where all the police were. He was told that the vice governor had ordered them to defend the governor's residence. Returning there furious, he found the house surrounded by policemen and his family highly alarmed. He ordered the police immediately back to their posts.

Soon Vice Governor Khvostov arrived. He reported that 23 bodies had been gathered, and there were many more wounded. The clash had been sudden and unexpected, and after a vicious exchange of fire both sides fled. The dead included "black hundreds" and revolutionaries, but most of them were chance passersby.

Later, the Communists turned "Bloody Friday" into a revolutionary myth. On its twentieth anniversary, the local Party in Tula issued a melodramatic but reasonably accurate report. In 1925 the art of rewriting history was not yet fully perfected, though the "mechanized speech" so favored by early revolutionaries was in full bloom:

> What happened in Tula on 21 October 1905?
>
> On that day a battle took place in Tula between activists of the revolution and the black forces of reaction.
>
> On that day black terror was unleashed on the revolutionaries in street battles marked by images of immeasurable savagery on the part of the nationalists with the support of the autocratic authorities.

In the Communist version, news of the manifesto was proclaimed in Tula by a young revolutionary named Rosa Raginskaya, who rushed into the Zaraisk Theater on the evening of October 18 and shouted: "Citizens, we have a constitution!" Everyone rose to their feet in confusion. "Hymn!" someone shouted from the audience. "Marseillaise!" retorted another. The crowd filed into the street, and Cossacks rushed in to beat them back.

As for the shooting, the Soviet account said that eighty leftists were leaving the governor's residence when they came face to face with a mob of nationalists. More nationalists appeared behind them, cutting off any possible retreat. The leftists formed a line across the street, singing the "Marseillaise" and "We Will Renounce the Old World." Then:

> *They built combat rows.*
> *They went a bit further.*
> *There was mortal silence.*
> *The weather worsened.*
> *The calm before the storm.*

On the day after the bloodshed, Governor Osorgin issued a proclamation:

The Lord our Emperor has granted new civil rights, which are listed in the Manifesto, and asks for peace and quiet. Be filled with love for one another, let us be tolerant of one another and of the views of each, and then we will truly have that peace which our tsar seeks, and which our motherland needs so much. As the head of the province, I answer before God and the tsar for the peace of all peaceful citizens, and I declare an unconditional ban on all meetings in the streets. I declare I will support order in the city with all legal means at my disposal, inclusive of the use of arms. May God preserve me from such extreme measures! May the animosities quiet, and may we live in peace, to the comfort of the tsar and the fatherland and in the glory of God.

In retrospect the appeal sounds pathetic, but this was still 1905, and a provincial city like Tula had no previous experience of political bloodshed.

If the Manifesto was confusing in the cities, it was utterly misunderstood in the villages. Several days after the bloodshed, a dirty and exhausted clerk named Pigulyovsky burst into the governor's residence with a strange and somber tale of a clash that had broken out in the town of Venev. After the Manifesto was published, the clerk said, he and several other left-leaning local officials, including one Chernosvitov, had taken a private room on the second floor of the local pub to celebrate. They were drinking champagne and shouting hurrah when some workers came up from the bar below and asked if the masters would please come down and explain this Manifesto, of which they had heard much but understood nothing.

Pigulyovsky and Chernosvitov went down to the bar and began trying to explain the Manifesto to the drunken workers. Looking for ways to illustrate what trade unions were, Chernosvitov said this meant that carpenters, for example, could get together and set prices. That got through to a carpenter in the pub, who shouted out, "Indeed, master, it's hard not to see the value of this. If we didn't join a union, it would be like cutting open our own stomach with an ax!" On hearing these last words, a totally drunk comrade leaped at the two clerks, bellowing: "Cut open my stomach, will you? Be damned! I'll cut your guts out!" The clerks ran for their lives.

The drunken workers ran amok, ransacking shops and smashing the windows of the house of Chernosvitov's father, the local miller. Chernosvitov grabbed his wife and child and tried to flee in the dark, but while crossing an earthen dam his wife fell into the water. He plunged after her into the freezing water, but she was already dead; he nearly died himself. Pigulyovsky hid at a teacher's house, but a worker found him and threatened to burn down the school if the teacher did not turn him out. Not bothering to put on his coat, he ran all the way to Tula.

More and more reports began reaching the governor of unrest in the countryside. The convening of a Peasant Union Congress in Moscow, one of many congresses held during what came to be known as the Days of Liberty following the Manifesto, contributed to a sense in the countryside that the government had endorsed all peasant demands, and therefore the time had come to seize the landlords' property. Osorgin's estate manager told him that after the Manifesto was published, some unknown men had galloped to Sergiyevskoye from the railway station, waving newspapers and yelling, "*Manekhvest!* Chop down the lords' forests!"

Sergiyevskoye remained reasonably quiet, but one neighboring manor, Borshchyovka, was destroyed. Just across the Oka River from Sergiyevksoye, it was the property of Mikhail Dmitrievich Yershov, a reasonably enlightened landowner active in the *zemstvo*. Like the Tula clash, the Borshchyovka incident was subsequently inflated into a Soviet legend.

The real problem was not Yershov but his estate manager, Zorin, who in the five years he worked at Borshchyovka came to be thoroughly despised by the peasants. He gave them little land in the best of times, and that year he had refused even to give them access to the river to water their cattle. The peasants' frustrations merged with revolutionary stirrings brought back by village men from their city jobs in distant factories.

Попрошо помешуигвего имамия в дер. Д. Борщевка.
1905г.

A stylized Soviet depiction of the trashing of the
Borshchyovka manor in 1905.

The clash was sparked on July 3, 1905, when peasants from the village of Dal'naya Borshchyovka went to cut hay on a meadow for which they had paid Zorin 390 rubles the previous day. When they got there, they found part of the grass trampled, and they sent for Zorin. He came out toward evening, carrying a gun. When the dispute became heated, he began threatening the peasants with the gun. After two hours of this, the angry peasants turned and marched on the manor. Zorin fled and locked himself in the house. He then fired two shots from a window. Infuriated, the peasants, about two hundred strong, broke down the fence and began smashing windows, doors, and furniture. Finally, they splashed kerosene inside the house and set it ablaze. Zorin escaped and ran barefoot to the river, rowed across to Sergiyevskoye, and alerted Lipko, the local police officer.

Lipko fired off a telegram to the Kaluga police chief ("3 JULY EVENING PEASANTS OF DAL'NAYA BORSHCHYOVKA BROKE INTO HOUSE OF YERSHOV ROBBED

POSSESSIONS. 4:10 a.m. 4 JULY 1905"). The Kaluga police immediately wired St. Petersburg, and at 10 p.m. on July 4, half a company of soldiers from the Lyubetsk military engineer camp arrived at the estate, along with the district police superintendent, the land captain, the district police chief, and several police officers. As they approached the house, peasants inside met them with taunts and stones. Eventually the peasants were dispersed, and soldiers were posted at each of their houses. Still, a fire broke out that night in the grain-drying barn. In the morning, 60 more soldiers arrived, and 28 peasants were arrested.

In a subsequent report to the governor of Kaluga, the district police superintendent wrote: "Many peasants returning to Borshchyovka from outside work told the others of agrarian troubles where they worked, and that nothing happened to peasants in retaliation. Vasily Konovalyov told them that after disturbances at Count Sheremetyev's, no peasants were punished. Several peasants shouted this during the fire."

Waves of unrest from Borshchyovka reached to Sergiyevskoye. A police report dated July 10 spoke of "noticeable disquiet on Osorgin's estate." The police reported that a soldier just back from the war had spoken approvingly of the Borshchyovka strike. "One of these days we'll do the same with Osorgin's estate," he was quoted as saying. "Maybe better; they harass us over every little thing. Whatever happens, they grab you by the beard and press charges. And we won't take into account that Osorgin is a governor. We'll do everything our own way."

With no guidance from St. Petersburg, Osorgin decided to distribute his own circulars to land captains and police chiefs in Tula Province explaining how the civil liberties proclaimed in the Manifesto should be applied in practice. He did so not because he supported the measure or agreed with the tsar, but because his monarchic convictions directed that the will of the monarch was law, and therefore all state officials must adopt the spirit of the Manifesto. The circulars—poignant appeals for tolerance and fairness in a land that has never put great stock in either—have been preserved in the Tula State Historical Archive.

To the land captains, he wrote: "We must struggle not to eliminate criticism but, on the contrary, to win confidence through loyalty and fairness."

To the police chiefs, he urged respect for freedom of speech and assembly: "Get closer to the people, gentlemen; become familiar with them—not to control their political thoughts or to impede them, but to restore balance to our social life."

Osorgin showed his circulars to two ideologically opposed brothers-in-law who were visiting at the time, and both their reactions dismayed him. The liberal Grigory Trubetskoi was thrilled and immediately took the documents to show Pyotr Struve, the leading liberal of the time, whom Osorgin looked upon as a dyed-in-the-wool Red. The conservative Fyodor Samarin, for his part, was very critical of the circular, arguing that rather than focus on the "spirit" of civil liberties, governors should make clear in their provinces that the Manifesto defined the limits of what the tsar was prepared to grant.

Soon Osorgin came to understand that the Manifesto was only a government tactic in a brutal political struggle. "In fact," he noted sadly, "the entire government, by the will of that same Gosudar, did everything it could to undercut all the freedom that the Godusar granted, and to reduce the effect of the Manifesto to the least possible."

Sensing which way the winds in St. Petersburg were blowing, Osorgin's vice governor, Khvostov, whose family had powerful connections in the capital, began urging Osorgin to join forces with the right, where he believed the governor's true feelings lay. But Osorgin's principles prescribed neutrality:

> My entire moral being and my conscience overwhelmingly demanded total nonpartisanship from me, whatever my tastes or sympathies.
>
> Later I often experienced ambivalence. Talking and consulting with leftist elements, I felt an affinity with many of their views, with their yearning for something higher than ordinary, narrow-minded comfort; but as soon as the question turned to their actual demands, their language pushed me away; that which they considered white was for me not so much black as awful, and it was with difficulty that I held back my dismay. It was much easier for me to find a common language with the bureaucratic world, entirely arch-conservative; but their narrowness, their self-serving opinions, based not on principle but on saving their own skins, vexed me.

Osorgin's neutrality had no place in the charged atmosphere of 1905. Prince Lvov, leader of the leftist forces in Tula, used every occasion to fan the fires, calling for opposition to a government that was "illegally limiting freedom." Osorgin eventually dismissed him as head of the provincial *zemstvo*. On the right, Count Bobrinsky organized his reactionary Union for Tsar and Order, while the boxer-baker Kolokolin demanded that the government rescind the Manifesto, "which the nation neither deserves nor wants," and went about beating up leftists whenever he could, for which he was arrested several times.

The next time Osorgin offered his resignation, the minister of the Interior, now Pyotr Nikolayevich Durnovo, promptly accepted. The final straw came with the Peasant Union Congress in Moscow, which turned into a radical forum. The authorities did nothing to curtail it, but when it ended, Durnovo sent a coded telegram to all provincial governors ordering them to arrest active participants immediately upon their return to their home provinces. Durnovo knew full well that Osorgin would refuse to participate in so blatant a violation of the spirit of the Manifesto. Unlike the messages to other governors, which were wired, Osorgin's was sent by courier and contained a handwritten addendum: "P.S.: If Your Excellency agrees to execute this order, please be so kind as to advise the director of the Police Department by telegram—'Will execute your message number such-and-such.' " Osorgin refused.

So ended Mikhail Mikhailovich's public-service career. Unlike his brother-in-law Sergei Trubetskoi, whose efforts to forestall violence made him a martyr, Osorgin left with little sympathy from either left or right. The only ones to publicly regret his departure were the Jews of Tula. One of their leaders called to ask if it was true that he was resigning, and when Osorgin said it was, the man replied: "That means there will be a pogrom! You alone, with your authority and tireless activity, were capable of precluding this. Under you, believing in your word, we were calm. Now I will be the first to advise my coreligionists to leave Tula."

Vice Governor Khvostov, who now became acting governor, insisted that Osorgin leave secretly, casting an additional pall over the inglorious end of Osorgin's tenure.

The Osorgins left Tula in early December of 1905. "I confess it was unbearably hard—not to part with Tula, not at all, but to cut short my service looking like a man who had been spat upon," he wrote. The train was late, and by the time the Osorgins arrived in Ferzikovo it was well after midnight. It was cruelly cold, and there was nobody waiting for them. The estate manager, Korchagin, had gotten tired of waiting for them and had left—something he never would have done in earlier years. Adding slight injury to the heavy insult, the hired sleigh carrying Mikhail Mikhailovich and Liza overturned on the way to Sergiyevskoye. Mikhail Mikhailovich was 44. His eldest son, Mikhail, was 18, and my grandfather was 17; their youngest sister, Tonia, was 4.

9

Soon It Will Be Ours

While all over Russia, landowners fled their manors in panic or went bankrupt, Sergiyevskoye remained a haven of relative calm and harmony.

"We returned to Sergiyevskoye in the knowledge that the revolutionary wave I experienced in Tula did not yet have the strength to swamp and destroy those patriarchal relations that had been formed long ago with our peasants," wrote Mikhail Mikhailovich with satisfaction. "But I nonetheless understood that much must change, and that there will be conflicts and problems with which we will have to deal. Panic is raging all around. Many landowners fled their villages and moved to the cities, and I was a touch proud that we, on the contrary, returned to our property in these times. . . . I was told that among themselves the peasants were saying, 'Look at that, all the lords are fleeing, and ours are coming back.' "

Still, a new day had dawned. Peasants worked reluctantly and violated their contracts more frequently. The manager at the time, Rodion Ivanovich Korchagin, tried to avoid direct contact with the villagers, and the burden of keeping things moving fell largely on the village foremen, Mikhail Glebov and Nikolai Shutov. "I confess I too was wary of the peasants," Osorgin wrote. Once, a group of women showed up to demand vodka. Not finding the manager, they burst into the Osorgin living room. When Osorgin ordered them out, one sturdy *baba* barked at him, "No, Mikhal Mikhalych, we have freedom now." He yelled back, "Right, and that's why I have the right to freely chase you out!" The other *babas* liked that and left, laughing.

Mikhail Mikhailovich now focused his bustling energy on the land, the parish, his family, and above all the school, where he managed to spend most of his days. At home, his seven children always had gaggles of cousins over, and their music, dances, charades, and courtships filled the house with life and laughter.

Soon after settling back at Sergiyevskoye, Osorgin decided to sell much of his farmland to the Peasant Land Bank for resale to his villagers, retaining only the manor and about 800 acres. He also sold off his wife's Tula properties, and his father sold their Volga lands to their former manager. For Mikhail Mikhailovich, the sale of Sergiyevskoye lands was a decision based less on commercial or personal considerations than on principle. After what he had witnessed in Tula, he believed that it was necessary to develop the holdings of competent peasants as quickly as possible.

"I came to the conviction that large estates could not now avoid tensions existing side by side with small peasant landholdings that had no chance to develop," he wrote. "I considered it essential to give real peasants, those who loved the land, a chance to broaden their holdings."

A similar conviction motivated the subsequent land reforms of Prime Minister Stolypin. But Osorgin proposed to practice what he preached immediately, selling to his peasants more than 3,000 of his ancestral acres at one half to one third of their market price.

For Osorgin it was more than a financial sacrifice; it was a voluntary and conscious parting with a patriarchal order that reached to the deepest recesses of his soul. "With this sale, I proposed to break at the root the entire structure of Sergiyevskoye's economy," he wrote. "The peasants would be totally removed from the economic influence of my office, and we would have to establish new relations as neighboring landowners. I felt I was breaking the last link of that chain which, [the radical poet] Nekrasov wrote, 'in breaking will strike with one end the *barin*, with the other, the *muzhik*.' "

But Russia is Russia, and Osorgin's best intentions quickly ran up against bureaucracy, shifting government policy, peasant suspiciousness, and general greed. St. Petersburg bureaucrats did nothing, while officials of the Kaluga Peasant Land Bank suspected that Osorgin was another in a long line of bankrupt landowners trying to dip into public funds. The logjam was broken when Alexander Vasilievich Krivoshein, an old friend, was appointed head of the nobility and peasant land banks in St. Petersburg. He did not understand what Osorgin was trying to do, but he hoped to recruit him to head the Kiev branch of the bank, and so decided to humor him.

At long last, Mikhail Mikhailovich took a deep breath, crossed himself, and signed the papers. But that was not the end of the ordeal. Instead of reselling his lands to peasants as it was supposed to, the bank began behaving like the worst of the landlords, demanding exorbitant rents from peasants who had always paid Osorgin for the use of these lands with labor. Osorgin rushed back to Kaluga to argue in behalf of the peasants. But his efforts now came in conflict with the reforms introduced by Stolypin. The new premier's intent was to break enterprising farmers out of the traditional village commune, and he mandated that the Peasant Land Bank should advance money only to independent farmers, and not to village collectives. Knowing the peasants, Osorgin believed most of them would refuse to buy land individually for fear of social reprisal in the village, and his idea was to sell his lands to the commune for subsequent distribution among the more active households. He rushed off to St. Petersburg to argue his case but was met by uninterested officials who could not understand his concern: "What's it to you? The land's not yours any more. You sold it; you have your money." Only one village, Zinovo, beat the deadline and bought communal lands; the other villages were refused, and, as Osorgin feared, most of the peasants refused to buy land. Outsiders rushed in to pick off the bargain properties.

To make matters worse, the bank disregarded Osorgin's survey and broke the land into indiscriminate small holdings. Some buyers made instant fortunes—for example, those who bought lots with large oak trees, which they immediately sold off. Osorgin fought a losing battle with the banks. He waged a particularly fierce fight to block the sale of a strategic lot to Sergei Trofimov Kuznetsov, a blacksmith who dealt in moonshine vodka and stolen horses and wanted to expand his enterprises. Mikhail Mikhailovich had tangled with Kuznetsov many times before as land captain and landowner, and he succeeded in blocking the sale.

Kuznetsov paid Osorgin back in an unexpected way. Years later, after the revolution, Mikhail Mikhailovich was arrested and jailed for refusing to pay some revolutionary tax, and this same Kuznetsov rushed to Kaluga at the head of a group of Sergiyevskoye villagers to bail out the old *barin*. When Osorgin walked out of jail, Kuznetsov embraced him with tears in his eyes. Ever the moralist, Osorgin concluded: "That is a bright example of the sense of fairness in the simple Russian. When he realizes that another is acting without a selfish aim, he respects him, even when he has to suffer because of him."

As his land schemes fell apart, Osorgin at least made sure that those villagers closest to him got to buy lots. "The result was that twenty or thirty families improved their condition, and even grew wealthy. The villagers of Zinovo prospered. But the others remained as they were, and since I now had 3,240 acres fewer, I could not help them as I had before," wrote Osorgin. "Thus my scheme to improve the use of land by peasants ended unsuccessfully. But my efforts were appreciated by the peasants, and relations grew better than before. Those who bought lots became especially loyal."

I find this story sadly familiar. So much of what went wrong then is going wrong now; the bureaucratic ignorance, the attempts to reform by mandate, the social inflexibility. Much like Stolypin, Boris Yeltsin belted out decrees in the first rush of post-Communism, enabling peasants to take land, and Western experts gushed assurances that as soon as they owned their own land, the farmers would prosper. I believed that, too—at least until I started visiting Koltsovo regularly. A few farmers did take land for themselves, but for most it was simply impossible. There was no system of markets or credits for commercial farmers; no place to buy fertilizer, tractors, or seed; no place to sell their grain or produce. That might have developed with time; the more difficult obstacle, as Osorgin understood from long experience, was the mindset. The communal mentality of the prerevolutionary countryside was only strengthened by collectivization, and those peasants who stayed on the land stayed there precisely for the sense of collective security it offered. To grab a large piece of land for oneself and to milk it for money was to spit in the face of the collective and to lose its protection.

The celebrated private plots on which collective farmers raised so much of the Soviet Union's produce were always misinterpreted in the West as evidence of an entrepreneurial spirit yearning to break free. In fact, the plots were more like an acceptable form of cheating the system, with well-defined bounds. I often noted that when old peasants criticized the persecution of *kulaks* in the 1930s, it was not because they saw nothing wrong in being rich and productive, but because they believed that "honest" peasants were being swept up along with the rich. "They grabbed my father, but he had only one horse and never hired anyone," an old woman complained, implying that if he had had a second horse and a hired hand, exiling him would have been justified.

I also recognized Kuznetsov, that Russian scoundrel who will do his utmost to cheat you, and, if he fails, embraces you almost with relief. If there is a Russian stereotype, this is it: the many officials I knew in the old Soviet Union whose job it was to follow me, misinform me, lie to me, and who now embrace me as an old buddy, assuring me that they always admired my work. And I'll be damned if I don't embrace them back—not because they were "just following orders," which they probably would not claim, but because I, too, am Russian, and feel some ridiculous (if marginal) guilt for having been spared their degradation.

A typical day for Mikhail Mikhailovich in the last years of the old regime began in church.

> I stand at the altar; it is already spring, and the sun brightly warms my usual place by the window. I cannot express how peaceful and good it is. The choir sings badly, but these children's voices are so dear that it is joyful to join with them in prayer.
>
> . . . The service is over, and I go with them to school, where I will substitute for the priest, who does not have time for classes during Lent. I stay for lunch. I taste the food and walk about the dining room with the duty teacher, giving instructions here and there—this one a haircut, this one sick call. Lunch is finished; they rise and say the prayer and rush off to get dressed for recess, and I rush home, where I'm late for lunch as usual, and my family rib me for that.
>
> Now it's dusk, time for the tour of the manor. Maria [his daughter] likes to come along, and we're joined en route by Shutov, the bookkeeper, and the steward. First the stables, where the young horses are returning from being watered and the old ones are being unharnessed. The foreman joins us here. We proceed to the granary, where seed is being prepared for sale. Then to the shop. We dally longer here—either they're working at the ripsaw or making shingles or bending shafts for the harness or preparing runners for the sleds. Here I have to give instructions—sometimes to argue about something that has not been done. From there we go to the mill, or the "machine," as they call it. We're met by the miller, the machinist, and the scale operator. It's especially cozy here when the lamps are lit. Having checked the machinery and the grind setting, and having made sure of the order of milling, and having taken some rudeness from Vasily (very competent, but with an impossible character), we go on. At the barn the last milking and feeding is underway.
>
> I particularly liked the last watering of the cattle. In those final years

they looked especially noble and beautiful. The calves romp; the cows drink and only occasionally butt heads, for which they get deserved reprimands. They understand, they know their names. Having drunk their fill, the cows return importantly, sniffing all along their way, and take their place in the barn waiting to be tied. I glance into the calf stalls, admire some new creature, stop in the sparkling clean dairy. It remains only to visit the garden and the hothouse. Walking by the basement kitchen, I inquire about the dinner menu; but then, if I have no lesson with my children, I release the managers and rush back to the school.

The two-room boarding school near the church became Osorgin's chief occupation. This school, and five elementary schools in villages belonging to the Sergiyevskoye parish, were under the jurisdiction of the Kaluga diocese, and the director was always the parish priest. But Osorgin became the patron and, by dint of his patriarchal standing in the village, unofficial headmaster, counselor, and disciplinarian. He knew each pupil, tutored the slow ones, dispensed punishment (more often a private reprimand), counseled the teachers, and substituted for absent ones.

Pupils of the Sergiyevskoye parish school.

"Our school became renowned for its religious and moral spirit," Osorgin wrote. "Alas, this proved an edifice built on sand. During the revolution I heard of pupils who remained true sons of the Church and did their Christian duty, but more often I heard of those who, even if they did not become Bolsheviks, attached themselves to them and drew gain from the disintegration."

It is my conviction that he was wrong, that the moral spirit imparted by that school survived among many of those who became Bolsheviks or adopted their cause. After the revolution the school became a teachers' training institute, with many of the same instructors, and its graduates included a remarkable number of idealistic, earnest Communists. I met some of them in their old age, and they described the reunions they started holding regularly in the 1960s, read me their poems, and showed me their photographs. They were proud of the school's prerevolutionary legacy; in 1987, the graduates stamped a medallion marking the centenary of the school.

The school still stands, the only structure from old Sergiyevskoye to survive intact. A wing and a second floor were added, but inside it still has its wide hall-ways and large windows. It was turned into an orphanage after the war, and in 1977 the school and the core of the old manor—the linden park, the bell tower, the forested descent to the Oka—were taken over by the Kaluga Turbine Works, which runs the school as a weekend "rest base." On my first visit to Sergiyevskoye, the director of the rest base, Gennady Mikhailovich Steshin, drove over from Kaluga to meet me. "We only hope that one day we can bring it back to the condition your forebears left it in," he said gallantly. He also said I could stay there any time I wished, and I often have, lying awake for a long time in the silence of the countryside and marveling at the fate that brought me to this place from which my forebears were torn.

One of the students of the school was Nina Semyonova, on whose reminis-cences I have drawn before. She was born at about the time Osorgin returned from Tula. The daughter of a peasant named Georgy Agentov, she grew up a typical village child, attending church, picking mushrooms, and learning crafts. The linden park and its white mushrooms were strictly off limits, and the *barin,* "Mikhal Mikhalych," was a magisterial figure with a grand beard.

After the Osorgins were expelled, Nina and other local youths became active members of the Komsomol, the Communist Youth League.

After I first wrote about Sergiyevskoye in *The New York Times* in the fall of 1991, Soviet television and several Soviet newspapers picked up the story. That piqued the interest of a number of people, including Nina Semyonova, who began jotting down her memories and sending them to me through Alexandra

Nikitichna Trunin. She was eighty-five and her eyesight was failing fast, and her last vignettes were in huge letters that often ran off the page.

I never met Semyonova, but I believe that her painful efforts in her last months to revive memories of a village childhood and a kind *barin*, and to share them with his descendant, were a sincere attempt at reconciliation and at restoring a link to the past. The recollections offered a unique glimpse of the final days of Sergiyevskoye through the eyes of a child on the other side of the social divide. The last parcel came with this letter to Alexandra Nikitichna:

> This last work about the peasants I am writing entirely without sight. Please help the great-grandson of our last landowner, Osorgin, to decipher my letter.
>
> The main subject of my story is the landowner M. M. Osorgin and his family, and their attitude toward the people on their main estate, Karovo. My memories of the distant past will have an episodic nature, various years and times and seasons, and only other events in this same time can confirm the truth of my memories. . . .
>
> . . . There are few left among my contemporaries from the village, but I think those still living often remember that Karovo miracle, the linden garden. True, it was someone else's, but this was precisely what drew us there. Why? There were white mushrooms [cèpes] there! The linden garden also beckoned us with its mystery and prohibition. This was the *barin*'s garden. We didn't even know their name then, we just called them the *bariny*.
>
> The linden garden was bordered on three sides by a broad brick fence, painted white, the height of a grown man, capped with iron. The garden was for us something fantastic, in the sense that it was inaccessible. Looking through the tiny cracks betwen the bricks, we tried to see what was happening inside. Nobody would have dared to climb over the fence, and in any case it was too tall. We knew that there were many white mushrooms in the garden, and once we did climb in there, precisely for the mushrooms.
>
> We went in through the fancy iron gates, which by chance had been left open. We gathered many mushrooms—we knew where they grew, by the last row of lindens before the fence, when facing Karovo. With full baskets and buckets we rushed to get out the same way we came in, but a woman in a white dress stood by the gates. This was the *barynia* herself. She looked at our baskets and buckets and said sternly, "Children, you

can't pick mushrooms here. But over there, behind the fence, in the firs, there are many *masliata* [a less prized mushroom]. There you can gather." Embarrassed at being caught red-handed, we stood there, not raising our eyes. It was good that we were caught by the *barynia* and not the foreman, Nikolai Shutov, or it would have been hard to avoid the rod.

. . . When Filka Fomichev organized the first Komsomol cell, we began taking care of the linden grove. On holidays we hung Chinese lanterns. . . .

When I was in the first or second grade, the *izba* one away from us, belonging to Dmitry Dronov, burned down. We were not allowed to leave school to see the fire, or to watch from the window. We ran home when all that remained were scorched logs. I stood among the *muzhiks* and *babas* who had put out the fire. When it began, none of the inhabitants of the house were in. It was probably September, if school was in session. Mikhal Mikhalych drove up to the crowd in his carriage, went up to the grieving Dmitry Dronov, and said, "Don't worry, Dmitry," and he patted one of the boys on the head. He took off his coat and hat, adding, "Here, take these in the meantime, and I'll help you rebuild."

When we had our reunion in 1968, an already aging house stood on the spot of the burned *izba*. I made a point of meeting with Masha, the wife of Dmitry, and she recounted how M.M. didn't forget his promise. The culprit in that distant disaster, Lenka, became a pilot and was killed in the war in 1943. His curiosity cost the family dearly. At 13, he wanted to see how flax burns. It was already spun into yarn and was lying in large bundles on the porch. He himself was barely saved: he hid in the stove. This was probably 1914/15, because the talk was of war. From my father, I heard that Mikhal Mikhalych was a big liberal then, but I didn't understand that word, and only later, studying in the elementary school after the first war with Germany, the meaning of that word became clear.

In September 1906, Mikhail Mikhailovich's two older sons entered Moscow University—Mikhail to study law; Sergei, the natural sciences. They moved in with their uncle Evgeny Trubetskoi, a professor of philosophy who had just been transferred from Kiev to Moscow.

Sergei loved everything about Moscow except its social obligations. The city was the natural complement to Sergiyevskoye; even after Peter the Great moved the imperial court to his new capital of St. Petersburg, Moscow remained the

The Osorgin family at Sergiyevskoye on August 28,
1906, with the boys in the uniform of students at Moscow
University. From left: Liza, Mikhail Mikhailovich,
Sofia, Mikhail, Liana, Sergei, Maria, Georgy, Tonia.

spiritual capital of Russia, where tsars came to be crowned and old families had
their primary residences. The architecture was decidedly provincial: the gentry
built their city houses much like their country ones, large neoclassical buildings
of painted plaster with porticos of six columns and overgrown gardens. Wealthy
merchants raised mansions in whimsical styles, ranging from pseudo-Russian to
pseudo-Gothic, while the poor lived in low, listing houses that stretched along
crooked streets. Moscow's glory was its Kremlin, its walled monasteries, and its
churches, whose number tradition put at "forty times forty," whose gilded cupolas sparkled like a field of diamonds from a distance, and whose bells raised a glorious cacophony on holy days.

Moscow had none of St. Petersburg's urban bustle. The street the Trubetskois lived on, Third Zachatievsky Pereulok, was so sleepy, Sergei wrote, that
gardeners had to weed it regularly; only two or three carriages passed by daily,
and the only sounds were the bells from the nearby Zachatie (Conception) Convent and the occasional cry of a street peddler. The *pereulok*, or side street, ran

between the convent and the fashionable Ostozhenka Street, which ended at the monolithic Church of Christ the Savior.

After the revolution, the Soviets renamed Ostozhenka, a lovely name from an archaic word for hayfield, Metrostroyevskaya ("Metro-Construction") Street, blew up the Church of Christ the Savior and built an outdoor pool in its place, and razed the Zachatie Convent, except for the east wall and a small church over the gate. Today the street is once again Ostozhenka; the pool has been drained and the church rebuilt; and the convent, founded in 1360, is functioning again. Nuns climb over scaffolding to reach the small surviving chapel over the gate, and bells once again call the faithful to vespers. On Third Zachatievsky Pereulok, the lone surviving building is being restored because the legendary bass Fyodor Chaliapin once lived there. And the Church of Christ the Savior stands again in all its massive splendor, rebuilt for untold billions on the orders of Moscow's popular post-Soviet mayor, Yuri Luzhkov.

Even in Soviet times the neighborhood never wholly lost its charm. Many of the modest old yellow houses with white columns and crumbling bas-relief wreaths in their pediments still stand, and many have been nicely restored since the collapse of Communism. My wife and I spent many a pleasant hour roaming these *pereulki* with our off-white Moscow mutt, Ahmed, conjuring up my grandfather's images of "an open window with a rounded top from which wafted real, serious music; the master's study lined with bookshelves; a small sitting room with armchairs upholstered in white or blue brocade, and if there was a canary in a cage, there were also display cases with Sèvres china and Meissen shepherds."

Sergei was a promising student. His professor singled him out early on as a potential successor: in Osorgin's fourth year, he appointed him an instructor, and that same year he sent Sergei for two months to study at a biological research institute on the Mediterranean, near Nice. Some of Sergei's research was published in German scientific journals, and his doctoral thesis was accepted by Leipzig University.

A highlight for every student at Moscow University was the celebrated lecture series on Russian history by Professor Vasily Klyuchevsky. Klyuchevsky was a celebrity; known abroad for his landmark *History of Russia*, he was a gifted speaker who sprinkled his lectures with witty asides and a wealth of detail that brought ancient tsars and boyars to life. Students from all faculties packed the largest auditorium in the university for his course, and many returned in subsequent years for particularly favorite lectures. Chaliapin spent long hours with Klyuchevsky in preparation for his opera roles as Rimsky-Korsakov's Ivan the Terrible and Mussorgsky's Boris Godunov.

Music was central in the life of the Osorgin brothers in Moscow, as it had been for their father in St. Petersburg and their family at Sergiyevskoye. "I threw myself at music like a starving man at food, and there was a lot of it in Moscow," wrote Sergei. The Russian Musical Society (co-founded by his grandfather, Prince Nikolai Petrovich Trubetskoi), the Philharmonic Society, and Serge Koussevitzky's Concert Society attracted the world's finest conductors and musicians for their subscription concerts, and the Osorgins heard the likes of Toscanini, Casals, and Rachmaninov. During Lent all Moscow theaters closed down, and music formed the only diversion—along with riding competitions at the Great Manège, across from the university, which Sergei regularly watched.

The downside to Moscow life for Sergei was society, which he viewed as unmitigated torture. Moscow's social life was not what it was before the revolution of 1905, and "high society" shifted markedly in the last years to St. Petersburg and the salons of rich merchants. But a gentry ball was still a grand ritual. A broad red carpet to the street, doormen in gilded livery, the grand stairway alive with flowers and plants, young ladies in décolleté gowns and white kid gloves to above the elbow, young men in the gold-embroidered uniforms of their university or *lycée* (military uniforms appeared in Moscow only if somebody's cousin happened to be on leave from his Guards regiment in St. Petersburg).

Like their father, Mikhail and Sergei were excruciatingly shy, but their "Moscow aunties" were inflexible, Sergei wrote:

> There was nothing to be done. We ordered frock coats and uniforms and plunged. Our first ball was at the Glebovs. My entrance and introductions passed without incident, though the sword swung awkwardly and the high embroidered collar of the uniform choked me. But my first social disaster was poising to pounce: The hosts' daughter, my cousin Manya Glebov, pulled me into a furious waltz. This in itself was not so bad, because I was a good dancer, but I forgot to take off the sword, which began slapping against passing couples, chairs, and the mamas sitting on them, until everybody was shouting, "Sword!" I stopped on a turn, took off the sword, and ran into the smoking room, where I hid until I could escape, before the mazurka.

I apologize for the disloyalty to my ancestor, but his brief description of this incident does not do full justice to his humiliation. Etiquette required anyone bearing arms, which came with virtually every uniform, to keep his sword on while greeting the hosts, after which the host was expected to invite the guest to set the weapon aside for the dancing. So the host, old Vladimir Petrovich Glebov, is at least partly to blame for what happened. But the fact that the host's daughter grabbed Sergei suggests that this was the opening waltz, in which case they circled the floor alone for a spell while everyone else watched from the upholstered chairs lining the wall. Poor Sergei must have hidden in the smoking room quite some time: following the opening waltz, a Moscow ball continued with the first quadrille, then another "small dance" (either a waltz or one of several traditional dances, like the Hungarian *cracovienne*, the *pas de patiner*, the *pas de quatre*, or the *pas d'Espagne*), then the second quadrille, then another "small dance," then the third quadrille, then the mazurka—or, if there was a fourth quadrille, the mazurka followed that.

The lady with whom a gentleman danced the mazurka was the one he led to supper, so the mazurka was very important. If invitations to a "small dance" could be spontaneous, invitations to the quadrilles, the cotillion, and especially the mazurka were usually made in advance. Young ladies "enjoying success" that season were usually booked solid for every quadrille, not to mention mazurka, weeks in advance. Not only were partners prearranged, but couples agreed on which other couples to join in a quadrille or to sit with at supper. At supper, waiters served only the gentlemen; it was the men who were expected to fill their lady's plate.

After supper came the cotillion, for which baskets of carnations imported from Nice were brought into the ballroom (at least by those hosts who could afford them), and gentlemen brought bouquets to the ladies they had contracted for the dance. Then the master of ceremonies and his helpers marched out with raised swords, from which hung garlands of colored silk ribbons with little bells attached; the gentlemen would pluck these and tie them around each dancing partner's wrist. The ladies were issued boutonnières to distribute to their beaux. By evening's end, a lady might have ribbons and bells up to her elbow, while a popular young man's tunic might be covered with flowers. Though the youths all knew each other and often were related, during the ball they maintained a strict formality, addressing each other by name and patronymic or title.

The finale was always a polonaise. The dancers would parade in pairs past "the icon stand"—the non-dancing mothers and chaperones arrayed along the wall—and would nod to the hosts to express their gratitude.

For Sergei, the torture continued into the next day. A young man was expected to call, in full uniform, on the parents of every young lady he had danced with. Approaching each house, Sergei prayed that he would not be received, and would get away with just leaving behind a calling card bent over at the corner to show that he had tried. But too often he heard the dreaded "Please come in," and, reddening and clenching his teeth, he would struggle to make coherent small talk until he could escape.

Summers were spent at Sergiyevskoye. Sergei liked to travel the last leg of the trip home up the Oka on a steam side-wheeler, and reading his description, I mourn that I never made the journey. (Regular summer river service on the Oka was suspended in 1992 for lack of fuel.) Here it is mid-June, when the night lasts only a few hours and the northern countryside is an explosion of life:

> The train arrived in Serpukhov at about two a.m., so we boarded before dawn: gray light, the smell of the river, fish jumping in the strong current by the high bank, the furnace coughing to clear its chilled steampipes. I always rushed to get the only single cabin, which was especially comfortable on the *Vladimir Svyatoi,* and lay down to sleep.
>
> The ship gradually comes to life: freight is loaded, passengers board, some merchants are already sitting down to tea. At last the *Vladimir Svyatoi* gives the first, the second, the third signal. After the third blast we still stand a long time while the captain argues with someone on the landing; all this I hear through a half-sleep, and at last I become distantly aware that the wheels of the ship have started slowly slapping the water. We turn grandly into the current; I hear the captain's terse command, "Full steam ahead!" and we are steaming up the Oka.
>
> Already far from Serpukhov, I am awakened because our motion has been disturbed. The ship is moving slowly, cautiously slapping its wheels, and I can hear the shouts of the sailor sounding the depth at the bow: "Five! Four and a half! Four! Three and a half! . . ." the bottom scrapes hard on the sand ". . . Four and a half! Five! Full ahead!" We have successfully passed the shallows, which in dry years were far worse. Sometimes they had to plant an anchor up ahead and pull the steamship to it on a towline, or the third-class passengers were disembarked in shallow water, and when the lightened vessel cleared the shallows the passengers, who by then had had a good swim, were gathered in boats. All this I lazily hear and watch from the window of the cabin, and I wash up and go on deck to have coffee. Those endlessly lovely, familiar sights! Pampered by a tender breeze, scanning the bank or squinting at the blinding river, I never thought that I might lose all this one day. What I would give now to see some tiny village on the bank of the Oka with little gray *izbas* roofed

with straw, a *baba* at the door of one shading her eyes to watch the steamship, an old grandpa untangling his nets in his fishing skiff by the bank! All this used to be—it is still, but not for me.

. . . Now we've passed Aleksin, with its railroad bridge, which we considered a bit ours—the stone for the piers was quarried at our Rock Mountain. More shallows—"Four! Three and a half! Four!"—and we arrive at Krasnyi, where for a long time we load lumber. To fill the remaining hour and a half, I always order the same cutlets with peas. At last, our Kashurki—from here the left bank of the Oka is already ours. The Borshchyovka church peeps over the high right bank, and behind the sand spit, our ferry. On the spit across from us a village herd has gone into the river and stands reflected in the motionless water, lazily shaking off the flies and gadflies while gazing dumbly at the ship. Somebody always met me at our landing, and we ride through our lovely Zaraza forest, where along the path each tree, each bush, each stone is linked to memories of childhood and youth.

Sonia and Marina Gagarin, spring 1917.

Among these trees, bushes, and stones was a tree stump that the unabashedly romantic Sergei Osorgin held particularly sacred. It was there that he first revealed his feelings to his true love, Sonia Gagarin. She was eight years his junior, and he had known her all his life because she was his first cousin. That was the rub; her mother, Princess Marina Nikolayevna Gagarin, was the youngest of Liza Osorgin's 12 Trubetskoi brothers and sisters. She had married into a very wealthy family: the Gagarins had a palace in Moscow on Novinsky Boulevard (now Tchaikovsky Street, where the American Embassy stands), as well as a striking hilltop mansion 40 miles outside Moscow in Nikolskoye-Gagarino. They also had a mansion in the Crimea; villas in Baden-Baden, San Moritz, and Dinar, near the Mediterranean; and a variety of other properties. My mother was born at their house in Baden-Baden, Villa Menshikov, which the Gagarins later sold to a German ballerina, whose daughter was still living there with a large number of dogs when we visited in 1987.

In 1907, the Gagarins spent the summer at Sergiyevskoye (and the fall, and part of the winter). The two older Gagarin girls, Sonia and Marina, were eleven and ten; they were still kids to Sergei, who was eighteen, but all the children were very close. For one game of charades, Sergei was to appear as a ghost, and for effect he perched both girls on his shoulders under a sheet: "True, they were thin and light as a feather, but it was hot under the sheet. Both still remember how wet my neck was. It's hard to imagine today that this was once possible!" (I presume he means socially, because my grandmother was never heavy.)

His perception began to change in the summer of 1911. His parents celebrated their silver anniversary in August, and many relatives descended on Sergiyevskoye for the celebration, at which the Kaluga military orchestra played. After dinner, the Gagarin girls performed the tarantella, a vivacious Neapolitan folk dance. "My future wife turned fifteen that summer, and I admired her in the tarantella already not purely as her older cousin," noted Sergei.

A year and a half later, the Gagarins came out for Sviatki (the 12 days between Christmas and Epiphany), and it was then that Sergei had his first serious talk with Sonia on that stump: "Basically, nothing was said, but all was clear!" She was 16—the age at which girls unwound their braid and put their hair up and officially became young ladies—and he was 24, "but from that day, I had no further doubts that our lives were fused forever. It was a quiet, frosty Epiphany, snowflakes tumbled and came to rest on her black sealskin jacket and hat, frost sparkled on the thin birch branches, and I talked, unclearly, inconsistently, unaware myself that I was talking of love."

My grandfather was in love. But marrying a first cousin was frowned upon by the Church, not to mention the family. Both sets of parents told him to "test his feelings," which was what parents said when they hoped that their children would change their minds.

On August 28, 1913, the Osorgins held a wedding in Sergiyevskoye for their eldest daughter, Sofia, the first of the Osorgin children to be married. The groom was Nikolai Sergeyevich Lopukhin, a Moscow magistrate and a cousin of her mother, Liza. Guests filled the house plus the neighboring manor and a ship leased for the occasion and docked at Sergiyevksoye, and by all accounts the wedding was splendid. But the recollections of both Mikhail Mikhailovich and his son Sergei are curiously downbeat. Mikhail Mikhailovich and his wife were so anguished by the thought of giving away their daughter that the poor girl nearly called off the wedding. Mikhail Mikhailovich wrote that he remembered the occasion as through a fog of grief: "It's hard, so hard, to give your first daughter away in marriage." Sergei had his own grief: the Gagarin girls attended the wedding, and he had to keep his distance.

That winter, the Osorgins took an apartment in Moscow, on the Patriarchal Ponds, to be near their newly married daughter. But things did not go as expected. The apartment was too small to be the family center that Mikhail Mikhailovich had hoped for; the love-struck Sergei delayed taking the government exams that could have given him a chair at the university; and the other children fell ill, Tonia seriously. Instead of returning to Sergiyevskoye for the summer, the Osorgins decided to take Tonia to the spa at Bad Kissingen, in Germany, which was where they were when they learned about the assassination of the Austrian archduke, Franz Ferdinand, in Sarajevo.

Reading these last pages of Mikhail Mikhailovich's memoirs, I realize how normal life appeared to be up to the very eve of the great cataclysm of war and revolution. Misha is elected a local official, Sonia is married, the Trubetskois are politicking, Sergei is in love, Tonia is sick, the Moscow apartment is disappointing. The assassination of the archduke is a scandal, of course, but it hardly prevented Osorgin from going to visit the Gagarins at San Moritz.

Yet the signs of impending upheaval were growing. At about this time, a peasant boy with a bent for drawing wandered into the Osorgin garden in

Sergiyevskoye in search of a subject to sketch, and there he encountered Tonia Osorgin. Several years after the revolution, when the boy, Misha Tinyakov, became the first chairman of the Koltsovo Komsomol cell, he described the encounter to a group of his comrades as they sat waiting for a meeting to start in the "People's House" they had set up in a wing of the former Osorgin house. One of those present was Nina Semyonova, who as administrative secretary of the Komsomol cell recorded Tinyakov's account under the title, "Two in the Gazebo."

As a youth I really liked to draw, and one fine summer day I was in search of a good view. This was before the revolution, 1916 or 1917, maybe even earlier. In Polivanovo, my village, I couldn't find a suitable subject. So I went to Karovo and decided to paint the other bank of the Oka. I went into the gazebo. It was morning; no one was around. I sat down on the left bench in the gazebo with the aim of drawing the Oka and the entire right bank beyond. I set up my homemade easel and began to work.

Suddenly I heard a noise. A pretty girl walked into the gazebo, holding a real easel and a large folio for paper. "Young man, what are you doing here?" she asked. "Drawing," I answered. "But this is our gazebo," she continued. "Soon it will be ours," I said. She pouted and sat down on the right bench, fixing her eyes on the left bank. For a while we worked silently. I would look at the right bank, she at the left, and our eyes would inadvertently meet.

She was the first to interrupt, saying, "Let's take a look at what we've done." And on my sheet we saw a few chunks of sandy shore, some small stretches of the Oka, and for some reason the top of a larch that was on the right side of the gazebo, plus something indistinct. On her sheet was a youth with unruly hair staring off into the distance. We both laughed. She said, "Our drawing didn't work. Well, let's get to know each other." And she stretched out her hand, saying "Osorgina, Antonina." "Mikhail Tinyakov," I managed to say, and clasped her slender fingers, smudged with paint.

"Tell you what, Misha," she said. "We'll have to work together, so you can come every day. I won't bother you. I'll find another subject." And we both began gathering our things. I suddenly felt uneasy and ashamed, and, not even thanking her, I left the gazebo. When I reached the white wall of the linden park, I looked back. She was standing next to the gazebo and waving to me. I didn't know what to do, so I pointed to the left with my right hand. She didn't know I lived in Polivanovo.

The scene is from a genteel nineteenth-century romance: a lovely summer morning in the gazebo, a chance encounter of a young lady from the manor with a talented but rude country lad, a shy exchange. And in the midst of it all, that casually delivered thunderbolt: "Soon it will be ours." Antonina Osorgin, my grandfather's youngest sister, would have been 15 or 16 then. Did she appreciate what this meant?

Even if she did, she could never have guessed how she would meet this village boy next. In December 1994, I was in Paris at the home of Juliana Samarin, and I told her Semyonova's story. "Wait," she said, rummaging through a folder. Soon she produced a clipping from a Russian-language émigré newspaper published in Paris. It was an article by Mikhail Mikhailovich's daughter Maria, who told of the family's expulsion from Sergiyevskoye and their subsequent years in Soviet Russia in a house on the outskirts of Moscow. One day in the spring of 1926, she wrote, several agents of the GPU—a precursor of the KGB—came with orders to search the house and to arrest her father.

During the search, a young commissar talked with my father and looked with great interest through photo albums from our Sergiyevskoye, especially those showing the festivals that we used to organize each summer for children from all the villages of our parish.

Then, pointing to the icons, this young commissar said to my father, "You are evidently a cultured person. Do you believe in this?" My father answered, "My friend, you have a mother, and she undoubtedly also believes in this." The young man's face changed somehow, and he quickly said: "My mother? She has cursed me!"

After a few hours the commissar announced that my father was free. When one of my sisters leaned over to take a close look at his signature, he turned around and said, "My name is Tinyakov." At that moment nobody remembered, but afterward we recalled that in the neighboring village of Polivanovo there was a family named Tinyakov, and they had two boys to whom my father paid special attention and whom he taught to be altar boys in the church.

Apparently this commissar was one of them, and, on coming to us, realized who we were, recognized our father, and lo!—did not arrest him.

Remarkably, Tinyakov would appear again in the saga of Sergiyevskoye/ Koltsovo. Soon after learning about the search, I had a series of interviews outside Moscow with another graduate of the Koltsovo teachers' institute, Nadezhda Sergeyevna Likhachev, the daughter of a priest in a neighboring village, who went on to become a loyal Communist, teacher, and chemist. She told me how her brother-in-law, Alexei Sergeyevich Subbotin, a veterinarian, was arrested in 1932 and taken to the Lubianka, the prison of the NKVD (the successor to the GPU). He had apparently triggered the suspicions of the political police because he regularly played cards with a group of friends, and any repeated gathering of the same people was certain to attract the attention of the secret police sooner or later. "And do you know the funniest thing?" Nadezhda Sergeyevna asked with a smile of anticipation. "He was questioned by Misha Tinyakov! He was the NKVD's chief interrogator at Lubianka!

"Misha Tinyakov threatened Alexei Sergeyevich: 'Tell me about your organization or I'll arrest Dunya'—that's his wife, my sister Maria,—'and Nastya'— that's me!" Nadezhda Sergeyevna paused for effect, then continued: "After each session, Misha wrote out the questions and answers, and gave Alexei Sergeyevich the paper to sign. But Alexei Sergeyevich only made a mark. He said he wouldn't sign any document that was so ungrammatical. He forced Misha to rewrite them!" She smiled at the notion of such boldness.

Like Maria Osorgin, Nadezhda Sergeyevna seemed to view Tinyakov's appearance as an ironic coincidence. I believe it is more likely that he was selected for both tasks because he knew the targets. Or it may be that he chose them himself. He certainly showed no great compassion for Subbotin. And when he scoured the Osorgin family photo albums, was he merely curious, or was he trying to make sure there was nothing there that might compromise him? Yet it may be that Mikhail Mikhailovich touched some human chord in Tinyakov, and that it was still possible in 1926 for an agent to spare a victim. By 1932, however, when Subbotin was questioned, an interrogator showed mercy only at the risk of his own life. Subbotin was held at the Lubianka and at the Butyrka prison in Moscow for two years, and then was exiled to Novosibirsk. He was released in 1937 and served in the army during World War II.

In a group picture from the 1920s, Tinyakov is a sturdy youth with narrow, deep-set eyes. (I came across the same picture in a newspaper clipping from the 1960s, but with Tinyakov cropped out.) Nadezhda Sergeyevna remembered him as a bossy and self-important Komsomol head whom the girls made fun of. She said he commanded no respect at the school but was feared by the teachers and the director as an informer. He informed on the popular director of the school, Afanasy Matveyevich Popov, for using a horse owned by the school for some personal tasks, and Popov was fired.

Nadezhda Sergeyevna said she heard that sometime before the war Tinyakov's mother was summoned to Moscow by the "organs of state security"—the euphemism for the secret police—and taken to an apartment that, she was told, was her son's. "Take whatever you want," they said, "he won't return." According to another of Tinyakov's former classmates, he died in 1937. The most common cause of death that year was a bullet in the back of the neck, so I suspect Misha Tinyakov was devoured by the same machine he served.

10

Hussars to Commissars

On a sunny day in August 1914, Sofia's husband, Nikolai Lopukhin, arrived in Sergiyevskoye from Moscow. Before the carriage had even come to a halt, he shouted: "Germany has declared war on us!" With him was Nikolai Shutov, the estate foreman, who abandoned all decorum and ran with Lopukhin onto the balcony to report that mobilization was already underway in Kaluga. Old Russia was sounding its last hurrah.

"The war that would ruin Russia struck like thunder from a clear sky," wrote Sergei. It swept up everybody. Young Mikhail Osorgin, the third of that name, set off as a reserve officer to serve as an aide to his uncle General Yakov Zhilinsky, who as governor general of Poland became commander of the northwestern front. Grigory Trubetskoi, Liza Osorgin's younger brother and a deputy minister of foreign affairs, was dispatched as ambassador to Serbia to monitor the war there. Mikhail Mikhailovich gave over a wing of Sergiyevskoye for a military hospital, where his wife and unmarried daughters Liana, Maria, and Tonia served as nurses and orderlies until war's end. Sergei, aged 25, and Georgy, 20, quit their studies at the university and entered the accelerated officer training course at the Nikolayevskoye Cavalry School in St. Petersburg. Sergei had only to pass his state exams to join the faculty of Moscow University, and Georgy had less than a year left in his undergraduate studies, but there was no holding them back.

"We thought it would be a short war, and we were uncontrollably drawn to combat," Sergei explained. "We'd have time after the war to study, to plunge into everyday life, but for now, hurrah! We're young; our blood is boiling."

They were not alone in the conviction that the war would be quickly over; Tsar Nicholas II, seeing Grigory Trubetskoi off to Serbia, said, "I am not releasing you for long. I will recall you by Easter, because I will need you to work out the peace treaty."

Reality returned with the first transport ship to reach Kaluga from the front, which brought 2,200 wounded soldiers, overwhelming all the province's preparations. The Sergiyevskoye clinic doubled its capacity: from the day it opened, on October 18, 1914, until it closed, in August 1917, more than five hundred seriously wounded soldiers were treated there. In late August, the ill-prepared Russian forces on the northwestern front were smashed at Stebark, and Zhilinsky, though he had tried to warn the High Command that the armies were not ready, was relieved of his command (he was subsequently appointed Russian representative to the Allied Council in Paris). Young Mikhail Osorgin, just starting as his aide, was reassigned to a medical train; he later transferred to an automobile unit and was in Romania when the war ended.

In March 1915, Sergei and Georgy were issued field binoculars, swords, and Nagant revolvers and dispatched to their regiments as newly commissioned *praporshchiki* (sub-ensigns, an entry-level officer rank used only in wartime). Georgy joined the Horse Grenadiers Life Guards regiment, whose commander was Dmitry Alexandrovich Lopukhin, Liza Osorgin's cousin and the brother of Alexei Lopukhin, the former director of the Police Department.

Sergei also initially intended to join the Horse Grenadiers but changed his mind and joined the Alexandriiskiye Hussars, a regiment known as the Immortal Hussars for its legendary feats of reckless bravado. He wrote that he did so "mainly" because the empress, Alexandra Fyodorovna, was the honorary commander. However, his father suspected that Sergei joined because the Immortal Hussars promised action, in which he sought to drown his love for his cousin.

By May, Sergei was en route to the front on a train that passed right by Sergiyevskoye. His parents rode with him to Kaluga and returned by steamboat. "Oh, how it hurt!" wrote his father. "The trip home on a steamship along a route on which every bush was familiar seemed to mock our sorrow. Could a regular life really continue? Was it possible to return to a normal routine? God is wise, that to us, His limited creations, He gives time to smooth and erase." In July, Georgy was off to the front, and the parental grief was doubled.

*A family picture taken during the First World War, with
the three Osorgin boys in uniform. Georgy is at the
bottom, Mikhail is directly behind him, and Sergei is at
the right.*

"I can say with pride that they both fulfilled their duty to their motherland
and tsar with great bravery, courage, and composure," wrote Mikhail
Mikhailovich. Indeed, the exploits of these two young officers are remarkable
to read. Both wildly romantic, both reared in an unquestioning love for tsar and
Russia, both born into a caste that glorified martial bravado, they plunged into
the war with all the desperate abandon of their fading empire.

"Although I was already 25, I again became a youth," wrote Sergei. "I
dreamed of bold charges, of a St. George's Cross, of recuperating from a
wound at Sergiyevskoye with my arm in a sling, the unexpected but inevitable
meeting with my Sonia, and beyond that, in the distant blue haze, a happiness of
which I never doubted."

Reading of their feats today—the cavalry charges with drawn sword against
machine-gun nests; the brazen patrols deep behind enemy lines; the yearning
for decorations, noble wounds, and self-sacrificing nurses; the Tolstoyan glam-

orization of the "simple Russian soldier," with his mournful songs and stoicism—one feels a great ambivalence. It is hard to resist the allure of the last great war in which there was a modicum of chivalry and romance. But it is also hard to dismiss the futility and foolishness of that adventure. "Fighting for Tsar and Motherland is immeasurably better than trashing them from the rostrum of the Duma," wrote Sergei. Immeasurably easier, perhaps, but better? The Duma was old Russia's last hope, after all, and the war its fatal folly.

In the summer of 1915, Sergei Osorgin's unit was assigned to harass the Germans along the Neman River to prevent them from massing for an attack on Vilnius. In late July, Sergei's squadron commander, Prince Eristov, sent him with three platoons to roust German infantry entrenched in the village of Kovarsk. To the right of his Hussars was a unit of Cuirassiers; to the left, a unit of Cossacks; between them and the Germans, an open field.

The light began to break; the birds in the forest awakened and, jumping from branch to branch, shook drops of dew on us. The Germans in the village came to life, and through binoculars I could see them getting down into the trenches just outside the village. Before they could settle in, I ordered my men to start advancing in sprints. There was no difference between the place where I had spent the night and the depression behind the haystack where I planned to make my first dash, but the depression somehow seemed far more dangerous than the birches to which I had already become accustomed, where I had tamped down a comfortable seat and had a special twig on which to hang my binoculars.

I sensed the same unease—not fear, but some sort of misgiving— among the soldiers, so I went first, running my forty or fifty steps shouting, "Ahead! Ahead! Don't fall behind!" The Germans immediately opened rifle and machine-gun fire, and their artillery showered us and our reserves with shrapnel, cutting them from us. The closer we got to the Germans, the more this unease gave way to arousal, especially when I saw that the Cuirassiers, who began their advance after us, were drawing close, and even passing us.

Only about a hundred and fifty steps remained to the German trenches, but the din of fire, flak, and "suitcases" [artillery rounds] exploding behind us was such that, trying to be heard, I rose to full height, signaled a charge with my drawn sword, and with a fierce cry of "Hurra-a-ah!" sprinted ahead. My Hussars rose as one, shooting on the run. I singled out the German machine-gun nest, freed my revolver, and, continuing to shout "Hurrah!" and waving my sword, ran with everything I had. One Hussar fell, then another, but I shouted, "We'll gather them after!" and continued running. The trenches were close, German helmets were popping up behind the parapets, when suddenly I felt something hit me in the back with great force. I turned around, thinking that one of my men had run into me, and . . . I remember nothing more. I came to lying on my back and saw above me a bright blue sky with occasional green bursts of shrapnel, but I heard nothing. I had received a concussion from the explosion of a "suitcase," and shrapnel had scratched my temple, from which blood trickled slowly. But what blessed, intoxicating silence!

A soldier hoisted Osorgin onto his back and carried him to the rear, but he had time to see his men jumping one after another into the machine-gun nest and the Germans fleeing back to Kovarsk. As Sergei was being carried off on a stretcher, the Cuirassier commander bent over and asked how he was. Though barely conscious, Osorgin's bravado was intact: "Trenches taken. First in were the Alexandriiskiye Hussars."

Osorgin was not awarded the St. George's Cross he so coveted. Only one was awarded per battle, and it went that day to a lieutenant of the Cuirassiers who was killed ("even though it was the Hussars who took the machine guns," groused Osorgin). But his request to be evacuated to Sergiyevskoye was granted. "What bliss it was to get to Sergiyevskoye, to our quiet nest, to be surrounded with the familiar care, love, and tenderness, to release nerves as taut as guitar strings, to drink morning coffee in bed, which we never did, and to sense how my stories gripped my listeners."

His mother, with three sons at the front, was delighted to get back at least one for a while. On August 18, 1915, she wrote to her sister Olga Trubetskoi: "How happy I am. I've been so worried the past month, and am so relieved that he has been taken out of the fire. Now, seeing him and hearing him, I thank God that He kept him alive through the horror he was in. He is visibly improving, walks about, and is not dizzy, only of course he's weak."

Within a month Sergei returned to his unit, but it soon became evident that the injury to his spine was far more serious than had initially appeared; he suffered its consequences for the rest of his life. He was sent back home again. During a stopover at his sister Sofia's house in Moscow, the phone rang: it was Sonia Gagarin summoning him. His sister made the sign of the cross over him, and he rushed off in his dirty field uniform to the Gagarin palace on Novinsky Boulevard. In the vestibule, his aunt Marina Gagarin met him and silently led him to Sonia. "It was our first meeting after so much suffering, after all the honest, heroic efforts to overcome my feelings, and we emerged as fiancés."

Two years and many battles later, Sergei Osorgin's regiment was settled in a "quiet positional war" on the Northern Dvina River.

> But here, over us, over all Russia, erupted that terrible disaster, revolution. I do not believe I could sustain a calm, factual tone telling you about the revolution. Anyone who lived through it will understand me. . . . We suffered too much blood, too many lies, too much hypocrisy. We had to endure too much humiliation, too many unbearable insults. May God be my judge, but there is too much blood-soaked hatred, too many unpunished crimes! I fear you might misunderstand, my children, you may find this dated; already one hears the appeasing speeches of the conciliators, "It's time to forget. . . ." No. I cannot forget. God have mercy on unfortunate Russia, mercy on the long-suffering Russian people.

There his memoirs end.

Eighty years later, in the Military Historical Archive in Moscow, I read the service records of Cornet Sergei Mikhailovich Osorgin. They record that he suffered a concussion on July 31, 1915, from an artillery shell that exploded to the right of him; it lists three decorations for valor and his promotion to cornet on May 12, 1916. The final entry in his file is order number 1359, dated December 4, 1917: "For absence without leave for more than two months, struck from the lists of the regiment." By then he and Sonia were in southern Russia, far from the Bolsheviks.

In that same archive I also rummaged through the records of my other grandfather's unit, the Semyonovsky Life Guards infantry regiment. Dmitry Nikolayevich Schmemann left no memoirs, but the cold idiom of regimental orders tells a story no less dramatic.

The daily order for October 27, 1915, posted at the village of Dugi, somewhere on the southern front, reports the arrival of several officers just commissioned after an accelerated course at the Corps of Pages school, among them Sublieutenant Schmemann and his future brother-in-law, Tikhon Shishkov. For the rest of that year, and until the regiment is ordered back by the revolutionary government two years later, the daily orders record a terrible toll in dead and wounded among soldiers and officers, most of them from artillery fire on their trenches in a succession of obscure Galician villages.

In the Central State Historical Archive in St. Petersburg (where Dmitry Schmemann's file is quaintly stamped "State Archive of the Feudal-Serf Epoch"), I found letters Dmitry wrote from the front to Elena Krivoshein, the wife of the minister of Agriculture, Alexander Krivoshein (with whom Osorgin had dealt when he was head of the Land Bank), and apparently the mother of one of Dmitry's friends. In a letter dated February 23, 1915, he writes: "Soon I shall have been four months in the regiment, but four months of unbroken life in the trenches is not attractive. The weather has been wonderful, though very cold, and this morning there arose a monstrous blizzard, and our trenches are full almost to the top with snow. We clear them with difficulty because they are immediately filled with drifts. Our position is generally calm, but we take losses almost daily."

The order for July 30, 1916, lists Schmemann among the wounded. An appendix to this order gives the doctor's report: contusion to the head from an exploding mine in the village of Belitsk; "both eardrums ruptured, blood flow from the ears, and almost complete loss of hearing in right ear and lowered hearing in left."

While recuperating in Petrograd (as St. Petersburg was renamed at the outset of the war), it fell to Schmemann to inform the Shishkovs that one of their sons had been killed and the other wounded, in the same battle. In a vicious battle on September 7, Tikhon Shishkov had been felled by an explosion. His brother, Nikolai, ran up to him and, seeing that Tikhon was still alive, exclaimed, "Thank God at least one of us will survive this day." Soon after, Nikolai was killed. It was while informing the family of this episode, his head in a bandage and his hearing all but gone, that Dmitry Schmemann proposed to Anna Shishkov. (A striking woman with a dash of Georgian blood, she later said that it was the bandage that swayed her—not because of any martial glory it reflected, but because it hid Dmitry's prominent ears.)

Schmemann returned to the front in November 1916 and fought until the end of the war. With the abdication of the tsar on March 2, 1917, the tone of the daily orders abruptly changes. Appeals from the Provisional Government take the place of crisp orders from the tsarist General Staff; soldiers' committees are formed; the designation "Life Guards"—first granted the Semyonovsky Regiment, in 1700, by its founder, Tsar Peter the Great—is scrapped, because the life that was being guarded was that of the monarch, who no longer existed. In June 1917, the army authorized the soldiers of individual military units to award a soldier's St. George's Cross to their officers for acts of exceptional bravery; Schmemann, now a staff captain, is awarded one for a battle on June 22 and 23.

In October 1917, he begins signing the orders as regimental adjutant; before long, a new signature is added to his and the regimental commander's—that of a "commissar."

On February 27, 1918, the Semyonovsky regiment is ordered back, and after an arduous march from Galicia it arrives in Petrograd on March 13. On April 1, the final order is posted, declaring the regiment dissolved. One of the three signatures is a large, distinct "Schmemann." It's silly, I know, but I looked for a long time at the fuzzy hectograph copy. The Semyonovsky Life Guards was one of the two oldest regiments of the Russian army, along with the Preobrazhensky infantry regiment. They were formed in 1687 by Peter the Great out of men from the villages of Preobrazhenskoye and Semyonovskoye (both now inside the Moscow city limits) with whom he had played soldiers as a boy. And it was my grandfather who co-signed the order dissolving the regiment.

Dmitry Schmemann's war was not yet over. While many of his fellow Semyonovsky officers fled revolutionary Petrograd or joined the White Guards, he stayed in the army, seeking to ensure that every man he had fought with was taken care of. On September 25, 1918, he married Anna Tikhonovna Shishkov; soon after, he was ordered to block the advancing anti-Bolshevik forces of General Nikolai Yudenich. Schmemann's entire unit, composed mostly of former Guardsmen, changed sides and joined Yudenich. After fighting to within a few miles of Petrograd, Yudenich's Northwest army was pushed back to Estonia, where it was disarmed and interned in appalling conditions. Alone in Petrograd, Dmitry's wife gave birth to their first child, a daughter, Elena, and soon after, using bribes and forged documents, she managed to join Dmitry in Reval (now Tallinn). There, on September 13, 1921, Anna gave birth to twin boys, Andrei and Alexander. The latter was my father. Elena died in her mother's arms of scarlet fever at the age of seven and is buried in Estonia. The Schmemanns eventually made their way to Serbia, and then to Paris, where my grandfather ran a wholesale wine business and my grandmother worked in an employment agency for refugees. Both are buried in France.

Liza Osorgin's letters to her sister Olga Trubetskoi from these years are filled with foreboding. "We were terribly frightened by the news brought by our Misha," she writes on December 20, 1916. "What horrible times! How crude and brutal we've all become. Take, for example, how we all feel about the killing of Rasputin. We must all share the guilt of Sumarokov [Prince Yusupov], who did what we all wished. Terrible! I fear that this is only the beginning. Where will it all end? It's terrible to have three sons now at the front. I try not to think of this, but to keep my mind on the present."

In another letter, Liza writes to Olga of an uprising by the Kaluga garrison that was brutally suppressed by Cossacks. She adds that Tonia, her youngest, has begun writing verse: "Amid these cataclysmic, awesome trials / Lord God preserve us. . . ."

Throughout the war, Mikhail Mikhailovich tried to keep in touch with villagers from Sergiyevskoye who were at the front, of whom there were about two hundred. In January 1917, he had the idea of sending each soldier an Easter gift from the school. The teachers and pupils responded enthusiastically. Contributions began flowing in; girls sewed tobacco pouches, boys built boxes for the parcels. Each soldier was to get stationery, a pen and pencil, needles and thread, buttons, tobacco, soap, sweets, an icon, a book, and postcards with views of Kaluga, along with Easter greetings from the parish priest. The parcels began going out at the start of Lent—just when the tsar abdicated.

The first thank-you note came in the fourth week of Lent. It was addressed to the pupils: "Thank you for remembering those of us who have been torn from our families by the will of the hated government. But now we have freedom. Remember, children, that this is a great thing. There are no more *barins*, landowners, or bosses. Cherish this freedom and use it fully."

Mikhail Mikhailovich's memoirs stop here.

For the soldier and peasant, this was the timeless dream: the land that they had tilled since time immemorial finally their own, without obligations to any parasitic landowner, without rapacious taxes, without the cruel burden of distant wars. This was "freedom"—not an abstract human or political right, not representation in some distant assembly, but the lifting of hated authority and alien sovereignty over their fields and meadows.

"What are they doing in your Moscow?" Liza Osorgin writes from Sergiyevskoye to her sister Olga Trubetskoi on October 4, 1917. "We get no papers and hear the worst rumors. The *muzhiks* tell us there are strikes over hunger and high prices. But then maybe you don't know, either. Ask around by telephone and let us know. I fear that the total outrage of the mob will lead us to catastrophe. We haven't even finished gathering potatoes, and the peas are just lying in the field. The roads are impassable."

Liza's next letter is dated October 30: "We sit for the second day without any news, since there are no newspapers. We find out about things from letters from our Seryozha, but we get them late. The telegraph is out—the telegraphist in Ferzikovo is devoted to us, but he sees nothing and knows nothing. I await the worst. But for now all is quiet and calm here."

The worst was well underway—that "terrible disaster" my grandfather and many other relatives could not discuss without revulsion and dismay. Most of the Osorgins' relatives fled Moscow and St. Petersburg, all in the certainty that they would return "as soon as the Bolsheviks leave." That's how they always said it, as if the Communists were a bad dream or a curable disease. Many headed south to lands controlled by the Cossacks; a few turned east to Siberia; others headed for the apparent security of their estates. Before leaving, many deposited their valuables, securities, and deeds in savings banks, certain that they would be there when they returned.

The Bolsheviks quickly set about taking charge. The Russian Soviet Federated Socialist Republic was proclaimed on October 25, 1917 (November 7 New Style), and on the next day the Bolsheviks issued a decree banning private ownership of land. Article 2 of the Decree on Land ordered the confiscation of all large properties owned by landowners and the Church, with all equipment, buildings, and livestock. Article 3 warned that any damage to confiscated lands would be punished by "revolutionary courts." On December 18, the People's Commissariat of Land Use issued "temporary instructions for transitional measures" toward the nationalization of all land; it declared that the task before local *soviets* was to "immediately expel . . . all former landowners and nonproductive renters and to take land under their control."

In those parts of central Russia that the Bolsheviks controlled, the confiscation went briskly. More than three quarters of the estates of central Russia were seized within six months, almost two thousand in Moscow Province alone. Many landowners abandoned their estates for the cities or for regions outside Soviet control, and many manors were destroyed or looted.

Both victors and victims kept lists. In Paris, the Friends of the Russian Book published catalogues of estate libraries that had been destroyed, vandalized, or burned. "Now, while the smell of smoke still covers all Russia, we would like to say a few words about what was destroyed in those fires," read one of their publications in 1925. In Soviet Russia, museums and libraries kept their own lists of what they salvaged and nationalized. A tally of valuables confiscated from Nikolskoye-Gagarino alone included 107 items of special value taken by the National Museum Fund, as well as four late-seventeenth-century Italian panels, furniture, five mirrors, and fifteen hundred books, all of which were signed over to the museum of the New Jerusalem monastery, in nearby Istra.

Not all landowners fled. The Osorgins were among those who stayed on their land, both because they had good relations with their neighboring villages and because, like many others, they presumed that the Bolshevik blight would pass. In the early days of the revolution, local *soviets* often allowed those landowners who did not openly oppose the Bolsheviks to stay on, albeit now on equal terms with the peasants.

Even in all this turmoil and confusion, and even among those with little sympathy for the abdicated tsar, the brief, five-line announcement in July 1918 of the execution of Nicholas II and his family in Ekaterinburg caused a terrible shock. Sergei Golitsyn, whose liberal father regarded Nicholas as the root cause of Russia's collapse (and whose sister would soon marry Georgy Osorgin), recalled how people at all levels of society wept and prayed, how he himself, as a nine-year-old boy, cried night after night into his pillow. "In those days, many houses in cities and villages had cheap color pictures of the tsar, the tsarina, their charming daughters in white dresses, and the good-looking boy in a sailor suit. Along with icons, they were the embellishment of a peasant hut. Millions of boys, myself included, revered the heir, who was only four years older than I. I was seized with horror. Killings in war were understandable. But how could someone raise a hand against this nice boy, these young beauties?!"

At Sergiyevskoye, the greatest torment was the lack of information. The Osorgins lost contact with their sons on the front and with their married daughter, Sofia, who had fled with her husband, Nikolai Lopukhin, to Tyumen, in Siberia.

"I hope you're back in Izmalkovo," an anguished Liza wrote to Olga in November 1917. "Moving about Moscow is dangerous for you. Sonia and Kolya are in Siberia. How hard it is for me! I find it very difficult to control myself. The fate of my boys tortures me. In general, life is not easy. I try to leave everything to the will of God, but it is very hard."

The next letter in the file is at Christmas. Sergei Osorgin has made his way with his fiancée and a slew of other relatives to Novorossisk, in southern Russia, in a region controlled by the Don Cossacks, where anti-Bolshevik forces were gathering and forming the volunteer (White) army, under General Anton Denikin. The other two sons are at home, but the tension is taking its toll on Mikhail Mikhailovich and Liza: "Misha's nerves are in an awful state. He is terribly tortured and shaken. I am very weak and can barely move from room to room. . . . We are extremely interested in the successes of Denikin. Hopes are rising in everyone's soul."

By the next letter, on January 29, 1918, the revolution has reached Sergiyevskoye. A "committee" has taken over the Osorgins' lands and farm equipment and moved into the children's wing of the house, leaving the Osorgins only five rooms. These self-appointed committees (the foreign word, supplanted later by the Russian *soviet*, was held in high regard in the countryside) differed widely from village to village but usually consisted of local peasants who took the Bolshevik decrees as authority to seize land and equipment.

However irksome the intrusion, the formation of the committee comes as almost a relief to Liza after the suspense and tension of the last four months:

> You're probably worried about us, so I want to calm you. The "coup" happened painlessly, quietly, and peacefully. The worst is that the committee took over part of the house, and emotionally that's very hard. You can understand how this defiles our children's bedrooms. Besides, they have many large gatherings, and of course this is unpleasant. It's also very hard on our servants. They all come to pour out their feelings. They've stayed on only for us, to defend our interests. It's very difficult. . . .
>
> The first days were unbearable. We should have anticipated it, but we never really believed it, and we were filled with unbearable grief. Misha [Mikhail Mikhailovich] was calm. He took everything serenely and modestly. The girls also. . . . Now we've all rallied and calmed down. I must say the chairman behaves correctly and even politely. We were left two cows and two horses. The servants tell them all the time not to bother us. "Let them live. We vouch for their safety and property. We want them treated as humanely as possible."
>
> . . . There are rumors that several villages are trying to evict the committees and return the estate to Misha. I don't know if this will happen, or if it's good for us. But we rejoice that there is a conscience in our people.

On March 8, 1918, Liza's youngest brother, Grigory Nikolayevich Trubetskoi, now 44, arrived at Sergiyevskoye. He had been ambassador to Serbia during the war, and afterward joined Denikin's White Army in southern Russia. Trubetskoi and his eldest son, Konstantin, had managed to escape from Novocherkassk, in the south, just before the White Army evacuated the city ahead of the advancing Reds. Traveling through Bolshevik-held territory on forged documents, and with many narrow escapes, they at last reached Moscow, and decided to rest awhile in the relative security of Sergiyevskoye.

Of Liza's 12 brothers and sisters, Grigory was the closest to the Osorgins; Mikhail Mikhailovich had tutored and befriended his young brother-in-law, and Grigory in turn became their favorite "Uncle Grishanchik" to his Osorgin nieces and nephews. In his memoirs, Trubetskoi portrayed those two months salvaged from the violence and destruction of the revolution as a leave-taking of the old world.

Even though the Bolsheviks had taken away the lands and a wing of the house, there was an illusion of continuity. As before, peasants came to the Osorgins for medical treatment and advice, or just to check up on the old masters. Mikhail Mikhailovich was only 57 in 1918, but he was increasingly assuming the role and style of a patriarch, complete with a grand beard, for which Grigory teased him mercilessly.

"These were the most profoundly patriarchal of relations, which could only have been formed through long, harmonious years together," wrote Trubetskoi.

> The peasants brought all they could to the *barins*. Although the area lived off itinerant traders (Kaluga never had enough grain to feed itself) the peasants still brought the Osorgins flour, sugar, kerosene, and cloth and refused to take any money. "Before, you fed us; now we have to feed you," the peasants said. Of course, it was only thanks to God's mercy that the former life was maintained so long. To a large degree, this was because the Church brought them together. All the Osorgins sang in the choir from childhood, the father was the church warden, and the services were celebrated with special luster. The peasants loved this and knew to whom they were obliged for it. The services were especially magnificent during Lent and Holy Week. . . . The Osorgins blended so thoroughly with their Sergiyevskoye that it was hard to imagine them outside of their beloved surroundings, in which they had the deepest roots.

After the *soviet* confiscated their estate, Mikhail Mikhailovich and his eldest son, Mikhail, were stripped of the central occupation of their lives. The father, accustomed to fussing eternally over something, could find no outlet for his energies and paced the halls, sometimes seizing a broom and sweeping the alleys in the garden. The son, then 31, never left his room and saw no one. Liza, suffering from phlebitis and worn down by the anxieties of war and revolution, was often confined to a wheelchair. Only 52, her hair was completely white.

The cheeriest spirit was the youngest son, Georgy. Twenty-five that summer, he returned a hero from the war, but still looked like a boy and was treated as such in the family. Seeking to make the best of things, he demanded an allotment of land, and the local *soviet* assigned him 40 acres of the best, along with two horses, two cows, seed, and whatever equipment he needed to farm.

Georgy Osorgin plowing lands allocated to him by the
local revolutionary "committee" after the Russian
Revolution, as drawn by Maria Osorgin.

Georgy spent all day in the field, from dawn to dusk, assisted by former servants and his three unmarried sisters. They were Liana (Juliana), 26, quiet, uncomplaining, and unassuming; Maria, 20, tall, and a talented artist whose sketches of those years have left a matchless record of the last days of the old order; and Tonia (Antonina), 17, petite, with huge eyes, bright, alive, and treated by everyone as the baby.

"They were capable, when time allowed, of spending whole hours on the bluff beyond the park, from which one could see the Oka snaking and disappearing into the horizon," Trubetskoi wrote.

In the evenings they played bridge while Maria sketched, or Liza and Liana would play Beethoven, Schumann, or their current favorite, Rimsky-Korsakov, four-hands.

News of the outside world sneaked in only through newspapers, or sometimes with arrivals from Kaluga. They lived from day to day in the hope that in two or three weeks, at most a month, the Bolsheviks would be thrown out. Mishan never missed a chance to reproach the people for betraying the tsar and thus touching off the collapse. The peasants liked it when "Mikhal Mikhalych" took them to task and readily came to him to lay out all their concerns.

In the fall of 1918, the Kaluga Bolsheviks abruptly ordered the Osorgins to quit Sergiyevskoye within three days. The eviction did not come as a total surprise. For many months already, landowners on all sides were being thrown out. In June, Liza Osorgin had written to Olga Trubetskoi in Moscow asking her to make inquiries about moving to Izmalkovo, the estate of their Samarin cousins, outside Moscow. The note, in pencil, is dated June 16, 1918:

> No one bothers us for now, but Red Guards are evicting people from Tula *uyezd* since late May. . . . Recently, Nikolai saw a landowner in Ferzikovo who was thrown out at night, without even being given a chance to get dressed. . . .
>
> Here the peasants say they'll never allow it, but you know how little is determined by them, and nobody has the time to take any measures.
>
> We need to know where to go, at least temporarily. Ask Misha to see, or find out yourself, if we can go to Izmalkovo. We'd try to send some things out there, that way we'd have something to live on at least temporarily.
>
> Don't sound the alarm yet, but we need to think of something in advance and to prepare without haste. Our peasants can't do anything. I doubt they would be able to protect us, they're unarmed. But their relations with us are of the best.

Liza's preparations were not in vain. When the inevitable expulsion order finally came, the Osorgins moved in with the Samarins at Izmalkovo. Five years later, in 1923 after a long legal battle, the Samarins were evicted from Izmalkovo, and the Osorgins had to move again. They had spent the years at Izmalkovo giving lessons to local children; the grateful parents of one pupil gave them the free use of their nearby dacha. For Maria Osorgin, that second eviction rekindled memories of the expulsion from Sergiyevskoye. In the fall of 1923 she wrote to a cousin in Paris, Nikolai Lermontov:

> I keep remembering our departure from Sergiyevskoye exactly five years ago and how it was different. Here the agony of eviction lasted so long, it was in a way worse, whereas we left Sergiyevskoye while our lovely life was at full tilt. We were ousted, after all, within three days. We were not even allowed to take anything except clothes, and where was there time to pack everything in our huge house? We left everything as it was. We arose from breakfast, leaving behind even the bowl with fruits, we went into the living room, where open music still lay on the piano, while in the other rooms, in the billiards room, in the study, the commissars were already acting like masters, lowering the curtains for some reason and putting locks on the doors. We rushed to go out on the stoop, so this would not happen in our presence, but they kept delaying the horses, and there was a terrible moment when we all, dressed, with all our things, sat there on the stoop. I

especially remember Papa's face, and we all kept silent, and endlessly and stupidly waited for the delayed cart. At the gates of the yard and the garden there was a mass of peasants, who wept and crossed themselves from a distance, but they were forbidden to come in to say goodbye, and one commissar started yelling at them rudely, something about landowners, bloodsuckers, and so forth. Inside the house there were loud and unfamiliar voices, the sound of doors slamming, laughter, it got entirely unbearable and we were happy when finally the cart came, hitched to our kind and beloved Bogatyr (remember?), who had taken us for so many rides. When we sat down and took off, the whole crowd removed their hats and stood bowing, crossing themselves, and wailing. But when we went past the yard around the island of flowers and past the windows of the dining room and study, and the acacias, and the children's windows, with our prim curtains with the familiar hole, for which we blamed each other all summer, and I glanced for the last time from the gates at the yard, at the round green island, the sandy paths, this whole huge, familiar, white mass of a house, so beloved—oh, how I began to weep, biting my lips until they hurt, and it was in a fog that I saw the rest of the road through the estate, our pigeon loft, stables, the crossroads, the church in the distance, never in my life have I felt such a heavy grief. You know yourself, Nikolai, how we loved our unique, dear Sergiyevskoye. . . . How much love was shown us, sympathy, so many devoted friends, what things they said in parting, they showered us with gifts and the most touching offerings, all three days before our departure, from morning to night, everyone, coming to say goodbye and flooding us with tears. And the last Liturgy, at which Papa and Mama took Communion on the very day of departure, after which literally everybody in church wept and covered us with blessings. One *muzhik*, whom Papa considered his enemy, called Tonia into a hidden corner behind the stove and handed her 25 rubles, flowing with tears and begging her to take it. There were innumerable such touching details, which created a common atmosphere of love, loyalty, sympathy, and assistance, so that we had a rise of spirit, as of some celebration, an awareness that this was a final chord of our life, of Papa's work with Sergiyevskoye. Along the road, in the villages we passed, there were virtual ambushes. . . .

The rest of the letter is missing.

Seventy-two years later, on my first visit to Koltsovo, I met Irina Yakovlevna Denisova, whose uncle was head of the "committee" that moved into the Osorgin house. A spry, retired schoolteacher who raised bees and incessantly tangled with the local authorities, she remembered the departure well. "We lived in your house," she said with pride. "After the masters left, all the furniture disappeared. We snuck in and played the piano, and got whipped for it. What toys they had! We never saw such toys."

The ties between the Osorgins and the villagers lasted for several more years. The peasants continued sending them food in Moscow even into the hungry twenties. Georgy Osorgin also made some foraging trips to Sergiyevskoye, which Liza Osorgin refers to in two brief notes to her sister. The notes have no dates but must be from the 1920s:

"Olga, how are you eating? Do you have milk? Georgy left on Saturday and we have no news yet. He was to have stopped in Kaluga to find out about Sergiyevskoye, then to go to the farm and gather supplies. God grant him success. I'm very scared, they're stopping people on the road and taking things away. We are risking a lot, we've risked a lot of money."

In the next note, Georgy has returned: "Georgy is working for everybody, stoking stoves, chopping wood. Anna will tell you how brilliantly successful his trip was. He brought four wagonloads of supplies, and presents from our servants and peasants—he saw so much kindness and good on the part of the peasants that it raised our spirits and again compelled us to recognize the mercy God has shown us."

On my last trip to Koltsovo, in March 1995, I met Polina Ivanovna Kushpil, who told me many stories she had heard from her late mother, Olga Akimovna Rogov, who was a young woman when the Osorgins were expelled and had sung in the church choir with them. One of the stories was about an Osorgin son who showed up secretly one day at the house of an aunt who was married to Kuzma, a former coachman. "He was there to gather supplies, he said. Everybody kissed and hugged and cried, and before he left, Osorgin told my mother, 'Remember, you didn't see me here.'"

The Osorgin home outside Moscow became a center for the relatives who stayed behind, some because they failed to flee, others by choice. Mikhail Mikhailovich and Liza stayed there with Georgy and their daughters Maria, Liana, and Tonia, until Georgy was executed in 1928. Then, accompanied by Georgy's widow and his two infant children, they bought their way out to Paris, where Mikhail Mikhailovich at last achieved his lifelong yearning to be ordained a priest.

Sergei Osorgin, along with assorted Trubetskoi, Gagarin, and Lermontov kin, quit his regiment after the revolution and made his way to Novocherkassk in November 1917. There, on January 29, 1918, he finally married Sonia Gagarin. The wedding was very tense because it took place the day after the White forces had decided to abandon Novocherkassk to the Reds. Just before the wedding service began, the leader of the Don Cossacks, General Alexei Kaledin, shot himself in despair over his inability to curb rebellion among his Cossacks or halt the anarchy in his land. Sergei's uncle Grigory Trubetskoi served as a stand-in father at the wedding. His wife, Maria, described the affair in a letter to her father:

"Sonia G. and Seryozha O. were married three days ago. It was a very strange and unusual wedding. We had to hurry it up because the situation was very bad, but within two days we even managed to prepare the *kornety* [sacks of candy with the date of the wedding stamped on it, which were traditionally distributed at weddings]. It was the day that Kaledin committed suicide, and in general an unusually difficult day, so it was even good to have a diversion."

It was also a rare treat. A mysterious woman named Alexandra Nikolayevna, who called herself Baroness Rosen and went about in Cossack dress with a St. George's medal pinned to it, and who seemed to be involved in everything going on in Moscow, had somehow attached herself to the Gagarins and came all the way to Novocherkassk for the wedding with 40 pounds of sugar, a great rarity, which enabled the Gagarin chef to bake up a storm of cookies and cakes.

Oblivious to the chaos about them, the radiant newlyweds went off to the Cossack village of Persianovka, where, according to Trubetskoi, "they lived immersed in their own happiness, which could not be eclipsed by anyone or anything." Two years later, with two children, they left Russia through the Crimea with the last of General Pyotr Wrangel's White armies.

The other Osorgin children, Sofia Lopukhin and Mikhail, also left Russia and made their way to France.

In later years, the Communists created a myth around the "Great October Revolution," depicting it as a momentous uprising of peasants and workers against their oppressors. But as I followed it through the stories of those who lived it, the revolution always seemed more a collapse of the old order than its overthrow, much as the Communist regime subsequently collapsed of exhaustion and bankruptcy rather than because of anything the West did.

By the time Nicholas stepped down, the Russian empire was battered and disintegrating. The loss to Japan and the 1905 insurrection had weakened the pillars of tsar, motherland, and faith, and the subsequent stabs at reform were too few, too patchy, and too late. When the First World War broke out, the central government was polarized and demoralized; Rasputin was using his mystical hold over the empress to foist a progression of pliant nonentities on the government; reactionary nationalists—who were probably responsible for the assassination of the reformist prime minister, Stolypin—grew rabid as traditional institutions unraveled. The four successive elected Dumas were paralyzed and divided. The military command was incompetent. What is remarkable is not that the Russian state collapsed in 1917 but that it managed to survive and even to sustain a European war for as long as it did.

The abdication of the monarch could not set things right in these conditions; it could only create chaos, in which every social class and ethnic group looked to its own interests—the Cossacks on the Don, the Tatars and Bashkirs in the steppes, the soldiers on the front, the workers in Tula, the merchants in Moscow. The Russian Church, gathered in a full council in Moscow as street battles raged on all sides, looked first to its own survival in the rapidly crumbling order. The actual battles in the civil war between Reds and Whites were fought with relatively small numbers; the majority of the population viewed the struggle as a plague that brought only death and destruction, regardless of who was winning.

The Bolsheviks emerged triumphant from this chaos not because they had the greater popular support or the greater truth, but because in times of trouble the best-organized and most ruthless force will prevail. Lenin was strong because he had no illusions of popular support, no particular feelings for "Mother Russia," and no time for fair play or democratic niceties. His ideology dictated the seizure of power, and with a tautly disciplined and zealous following, unencumbered by scruples or patriotism, seize it he did.

The common wisdom is that the peasants played no part in the revolution. Indeed, they were not at its forefront as Red Guards or ideologues, and for the most part they stayed out of the revolutionary battles and the civil war. They felt no solidarity with the beardless urban radicals, and often no great hatred for the landowning class. In many places they seized the land because it was there to be seized, and because they had always believed that the land they cultivated was theirs: "I may belong to the *barin*, but the land belongs to me," was their timeless credo. If the *pomeshchik* or his estate manager had been cruel, they might drive him off and torch the manor house; if the *barin* had been kindly, as Osorgin was, they treated him with humanity and generosity. Either way, they believed they were taking charge of what was theirs by right.

Yet to conclude that the peasants passively submitted to the Bolsheviks as simply the latest in a long line of repressive exploiters is also false. There is no question that the Communists' promise of equality, communal ownership, and universal literacy found fertile ground among the young and the disenfranchised, both urban and rural. Many youths in the village were fired by what they viewed as liberation from poverty, ignorance, and bondage to the land. Those same students in whom Mikhail Mikhailovich Osorgin planted notions of morality and piety now plunged ardently into building a new world, traveling as Young Communist activists among villages to preach the coming of a new order, to "liquidate illiteracy," to create communes, and to close the churches.

The new faith *was* liberating. On the eve of the revolution, despite whatever changes were underway in the countryside, the village was a dark and backward place. Most peasants were illiterate, only half had iron plows, reaping was still done with sickles, threshing with flails. The "three-field" cycle of cultivation, which Europe abandoned after the Middle Ages and General Kar tried to eradicate on his estate, was still the norm. The average yield of grain from peasant lands was only slightly better than that of a fourteenth-century English estate.

The Osorgins always took pride in their close, patrimonial relations with "their people," and I don't doubt they understood the peasants better than the intellectuals, revolutionaries, or politicians. Yet I wonder if they really knew the squalor and poverty in which their people lived. Irina Yakovlevna Denisova described to me how she and other village girls marveled at the lovely smocks of the "young ladies" as they rode past to go to church, and her awe at the toys she found inside the Osorgin house after they were evicted. She also remembered life as the youngest of ten children in a fetid log house with an earthen floor, filled with thick black smoke because her father could not afford to fix the chimney or to burn fuel other than straw. In winter, calves and goats moved in and shared the stale air. Many of the children died young.

Irina Yakovlevna, like many other village youths, rushed enthusiastically to join the Komsomol and to enroll in the new teachers' training school set up at Koltsovo. She remembered how the young people cried when Lenin died, and how young Filip Golubkov, whose father farmed his own small plot of land by the river, worked all night to paint a portrait of Lenin that they could display in mourning. A year later the village youths traveled to Moscow to pay their respects at Lenin's mausoleum, much as their parents had bowed before the relics of their saints.

When they left, the Osorgins took with them the old Sergiyevskoye and forever closed the 150-year-old nest of gentry on the Oka. The peasants had never called it Sergiyevskoye anyway: they always called the village Karovo, and for a while continued to do so. Then the builders of the new world determined that it was politically improper to have a place named after a tsarist general, and a "foreigner" at that, so in 1919, "in years of revolutionary creativity," as the Soviet records have it, the Bolsheviks renamed it after Alexei Koltsov, a writer of literary folk songs in the early nineteenth century with no connection whatsoever to the village.

It was as Koltsovo that the old village began the next chapter of its existence. Everything inside the old Osorgin house was confiscated, stolen, or broken, and before long it was taken over by the First Workers' Agricultural Commune. The parish school into which Mikhail Mikhailovich had poured so much love and labor became the Karovo Pedtekhnikum, a "pedagogical vocational school" to train elementary-school teachers. The director and most of the old teachers, many of them graduates of seminaries, stayed on, now as ardent revolutionaries, training an entire generation of village children to be upstanding Communists and missionaries of the new order.

I I

The Classes Struggle and a Tractor Arrives

Among the peasants of Koltsovo, the 1917 revolution was not particularly memorable. Fyodor Akimovich Glebov, who was 13 at the time and would become a staunch Communist, wrote some decades later, "The Great October Revolution I don't remember, only that we boys walked and sang ditties, 'We'll climb up to heaven and chase out the gods.'" But the process of Sovietizing the village began almost immediately after, when the "committee" moved into the Osorgin house and took charge of their lands. According to local records, in May 1918 the committee held 270 acres of land, two fruit orchards, and some livestock.

These ad hoc committees of local peasants popped up all over the countryside. For the brief time they existed, the committees were about as close as the peasants ever came to realizing their dream of possessing the land. But after a few months the Bolsheviks crushed the committees, and all the subsequent local institutions, from the Committees of the Poor through the collective and state farms, became tightly controlled instruments of central Soviet control.

What spelled the doom of the committees was their resistance to turning their wheat over to the Bolsheviks. In the files of the Ferzikovo *Red Banner*, I read the Soviet version of this period: "The class struggle in the village sharply escalated in connection with the practical application of the Decree on Land. *Kulaks* grabbed the best lands and got onto local committees, and they refused to sell wheat to the government at fixed prices." Ten years later, the struggle was still raging: another report told how Communist youths "blocked efforts by *kulaks* to raise an insurrection against collectivization."

The first congress of Bolsheviks in Kaluga was held in January 1918. Following Moscow's instructions, it ordered the nationalization of all banks, factories, trade, and river transport. On February 20, provincial commissars were appointed for justice, land, the post, and the railroads, followed in May by commissars responsible for food, education, social services, and health.

The congress also ordered that 5.4 million rubles be raised through a special tax on "landowners, *kulaks*, traders, and speculators." Mikhail Mikhailovich Osorgin, still living at Sergiyevskoye, categorically refused to pay and was hauled off to jail in Kaluga. That was when Sergei Trofimov Kuznetsov, the dealer in illegal vodka whom Osorgin had so relentlessly prosecuted before the revolution, rushed off at the head of a group of peasants to ransom their former *barin*—and, while they were at it, also free the former owner of the small neighboring estate. Describing in his memoirs how he undid Kuznetsov's moonshine business, Osorgin added: "Sergei Kuznetsov paid me back for this matter, but with such kindness that God grant everyone be like this."

In June 1918, the Bolsheviks created a new weapon in the war with the village—the *kombed*, a portmanteau word for "committees of the poor." The *kombedy* purportedly represented the poorest peasants, in whose name they were charged with redistributing land and equipment. The tactic was elementary divide-and-conquer: in the first stage, peasant was turned against landowner; now "poor" peasant was being turned against "rich" peasant. The labels were highly relative. Poor peasants, *bednyaki*, were defined as those who owned virtually nothing. Next up the ladder of socialist worthiness were the *srednyaki*, who might have a horse and a couple of cows. Anyone who had more, and especially anyone who used hired labor, was a *kulak*, an exploiter and sworn enemy of the new order. Needless to say, the *bednyak* was usually the laziest and most drunken of the villagers, while anyone who resisted Soviet power was by definition a *kulak*. Not that these categories made much difference in the work of the *kombedy*, since all the committees were tightly controlled by professional Bolshevik cadres, and it was they who decided whom to advance and whom to repress.

Under the cover of redistributing peasant wealth, the real job of the *kombedy* was to requisition grain—by force if necessary—to sustain the Reds in the civil war. The resistance was vicious. In August 1918, regional Bolsheviks held a congress at Sugonovo, near Koltsovo, to organize the collection of grain in the region. They formed a *prodotriad* (supply detachment) under a hardened Bolshevik named Nazarov, leader of the local *kombed*. According to local records, "*kulak* bandits" massacred the entire detachment—except for Nazarov, who was taken alive, disemboweled, and stuffed with grain. Nazarov was succeeded by Andrei Porfirievich Kondratiev, a bloodied veteran of battles with peasants in Tambov, who resumed the Kaluga requisitioning, now backed up by a unit of Red Army soldiers.

The longer-range Soviet goal was to eliminate all independent farming and to put agriculture on the same mechanized footing as socialized industry. Already on December 9, 1918, the Communist administration in Kaluga launched the first drive to collectivize farming. The proclamation reveals the dream behind what would soon become one of the most brutal aspects of Communist rule:

> Only those will be considered members of a commune who give themselves wholly to the commune, entering it with *all* their property, living and inanimate, which from the moment of their entering the commune becomes its property.
>
> Every person who enters the commune must be free of any other work that would hamper the main goals of developing the commune movement. The fundamental task of the commune is to develop socialist agriculture, applying all the achievements of science and technology. A person involved in outside agricultural work is probably incapable of giving himself wholly to this development, and extra time is precisely that, time for rest and study.

In February 1919, a group of Bolshevik officials arrived in Koltsovo, among them the heads of the Kaluga *soviet*, the local *kombed*, and the local land department. According to a report on their visit, "they sought in heated debate to convince peasants that a commune would bring a new life based on social principles and a just order." They also pledged that "nobody will be compelled to join by force." On the tenth, the "First Workers' Agricultural Commune" was duly inaugurated (when Lenin died in 1924 it adopted his patronymic, Ilyich, as its name).

There was not a single local peasant among the commune's founding members. The initial *kommunary* were several outsiders and a few former villagers who had left to work in Tula and Moscow, as well as two widows with their children. The chairman was a veteran revolutionary from Moscow, a printer named

Alexander Vasilievich Lebedev, who was described in newspaper reports of the time as "the soul of the collective; an energetic, fair, politically literate person with prerevolutionary membership in the Party." Lebedev wrote a charter for the commune and, true to the time-honored tradition of the Russian radical, died soon afterward of consumption.

The *kommunary* moved into the Osorgin house, hoisted the mandatory Red propaganda placards ("All to the War with Kolchak!"), and set about recovering the Osorgins' equipment, horses, and cattle that had been appropriated by the "committee"—which was now condemned by the Bolsheviks as reactionary. Soon the *kommunary* had 300 acres under cultivation, about a hundred head of cattle, six sows, and poultry. Like the industrial laborers they were meant to emulate (and unlike the peasants), they tallied their labor in money and man-hours. For a while, the commune had the only elementary school in the village.

The commune was supposed to become the model for the village. In fact, villagers viewed their new neighbors as carpetbaggers and neo-*barins* out to grab the best land and cattle. The resentment was so high that despite the abundance of rooms in the old Osorgin house, all members of the new commune slept together in two rooms, the men taking turns standing guard with loaded rifles. On May 1, 1923, the main part of the manor burned down. The Soviets automatically blamed former landowners and *kulaks,* but everyone else believed the house was torched by villagers while the *kommunary* were out celebrating May Day. Now only the two wings and their "English" towers remained. The commune moved into one wing and gave the other to the local branch of the Komsomol for a "People's House."

In March 1919, commissars from Kaluga organized a meeting with peasants in a neighboring district, newly christened Karl-Marx Volost. A report has survived:

> The meeting was at 20:00 hours. *Kulaks* yelled "Godless authority," "Out with Communists," "You get 1,500 each, give us bread, exploiters, then talk!" The speaker set as his goal to bolster the ranks of the poor and to squeeze out the *kulak*–White Guardist scum. He concluded his remarks by saying, "If the citizens of Karl-Marx Volost are thinking of setting up an independent republic, then the hand of the proletariat will not spare its enemies. The poor are obliged to chase wolves in sheep's clothing out of their midst." But nobody listened and they threw stones. It was hard to work. *Kulaks* crushed everything. Everywhere, everything was sabo-

taged. Students did not help, either. There was not a single Communist or sympathizer among the students.

Though there were no actual battles between Whites and Reds in the area of Koltsovo during the civil war, there was many a fierce struggle between the Bolsheviks and their foes. According to another report, "Often in the first years of Soviet power, there were instances of sabotage even from teachers and doctors, and in the beginning of 1918 some schools and clinics were not working because of them." On the railroad station in Ferzikovo, there is a memorial plaque to one Nikolai Ippolitovich Kolosov, "a Chekist and active participant in the battle for Soviet power, killed 19 May 1923 by enemies of the people." A book about the feats of the local Cheka—as the secret political police was originally known—said this Kolosov was followed out of Kaluga by a red-haired White Guard officer intent on killing him. When Kolosov tried to elude the officer by jumping off the train at Ferzikovo, the red-haired man came after him and gunned him down.

But the Bolsheviks persisted: "The construction [of socialism] continued: By fall, there were 23 communes, 87 state farms, 133 agricultural *artels* [cooperatives], and 62 *tovarishchestvos* [associations]" in the province.

However unpopular the commune was in the village, it ranked sufficiently high in Bolshevik circles to receive one of the first tractors distributed by the Soviet authorities. In 1924 there were only 117 tractors in all of Soviet Russia, so the selection of Koltsovo for one of them indicated that the First Workers' Agricultural Commune was highly regarded by the new regime.

The 20-horsepower Fordzon tractor that arrived in the summer of 1924 was the first internal-combustion engine of any sort to make an appearance at Koltsovo, and peasants gathered from all the surrounding villages for the event. Ivan Pyzhukhin and his wife, Mavra Nikiforovna, never forgot the day: "When we learned that they had brought a tractor, we all ran out into the street and surrounded it. Children touched it with their hands. When it began moving forward, old women began crossing themselves and muttering, 'Lord, take away this evil power.' "

The regional newspaper of the commune movement, *Kommuna*, splashed the news under a banner headline: "TRACTOR ARRIVES." The article stressed the advantages of communal ownership of such equipment: "Many began thinking how they might get a tractor, and how this was not expensive, since it could be paid for over five years, and the payments were easy for a village of fifty households."

"Graybeards with measuring sticks followed after the tractor measuring the width and depth of the furrow, and they wagged their heads in amazement and delight," the article continued. "A machine plowing? This was unseen and unheard of. That led to thoughts of collective farming."

The honor of becoming the first tractor operator fell to Vasily Mikhailovich Artamonov, the chairman of the commune. He kept careful records of the tractor's work. On October 24 and 25, for example, it was used to plow 99 *desiatins* (267 acres), to harrow 48 *desiatins* (130 acres), and to move 26,250 tons of freight.

What really gave the Communists a firm foothold in Koltsovo, however, was not the commune or the tractor, but the reorganization of the old two-room school that Mikhail Mikhailovich Osorgin so cherished into a teachers' training school, a *pedtekhnikum*. Already in 1920, the director of the school, Afanasy Matveyevich Popov, organized crash classes to prepare youths for the Liquidation of Illiteracy campaign, and in the summer of 1921 the school was formally

Students of the Karovo Pedtekhnikum. The director, Arkhangelsky, is at the center. Second from the left in the back row is Misha Tinyakov, who as a Cheka agent would send classmates to the Gulag and would search Mikhail Osorgin's home.

reorganized as the Karovo Pedtekhnikum (for some reason, it kept the name Karovo even after the village was renamed Koltsovo). What was left of the Osorgins' library was now taken over by the school.

The influence of the *pedtekhnikum* spread far beyond Koltsovo. "This was the cultural center for the whole *raion*," wrote Vasily Stepanovich Bocharov, one of the first graduates. "It was known far and wide. Each year, even when Soviet power was barely established in the village, the Karovo *pedtekhnikum* sent teachers to spread grammar, Soviet culture, and light to all the dark corners of the county and the province. In addition to raising the youths in the Soviet spirit, the teachers battled the darkness, ignorance, and illiteracy of the village, especially among women."

It is noteworthy that the heart of the new school was teachers who had taught there before the revolution, when it was a parish school, and who had been trained in seminaries. Popov, for example, had joined the staff before the revolution as a teacher of mathematics and church singing. Mikhail Mikhailovich Osorgin described him as "an urbanized peasant from Zhisdrinsk who finished the teachers' seminary in Smolensk." The Smolensk seminary was disbanded in 1905 as a hotbed of revolutionary activity, Osorgin noted, and Popov was regarded as suspect.

Graduates of the school whose letters I read all spoke glowingly of Popov as a champion of the new order. "He was devoted to Soviet power and instilled in us a love of labor, honesty, high moral behavior, love for the people, and patriotic feelings for the fatherland," wrote Nina Semyonova. Yet neither she nor anyone else thought it noteworthy that he was fired "at the request of students" in 1925 for using a school cart for his own needs (an inventory of school property listed 50 acres of arable land, two horses, two plows, two carts, a harrow, 14 kerosene lamps, 2,000 pounds of kerosene, and 12 boxes of matches). I chanced on the story of Popov's firing in a history of vocational education in Kaluga. The student who turned him in was the secretary of the Komsomol, Mikhail Tinyakov—the same Misha Tinyakov who graduated to become an NKVD interrogator.

Popov was replaced as director by Ivan Ivanovich Arkhangelsky, a priest's son who had graduated from the Kiev Theological Academy in 1910 and taught at a seminary in Kaluga before coming to Sergiyevskoye. One of Arkhangelsky's ten children wrote of him that he was fascinated by the theories of Ivan Pavlov, the physiologist of "Pavlov's dogs" fame who conditioned dogs to salivate at the expectation of food. Arkhangelsky once traveled all the way to Leningrad to meet Pavlov.

Spreading the new word was not easy. Arkhangelsky's daughter wrote that he had a rough time "in the difficult twenties, in conditions of breaking the old, of naked class struggle, when there existed the well-known distrust of the intelligentsia." And there was also basic survival to think of. One graduate recalled that breaks between classes lasted as long as it took the teacher to milk the cow and feed the chickens.

In the early years, students had to support themselves. This was one reason why most of the 130 original students were children of clergy or better-off peasants. It was only in 1924 that the school began granting stipends and paying "special attention to social selection."

The school was the only building of old Sergiyevskoye still in use when I arrived. Mikhail Mikhailovich had built it with brick salvaged after his barn burned down, and the *pedtekhnikum* had added a wing and a second floor in the 1920s with brick from the burned-out manor. When I was last there, in March 1995, it was still a rest base, or weekend retreat, for workers of the Kaluga Turbine Works, but with the withering of Soviet subsidies, the workers had stopped coming. It was clean and spacious, and I often took advantage of the director's invitation to stay the night.

On that last visit, I sat late into the night with my old Moscow mutt Ahmed in the one-room "museum" that Alexandra Nikitichna Trunin had set up in the old school, poring over musty piles of letters, poems, and fuzzy snapshots that she had amassed over the years. It was cold and silent, save for a mouse that emerged now and again to check on us, and an occasional outburst from the village dogs that would elicit a tentative "woof" from mine. A quarter-moon cast a thin light over the linden park, and I keenly felt the presence of all those who had lived here, whom I had come to know so well.

Alexandra Nikitichna had worked many years at the orphanage, and when it was closed down she stayed on at the rest base as the keeper of local lore, regaling workers with her stories. In the Soviet Union, virtually every organization—city, factory, ministry, school—had a "museum," one or more rooms where the history and the socialist achievements of the place could be displayed. When alumni of the old teacher-training school held a reunion in 1967, Alexandra Nikitichna decided to set up a museum, where her orphans and the village children could draw inspiration from the stories and achievements of their predecessors. She sent letters to all the graduates of the *pedtekhnikum* and orphanage she could locate, asking them to send their recollections and pictures. Many replied, and Alexandra Nikitichna set up a nice exhibit. Landscapes by Filip Golubkov, the local boy who discovered the tunnel entrance and became a professional artist, lined the walls, along with photographs of successful graduates and albums of letters, poems, and sketches. A mural on one wall depicted spaceships and cosmonauts, celebrating a visit to the area (though not actually to Koltsovo, nor anywhere near, really) by Yuri Gagarin, the first man in space.

The history of the old gentry was originally represented by a picture of an obscure mansion cut out of a magazine and an ideologically correct text about "social exploiters." But in a drawer, Alexandra Nikitichna kept some of the old Osorgin letters and photographs that had been discovered in the 1960s when workers were dismantling the chimney and found the urn hidden there. The discovery caused Alexandra Nikitichna no small trouble, she told me: The KGB heard about old tsarist-era letters circulating in the village and came around to check. "It didn't sound right when I told them they just fell out of the chimney,"

The one-room museum set up by Alexandra Nikitichna
Trunin at the school in Koltsovo. The paintings are by
Filip Golubkov.

she recalled. The letters disappeared, but after the collapse of the Soviet Union, Alexandra Nikitichna updated the exhibit about the past with photographs I contributed of the old mansion and park.

For long hours I sat there under a flickering lightbulb, surrounded by Golubkov's landscapes, poring over the crumbling albums, the photographs of jowly commissars with rows of ribbons on their ill-fitting suits and stern matrons with beehive hairdos and the same rows of ribbons on their heroic bosoms.

Little by little they came in focus. I could see those matrons and commissars in this same room as hungry, barefoot kids in homespun cotton smocks, taking turns shaping letters with beet juice in the single notebook. The poorest among them lived in chimneyless huts where disease and death stalked the squalor. It is difficult to fault those of them who found hope in the Bolshevik dream.

One was Fyodor Akimovich Glebov, or "Glebich," born in 1904, and a founding member of the first Komsomol cell. In 1922, aroused by celebrations marking the designation of the Komsomol as the patron of the Red fleet, he enlisted; he spent the next 58 years in the Baltic fleet. Among the ships on which he served was the *Aurora*, the warship that fired blanks at the Winter Palace in 1917 and stands to this day in the Neva River as a monument to the revolution (and now a rallying point for diehard Communists).

"I was born in a hut with icons in the corner and a calf as my neighbor," he wrote. "From childhood, they scared us with God and the devil, and when we asked if anyone had ever seen God, the policeman threatened us with jail. Many years have passed since then, Holy Russia is gone forever, and as for me, I have lived to see the Victory of Labor."

Another founding member of the Komsomol was Vasily Stepanovich Bocharov. He believed that the revolution rescued him from the wretched life of his parents, scratching a bare subsistence from the soil:

We had a large family, nine children, of whom I was the oldest. I saw and understood our poverty, and I wanted to help my father and mother improve our material situation. We lived in constant need. Our daily life was one of systematic shortages of food and occasional famine. Our old, small house was sunk up to its windows in mud because of its age and the weight of its many inhabitants (in winter they included goats, cows, and pigs). Half of it was taken up by the Russian stove and by benches and pens for young animals. We had no permanent place to sleep, only sacks of straw. Grandpa Daniil wheezed, and the stench of old harness, tanned skins, and tar filled the hut. The horribly heavy air and the systematic shortage of food undermined the health of both children and adults. Pale, with swollen stomachs, skinny arms and legs, in torn caftans, we emerged in early spring to gulp fresh air and bake in the sun.

All this led one to think about escaping poverty, and not about studying. When I was in the seventh grade, I decided to quit school and to become an apprentice under the cobbler Nikanor Timaryov in Shakhovo. I didn't tell my parents, and every day I pretended I was leaving for school with my schoolbag. Eventually the teacher came to our house to see if I was sick. Despite our poverty, my father did not agree with my decision and insisted that I finish the seventh grade and enter the *pedtekhnikum*.

. . . In June 1929, I received a certificate testifying that I had graduated from the *pedtekhnikum* and was qualified as an elementary-school teacher. You can understand my joy and pride! I, the son of a poor peasant, had become a teacher! This was possible only in our great Motherland, at whose head after the Great October Revolution stood the party of Lenin, the Communist Party!

The leader of the Komsomol, a figure who dominates all the records, was Filip Ivanovich Fomichev. It was he who formed the first Komsomol cell, as early as the fall of 1919, then the first detachment of Pioneers, the communist children's organization, then the first agricultural *artel* (cooperative), then the first *kolkhoz* (collective). It was he who led the assault on the Church and who organized every Communist celebration. There are people in the village who assert that Fomichev is at least partly responsible for the fact that not a single church was left open between Kaluga and Aleksin.

Like a Leninist sower, Fomichev scattered the mechanized speech of the new order in the old village: a log hut filled with furniture taken from the Osorgin house became a *nardom* (people's house), from which the *komsomol* (Communist union of youth) dispensed *agitprop* (agitation and propaganda), *likbez* (liquidation of illiteracy), and *proletkult* (proletarian culture). They organized talks and spectacles, held public newspaper readings, and published their own paper, *Na chistuyu vodu* (Toward open water). When the *nardom* burned down—or was torched—along with the Osorgin furniture, the Komsomoltsy moved into a wing of the old manor.

Fomichev was the star graduate and the last director of the *pedtekhnikum*. In 1930 he moved the school to Maloyaroslavets, closer to Moscow. From there he rose to become instructor in Marxism-Leninism and director of the Pedagogical Institute in the city of Orekhovo-Zuyevo. Until his death in 1980, he regularly churned out books and articles in the newspeak of his adopted religion. ("The most important condition of the victory of socialist construction was the annihilation by the Party of anti-Leninist opposition groupings—the Trotsky-Zinoviev bloc, the Right Capitulationists, the Nationalist-Deviationists—whose views were recognized as being incompatible with membership in the Communist Party.")

Sitting in the old school on that cold March night, I waded through Fomichev's memories and some verse, all in the mind-numbing idiom of the professional ideologue. I suspect he knew no other language; like many youths of the time, he went directly from illiteracy to Marxism. The old snapshots depict a jovial little Khrushchev, bald and pudgy, hugging, laughing, posing. I even found out that Fomichev was involved in a lifelong love triangle. In his youth he had loved Irina Zybina, but a more nimble classmate managed to nab the rising Communist star by subterfuge. For years thereafter he and Irina held regular trysts, of which his pragmatic wife was fully aware, and even supportive. In their old age, Filip and Irina were widowed almost simultaneously and tried, at last, to join their lives. But after a few days they returned to their separate homes, and they finished out their lives apart.

As Komsomol chief, Fomichev was a true zealot, banning dancing and even the wearing of rings at the Nardom. He strictly observed all the new Soviet holidays and campaigns: Days of the Paris Commune, Red Army Day, Red Navy Week, Air Force Assistance Week, Harvest Day, May Day, Front and Transport Week, Red Youth Week, Week of the Homeless Child, International Week of the Child, Lumber Day, Day of Protest Against the Killing of V. V. Vorovsky. . . .

One of the original Komsomol members recalled how such days were marked: "Usually two or three people were dispatched to a specific village with speeches and appropriate poems. They'd go in the evening, since people could be gathered only after the peasant working day. Not every village had a reading room. More often we gathered in the home of a peasant who had agreed to it in advance. Since they had no idea yet of radio (or of a *kolkhoz*), the people were relatively willing to listen to a living person."

A major local event in 1920 was the first village wedding ever held outside the church. The Komsomol weddings were businesslike and brief, as befitted the vanguard of scientific materialism. One of the women so wed was Evdokiya Timofeyevna Pokrovsky. "The wedding consisted of signing a book and returning to the dormitory. Anything more was regarded as 'vestiges of capitalism,' " she recalled. Furthermore, she said that in ten years of marriage, she learned only vague details of her husband's past, and he of hers. "Those were years when it was not considered proper to talk of the past. I never asked about his, and I don't think he ever asked about mine. In general, there was not much communication between couples."

You could also learn things you did not want to know. Evdokiya Timofeyevna's maiden name was Khokhlov, and a peasant couple of that name had been exiled from the village as enemies of the people. Her husband, Konstantin Ilyich Pokrovsky, was even worse: he was the son of the last subdeacon at Sergiyevskoye, and so by definition a "class enemy."

In the first postrevolutionary years, the greatest danger was not from the political police but from the older peasants, who viewed the Communists and the Komsomol as godless parasites who threatened traditional village ways and ethics.

"It was hard work, especially with village women, to pry them away from their looms in the evening," recalled Bocharov. "If they came, it was not without threats from their husbands. Our first talks with young girls also produced no results. They submitted to their stern mothers, who saw their daughters as future brides with large trunks of cotton, competent in housework and field work; that is, ready for family life."

The first three girls who joined made it a condition that their membership be kept secret from their parents. When they came to meetings they told their parents they were going to a dance. "But the secret could not be kept for long. The parents found out and punished the daughters, and talked sternly to us," Bocharov recalled. Another new female member was grabbed during a spectacle in a village and peasants cut off her braid.

In its first year, the Koltsovo Komsomol cell held twelve meetings and seven conferences, as well as fifteen gatherings in other villages. Bocharov wrote: "We began our work studying the Program and Rules of the Komsomol and the speech of V. I. Lenin at the Third Congress of the Komsomol, on 6 Oct. 1920, 'The Tasks of the Unions of Youth.' One thing that entered the heart of each of us especially clearly was where V. I. Lenin said: '. . . every day in any village and in any city, the youth resolve practical and other tasks through common labor, even the smallest, most basic tasks' (Lenin 41, p. 318)."

Program, rules, tasks; the military discipline of the language, the cells, and political bureaus; the official-sounding committees, *soviets*, congresses, and plenums—all this had the appeal of order. It is said that Russians compensate for the severity of their laws by disregarding them. The opposite is also true—that Russians compensate for their proclivity to anarchy by forever seeking regimentation. I have known more than one Russian driver to barrel recklessly through a red light and then curse the police for not being there to stop him.

The "Time of Troubles" that preceded the accession of the Romanov dynasty was a strong factor in the sweeping efforts of Peter the Great to impose a military order on his subjects. He graded all civil, military, and court officials in 14 ranks, each with its honorific, uniform, and privileges. A gentleman who had no rank or uniform was by definition either a foreigner or in disgrace. Succeeding emperors and empresses continued to regard the military as the image of perfect organization, and each of them spent considerable time designing new uniforms and drilling troops. Peter III did his soldiers up in Prussian dress, Alexander III in native Russian garb; the last emperor, Nicholas II, wore civilian garb only when he traveled "incognito" to Germany to take the waters, and then reluctantly.

The dream of regimenting Russia's chaos was transferred to the Soviets, who quickly abandoned their revolutionary affectations of egalitarianism and permissiveness and redoubled the search for martial order. Military imagery came to pervade their system: A central "command economy" was imposed; workers were formed into "brigades"; pensioners were "veterans of labor"; harvests were "campaigns." Uniforms, ranks, medals, and titles proliferated beyond the wildest dreams of the tsars. But in the end, the chaos always reasserted itself. Today Russia is once again plunged into lawlessness, with crime syndicates peddling raw materials, generals smuggling weapons, and former Communist apparatchiks "privatizing" whatever they can.

But after the chaos of a crumbling monarchy, disastrous wars, and revolution, the Komsomol stalwarts in the village genuinely believed that they were the chosen bearers of order, enlightenment, and freedom. Many recalled with especial excitement the campaign against illiteracy. "It was enough to see how our mamas and papas, our older sisters and brothers, painstakingly shaped letters, then syllables, then words on the blackboard," wrote Bocharov. "Their desire, their determination showed good results. At the end, we gave each a certificate showing that they had attended a *likbezpunkt* [illiteracy liquidation point]. What pride and joy it was when somebody who had been illiterate or semiliterate had a newspaper or magazine in his hands!"

Besides, it was not all Lenin and *likbez*. Many alumni recalled the theater group, led by an old Bolshevik from the commune, Elena Konstantinovna

Markevich, who also supervised the Political Enlightenment Circle. The students put on plays by Ostrovsky, Gogol, and Pushkin.

Fomichev's stricture against dancing in the Nardom did not apply in the school. There, recalled Glebov, "we danced the waltz, the polka, the cracovienne, the karapet-two-step, and, of course, our Russian dances, with concertinas and accordions, all led by the teacher Lidya Nikolayevna Vatolin" (one of the early Communist activists at the school, and a niece of the last parish priest, Father Sergei Vatolin).

There were other tasks, however, to which the alumni alluded with cautious brevity. In one letter Glebov noted that one of the duties of the Komsomol was to "help the military in the battle against deserters, against people who ran from the front in the civil war." What that entailed he did not say, but I know that deserters hid in the caves on Stone Mountain, and I suspect the Komsomol youths informed on them.

The Komsomol also helped Soviet authorities "correctly apply tax policies, aiming their point against the *kulaks*." Again there are no details, but the image of young zealots shaking down resisting old peasants comes readily to mind.

Bocharov noted in another letter that several village youths served as "Chonovtsy." The title derives from Chasti Osobovo Naznacheniya, "Units of Special Designation," which were formed "to struggle with internal counter-revolution." One Chonovets was Andrei Gavrilovich Zakharov, who helped Fomichev organize his institute and died in the last days of the Second World War. I'm sure Mikhail Tinyakov was another. But how many others were there? And how many denunciations and secret reports did that "struggle" entail?

When Lenin died, the students were genuinely grief-stricken, as was much of the nation. "I remember that cold January day in 1924 when we were told of the death of V. I. Lenin," wrote Bocharov. "We were shaken by the tragic news. I will never forget it. The memorial meeting filled the People's House to capacity. A year later, a delegation of students from the Komsomol and the school went to Moscow for the funeral of V. I. Lenin, led by Nikolai Shmanenkov, now professor and academician."

After hearing of Lenin's death, Filip Golubkov stayed up all night painting a portrait of Lenin to display in mourning in the People's House. The painting came out quite well, and Golubkov found his calling. He went on to attend Igor Grabar's renowned art academy in Moscow and became a leading iconographer of Lenin, Stalin, and other Soviet leaders. His *First Leaflet*, showing a young Lenin presiding over the preparation of a propaganda flyer, is included in the

*Students from the Koltsovo Pedtekhnikum visit Lenin's
mausoleum on Red Square in Moscow on the first
anniversary of his death.*

permanent collection of the Lenin Museum in Moscow, and his *Lenin and Wells*
was presented by Nikita Khrushchev to Hungarian leaders during the first
Soviet-Hungarian meeting after Moscow crushed the Hungarian uprising of
1956. What the Hungarians really thought of the gift can only be guessed at, but
a photograph of Khrushchev with Golubkov's painting and a gaggle of Hungarian commissars, published in *Pravda*, is proudly displayed in Koltsovo.

By the time I met Golubkov in his Moscow studio—a vast room with 16-
foot-high ceilings that testified to his former prestige—he was 80, the Soviet
Union had collapsed, and the demand for his Soviet icons had all but vanished.
"Not even the French buy them any more," he groused, leaving me to wonder
about the vagaries of French tastes. The floor of the studio was lined with studies for paintings of Lenin and Stalin (there were strict iconographic rules for
portraits of the leaders, and every project required approval from a special
committee). Many paintings had scenes of people adulating the leader, in which
Golubkov always included his wife or his daughter. A hearty man who dressed
in Levi's and Western shirts sent to him from America by his daughter, who

married a Jewish emigrant and worked as an artist in New York City, Golubkov became a good friend, and he gave me two lovely pastel sketches of the Oka that he had made in his youth.

Golubkov made no effort to romanticize his past. His father, Ivan, was one of the first villagers to buy his own plot of land, by the river, and there he worked from dawn to dusk, driving his family mercilessly to do the same and beating them when they fell behind. On market days, Ivan drank. He would return from town with vodka, chase his wife and daughter out of the house, and fill his first glass. But it was considered bad form for a peasant to drink alone, so if no one else was around he would sit eight-year-old Filip down across from him and make the boy take a sip every time he downed a glass. The vodka eventually killed Ivan, as it had killed his father and his father's father before him. It nearly killed Filip, but he escaped in time.

Anxious to increase his family, and thereby his labor force, Ivan Golubkov compelled his eldest son, also named Ivan, to marry young (women did the milking, haying, weaving, harvesting, and many other chores). But young Ivan soon fled to work in a city, leaving his teenage bride and an infant son behind. They stayed on in the village, and the boy grew up to be the Mikhail Ivanovich Golubkov who, as village council chairman, told the KGB in 1985 that it was not wise to let an inquiring reporter visit the village, and so kept me away another five years.

Young Filip was raised largely by his remaining brother, Sergei. "Seryozha had been baptized by one of the *pomeshchiki,* and everyone used to say how lucky he was," Filip recalled. "He was handsome, he was everybody's friend, he did everything for me. He wanted to become a teacher, but Uspensky, who was in charge of studies at the school, lured him into the organs. Seryozha was sent out in the collectivization drive, but what he saw filled him with horror. He wrote to the Central Committee that this was wrong. On March 8, 1932, they told us he shot himself. Of course, *they* killed him, the bastards."

Golubkov remembered the campaign against the *kulaks* at Koltsovo. "But we had no *kulaks.* Just babblers, who talked against Soviet power. Those were the ones they threw out." He remembered, too, how the church was robbed of icons and valuables one night while he and Tikhon Kuznetsov, a friend from the village, secretly watched, too scared to do anything. "Afterward, Fomichev took it apart brick-by-brick, the son of a bitch. He dismantled and drank, dismantled and drank."

With his brother gone, Filip quit the village. He worked for a while on the railroads, then entered the art institute in Moscow. He spent the war in Central

Asia at a studio producing inspiring tableaux for the army, then moved to Moscow. And he drank. There were times in his life, Alexandra Nikitichna told me, such as after the death of his first wife, when friends thought he was trying to drink himself to death.

"It wasn't hard. If we needed booze, I'd quickly do a couple of Stalins and go to some *kolkhoz*. Let them try to say no! The sale was enough to drink a whole week."

Yet Golubkov was not a cynic. His life paralleled that of the Soviet state, and the Lenin he painted really was his hero. "I tell you, Lenin and Marx were not some adventurers. This was a true historical movement. Sorry, I'm not a propagandist. There were others who also said that the world must change, and I suppose it would have changed gradually, if not for the petty cheats who took over and failed.

"Only Lenin could have turned such a huge machine upside down. How can I say he was a louse? I consider him one of the smartest men in history. He didn't do it for a career, like the others. Stalin never understood Lenin. He tried to hasten history by force, but he was not suitable for a new page of history. How can you create Communism by force? That's how it perished."

12

On the Path to Communism

I think Filip Golubkov was right: Lenin did turn the huge machine of Russia upside down, and history cannot be hastened by force.

Peasants who had been held for ages as chattel and cannon fodder could easily identify with the slogans of the revolution: land to the people; out with merchants, landowners, and officers; a pox on the state and foreign wars. But that same heritage was woefully unsuitable for creating a modern state. Long segregated from the political and economic life of their nation, the peasants equated authority with force, and survival with dissembling. Living at the mercy of a fickle climate and capricious masters, they put their faith in wonder-working icons and a mythical father-tsar, not in law or government officials. What loyalty they had was to family and village. Their only constant was the land and its yield, which had to be shared according to need. In this zero-sum universe, he who had too little was due more, and he who grabbed too much was denying it to others.

These were tactics evolved for survival under serfdom, not for being masters of their own fate. "The absence of inner discipline and respect for law required order to be imposed from the outside," wrote Richard Pipes in his landmark study of the revolution and its aftermath. "When despotism ceased to be viable, anarchy ensued; and once anarchy had run its course, it inevitably gave rise to a new despotism."

So it was that the unnatural union of a utopian ideology and the backward village gave rise to the world's first true police state.

Will despotism return? There is something drearily familiar in the failure of the basic institutions of democracy to take root in Russia since the collapse of Communism—whether it be the legislature, the Constitutional Court, or the presidency—and in the constant power struggles at all levels of government. The old village instincts still run deep: many Russians still look upon private ownership of land with hostility and distrust, on those who amass riches as bandits, and on the law as an arbitrary instrument of power. More and more, Russians are yearning for a strong hand at the helm.

If the heritage of the village complicated the creation of a modern state in the new Soviet Union, the ideology that seized power ensured that it would fail. The Bolsheviks were never interested in simply replacing one regime with another, or just changing the economic system, much less introducing democracy. Their goal from the outset was nothing less than to create an entirely new system of social and economic relationships—virtually a new world. It was an ambition of dazzling arrogance and delusion, and it required that the old be utterly uprooted and destroyed. That meant, first of all, religion.

The struggle against religion reached Kaluga within weeks of the October revolution. In February 1918, a commissar was appointed to monitor the venerable St. Tikhon Pustyn monastery, outside Kaluga, and on October 11, a year after the revolution, the Kaluga Bolsheviks ordered the monastery shut down altogether, along with a convent in Dugna.

By chance, Kaluga was the first provincial city I visited when I first came to the Soviet Union, in 1980, so it was there I first looked upon the dismal landscape of an old Russian city after seventy years of systematic defilement by the Communists. Trees and chimneys sprouted from battered belfries, and rusted factories peered through crumbling stretches of ancient monastic walls, all ringed by the soulless, unkempt tenements of the Soviet era. Only one church was left open in Kaluga, none in the surrounding villages. Perhaps 650 churches had been excessive, but why such wanton destruction of everything that had charm or soul?

The campaign against religion was ruthless. The popular and visionary Patriarch Tikhon, who had served many years as a bishop in America and was elected to the newly restored patriarchal throne of the Russian Orthodox Church in 1917, died in 1925 while under house arrest—possibly killed by the Bolsheviks. Tens of thousands of priests, bishops, and believers perished in the Gulag, and the Communists backed off only when the Second World War broke out and they needed all the support they could muster, including the patriotic backing of the Church.

But the religion that the Communists permitted thereafter was a shell. A small number of ill-trained priests, ministers, imams, and rabbis were permitted to "serve their cults" within the confines of a handful of temples, but never to preach, teach, do humanitarian work, or otherwise minister to their faithful. My memories of church services in my first years in Moscow are of magnificent choirs and richly bearded clerics in glittering vestments, but I usually went away with the same melancholy feeling I get from art museums. Just as a painting pinned to a cream-colored wall in the sterile air of a museum seems stripped of soul and life, so those church services seemed no more than elaborate pantomimes.

In 1925, Filip Fomichev, the leading village Bolshevik, decided to attack the very heart of village piety, the feast of Easter. A half century later, one of Fomichev's comrades in the campaign, Vasily Stepanovich Bocharov, wrote a history of what happened to deposit for posterity in the Koltsovo museum. Even after so many years and so much suffering, that long-past spring was still vivid for Bocharov when he penned his report.

For the Komsomol, the war on "the opiate of the people" was a central duty. On all major holy days, and especially on Easter, the Komsomol cell in Koltsovo organized special antireligious shows and lectures. Now, Bocharov recounted, Fomichev decided to escalate the struggle:

> One night before Easter of 1925 we decided at our Komsomol gathering to hold an antireligious carnival on Easter night. This idea came, as usual, from Filip Fomichev. We began thorough preparations. Since the nights were still dark, we decided to prepare torches. We took old galoshes and rags and soaked them in oil for several days. They burned long and bright. The chairman of the commune, Vasily Mikhailovich Artamonov, let us use a horse and carriage. We also prepared our improvised "clergy"—a "pope" (Sergei Ermolkov), a "deac" (Alyosha Fomichev), and a "subdeac" (Seryozha Makarov). We found some old priest's caps and cassocks (the watchman at the church, Uncle Alexei, helped us, giving us some old stuff). On the night before Easter, we had lectures at the People's House on the "Sources of Easter" by one of the teachers at the school, Evgeny

Vasilievich Baranov, and we showed pictures through the projector; then we had a show, followed by singing and dancing. The People's House was full of youths; there were also some adults, and even old-timers. The evening was widely advertised, but we kept the carnival a secret. The evening was a success.

When the clock showed midnight, the church bells began ringing, summoning people to the Easter midnight service. We began our procession from the People's House, following the alleys through the park to the church square. We put our "pope," "deac," and "subdeac" on the wagon, with vodka bottles and glasses in their hands as symbols of the feast, then we lit our torches and began singing antireligious ditties. Our scouts reported that a group of men armed with sticks and stones was waiting for us behind the church fence to block us from entering the gates. We decided that a clash would be of no use to either side, so after standing and singing next to the fence we returned.

News of the carnival spread throughout the surrounding villages. The parents of the participants took it very badly. Some youths were punished physically for such an unheard-of audacity. But the battle spirit of the Komsomoltsy was not broken.

The Komsomoltsy were not finished. The custom was for the clergy to march in procession through the village with the icon of the Resurrection, stopping at every house to bestow a blessing and receive a bit of Easter fare, including a dollop of vodka. But Filip Fomichev and Vasily Bocharov had managed to prevail upon their parents to keep the priest out of their houses. The boycott was a horrible shock. "Our parents fell out with the priest and believing villagers," Bocharov wrote.

But they survived the judgments. The battle with religious prejudice had begun. The ice was moving. The authority of the clergy was undermined. After the death of the old priest, Sergei Vatolin, our parish was sent one of the so-called red popes (they were called "clipped" for wearing short hair). They were indifferent to their duties and rites, and hastened the fall of the Church's authority.

. . . Of course, our carnival night and our refusal to receive the icon and the priest in our houses was not heroism. But it brought doubts about the usefulness of religion into the heads of believers. . . . Did the Komsomol and Communism lose authority that night? No, and again, no. Our audacity and decisiveness filled us with new strength and boosted the authority of the Komsomol among youths, adults, and the old. In '25 this was a major achievement.

As Bocharov suggests, the deliberate sacrilege on the most sacred night of the year must have been an enormous shock in Koltsovo and the surrounding villages. "There never was, and never will be, anything better than Easter at Sergiyevskoye," Georgy Osorgin would write from his prison cell, recalling what to him was the very soul and spirit of the old order. This was as true for the parents of the Bocharovs and Fomichevs as for the Osorgins. Easter was the Resurrection, the promise of eternal life, the triumph over death and the long, bitter winter. Raised in the village, in a log house with a red votive light flickering reassuringly before the icon through the night, nourished from infancy on catechism and the chants of the Church, Fomichev and Bocharov knew full well that to defile Easter was to deal a terrible blow to the entire universe of their mothers and fathers. In his old age and nearly blind, Bocharov still seemed awed and slightly troubled by his daring.

It was over the Church, too, that the villagers of Koltsovo made their last recorded stand against the Communists. That was in early 1930, when the Bolsheviks declared an all-out campaign to collectivize agriculture and crush the last resistance among peasants.

On the last day of 1929, the local Communist Party organization, following Moscow's lead, declared it "imperative" to collectivize 60 percent of the peasant holdings within a year, and the entire *raion* within two years. January 15, 1930, was proclaimed the "Day of Mass Collectivization," and the party called on all "social activists, *kolkhozniks,* hired laborers, *bednyaki,* and the best *srednyaki*" to join in the campaign.

Filip Fomichev needed no summons. Already in 1929 he had drawn the curtain on the First Workers' Agricultural Commune and merged it into a new *selkhozartel,* an early version of the collective farm, named Day of Harvest and Collectivization.

But the resistance proved unexpectedly vicious. A report from Koltsovo at the time said that "*kulaks* and prosperous elements are waging a fierce battle to destroy the *kolkhoz.* The initiator of the poisoning is the wife of the *kulak* Khokhlov. Party and Komsomol cells must take full leadership of this *kolkhoz.*"

In the nearby village of Ladygino, only 8 of the 63 households signed up. "The brake in Ladygino, in addition to provocateurs, is bad preparatory work," the Party reported. "Peasants do not have the most elementary idea of what a *kolkhoz* is. The *bednyaki* are not taking the initiative, and in fact sometimes resist collectivization. At a meeting on February 8, the *bednyachka* Kosichkina actively spoke out against the *kolkhoz*."

In naming Kosichkina in Ladygino and Khokhlov in Koltsovo, the Communists were already manifesting a major tool of repression—identifying an individual or group as the foe. There was an ideological reason for this: the party and its historical mission could not be wrong or unpopular, so if there were any glitches, there had to be someone deliberately sabotaging its efforts—someone who could be publicly identified and eliminated. The logic would blossom into brutal purges and the creation of the greatest system of repression the world had ever known.

The fact was that the poor peasants, so often betrayed in the past, simply refused to be the first to join the collective. "There were endless provocations. Some said old people would be killed in the *kolkhoz*. Others said, 'What if war begins and the rulers change? What will we do then?' Others: 'Will they let us pray in the *kolkhoz*?' " Subsequent history demonstrated that these reservations were fully justified, but they did little good. The Communist response was to exile seven *"kulak"* households and to confiscate their property.

To the Communists' surprise and delight, the women of one village did rush to join the collective farm (peasant men spent their winters working in towns and cities, so these early campaigners dealt largely with women). In early February, the village of Vislyayevo, across the river from Koltsovo, proudly reported that 94.5 percent of the peasants there had joined the *kolkhoz*. Two weeks later, all the women asked to resign. It turned out that a unit of the Red Army had been stationed in Vislyayevo in early February, and the women had believed they would be shot if they resisted joining. As soon as the soldiers moved on, they declared: "They say in the papers that the *kolkhoz* is voluntary, so count us out, and stop trying to convince us. The men will leave for seasonal work, we will argue and fight, and nothing will come of it." There was nothing left for the Party to do but to find a scapegoat. The ringleader, they declared, was one Efrosiya Bespalova, who "acted on instructions from petty-bourgeois representatives of peasant seasonal workers."

The campaign continued, but so did the resistance. With the approach of the sowing season, the Party noted with alarm that "preparations for spring field work passed in conditions of acute class struggle, including anticollectivization demonstrations." Koltsovo, where students of the *pedtekhnikum* actively backed collectivization, had some of the angriest confrontations, including a showdown that nearly came to bloodshed when Fomichev tried to bunch 13 villages in a single *kolkhoz* and, far more provocatively, tried to close down the church. It was the last recorded stand of the Koltsovo peasants.

I learned about the incident from one of Fomichev's letters in the museum. The language is smug Sovietese, but tension seethes in every line:

> Great successes in the whole of collectivization were accompanied by some mistakes and miscalculations, which found their expression in the winter–spring period of 1930 in Koltsovo in the form of attempts to create a united *kolkhoz* of 13 villages, and to close, with the agreement of an absolute majority of peasants, the Koltsovo church, on whose cross some hothead had hung a red flag (it was Krylov, a department head at the pedagogical *tekhnikum*).

There it was again: the Party and its Leninist strategy were always right and always supported by the people, but some politically unripe individuals made "mistakes." Fomichev never made mistakes: he knew that the key to survival was to finger a scapegoat before someone fingered you.

> . . . *Kulaks* tried to use these distortions of the Party line to organize peasants against the collective. In February 1930, a large number of women from surrounding villages gathered at the ringing of the large bell. A group of men quickly followed, watching how Communists and representatives of Soviet power would behave toward the women who came to this gathering, which was organized by *kulaks*.
>
> Communists, Komsomoltsy, teachers from the pedagogical *tekhnikum* and from the seven-year school showed courage and restraint. They did not lose control over themselves, but insistently and convincingly explained to the women that they will compel those who put the red flag on the cross to take it down, and urged them to calmly return home. They worked also with the men, telling them that there would be no administrative measures taken against the women.

The women dispersed, the flag was taken off the cross, the church was reopened, and Fomichev proclaimed that "the conviction of Communists, Komsomol, and working peasants won out as a result of its correctness." His letter is a classic example of the retrospective reinterpretation of history, which in fact Fomichev did for a living as a professional ideologue.

Fomichev was smart to back off in time. Immediately after the incident he describes, just as the resistance to collectivization was about to break into open warfare, Stalin stepped in. On March 2, 1930, *Pravda* printed an article by the Great Leader titled "Dizzy with Success," in which he accused overzealous Party officials of pushing collectivization too fast, of "administrative willfulness," "violating revolutionary legality," and other excessive measures that "caused the political situation in the country to deteriorate, threatening the alliance of workers and peasants."

It was another typical Soviet retreat—blaming underlings for an ill-conceived policy. Many a local commissar who had loyally undertaken to collectivize at full tilt was left in the lurch. Many of them had not yet learned in 1930 that survival in such situations required immediate and incessant groveling. Records of a Party meeting in Kaluga at the time note: "The article of I. V. Stalin was met with hostility from individual members of the Party. Comments were heard to the effect that we are retreating." I wonder how many of these "individual members" survived the purges.

Fomichev, of course, was not among the critics. Though he was obviously at the forefront of the ill-fated attempt to form a united *kolkhoz* and to close the church, he was sufficiently cunning—"politically mature," in Sovietese—to catch Stalin's drift in time, to reverse his position 180 degrees, and to throw the unfortunate Krylov (who had hung the flag on the bell tower) to the wolves.

In Koltsovo, as across the Soviet Union, Stalin's article triggered an immediate and massive exodus from the collectives. Four weeks after it appeared, only five households remained in the Koltsovo *kolkhoz*. Many others in the region were disbanded. But the same plenum in Kaluga that reported the resistance of "individual members" also concluded with a resolution expressing "total conviction that decisively crushing and eliminating all mistakes and distortions, organizing the poor and middle-level peasant masses, consolidating successes, rebuffing all right-opportunist attitudes and leftist excesses, and making further advances against the *kulaks,* the *raipartorg* [regional Party organizer] will achieve a further increase in the collective movement on the basis of total collectivization and the liquidation of the *kulaks* as a class."

And that's exactly what happened. When the campaign resumed, "mistakes" and "distortions" were duly eliminated, leftist and rightist "excesses" were rebuffed, *kulaks* were liquidated, all resistance to collectivization was crushed, and Stalin emerged as the unchallenged master of the Soviet empire. The Koltsovo church was soon closed for good. If there was resistance this time, it was not recorded or remembered.

Fomichev left Koltsovo soon after the confrontation, taking the *pedtekhnikum* with him to Maloyaroslavets. The official explanation was that he wanted to transfer the school to a more substantial town and nearer Moscow, but I suspect he left because he had to. It was one thing, in that great Russian expression, to hang noodles on the ears of Bolshevik commissars about "mistakes" and "distortions," another altogether to betray parents, neighbors, and comrades. Fomichev survived and flourished through Stalinism, the Terror, the war, and de-Stalinization, and his last letters before his death in 1980 reveal no doubts or regrets.

In 1967, on the fiftieth anniversary of the Russian Revolution, two of the most prominent graduates of the old Karovo Pedtekhnikum ran into each other at a conference. One was Filip Fomichev, by then director of the Pedagogical Institute at Orekhovo-Zuyevo, outside Moscow, and a professional ideologue. The other was Nikolai Alexandrovich Shmanenkov, who as a youth had led the delegation to Lenin's funeral, and who became the founder and director of the Scientific-Research Institute of the Physiology of Biotechnology and the Feeding of Farm Animals and a full member of the Academy of Agricultural Sciences.

Fomichev and Shmanenkov got to talking about the old days, and they decided to organize a reunion of alumni of the Karovo Pedtekhnikum. Senior Party members both, it was easy for them to track down surviving graduates through the "organs" and to print up invitations, which included a snippet of Fomichev's verse:

Proletariat of the world, unite!

Comrade Koltsovite! Remember our school
Back in those hungry 'twenties?
While studying you built the Komsomol
The guardian of our freedom and soviets.

Nadezhda Likhachev remembered how she and a group of other women arrived at the first reunion. After reaching the Ferzikovo station they hired a battered old taxi for the 8-mile trip to Koltsovo. "The road was rutted and muddy, and the driver cursed while we shrieked with delight at every view. When we saw the cross over the distant trees we all wept. Our youth had passed here."

Many of the old Komsomoltsy could barely recognize each other at first, but the gathering was a smashing success as the heavyset, gold-toothed veterans of wars, labor, and Soviet politics hugged, wept, recited poems, and reveled in memories of a youth spent on the beautiful Oka, in the selfless pursuit of

Graduates of the Koltsovo Pedtekhnikum at their
reunion in 1967.

progress. The old alumni told their war stories to the children in the orphanage and the village school; the local paper carried paeans to their accomplishments; the weather was splendid. It was all so good that the old Koltsovites held three more reunions, in 1968, 1970, and 1972, and then gathered in Moscow in 1987 on the hundredth anniversary of the school. By then their ranks were rapidly dwindling.

I read many recollections of that reunion, talked to a few surviving participants, and pored over many a fuzzy snapshot of heavyset men in loose blousons and stout women in floral-printed cotton smocks basking in the sunshine and camaraderie in their native fields. These were the flower children of the Soviet era, I thought, and Koltsovo was their modest Woodstock before the realities of war and repression came crashing in.

All of them were convinced that they had helped set the Soviet Union on a course of happiness and prosperity. "When those of us who are still alive meet these days, we say to each other that our youth was difficult but also wonderful, and necessary for the generations that will come after us," Nina Semyonova wrote confidently.

Many of them had done well in life. Shmanenkov and Fomichev were directors of institutes; Golubkov was a leading Soviet painter; Nina Semyonova was director of the Moskva Hotel in Moscow, where many Party officials stayed; Mikhail Gribanov was the Soviet ambassador to Norway; Zakhar Osipov, who as a kid used to harass the girls, was a major general in the political corps. Alexander Timarev was deputy head of the city council in Riga; Vasily Bocharov was director of a school in Barovsk and a decorated war veteran; Fyodor Glebov was a naval captain. Mitya Khokhlov, who as a schoolboy was nicknamed "Ryazan *baba*" because he liked to sew and knit, went on to earn a graduate degree in chemistry at Moscow University. Nadezhda Likhachev worked as a chemist at a KGB factory. Irina Denisova, who joined the Komsomol over the protests of her parents, was head of a children's library in Tula. Dmitry Rodionov, a retired army colonel who now raised gladioli at his house in a nearby village, produced a huge hybrid for the gathering, which he named "Karovo Reunion."

It was the august gathering that persuaded Alexandra Nikitichna Trunin to organize a museum at Koltsovo. "You have done a great deed, Alexandra Nikitichna," they proudly declared in a resolution when the museum began to take shape. "You have collected and preserved for the next generation our labors, our first steps in life in those distant, alarming, and dangerous years, when the finest young men and women of our generation died in combat with enemies of Soviet power. We will be deeply pleased if our humble deeds of those years come to serve as an example for Komsomoltsy of all generations. Let the methods be different, but the goal will always be the same, the path to Communism."

A noble sentiment indeed, except that it made no mention of those who stumbled or were pushed off that path. Here and there, in conversations and letters, I found their traces: Sergei Golubkov, who "shot himself" after protesting against collectivization; Misha Tinyakov, who rose high in the political police and disappeared in 1937; Nadezhda Likhacheva's brother and two brothers-in-law, sent off to concentration camps or killed. Even among those who lived to be honored at the reunion, there were a few with dark holes in their pasts, like Timofei Gavrilovich Zakharov, an original member of the Komsomol, who provided this biography:

Well, as for me, I studied in Koltsovo from '24 to '28, and finished with the second graduating class at the Pedtekhnikum. I was a member of the bureau of the Komsomol. I performed Komsomol work at the Petrovskoye Machine Building Factory, then in the Aleksin *raion* Komsomol. The TsK of the VKLSM [Komsomol Central Committee] sent me to Ivanovsky *oblast*, where I was chosen secretary of the Komsomol *raikom* [*raion* committee]. There I also worked as secretary of the *partkom* [Party committee]. After repression (1937–1956, Kolyma), I was rehabilitated by the TsK of the KPSS [Communist Party Central Committee]. Member of the KPSS from 1930, member of the Komsomol from 1925.

For ten years I worked on the River Amur and the River Zeya. I was often sent to KNR [North Korea] to work. Now I am a pensioner, chairman of the Party commission of the Leninsky *raion* in Izhevsk.

"After repression (1937–1956, Kolyma) . . ."! For 19 years, Zakharov was a *zek*, a political prisoner, in the most brutal camps of the Gulag. And after that he worked for ten years in the Far East, probably barred from returning to European Russia. Yet as a pensioner he was still proudly waving his Party card.

What kind of faith was that? What blind loyalty enabled these people to ignore the repression of their friends and relatives, to overlook all the horrors of collectivization and mass repression, and to remain such stalwart Communists?

I looked for an answer in my long afternoons with Nadezhda Sergeyevna Likhachev, the retired chemist and teacher who told me how Tinyakov interrogated her brother. She saw me on television one day and wrote me a letter about herself, and in the spring of 1994 we finally met at her home in Kaliningrad, the "space city" just north of Moscow. She was 86, energetic, sprightly, and enormously thrilled that someone was interested in her past.

The Likhachev family had been one of the most active in Koltsovo in the 1920s, two brothers and three sisters who made their mark in every cultural and social campaign. Four became teachers, one a doctor. The eldest, Alexander Likhachev, a teacher of economics and the author of several books, volunteered for the army on the day after the Germans invaded Russia and was one of the first Soviet soldiers to die. His brother Pavel served as a frontline doctor in the Finnish war and through the entire Second World War, including service in the battle of Stalingrad. After the war, he worked with the broken and the uprooted.

Ardent participants in all the activities of the *pedtekhnikum*, the Likhachevs for many years were barred from joining the Komsomol or the Party because their "social origins" were flawed: their father was a priest. Nadezhda Sergeyevna spoke of her father with love and pride. She described him as the beloved village pastor in Ilyinskoye, a village near Sergiyevskoye, and she showed me photographs of a handsome young man in beard and cassock, proudly posing with his large brood. Father Sergei died in 1914, at the age of 46, of tuberculosis, which he contracted while ministering to a dying nephew.

Nadezhda Sergeyevna had photographs of his funeral, with hundreds of griev-ing peasants, workers, and landowners gathered to bid him farewell.

In our conversations, I could find no conflict in Nadezhda Sergeyevna be-tween a happy childhood spent in church and a youth spent eagerly serving an ideology that denounced everything her father had stood for. In her old age she began attending church again, but even then she remained proud of the Party card she had finally received in 1952.

On one of my visits I asked Nadezhda Sergeyevna about repression in the 1920s and 1930s in Koltsovo. She thought and thought, but said she could not re-member any. I was dubious—there was not a corner of Soviet Russia that es-caped the Terror—but I thought there might be reasons for her "forgetfulness" and did not press the point. The next time I went to see her she was waiting right by the door, very excited. "Sergei Alexandrovich, how could I not remember?"

That was when she told me how Misha Tinyakov had arrested and interro-gated her brother-in-law. And there was more: Her brother Pavel, a doctor, was arrested in the Far East in 1937. He was released in 1939 when the Finnish war began and served as a frontline doctor throughout World War II. Pavel's brother-in-law, Isaac Markovich Vargaftik, a senior commissar in charge of grain procurement for all Russia after the revolution, and a Jew, disappeared without a trace in the purges of the early thirties. Her uncle, a priest in Malo-yaroslavets, was taken one day and vanished. . . .

I wondered how she could have forgotten all this. These were close relatives, people she had known well; she still had many photographs of them. Yet I be-lieve she really did not remember them the first time we spoke. She was old, and like so many of her peers, she had had to suppress whole categories of thoughts and memories in order to survive, filing them away in some inaccessible corner of her mind.

Arrests and disappearances were things that you did not talk about, not even at home. Nadezhda Sergeyevna said her brother Pavel never said a thing about his time in the Gulag, even to his own family. If an acquaintance or neighbor was arrested, people would murmur that he or she had "fallen ill," and every-body knew better than to ask how or why. You never knew if there was an in-former in the room, and even if there was none, there was no telling when someone might fall into "their" hands and be forced to talk. I heard innumer-able accounts of arrests and interrogations in my years in Moscow, and there were few who survived the ordeal of a KGB grilling without leaving behind something "they" could exploit—if not right away, then later, sometimes many years later.

But Nadezhda Sergeyevna had still another surprise in store for me. After graduating from the *pedtekhnikum*, she continued matter-of-factly, she worked first as a chemistry teacher and then as a chemist at a secret KGB plant in Moscow.

What?

"Oh, that's where they processed the cult paraphernalia taken from the churches. You know, icons, chalices, miters," she explained. Her job was to analyze the metal content before the confiscated church treasures were melted down. I was stunned that the KGB ran such a factory in the first place, but even more so that this loving daughter of a village priest had sat there dutifully analyzing items for destruction that she had been raised to hold sacred.

"It was our youth. We were convinced we were ushering in a better world!" she exclaimed earnestly. "The village awoke. We were very poor, but we went around the villages, raring to 'liquidate illiteracy.' We gave concerts, we were met with cheers, we tried to teach everybody. They were raring to learn: 'Give us knowledge,' they said. Study, study, study! This was our passion! We wanted to learn everything. The teachers never had to prod us, we had such enthusiasm!"

Yes, I can understand that; I can see the liberating power of learning, the giddy excitement of spreading enlightenment to the village, the thrill of serving progress and science. But when her brother was thrown in the Gulag for no reason; when her friend Isaac Vargaftik disappeared; when Misha Tinyakov, her classmate, exiled her brother-in-law for playing cards and threatened her as well; when her uncle was taken away forever; when her closest friends, the children of the miller Alexeyev, were thrown out of their house in the middle of the night as *kulaks* (a horror whose recollection made her cry 65 years later); when she herself was refused Communist Party membership because her father was a priest—how could she not doubt? Could she not see that the Bolsheviks had betrayed them all?

"No! The village did not fall asleep again!" the old woman cried. "Look, after the 1914 war, after the civil war, it was all destruction. We worked hard, we built a powerful state in just ten years! In the war it was all motherland, motherland, motherland!"

I knew that mantra by heart—the list of awesome achievements that so many Russians looked on with such pride: the incredible victory over Germany, the first man in space, the Olympic medals, the pinnacle of global power. . . . Never mind the cost: We did it!

But she knew full well—they all did—that these triumphs were tainted. "Ah, if only this had not happened," she said, pointing sadly to the volume of

Solzhenitsyn's *Gulag Archipelago* lying on her table, thinking back to the Var-gaftiks, her brother, all the millions of others who had fallen victim. "I know they did nothing wrong," she said quietly. "Why did it happen? It's terrible. It's inexplicable. People came to power with no conscience, no decency. They lost their honor. And now again it's back to hand-to-hand combat for power." She turned to a photograph of her late husband, a factory worker and lifelong Com-munist. "If he was here, he'd be so horrified! Ah, where have all the honest people gone?"

In the days I spent interviewing Nadezhda Sergeyevna, her daughter and her adult grandson often came to listen. Not trusting her memory, Nadezhda Sergeyevna prepared notes and documents for my every visit, and it struck me that her own family had never seen these albums and photographs, had never heard these memories. I was the first person outside her generation who had ever shown an interest in her life. As I prepared to leave after our last interview, she became very sad. "Tell me," she asked, "is there any chance you might need more?" "Of course I will," I said. Her face lit up: "Then I have something left to live for!"

* * *

Nadezhda Sergeyevna Likhachev, surrounded by her family. I'm on the left.

Dreams die hard, and those die hardest that exacted the heaviest cost. It is difficult for us to fathom what that generation which is now finishing its life in Russia endured: revolution, war, terror, purges, camps. I know no Russian over 70 who does not carry some terrible physical or emotional scar. Like all survivors of horrible ordeals and injustice, they need to believe there is a reason, an explanation, a lesson. Lev Kopelev, one of the great Russian dissidents (and the model for Rubin in Solzhenitsyn's *First Circle*), maintained his faith in the sanctity of the Communist cause through nine and a half years of the Gulag and for at least a decade beyond: "I stubbornly believed, wanted to believe, that the cruel baseness and dull heartlessness of our organs of state security, procurators, judges, and prison and camp officers, as well as the shameless lies of our press, official propaganda, and official literature—all were merely unnatural, irregular perversions," he wrote in his memoirs. Only when the people he most respected were arrested one by one did he finally—reluctantly and agonizingly—abandon his faith in Communism.

Among the people who came to the first Koltsovo reunion in 1967 was Nadezhda Likhacheva's elder sister Antonina, a modest retired teacher who also wrote poetry. When I told her I was doing a book on Koltsovo, she rummaged through a stack of crumbling albums and found a poem she had written after the reunion, her first visit to her childhood haunts. Unlike Fomichev's Soviet bombast or the smug reminiscences in Alexandra Nikitichna's museum, Antonina Sergeyevna's verse expressed the sadness that most of them probably shared:

> *Greetings, my birthplace! You see, I've come back*
> *After so many years have gone by.*
> *I ask you, my dearest, don't look at me sternly.*
> *I too have seen suffering and grief.*
> > *Open to me your embrace*
> > *Hold me, as gentle and tender*
> > *As when I was small, let me snuggle*
> > *As before to your breast.*
> *The path I have walked is honest and straight*
> *I've done nothing that you can reproach*
> *This is why now when I come back to you*
> *I dare be so bold and so calm.*
> > *How many winters have passed!*
> > *How much we both have endured!*

So many sorrows, and joys . . .
But tell me, how about you?

. . .

Now our autumn has come
In its beauty, everything's calm
The birds are preparing to leave
The cobwebs lie in the grass.
And now that I've seen you, my dear,
I too can depart.
My autumn is with me to stay.
Not that I'll ever forget . . .
Only forgive me, as keepsake
I've taken two poplars with roots.
There, in the place where I live now,
There by my window they'll grow.

Seventeenth Versta

Russia reveals her greatest charm in winter, on those rare days when the sky is clear and the low sun sends long shadows across the gilded snow. Walking out-doors on days like this, Russians pause to close their eyes and take a deep, rap-turous breath, as if the frosty air were a life-giving elixir. Mothers keep their heavily bundled children out-of-doors, convinced that it is impossible to catch cold as long as temperatures stay securely below freezing.

On such a day in February 1995, my wife and I and two Russian relatives drove out to Peredelkino, about 10 miles west of Moscow. We had been there often in our years in Moscow, to visit acquaintances in the celebrated writers' compound, to take visitors to Boris Pasternak's grave, or to ski in the lovely fields and forests. This time, we went to find the house where the Osorgins had spent their last years in Russia.

After their expulsion from Sergiyevskoye, the Osorgins lived for five years at the Samarin house outside Moscow. When that was expropriated in 1923, they moved into the modest nearby dacha put at their disposal by the parents of a child they tutored. Everyone called the house by the name of the nearby rail-road station, Seventeenth Versta, which was its distance from Moscow (about 12 miles). The Osorgins lived there eight years, until they left Russia in 1931. Soon after, Maxim Gorky secured the lovely environs, including the village of Peredelki (hence its new name, Peredelkino), to build dachas for Soviet writers, of whose newly formed union he was president.

Our companions on that winter day were Andrei Vladimirovich Trubetskoi and Ekaterina Mikhailovna Pertseva (nee Golitsyn)—Uncle Andrei and Aunt Katya, once we came to know them well. Both were distant relatives whose families had remained in the Soviet Union after the revolution and endured great suffering and pain. Many of their relatives and friends had vanished or suffered in the Gulag and World War II, and as "former people" (as the Soviets called their kind), they and their families were systematically humiliated, distrusted, and repressed throughout the first decades of Communist rule.

During our first stint in Moscow, from 1980 to 1986, my wife and I maintained a cautious distance from whatever Soviet relatives we were aware of. Most of them had endured too much to risk their tenuous security for a meeting with an American correspondent (and especially one occasionally lambasted in the Soviet press). We knew very little about them or their lives. In the first years after the revolution, Russians abroad maintained contact with relatives in the Soviet Union and sent them packages, but any links grew dangerous by the 1930s, and then impossible, and the lives of the emigrants and their former homeland diverged.

In a sense, we were returning to the place where our worlds had parted ways. Andrei's wife, Elena Vladimirovna Golitsyn, remembered coming out to Seventeenth Versta to take lessons from "Uncle Misha" Osorgin (as he grew older and more patriarchal, Mikhail Mikhailovich insisted that all young relatives address him as "uncle"). Aunt Katya Pertseva was another frequent visitor; her elder sister Lina married Georgy Osorgin and had lived with the Osorgins at Seventeenth Versta.

Aunt Katya, now 80, her head shaking with Parkinson's disease, was certain she could still find the Osorgin house. She led us through deep snow, between new houses, down slippery slopes, and through woods, and finally pointed at a wooden house on a large lot. The barking of a dog drew a woman to the door. She was delighted to meet us. Her grandparents had purchased the dacha after the Osorgins left in 1931, and she knew only that the former residents had gone abroad.

In the 1920s, the totalitarian ambitions of the Bolsheviks were still held in check by the lingering anarchic spirit of revolution and the freedoms of the New Economic Policy. In retrospect, the first decade after the revolution seems

remarkably permissive. These were years when Ilf and Petrov could still publish brilliant satires on Soviet life; when writers, artists, and musicians explored
brave new forms; when a measure of public debate was still possible. Theaters
and churches could still function, Russians could still mingle with foreigners,
the Samarins could still challenge the expropriation of their house in the courts,
Georgy could still sell the jewelry of the "former people," nightlife could still
be fun. Yet it was in these same years that searches and arrests began to come
ever more frequently, that informers were recruited in ever greater numbers,
that concentration camps were rapidly expanding and proliferating.

By the time the Osorgins settled at Seventeenth Versta in 1923, the family
was partly dispersed: the three eldest children, Mikhail, Sergei, and Sofia, had
already reached the West with their families. Mikhail Mikhailovich, Liza, and
their unmarried daughters, Maria and Tonia, earned a modest living giving
lessons. Georgy married Alexandra Mikhailovna (Lina) Golitsyn, a granddaughter of a liberal governor general of Moscow, in 1923 and worked as a middleman for "former people" who had to sell off the baubles of their former
life—the brooches, coins, and silverware that are now reappearing in such
surprising profusion in the flea markets of the Old Arbat and Izmailovo.
Juliana (Liana) Osorgin married Sergei Dimitrievich Samarin, a member of a
renowned family of prerevolutionary Slavophile intellectuals and politicians,
who owned Izmalkovo. A nanny who had worked many years for the Samarins
became governess to Stalin's daughter, Svetlana Alliluyeva, born in 1927, and
helped the Samarins and Osorgins by smuggling food to them.

In the beginning, the Osorgin home at Seventeenth Versta was always full.
Relatives and friends came regularly from Moscow to rest from the city, to court
the girls, and to draw on the wisdom and spirituality of Mikhail Mikhailovich.
One frequent visitor was Sergei Golitsyn, the brother of Georgy's wife, Lina,
and of our companion that day, Katya Pertseva. He was eight at the time of the
revolution, and in his memoirs, *Notes of a Survivor*, which were published in
1990, a year after his death, he included a moving description of the Osorgin
home:

> How many memories, dark and sad, bright and joyous, but always poetic,
> are linked for me with this house and the Osorgin family!
> . . . After skiing, we would get warm, and with our clothes still moist
> we would sit around the table, greedily eating noodles with sunflower oil
> and millet porridge, drinking carrot tea through chunks of sugar clenched
> in our teeth.

Then Uncle Misha would take his place on the soft divan and we would all fall quiet. He taught us catechism. For this, people were being persecuted. We were drawn by the romance of conspiracy. Uncle Misha talked passionately, trying to build in each of us a firm belief in God.

Music remained a central part of life at the Osorgin home. Golitsyn recalled that one frequent visitor was a famed professor of microbiology, named Barykin, who played the violin. He had been exiled as a Menshevik before the revolution, and Golitsyn remembered the passionate debates he would have with Mikhail Mikhailovich: "Uncle Misha was profoundly and philosophically religious, Barykin just as deeply and philosophically an atheist; the one would get all worked up, the other would calmly and logically hold his own. These debates did not affect their respect for each other."

Barykin's integrity proved to be his undoing. Soviet authorities offered him the use of inmates instead of expensive monkeys for his experiments in microbiology. He refused, was arrested, and disappeared.

It was a time when the "dictatorship of the proletariat" was identifying ever more enemies. There were the *kulaks,* peasants who dared work for themselves;

Liza Osorgin accompanying a guest at Seventeenth Versta, as drawn by Maria Osorgin.

then engineers, scholars, and white-collar workers, who were forever conspiring against socialism; then the "popes," as all clergymen were indiscriminately labeled, who spread superstition and hostile propaganda in their temples. Finally, there were the "former people"—the titled aristocrats, landowners, manufacturers, tsarist officers, and civil servants, who were deemed innate and mortal foes of the new order. Those who failed to leave in time after the revolution now found it increasingly hard to get out; either they lacked the money to buy their way out, or a person dear to them was in prison and they did not want to leave him or her behind.

Someone was always getting arrested. One of the favored techniques of the fledgling political police, initially known as the Cheka, was the *zasada,* or ambush. Plainclothesmen would burst into a suspect apartment and grab everyone there, and then would stay and nab anybody else who came by. Most people thus detained were eventually released, but thereafter they were marked.

It was possible in the early years to appeal to the International Red Cross or to senior commissars for help. Officials who were amenable to such appeals were known as *ruchnye,* "tame ones." "Go to Maria Ivanovna," the relatives of someone who had fallen prey to the political police would be advised. "She has a *ruchnoi* Communist." One extraordinary woman who extended considerable help to the Osorgins and to many others was Ekaterina Pavlovna Peshkova, head of the Political Red Cross and the wife of the writer Maxim Gorky. Peshkova tirelessly used her husband's standing with Stalin to extract people caught in the Cheka's spreading nets.

Georgy Osorgin was first snared on September 12, 1921, when Cheka agents swarmed over his aunt Olga Trubetskoi's apartment in Moscow. By then, people in Moscow had learned to write to their relatives abroad in code. An arrest was an illness; a prison was a hospital. "Nobody knows the condition of the ailing Georgy, who is in the same hospital where Seryozha Trub. was initially held," Georgy's aunt, Vera Trubetskoi, wrote to her brother-in-law Grigory in Paris. This time, Georgy was set free after a few weeks.

In those first years, it all still seemed a temporary nightmare. Soon after his release, on January 19, 1922, Georgy sent a penciled note to his uncle Grigory Trubetskoi in Paris: "I firmly hope that our separation from you will not last forever. . . ."

On the last day of 1922, Georgy wrote to Trubetskoi again, but this time the tone was very different: "On 16 October I returned home, but I don't know for how long, how, or what will happen next. . . . My parents, and especially Papa, have begun horribly losing spirit, he's fallen into some unbearable grief that

*The mug shot from Georgy
Osorgin's first arrest.*

gives him no peace. I have set myself two tasks: 1) to move the family from the Izmailovo swamp to Moscow, which is absolutely vital for Maria and Tonia, 2) this is frightening even to think about—to prepare to move Papa, Mama, and the girls to you."

Life grew ever harder. Hunger and famine ravaged the cities and villages, typhus stalked the weakened population, inflation soared out of control: in 1922, 1 prerevolutionary ruble was worth 10,000 rubles; a year later it was down to 1 million rubles. Schools and hospitals shut down for lack of funds or staff. Desperate for revenues, the Bolsheviks taxed everything and everyone. And all the while, the arrests intensified.

"Since Christmas, they have begun 'cleansing Moscow of harmful elements,' " Georgy wrote in 1924 to Grigory Trubetskoi.

Over one or two nights they arrest hundreds, sometimes thousands of people, and after two or three weeks the smaller part ends up in prison, a larger part is shipped in stages to the north or to the Urals, with the confiscation of all property, and the largest part is made to sign an agreement to leave Moscow and Moscow Province with their whole family in the course of one week. In one night, more than thirty of our close

The Osorgin family at Seventeenth Versta. Seated:
Mikhail Mikhailovich and Liʐa. Standing, from left:
Maria, Liana, Georgy, and Tonia.

acquaintances were taken, among them very many women, and some
were taken away with their families. Yes, Uncle Grisha, life has become
bleak, not because of the constantly poised sword of Damocles, but because it seems there is no hope of any change.

On March 6, 1925, Georgy went to the apartment of a young woman named
Sandra Meyendorff to drop something off and walked directly into a ʐasada.
Sandra worked as a secretary to John Speed Elliott, an American who was
working for W. Averell Harriman on a mining venture in Georgia, in the Caucasus. She often had Americans to her apartment, which inevitably attracted the
attention of the secret police. Osorgin was carted off to the Lubianskaya prison,
the infamous "Lubianka" of the secret police, but he managed to leave a note
behind for his wife. He listed what money he owed and to whom, and added:

"So now your turn has come, my darling, to be tested. May God help you all. Pray also for me, and be completely calm: I don't worry about myself for a minute, and my thoughts are of you who remain." He gave some more encouragement and concluded, somewhat patronizingly: "I bless you and pray for you, but remember that I will hold my banner high and expect the same from you."

Georgy was soon transferred from the Lubianka to the Butyrskaya prison, in northern Moscow, and his wife and relatives immediately set about trying to get him released. But he undermined their best efforts with his defiant behavior. He acknowledged as much in two letters smuggled out in the seam of a jacket worn by a prisoner who was released. In the first, Georgy wrote that two weeks after his arrest he was charged with counterrevolution and then taken to the Lubianka for questioning. The interrogator first asked about some acquaintances and relatives, Georgy wrote, "after which we talked for almost three hours, and here, I confess, I lost my temper and told the interrogator many unnecessary things about himself, his institution, and Soviet power in general."

Georgy's outburst sealed his fate. The best that Ekaterina Peshkova could do was to prevail on Genrikh Yagoda, the deputy director of the GPU (who as director would give his name to the first great purge and then would be swept up in it himself), to commute Georgy's death sentence to ten years of labor camp.

The protocol of October 12, 1925, noting that Georgy
was sentenced to be shot, and that the sentence was
reduced to a term of ten years in a concentration camp.

Georgy remained at the Butyrskaya prison for more than three years. He worked in the library, which enabled him to circulate through different wards and, in the guise of reading French book titles, to spread news among his acquaintances, who all knew French. Georgy also managed to smuggle several letters out. Most survive, and in each of them he seems to be readying himself and his family for his death.

In one letter to Lina, written in ink on a handkerchief and smuggled out at the end of 1925 in the lining of someone's coat, he wrote: "When I sat in solitary, I suffered so much for you, that I cannot describe it. I was not afraid of death (now I know that I will always know how to die), but for you, your life with Bubik [their daughter, Marina] without me. . . ."

Another letter, also on a handkerchief, was addressed to his mother-in-law, Anna Sergeyevna Golitsyn: "I would like, if it is my fate to die in prison, that Lina and my family would know that I die peacefully, praying that Lina might still find happiness and that her life on earth will not be limited to that chain of suffering and grief that bound her on marrying me; poor, poor Lina, why did you let her marry me?!"

Early in May 1926, a few days after Easter, Seventeenth Versta was searched from top to bottom by a crew led by Misha Tinyakov, the former Sergiyevskoye altar boy turned Bolshevik enforcer. On the morning after, Lina was arrested and interrogated for several days. Ekaterina Peshkova managed to get her released after a week. Was it Tinyakov who arrested and questioned Lina? Did he interrogate Georgy?

Two years later, in 1928, Georgy spent Easter night sitting by the barred window of his cell, awaiting the midnight bells. He and the 24 other "counterrevolutionaries" in cell number 8, many of them his relatives or acquaintances, had received from their families the basics of an Easter feast, which lay outspread on their table. Georgy was 32. As he waited, he resumed writing a letter he had begun earlier in the week to Grigory Trubetskoi in Paris, his dear "Uncle Grishanchik," recalling their last Easter at Sergiyevksoye, ten years earlier, in 1918, during that final visit that left so powerful an impression on Trubetskoi. For me, this letter is the finest expression of the spiritual legacy of Sergiyevskoye, and of the spirit of this remarkable man.

30 March/ 12 April 1928

Christ is Risen!

Dear Uncle Grishanchik, I greet you and Aunt Masha with the impending Holy Day, and I wish you all the very best. For a long, long time I have wanted to write to you, dear Uncle Grishanchik; you always showed such concern for me, you helped me so generously in a difficult moment of my life, and, mainly, your entire image is so inseparably linked for each of us, your nephews, with such wonderful memories; you always are, were, and will be our dearest, most beloved uncle.

I am approaching the fourth Easter that I will spend behind these walls, separated from my family, but the feelings for these holy days which were infused in me from earliest childhood do not fail me now; from the beginning of Holy Week I have felt the approach of the Feast, I follow the life of the Church, I repeat to myself the hymns of the Holy Week services, and in my soul there arise those feelings of tender reverence that I used to feel as a child going to confession or communion. At 35 those feelings are as strong and as deep as in those childhood years.

My dear Uncle Grishanchik, going over past Easters in my memory, I remembered our last Easter at Sergiyevskoye, which we spent with you and Aunt Masha, and I felt the immediate need to write you. If you have not forgotten, Easter in 1918 was rather late, and spring was early and very warm, so when in the last weeks of Lent I had to take Aunt Masha to Ferzikovo, the roads were impassable. I remember that trip as now; it was a warm, heavy, and humid day, which consumed the last snow in the forests and gullies faster than the hottest sun; wherever you looked, water, water, and more water, and all the sounds seemed to rise from it, from the burbling and rushing of the streams on all sides to the ceaseless ring of countless larks. We had to go by sleigh—not on the road, which wound through the half-naked fields in a single muddy ridge, but alongside, carefully choosing the route. Each hoofprint, each track left by the runners, immediately turned into a small muddy stream, busily rushing off somewhere. We drove forever, exhausting the poor horse, and, finally, after successfully eluding the Polivanovo field, one of the most difficult places, I became too bold and got Aunt Masha so mired that I nearly drowned the horse and the sleigh; we had to unharness to pull it out and got wet to the eyebrows; in a word, total "local color."

I remember the feeling I had that spring of growing strength, but that entire happy springtime din, for all the beauty and joy of awakening nature, could not muffle the sense of alarm that squeezed the heart in each of us. Either some hand rose in senseless fury to profane our Sergiyevskoye, or there was the troubling sense that our loving and closely welded family was being broken up: Sonia far off somewhere with a pile of kids, alone, separated from her husband; Seryozha, just married, we don't know where or how, and you, my dear Uncle Grisha and Aunt Masha, separated from your young ones, in constant worry over them. It was a hard and difficult time. But I believe that beyond these specific problems, this spiritual fog had a deeper common source: we all, old and young, stood then at a critical turning point: unaware of it, we were bidding farewell to a past filled with beloved memories, while ahead there loomed some hostile, utterly unknown future.

And in the midst of all this came Holy Week. The spring was in that stage when nature, after a big shove to cast off winter's shackles, suddenly grows quiet, as if resting from the first victory. But below this apparent calm there is always the sense of a complex, hidden process taking place somewhere deep in the earth, which is preparing to open up in all its force, in all the beauty of growth and flowering. Plowing and seeding the earth raised rich scents, and, following the plow on the sweaty, softly turning furrow, you were enveloped in the marvelous smell of moist earth. I always became intoxicated by that smell, because in it one senses the limitless creative power of nature.

I don't know how you all felt at the time, because I lived a totally separate life and worked from morning to night in the fields, not seeing, and, yes, not wanting to see, anything else. It was too painful to think, and only total physical exhaustion gave one a chance, if not to forget, then at least to forget oneself. But with Holy Week began the services in church and at home, I had to lead the choir in rehearsal and in church; on Holy Wednesday I finished the sowing of oats and, putting away the plow and harrow, gave myself entirely over to the tuning fork. And here began that which I will never forget!

Dear Uncle Grishanchik! Do you remember the service of the Twelve Gospels in our Sergiyevskoye church? Do you remember that marvelous, inimitable manner of our little parson? This spring will be nine years that he passed away during the midnight Easter service, but even now, when I hear certain litanies or certain Gospel readings, I can hear the exhilarated voice of our kind parson, his intonations piercing to the very soul. I remember that you were taken by this service, that it had a large impact on you. I see as now the huge crucifix rising in the midst of the church, with figures of the Mother of God on one side and the Apostle John on the other, framed by multicolored votive lights, the waving flame of many candles, and, among the thoroughly familiar throng of Sergiyevskoye peasants, your figure by the right wall in front of the candle counter, with a contemplative expression on your face. If you only knew what was happening in my soul at that time!! It was an entire turnover, some huge, healing revelation!

Don't be surprised that I'm writing this way; I don't think I'm exaggerating anything, it's just that I feel great emotion remembering all these things, because I am continuously breaking off to go to the window and listen. A quiet, starry night hangs over Moscow, and I can hear first one, then another church mark the successive Gospels with slow, measured strikes of the bell. I think of my Lina and our Marinochka, of Papa, Mama, my sisters, brothers, of all of you, feeling the sadness of expatriation in these days, all so dear and close. However painful, especially at this time, the awareness of our separation, I firmly, unshakably believe all the same that the hour will come when we will all gather together, just as you are all gathered now in my thoughts.

1/14 April—They've allowed me to finish writing letters, and I deliberately sat down to finish it this night. Any minute now the Easter matins will start; in our cell everything is clean, and on our large common table stand *kulichi* and *paskha*, a huge "X.B." from fresh watercress is beautifully arranged on a white tablecloth with brightly colored eggs all around. It's unusually quiet in the cell; in order not to arouse the guards, we all lay down on lowered cots (there are 24 of us) in anticipation of the bells, and I sat down to write to you again.

I remember I walked out of the Sergiyevskoye church at that time overwhelmed by a mass of feelings and sensations, and my earlier spiritual fog seemed a trifle, deserving of no attention. In the great images of the Holy Week services, the horror of man's sin and the suffering of the Creator leading to the great triumph of the resurrection, I suddenly discovered that eternal, indestructible beginning, which was also in that temporarily quiet spring, hiding in itself the seed of a total renewal of all that lives. The services continued in their stern, rich order; images replaced images, and when, on Holy Saturday, after the singing of "Arise, O Lord," the deacon, having changed into a white robe, walked into the center of the church to the burial cloth to read the gospel about the resurrection, it seemed to me that we are all equally shaken, that we all feel and pray as one.

In the meantime, spring went on the offensive. When we walked to the Easter matins, the night was humid, heavy clouds covered the sky, and walking through the dark alleys of the linden park, I imagined a motion in the ground, as if innumerable invisible plants were pushing through the earth toward air and light.

I don't know if our midnight Easter matins made any impression on you then. For me there never was, and never will be, anything better than Easter at Sergiyevskoye. We are all too organically tied to Sergiyevskoye for anything to transcend it, to evoke so much good. This is not blind patriotism, because for all of us Sergiyevskoye was that spiritual cradle in which everything by which each of us lives and breathes was born and raised.

My dear Uncle Grishanchik, as I've been writing to you the scattered ringing around Moscow has become a mighty, festive peal. Processions have begun, the sounds of firecrackers reach us, one church after another joins the growing din of bells. The wave of sound swells. There! Somewhere entirely nearby, a small church breaks brightly through the common chord with such a joyous, exultant little voice. Sometimes it seems that the tumult has begun to wane, and suddenly a new wave rushes in with unexpected strength, a grand hymn between heaven and earth.

I cannot write any more! That which I now hear is too overwhelming, too good, to try to convey in words. The incontrovertible sermon of the Resurrection seems to rise from this mighty peal of praise. My dear Uncle Grishanchik, it is so good in my soul that the only way I can express my spirit is to say to you once again, Christ is Risen!

Georgy

Outside, despite the intensifying repression, or perhaps because of it, the "former people" continued to lead a full life. They gathered at their cousin Masha Golitsyn's to dance the foxtrot to her new gramophone, they went to concerts and the theater, and on Sundays they took the train out to the Osorgins at Seventeenth Versta. But Mikhail Mikhailovich no longer gave catechism lessons; it was too dangerous now. The music-making stopped; those whom Liza had accompanied on the piano were in prison. Maria was no longer there; she had been arrested and exiled to Maloyaroslavets, a small city between Moscow and Kaluga where the Sergiyevskoye school would move in 1930. Life at Seventeenth Versta had changed. "The main thing that was always on the minds of the family, but hardly ever talked about, was their Georgy, languishing in Butyrka," wrote Sergei Golitsyn.

Georgy did not return. In retrospect, his death seems almost accidental—a badly timed visit, a misguided burst of temper, being in the wrong place when the camp authorities needed someone to kill. But then, there was really no logic to any of the millions of deaths in the orgy of terror unleashed by Lenin (as the Communist Party archives now establish beyond doubt) and carried to insane lengths by Stalin. It was enough to utter an unguarded crack about the Bolsheviks to be denounced by an informer. Informers spread through society like a contagious disease. People informed to protect themselves, out of jealousy, out of spite, to free up a room in a communal apartment. False witnesses were never punished; on the contrary, they were encouraged. Children were taught to emulate Pavlik Morozov, a peasant youth who informed on his parents and was "martyred" by villagers. The disease was still rampant during our first years in Moscow.

And once someone was arrested, in those decades before Khrushchev called off the killing, it was simply a question of luck whether he survived. Death hovered over prisoners from the day of their arrest. They were executed outright, they died under interrogation, they froze to death, they died "trying to escape," they died under the fists and cudgels of guards. A favorite pastime among guards at the Solovki prison camp was forcing prisoners to stand on the edge of a steep drop until they lost their balance and fell. Others succumbed to disease, hunger, or despair. And with every death, life became cheaper. Guards sank to primeval brutality; sadists found their calling; prisoners lost the will to live.

The horror of the modern police state lies in the enormous cruelty and single-mindedness of its pursuit of total control. But the drama is in the confrontation of individual men and women with the internal boundary that defines for them the limit of compromise and acquiescence.

It is different for every person, but it is the point in his own conscience at which he either surrenders to the state or manages to retain his dignity. The skill of the interrogator in a police state is to find that line and to push his victim across it and thus claim him for the state. In his first interrogation, when he was still a teenager, Sergei Golitsyn recalled that he was prepared to debunk the tsar and to declare full loyalty to the Soviet state. But the one question he really feared, the one he knew he would have to answer honestly, was: "Do you believe in God?" "There was no way I could deny it," he wrote. "I intended to broadly expound my beliefs, to explain that I am simultaneously a Christian and not opposed to Soviet power. . . . Thank God, the interrogator never asked the question."

In the end, for Golitsyn and for the others who did not succumb, the very fact of outliving the Soviet state and giving voice to what they witnessed was their triumph and their memorial to those who perished. Solzhenitsyn's *Gulag Archipelago* stands as the unsurpassed monument to the terror, and with glasnost, an entire literature of the Gulag found its voice. Interest has abated with the collapse of the Soviet Union and all the new problems that has created, but the testimonies will survive. Evil of such proportions cannot be swept away or forgotten.

Georgy had no chance to survive. He embodied an uncompromising faith and a code of honor that were incompatible with the Bolshevik demand for betrayal, compromise, and fear. His death was not accidental; it only came earlier rather than later. His only good fortune was to escape the anonymity of the millions whose names and fates will never be known. On leaving Russia, his widow exacted a promise from her brother to find out what happened to Georgy, and Sergei Golitsyn tracked down and questioned every survivor of the Solovki he could find, including Dmitry Sergeyevich Likhachev, the historian and academician who came to be known as "the conscience of Russia" for his lifelong witness to Russia's spiritual and esthetic legacy. Another of Georgy's fellow inmates who lived to tell the story was Oleg Vasiliyevich Volkov, who was in and out of the Gulag for thirty years and recorded the ordeal in a powerful chronicle, *Descent into Darkness*. Solzhenitsyn in his *Gulag* also paid tribute to Georgy Osorgin. From these records, and from letters and recollections in family archives, I pieced together Georgy's final months.

On April 14, 1928, two days after writing the Easter letter to Grigory Trubetskoi, Georgy was shipped to the "Solovki," the Solovetski Islands, in the White Sea. A famed monastery there, dating from 1429, had been converted by the Bolsheviks into the first concentration camp of the infamous Gulag, known formally as the Solovetski Camp of Special Designation (the camp's Russian initials, SLON, also spelled the Russian word for elephant).

Georgy's wife somehow learned that the train in which *zeks* were being transported was standing on a siding at the Nikolayev terminal in Moscow, and she went there with her brother and sister. They waved handkerchiefs, and soon Georgy's head appeared at a small window, with the long beard he had grown in prison. How beautiful the spring air was, he said. A guard walked up and ordered Lina away, but she begged for ten minutes more and he relented.

The next time Lina saw Georgy was in the Solovki, in August 1928, on a visit that the brave Peshkova helped to arrange. Lina was allowed to stay with Georgy a full month in a cabin on a ship moored off the island. The churches of

*A file entry dated September 3, 1928, reporting that
Georgy Mikhailovich Osorgin arrived at the Solovki
labor camp on May 29, 1928.*

the monastery were still functioning then, though at the services the local monks stood on the right, while inmate priests and monks stood to the left. On that visit Georgy and Lina conceived their second child, Mikhail.

Peshkova managed to wangle another visit, in October 1929. The Solovki was far different now. The number of prisoners had increased tenfold, all the monastic churches were closed, and the monks had been either driven off or arrested. The guards were crueler, and prisoners lived in terror. Later, when she learned of Georgy's death, Lina was tortured by the thought that had she not made that visit, Georgy might have survived. "Since spring, he was living in another place, not on the main island but in the north, on Anzersky Island, where he was sent as punishment for secretly passing the bread and wine of Holy Communion to a dying bishop, Pyotr Zverev of Voronezh," she wrote many years later. "When this was discovered, Georgy was put in the punishment cell. But at this time Maxim Gorky came to visit, and everybody was freed from the punishment cells. What if he had remained there [on Anzersky] and had not come in view of the infuriated leadership?!" Yet when her two-week visit ended on October 13, 1929, the day after Georgy's thirty-sixth birthday, Lina was radiant. "Lina said later that these were the happiest days of her brief married life with Georgy," wrote her brother, Sergei Golitsyn. "He had already served four of his ten years, and she dreamed of how he would be set free, and though they would not be allowed to live in Moscow, even with Peshkova's best efforts, they would go off to some place of exile, and there would live together and be happy."

Then relatives of other inmates began receiving ominous letters: "Please express to Lina our deepest sympathy in the grief that has befallen her." Soon after, Ekaterina Peshkova broke the news to Lina.

Three days after Lina left, on October 16, 1929, Georgy and a group of other prisoners were marched out of the camp through the former Holy Gates of the monastery. One witness remembered that Georgy chanted "Christ is risen!" and recited prayers as he walked. The prisoners were lined up against a wall by the cemetery, near the women's barracks, and shot. The commander of the execution squad, Dmitry Uspensky, was drunk, as probably were his men, and they did the job badly. Many of the condemned men were still alive when they were thrown into a shallow grave, and the ground thrown over them was still moving in places in the morning. Uspensky, still drunk, went out with a pistol and walked around shooting into the earth until it fell still. A woman prisoner, Yulia Nikolayevna Danzas, recalled later that the shooting spread hysteria among the women.

The executions were ordered in retribution for the first mass escape from Solovki. There had been many unsuccessful attempts at flight, and at last, in 1929, three former naval officers managed to reach Finland. Their appearance created an enormous stir in the West, where there had been no inkling until then of the existence of Soviet concentration camps. The stories of the escapees gained further impact from the discovery at about the same time of desperate messages scrawled by inmates onto logs exported from northern Russia: "If you knew how much suffering these logs cost!"

The outcry in the West infuriated Stalin. Soviet newspapers issued a stream of denials under Premier Vyacheslav Molotov's signature, accusing the Western press of vile slander and anti-Communist hysteria. Yagoda, the deputy chief of the secret police, sent a special commission to the Solovki to investigate the escape. To teach the inmates a lesson, Yagoda ordered the execution of a random batch of prisoners—either forty or four hundred, depending on the source. Georgy was among those swept up.

One of the prisoners who remembered the shootings was Dmitry Sergeyevich Likhachev, and sixty years later, Sergei Golitsyn's son sat down with Likhachev and recorded his account. Likhachev himself landed in the Solovki because of a practical joke. Twenty-three at the time, he was with a group of students who were celebrating an anniversary, and a friend of theirs sent them a telegram pretending to be congratulations from the Pope. The entire group was arrested. When Likhachev arrived at Solovki, Osorgin was working in the medical section, helping to examine arriving prisoners. His supervisor was a former professor of medicine named Zhizhelenko, who had taken monastic vows during the revolution and by the time of his arrest was a bishop. Zhizhelenko determined that Likhachev was too emaciated after prison to perform any physical labor, and he was assigned to work with the many *bezprizornye*—waifs who roamed Russia in half-wild bands after the revolution and civil war—who were being rounded up and shipped to Solovki.

In late September, 1929, Likhachev told Golitsyn, the order came down to execute four hundred prisoners, including any deemed "potentially dangerous." This included all former military officers and anyone who had any standing among fellow *zeks*. The roundup began at the start of October, and those selected were packed into a punishment cell. Among them was Georgy Osorgin.

At the same time, Likhachev said, visits were still being allowed. His own parents came in early October, and then Lina Osorgin arrived. Georgy was already in the punishment cell, but, according to Likhachev, he was released after giving his word that he would reveal nothing to her. He and other *zeks* remembered Lina's visit well, how they would look over the wall and see the tall woman walking arm-in-arm on the shore with the slight, bearded Georgy.

Likhachev said the condemned were led in groups to their execution. Pokrovsky, a one-legged former instructor in ballistics at the Artillery Academy, attacked the guards with a wooden stave and was shot on the spot. Likhachev clearly remembered Dmitry Uspensky, the supervisor of the execution; on the morning after the killings, Uspensky, still drunk, came to the criminological office, where Likhachev worked, and he watched as Uspensky washed blood and mud off his boots.

There was another reason Likhachev always remembered the executions: He was among those slated to die. It was the visit of his parents that saved him. On his way to greet them, he saw a list in the guardhouse of the prisoners who were to be shot the next day, and his name was on it. So he hid all night behind a pile of wood. "When dawn came, I counted the number of shots they made," he later recounted. "There was a shot for me; someone had died in my place. So, you see, ever since then I have had to live two lives: my own and the life of a man whose name I do not even know."

In 1988, Likhachev returned to the Solovki. A blue house stood on the spot where the prisoners were shot, and people who lived there told him that when they planted their potatoes they regularly unearthed bones and skulls.

Georgy's widow refused to believe Likhachev's version. She insisted that her husband could not have concealed from her that he knew he was about to die. She said that during the visit, he talked to her of an attempted escape, and of an escape plot that had been discovered, but he never mentioned any retributions or executions. She did recall, however, that one night while they were together, Georgy was called away and spent a long time talking to someone at the door. When he returned, he said it was nothing.

I have found no conclusive evidence that Georgy knew or did not know of his impending death. But Likhachev and others were there with him, and from everything I know about Georgy, I believe he had long prepared himself for death. I believe that he had the strength, the character, and the faith to accept it and to hide his terrible knowledge even from his wife, and to fill their last moments together with happiness.

In Moscow, the family wanted to hold a memorial service in secret, out of fear of bringing trouble down on others, but news of the execution spread, and the church was filled with friends and relatives. The Church of Sts. Boris and Gleb on Pokrovskaya, where Georgy had been reader and where he and Lina had been married five years earlier, had been shut down by the Communists, so the service was held at the nearby Church of the Rzhevsk Icon of the Mother of God (which was torn down shortly afterward). Lina and the Osorgins stood with stone faces. The priest was Mikhail Shik, a popular and charismatic pastor who would also soon perish in the camps with his wife.

For Lina, it became a mission to find out everything she could about her husband's end. In 1974, aged 74 and living in Paris, she recorded some of her recollections in a letter to a cousin:

> I met many [former prisoners] then, many who tried to confirm that he was shot dead and not buried alive. One told me that Georgy walked out of the Holy Gate to the execution site with the others singing "Christ is Risen" and other prayers. I remember well these gates, they went out to the bay where the old ship was moored in which Georgy and I had a cabin when I went to Solovki in August 1928 for the first meeting. . . . After I learned the whole truth from Peshkova, I asked her to help get us out so that the children would never become Young Pioneers.

The execution of his brother-in-law made a large impression on Sergei Golitsyn. "I fantasized and compared Georgy to the heroes of *War and Peace,*" he wrote. "How would they have behaved had they lived in the time of the revolution? For me, Georgy was Prince Andrei, who would never have betrayed his principles and convictions, and, of course, would have perished likewise."

Many months later, Golitsyn was boarding a train for a job in the Caucasus when Lina ran up. She showed him six new passports she had just picked up for herself and her Osorgin in-laws and said they were leaving. That is when she made him promise that he would find out for her everything he could about Georgy's fate.

Among others, he tracked down Dmitry Uspensky, Georgy's executioner, who lived to an honored old age. In 1933, when a group of Soviet writers were taken on a trip down the new White Sea–Baltic Canal, they were greeted and guided by Uspensky. Their accounts were universally glowing. Presumably they were not told that the canal was built almost entirely with prison labor, and that Uspensky was the slave-master; or maybe they were and saw nothing wrong in that. Golitsyn next ran into Uspensky many years later, when he was the deputy head of the Moscow–Volga Canal project; after that, Uspensky worked on the Kyubishev hydroelectric plant. When glasnost lifted the curtain of secrecy from the Gulag, a group of filmmakers made a documentary about Solovki, *Solovetskaya vlast* (Masters of the Solovki), and their cameras caught Uspensky walking down a street, an old man with a slight limp, clutching the mandatory Soviet shopping sack, six rows of ribbons on his chest.

The Osorgins, with Lina and her two small children, left for Paris in 1931. They were joined by Maria, who was taken directly from her place of exile in Maloyaroslavets to the Soviet frontier. When Mikhail Mikhailovich and Liza Osorgin rejoined their other children in Paris, my mother, who was eight years old, remembered that the grandparents she was seeing for the first time already seemed somewhat "Soviet"—rumpled, timid, and musty.

The head of the émigré Russian Orthodox Church in France, Metropolitan Evlogy, finally fulfilled Mikhail Mikhailovich's youthful yearning and ordained him, at the age of 71, to the priesthood. He was assigned to the small, family-built chapel at the Trubetskoi–Chreptowicz-Butenev villa in the suburb of Clamart. The ordination effectively confirmed Mikhail Mikhailovich's role as the spiritual father of his large clan. Metropolitan Evlogy wrote that among his relatives, Father Mikhail "is a sort of patriarch: he judges and reconciles, consoles and condones, baptizes, weds, and buries. He is a kind, evangelical pastor."

*The Osorgin family in Clamart, France. Front row, from
left: Tonia, Sofia, Father Mikhail Mikhailovich, Liza,
the third Mikhail Mikhailovich. Back row, from left:
Maria, Sergei (my grandfather), Liana. This is one of
the rare photographs of Mikhail Mikhailovich's entire
family in emigration.*

Mikhail Mikhailovich died in 1950, outliving Liza by 11 years. The chapel in
Clamart still stands.

Five years after Georgy's execution, Lina married his friend and cousin
Alexander Evgeniyevich Trubetskoi, with whom she had another son. She died
in 1991. Her first daughter, Marina, of whom Georgy wrote with such longing
in his letters from prison, married in Paris and had ten children. In 1974, after
saving one of her children from drowning, she collapsed and died. Georgy's
son, Mikhail, conceived at Solovki, is a Russian Orthodox priest serving
parishes in Paris and Rome. Maria and Tonia Osorgin never married. Maria
died in 1977. Tonia, who took holy orders as Mother Serafima, died in 1985.

All in all, Mikhail Mikhailovich and Liza had 21 grandchildren and 48 great-
grandchildren, of whom I am one.

$$\boxed{14}$$

Thank You, Comrade Stalin

What documents I found about Koltsovo in the 1930s give no further hints of resistance to the Bolsheviks, only the steady consolidation of Soviet control. By the spring of 1930, two hundred thirty families in the Ferzikovo *raion* had been repressed or expelled as *kulaks,* and the rest had been herded into collective farms.

Old people in the village do not like to talk of collectivization, especially to an outsider. Of all their memories, World War II alone is free of moral ambiguity. For all its destruction and bloodshed and mishandling, the "Great Patriotic War" was the one Soviet feat in which the people joined in a single cause. As for the rest of their lives, perhaps there is guilt simply at having survived, and all the compromises that required; perhaps it is just too confusing to have endured so much in the name of promises and dreams that now lie shattered and ridiculed. I always found something terribly sad in the anger of the old Communists who came out on Soviet holidays to curse the present in the name of the illusion for which they sacrificed so much.

I asked Sasha Trunin, Alexandra Nikitichna's son, who had grown up in the village and still spent his summers there, to see if people would talk to him about collectivization. This was already after the Soviet Union was gone, and the past was being openly dissected in the press. This is what he wrote to me:

From childhood, I remember the doleful asides—"Two cows they had, and six children, and I guess they dressed neater than the rest, and for that they were repressed as *kulaks*." But try to learn more, and they abruptly changed their tone: "Nobody was touched here, everybody voluntarily joined the *kolkhoz!*" And, of course, nobody was put away. And everybody lived well. But then it'll slip out again: "How many years we worked for sticks!" They meant that literally: in those years, if the *kolkhoz* authorities had no money to pay a peasant, they recorded a day's work as a notch in a stick. One has to assume that among some of those who were witnesses or participants, these memories touch a guilty conscience. Among others they touch a wound, and among all of them, by long habit, it just seems dangerous to talk about it.

As fear took hold as an instrument of state control, people learned not to talk about such things, and eventually silence became a habit. Filip Golubkov told me how it was instilled: "I once asked in school, if things were so bad in the capitalist countries, why not let us go there to see for ourselves? The teacher called me over after class and said, 'If you want to live normally, never ask questions like that.' 'Why?' I asked. 'Do as I say,' she said, 'and you will always thank me.' "

"There were thoughts we just didn't let in," Alexandra Nikitichna told me.

You never talked about *kulaks* or prisoners. We all knew who disappeared, but we never talked about them. You'd just hear a whisper: "They took Seryozha Soldatov." Or "Where's Soldatov?" "He's no longer here." "Oh, yes," and you quietly crossed out his name. Or the teacher would say, "Where's Soldatov?" And when there was no answer, she would cross out his name. You never asked further.

And all the while we sang patriotic songs! "Moscow, My Happiest Homeland." Everyone sang loudly, me loudest of all. There is still an old man who works here who will not apply for a pension because he was a prisoner of war. He's still so scared of what they might do that he won't apply!

Yet the old people did remember. Valentin Zabotin told how his great-grandfather Grigory built a large brick house after the revolution. His brother helped him. They made the bricks themselves. When the commune was set up, they had to surrender the house. Grigory left, not waiting to see what else the future had in store in the village. Zabotin's other great-grandfather, a smart and literate *muzhik*, worked as an accountant at the *kolkhoz*. During the German occupation, he was chosen village elder. He left with the Germans and never returned.

Sergei Kholshchyov also knew something about his great-grandfathers. One had a rather large lot, which he had bought from Osorgin. His brother, who joined the Bolsheviks, warned him in time that he was about to be repressed as a *kulak,* and he gave his four cows and everything else to the *kolkhoz* and left to work in Kaluga. He remained bitter to the end, and did not like to talk about it.

We were sitting on a bench outside Alexandra Nikitichna's neat log house in the oldest part of the village, a U-shaped stretch of huts on a hilltop across the Ozhzhyonka stream from the old Osorgin apple orchards. She went house by house: In that first one, the Ionovs were thrown out as *kulaks;* in that red one, they got Uncle Borya, a simple *muzhik* whose only crime was a badly timed curse; the Khokhlovs were driven out of the next one, where the Lagutins now live. . . . She continued down the row: eight of the fifteen households were thrown out as *kulaks.*

"I remember they were looking for the Khokhlovs, who had come to us with grain to hide," said Tatiana Tikhonovna Savitsky, a retired teacher whose own family was stripped of its property and narrowly escaped exile to Kazakhstan. "I remember how my mother said to us, 'Quiet! Don't say anything!' I remember well the atmosphere of fear." She glanced down the hill. "The Zabotnys, over there, where the telephone is. They took everything and exiled them. They'd had some disagreement with the leadership."

"They got our neighbor, too," said Sergei Afanasievich Razumov, beekeeper, war veteran, and poet. "He had flour and baked bread. He had a horse."

That was all it took to be condemned, to lose everything, to be exiled and possibly killed—flour and a horse, or a second cow, or four windows across the front of the hut instead of three.

Koltsovo, like much of Russia, was utterly unprepared for the war. Stalin publicly scorned Western warnings about German intentions and seemed intent on sitting out the "imperialist war." So when the Germans rolled into the Soviet Union, Communist *agitprop* units rushed to mobilize complacent populations.

On August 5, the head of the *agitkollektiv* (agitation collective) in Polivanovo, Comrade Tinyakova (Misha's relative?), gathered her comrades and "correctly explained the appeal of Comrade Stalin on how the *kolkhoz* must help the front." The task of agitators, she said, was "to impress on the population the depth of the danger and to put a decisive end to the attitudes of apathy and detachment, to raise vigilance, and to mobilize all the will and energy of the Soviet people to help the front and the country." Later that month, a representative of the NKVD (the current incarnation of the secret police) arrived in Koltsovo and raised the question of organizing a partisan unit, scouring the area for potential bases.

On October 12, with the Germans only a few miles away, two officials from the Kaluga Oblast Party Committee arrived and designated 22 local men as a partisan detachment. A peasant named Kashirin was appointed their head, and they were issued old French rifles with one cartridge each and an old English-made Lewis machine gun which usually jammed. They were assigned to observe the Germans and to deny them means of crossing the Oka.

The Germans duly arrived two days later and occupied the left bank of the Oka, including Koltsovo and 12 surrounding villages. On the right bank there were neither Germans nor the Red Army, and from there the partisans monitored German movements. Seventeen days later, when the Germans began marching up the right bank, the detachment "decided against entering into action against an enemy armed to the teeth." The partisans destroyed all the boats they could find, cut phone wires, and retreated to Aleksin, a town still under Red Army control. One partisan was killed. By October 30, the entire *raion* was occupied.

Koltsovo spent two months under the Germans. A unit led by an officer named Hoffmann, charged with monitoring Russian movements, moved into the village, turning the school into a stable and taking everything from the shop, including all the salt, matches, and heating oil.

Two incidents from this time entered local lore. First, a Soviet plane was shot down and two airmen parachuted into Koltsovo. The first was uninjured, and village women dressed him up as a peasant woman and walked him through the German lines to Aleksin. The second pilot was badly hurt, so one of the village women went to the German medic at Koltsovo with eggs and honey and told him that her husband had fallen in the forest and injured himself. The medic treated the man, and he remained in the village until the Red Army arrived. After the war both pilots visited Koltsovo to thank the women.

The second incident occurred as the Red Army was approaching. The Germans constantly required stout trees to support their tanks in the mud and snow, and Hoffmann ordered village women to cut down the soaring larches lining the old Alley of Love, planted many decades earlier by the Osorgins. The women refused.

Hoffmann's interpreter in Koltsovo was a Russian-German named Natalia

Nikolayevna Andreyeva; it was she who subsequently told the story to Alexandra Nikitichna. Recognizing that the refusal could have serious consequences, she told Hoffmann that the women wanted him to enjoy the beauty of the lane. Hoffmann would have none of it, and he ordered the Communist ringleader to be brought forward. One of the women, Natalia Semyonovna, had just lost her husband and son at the front. Believing that she had the least to live for, she stepped forward. At this time, the Soviet radio and press was trumpeting the heroism of Zoya Kosmodemianskaya, an 18-year-old schoolgirl who had joined the partisans and was caught and hanged by the Germans in a nearby village. Seeking to emulate Kosmodemianskaya, Natalia Semyonovna stepped up to Hoffmann and began gesticulating and shouting: "Our Red Army will come! Comrade Stalin will save us! We'll drive you off our Soviet land, we'll defeat you!" Natalia Nikolayevna, the interpreter, deciding that discretion was the better part of valor, gave Hoffmann a markedly different version in German. The poor woman was gesticulating that she had four children, she said, and she was pointing at the Iron Cross on his neck and saying that as a Christian, could he grant her a last request and let her say goodbye to her children. Hoffmann softened and said she could go, but that she must return in 20 minutes. Natalia Semyonovna and the other women quickly scattered, and with Soviet tanks rumbling in the distance, Hoffmann had no time to chase them.

The Germans left Koltsovo on December 20, retreating toward Kaluga. They took all the cattle and horses, and what grain and meat they could find, but the women managed to conceal some stores, and when the Red Army arrived the villagers proudly met them with boiled potatoes, bread, and milk.

Some neighboring farms were not as fortunate as Koltsovo. On their way out, the Germans burned and pillaged 15 nearby *kolkhozes*, whose names resound with the forced optimism of collectivization: Red Partisan, Our Victory, New Village, Labor, Victory, New Way, Path to Socialism, First of May, First of August, Freedom, Lenin, New Life, Activist, 15th Anniversary of October, Voluntary Labor. A survey of the losses lists 520 houses, 7 schools, and 156 farm buildings that were burned down. In addition, the Germans took or burned wheat from 6 depots, took 1,500 horses, 1,000 cows, 1,500 sheep, 15,000 chickens, and 376 pigs. Why such precision in tallying the lost pigs? I suspect because these were all privately owned, while the other animals and birds were *kolkhoz* property. In addition, 23 men and women were led away as prisoners.

Because Koltsovo was spared destruction, it was chosen as a base by the Soviet 5th Guards Aviation division for one of its surveillance wings, the 128th Aviation regiment. In 1943, a team of youths with forty horses arrived and, working nonstop for twenty days and nights, converted a meadow into a landing field. (Neighboring Grabtsevo became the base for the celebrated 125th Women's Aviation regiment, commanded by Marina Mikhailovna Raskova.)

German planes never spotted the Koltsovo field. When the Soviet planes were not on a mission, they were concealed in a birch grove, and when Germans flew over, women would quickly go out onto the landing strip as if hunting for mushrooms in a meadow.

In 1975, Alexander Viktorovich Kandidov, the editor of the Ferzikovo *Vesti*, tracked down a veteran of the 128th, Grigory Klementiyevich Kadola, the former head of air reconnaissance. The regiment, he told Kandidov in an interview, flew on all the major fronts—over Leningrad and Moscow, the northern Caucasus, the Oryol-Kursk salient, Crimea, Ukraine, Byelorussia and the Baltics, and finally eastern Prussia. It was awarded the Order of the Red Banner and the Order of Suvorov.

Kadola produced photographs from the time the unit was in Koltsovo, showing smiling pilots posing next to battered twin-engine NE-2 bombers with fangs painted on their cowling, or airmen being briefed in a forest of tall birches. Al-

Men of the 128th Aviation regiment, which was
stationed at Koltsovo in 1943, preparing for a mission.

most all the airmen perished. In the time the 128th stood at Koltsovo, Kadola said, 201 men were lost, half the unit's total strength, including the commander, Lieutenant Colonel Gorelov. Of all those who flew out of Koltsovo, Kadola was the only one still alive thirty years after the war.

When the war ended, the men and women of Koltsovo began coming home. People who had left as simple peasants came back hardened and scarred. Mikhail Alexeyevich Golubkov, another member of the large Golubkov clan, fought in Stalingrad, Voronezh, Kharkov, the Dnieper, Yugoslavia, Romania, Bulgaria, and Hungary, ending up in Austria. Mikhail Georgievich Gusev spent five months in a hospital with a shattered left hand. Ivan Zakharovich Balashenko fought with the partisans in the Crimea. Vasily Ivanovich Trunin, Alexandra Nikitichna's husband, fought in Ukraine, Byelorussia, and Czechoslovakia, where he lost his right leg. Vasily Tikhonovich Platonov, a pilot, was shot down during the very last days of the war, April 27, 1945, and captured by the Germans. For that, he spent the next 11 years in a Soviet labor camp.

The postwar years were both a time of simple joys after four years of sacrifice and slaughter and a time of renewed oppression as an aging and increasingly paranoid Stalin strove to reassert total control.

It was at this time that the Koltsovo church was dismantled for brick. Who gave the order is not clear—some say it came from the Kaluga Party organization, others that it was given by Polina Stepanovna Likhachev, the tough chairman of the village council. Either way, it is generally agreed that the work was done by Prokhor Sergeyevich Fomichev, an old alcoholic who had already dismantled three churches. He alternated between work and drinking binges, swapping a hundred bricks for a bottle of moonshine. He was about to start on the bell tower when villagers turned on him. Soon after, he was arrested, and he spent seven years in a labor camp for "parasitism." When he came back he drank himself to death in his cabin.

Still, most people remembered the postwar years as a happy time. Alexei Andreyevich Lagutin, who settled in Koltsovo with his mother after the war because their village had been destroyed, remembered long summer days spent restoring the *kolkhoz* and long summer evenings with friends in the sweet-smelling linden park, playing his accordion.

Once I started returning regularly to Koltsovo, Alexandra Nikitichna Trunin became my friend and guide. Her son Sasha, Moscow University graduate and poet, was suffocating in the village, so in 1991, to enable him to move to Saratov with his wife and small daughter, I bought their house. I did it on the understanding that it would stay in Alexandra Nikitichna's name and that the family would spend their summers there. It was not yet legal for a foreigner to own property in Russia, and what I really wanted was to secure Alexandra Nikitichna there as the custodian of local history and to have a place in the old village that I could call home whenever I was visiting. Alexandra Nikitichna stayed in Koltsovo from spring through fall, writing me detailed letters about what was sprouting in "our" garden, what was in bloom, who had died, who was trying to find me.

October 4, 1992: "Deeply esteemed Sergei Alexandrovich and Maria Alexeyevna, It is already golden autumn: all the lindens and the paths in the park are gilded, and the maples are red. The leaves have begun to fall. I had part of the garden turned and fertilized for potatoes, I planted winter garlic and onion and strawberry, and I'll do the rest of the work in the spring. . . ."

Whenever I came, she would feed me with produce from "our" plot, and I would leave with bagfuls of vegetables, fruits, and preserves. And she would talk to me of Koltsovo, of her life, of the orphans she had raised, of the total faith in Communism that had sustained her through a rough life—a faith that

Alexandra Nikitichna Trunin. The house behind her is the one I purchased.

began to erode only when glasnost began to shatter the myths about Lenin. As she talked, she would fill my cup with tea and spoon wild-strawberry preserves into the small plate that Russians set at teatime.

Alexandra Nikitichna's life was the saga of her generation. She came from a village near Kaluga. Her mother, Feodosina, was deeply religious and covered her wall with icons. Her father, Nikita Dumkin, was among those who embraced the new order and was devoured by it. He joined the Party during the 1917 revolution and plunged into political work in the local commune. But that was of no help when the collectivization campaign got underway. Alexandra Nikitichna remembered coming home from third grade to find men going through their house, and hearing her mother whisper, *"Nas raskulacheli"*— we've been condemned as *kulaks.* They lost everything—horse, cow, photos, even Alexandra Nikitichna's red Young Pioneer scarf, which was torn up into May Day ribbons. Later someone warned the family that they were slated for exile, and they hid in her grandmother's village.

Undeterred, Nikita Dumkin continued to serve the Party. One day in 1933, officials came and told his wife that he was dead, that he had fallen under a train—an accident, they said. Alexandra Nikitichna assumed that he was murdered, but by whom? By those who hated him as a Communist? By Communists who had no further need of him? Feodosina moved with her four children into a basement room in Kaluga which they shared with another family—13 people in all. One had tuberculosis and coughed blood all night. Alexandra Nikitichna remembered how when she was 16, the teacher asked the class to describe what they imagined as "happiness." To get her first wages, she replied, and to buy a dress and high heels, to have a glass of champagne, to dance. . . .

Her dominant memory of childhood was hunger. A meal was a potato fried in tallow and served with salt, supplemented in summer by dandelion soup. If they found milk, the mother diluted it with boiled water so that there would be enough to go around. Alexandra Nikitichna remembers standing in line for bread and passing out when she caught a whiff from inside the bakery. She remembers her mother bringing home pieces of a dead horse; she remembers how her little brother Vanya would fall asleep whimpering, "I want a piece of bread." When Vanya was 13 years old, he disappeared. A half year later, they received a letter: "Don't worry, I'm a sailor on the Black Sea. I work in the kitchen. I eat!" Soon after the war broke out, an officer came to report that Vanya had been killed, and he even described how he had been buried in a mass grave, one of the "fraternal tombs" scattered across eastern regions of the old USSR. But then a letter came from Vanya. He had been wounded badly in the face and presumed dead, but on the way to be buried he had come to. His eyes were gone. When he finally came home, helpless and disfigured, he tried to kill himself, and Alexandra Nikitichna's mother had to care for him full-time. Her mother lived to 92, Alexandra Nikitichna said, and it was only at the end that she found a bit of peace.

Vanya pulled himself together. He learned to play the accordion, married, and made a decent living as a musician. It was Vanya who first discovered that there were descendants of the old Sergiyevskoye *pomeshchiki* living in France. Unable to read, he spent hours by the radio, often tuning in illicitly to Radio Liberty, the station then financed by the Central Intelligence Agency to broadcast into the Soviet Union over shortwaves. One day he heard an interview with an Osorgin in Paris who talked about Sergiyevskoye, and he realized they were talking of Koltsovo.

When Alexandra Nikitichna was in the seventh grade, a worker who had once met Lenin, Efim Petrovich, came to address her class. As Lenin became increasingly deified in Soviet ideology, anyone who had ever met him, however briefly, gained a standing as something akin to an apostle, spreading the gospel of the infallible "Ilyich." As she listened, Alexandra Nikitichna was fired with faith, and Efim Petrovich became like a second father to her. Her dream became to be a history teacher, and she succeeded in entering a teachers' college. By the time war broke out in 1941, she was a teacher, engaged to marry a military aviator, and a proud candidate-member of the Communist Party.

The Germans marched into Kaluga on October 11, 1941, less than four months after they invaded the USSR. Alexandra Nikitichna remembers how the first German soldiers marched in friendly and laughing, but they were soon followed by the SS, who started shooting partisans and hostages and hunting down Communists. If a telephone wire was cut, SS troops would seize the first twenty Russians they found and shoot them. Communists were hanged. Alexandra Nikitichna eluded one search, but in December, with the Red Army fast approaching, the Germans nabbed her and marched her off with a group of others. "*Wohin wir gehen?*" she asked in what little German she knew. "*Schiessen,*" a soldier replied, and mimicked the firing of a gun. Rounding a corner, she jumped behind a fence and ran for her life. When she eventually returned home, she found that the house had been burned down in an air raid. Her mother had managed to salvage only two pillows and a samovar.

The Kalugans exacted a revenge. On December 24, 1941, a group of German officers gathered in a public bathhouse to celebrate Christmas. As they got drunker, they kept demanding more heat. The Russian women serving them, all smiles and giggles, packed straw around the bathhouse and set it ablaze, incinerating all inside. A week later, on December 30, 1941, Kaluga was liberated by the 50th Army under Lieutenant General Ivan Vasilievich Boldin. As the Soviet troops marched in, a German train was pulling into the Kaluga station, full of Christmas gifts for the German soldiers.

Alexandra Nikitichna went directly to the recruiting station and joined up. She was assigned first as an orderly at a field hospital, then as a clerk, and finally as chief of the hospital commander's staff, rising to the rank of lieutenant. Her aviator fiancé was killed, and she married a tank commander in the field. She served on the front all the way to Königsberg, in eastern Prussia; there, her continuing devotion to Communism was rewarded with an invitation to join the Party. She told the political commissar that she was already a candidate-member, and a routine query to the Kaluga Party organization turned up the fact that she had been under German occupation for three months. She was promptly expelled; anyone who had been under occupation was automatically suspect, just as any soldier who was a prisoner of war was treated as a traitor. In October 1944, Alexandra Nikitichna became pregnant and returned home. She never joined the Party, and for the rest of her career as a teacher of history, a subject that was regarded as ideologically sensitive, the local Party sent someone else to test her students.

With the end of the war, Stalinism returned with even greater force. Alexandra Nikitichna remembers a boy who told a joke in school: Roosevelt, Churchill, and Stalin are meeting, and bees keep buzzing around Roosevelt. Why are the bees around me? he asks. Because you smell of *lipa*, Stalin tells him. The word means both "linden tree" and "fib" in Russian, and so the joke was aimed against the capitalist leader, not Stalin. But to mention Stalin in any form other than those prescribed for his adulation was considered blasphemy. The boy never reappeared in school. Alexandra Nikitichna also remembered a German teacher who burst out in exasperation to a student one day, "Why are you Russians so unpunctual?" He, too, disappeared.

"But I remained true to Communism," she said, shrugging her shoulders in wonderment. "When the KGB came to take down the portraits of Stalin in school, I resisted: 'No, I will not allow this, I fought at the front for Stalin!' I remember once hearing a friend say, 'We don't need Stalin, only Lenin,' and my first thought was, 'Enemy of the people! I must report him!' Thank God, I didn't."

Alexandra Nikitichna's husband, the father of her baby girl, did not return with her from the war, and one day his letters stopped coming. When she asked about him, army officials were evasive. Other men tried to court her, but she kept waiting. Finally, after five years had passed, a frustrated suitor insisted that she demand an explanation from the Ministry of Defense in Moscow. She soon received a letter telling her that her husband was in Birobidjan, the "Jewish Autonomous Region" that Stalin had set up in the Far East. She wrote him a letter, but the reply came from a woman: "Your husband is now mine." It turned out that after the war he was sent as a military adviser to Mao Tse-tung in China, and on his way back he moved in with another woman. In those days it was common for those sent abroad on military or intelligence missions to "disappear" at home. Alexandra Nikitichna said that her husband and his family tried hard to persuade her to have him back, but she absolutely refused, and she married the first man who proposed. He was Vasily Ivanovich Trunin, a veteran who had lost a leg in the war, and a fellow teacher at the orphanage at Koltsovo. Together they built the log house that I eventually bought and raised Alexandra Nikitichna's daughter and two children of their own. Vasily Ivanovich died in 1976 and is buried in Koltsovo.

I asked Alexandra Nikitichna when was it that she began to have doubts about Communism? "It was when a friend I trusted told me that Lenin had ordered people killed," she said. That was the moment of truth for many, when the sainted Lenin was revealed to have been as conniving and murderous as Stalin, only on a smaller scale. They knew about the Gulag, Stalin, the purges, the economic failures, but they kept Lenin intact in their hearts. They were raised to worship him. They remembered how they trembled the first time they entered his mausoleum. They believed that he was one of history's greatest figures.

"After that, I was amazed how blind I had been, how fooled we all had been," she said. "We were always hungry, but our way was always good, always right. Under Brezhnev we began seeing things, but we still believed in the 'sacred future.' "

Could Communism have been made to work?

"Let some other country find out, not ours," she said. "Why was our poor Russia the one to take this on? Why couldn't Sweden try it first? No, I don't need any more of our 'camp Communism.' "

In the summer of 1994, Alexandra Nikitichna told me, she went to a Baptist meeting with a nephew who had become active in a local fellowship to explore a faith she had dutifully ridiculed for most of her Communist life. She sympathized and approved of what she saw, she said, but it was too late for her to find a new faith.

* * *

During her years on the front, Alexandra Nikitichna saw many roaming bands of *bezprizornye*, the thousands of children left parentless and homeless by the conflict. She vowed that after the war she would try to help them, and in 1946 she was assigned to a new orphanage set up in the old school in Koltsovo. There she married and there she stayed, burrowing deeply into the life and history of the village.

Lev Vasilievich Savitsky, the first man I met on my initial visit to Koltsovo, became the orphanage's director. He had lost the fingers of his right hand working as a carpenter before the war and spent the war years working in Sverdlovsk. After the war he joined the Party and was sent to the new orphanage at Koltsovo. There he met and married Tatiana Tikhonovna, a woman from the village who had survived the Leningrad blockade and returned to Koltsovo to be a teacher.

The orphanage soon had a staff of 14 and 180 children, all packed like sardines into the schoolhouse but bound in a common endeavor to create a household almost from scratch. The school had last been used as a stable by the Germans, and it took a long time to clean. The first children slept on straw mattresses laid on wooden pallets, the only lighting was from kerosene lamps, and water was dragged from the well by two old horses.

In the beginning, the orphanage got what food it could from the *kolkhoz*. Then one day an old woman came leading a little girl. Her parents had died in the war, the old woman said, and she was too weak to care for her. With the girl, the old woman left a cow. Now the orphanage had its own fresh milk, which at first was given only to the weakest children. Then the chairman of the *kolkhoz* gave the children another cow, and with time they became almost self-sufficient, with 14 cows as well as pigs, chickens, rabbits, and horses, and 30 beehives. They worked their own vegetable plot. Besides the farmwork and schoolwork, the children had a Young Pioneer organization, a choir, and a wind ensemble, which traveled around surrounding villages to play at funerals.

In 1950, using salvaged brick, a second floor was added to the schoolhouse. The next year Lev Vasilievich found an old diesel engine, and on a trip to Moscow he managed to scrounge up a generator. He and the children set it up and wired the school themselves. The year after, he wangled some cast-iron pipes in Kaluga, and water was run to the house and bathhouse. Then a refugee Polish tailor turned up and set up a sewing machine at the school to teach the children to sew their own clothing. In the end, they were even making their own felt boots. Filip Golubkov donated a large painting, *Stalin and Children*, which was framed and hung in the dining room. (It was taken down in 1961, when Nikita Khrushchev ordered Stalin expunged from Soviet history, though Alexandra Nikitichna indignantly resisted at first.)

Though the tsarist past was a stern taboo, everyone was keenly aware that a great manor was once located here—a palace, they said. The cellars of the old house were used to store potatoes and apples, and now and then someone would turn up a piece of china with the monogram *MMO*. Then, when they took apart the old chimney and the urn full of Osorgin letters and photos fell out, Alexandra Nikitichna and her colleagues saw for the first time the faces of the former tenants and read their words. There was a postcard from Tonia from Lake Geneva, and a description of a ball—"Mama, the Empress herself was there!" There were intimate letters about suitors—"He's very nice, and I really don't want to hurt him"—and letters from the boys at the front. They all ended the same way: "May God keep you."

As on other former estates, legends persisted that the departing grandees had left behind a buried treasure. Enough treasures were regularly uncovered in former townhouses and estates to keep such hopes alive. (When Stalin ordered a major thoroughfare bulldozed through the genteel district of the Arbat in Moscow, many houses were discovered to have a *faux étage*, a hidden floor to conceal various family treasures.)

Two incidents in the 1960s made Alexandra Nikitichna wonder whether perhaps there was something hidden at Koltsovo. The first was a visitor who arrived in a red car, introduced himself as a journalist from the magazine *Family and School*, and said he wanted to write a feature about the orphanage. Alexandra Nikitichna made him welcome, but she soon grew suspicious. Every day, she said, the man would come and ask if a boy could guide him on a walk through the park, and of everyone he met he would ask the same thing: "What was here before?" When he heard of the Osorgins he became very interested, and Alexandra Nikitichna's immediate reaction was, "Spy! He's secretly taping what I say, it'll be played back on Radio Liberty, and I'll be shot!" So she started answering with the strict Party line about oppressors and serfdom. The man grew angry and soon disappeared.

The next spring, another man arrived, Osmolov, accompanied by two pretty girls he introduced as his daughters, though they did not resemble him or each other. "I am a student of modern agricultural methods, and I will show you how to grow melons," he announced. The school offered him a room, but he insisted on staying in the former Osorgin stable, in the corner of the park.

He did produce some fine melons. But Osmolov could also be seen every evening digging in the linden park; by morning, the hole would be filled. One night Alexandra Nikitichna was taking a shortcut home through the park and ran smack into Osmolov. "What are you doing here?" she asked in alarm. "I am communing with the land, daughter," he replied. "There is strength in the earth. Now you had better be moving on."

One morning Osmolov and the girls were gone, leaving a large pit in the park. Alexandra Nikitichna showed me the hole; it was about 5 feet across and 2 feet deep, and was grown over with wild strawberries. What did he find? I doubt it was anything the Osorgins buried, but they left a lot behind when they departed, and their servants may have buried some things to hide them from the commune or the Bolsheviks. Or maybe it was something buried during the war.

In the 31 years that the orphanage functioned, from 1946 to 1977, a total of 988 children passed through it, and Alexandra Nikitichna remembered each of them clearly. "The first group arrived on March 29, 1946. Each had his own tragedy. Vitya Filipenkov lost an eye after an enemy air attack; his sister Valya had a scar on her forehead. Their mother was killed by fascists; their father died at the front. Nina Alferova had only one grandmother left alive, she often shouted in her sleep and would try to hide from the bombs." When little Nina Korneyeva first arrived, she was befuddled by the sound of a gramophone playing a recording of Leonid Utyosov, a pioneer of Russian jazz, since there were only girls in the room. "Where is he?" she asked. "In this box," the other girls said laughing. Nina looked at it for a while, and then said, "Poor man, he's hoarse." After dinner, Nina brought a piece of bread and some milk she had saved and put them on the gramophone for the person inside.

Alexandra Nikitichna remembered trying to answer all her charges' questions when Yuri Gagarin became the first man in space, as well as teaching them when they reached adolescence about the facts of life. Her instruction on the latter subject seems to have consisted chiefly of dire warnings of the consequences of "misbehavior." The memories made her laugh and cover her face in embarrassment.

Many of the early charges, now men and women in their fifties, still kept in touch with Alexandra Nikitichna. One became a merchant marine, another a nurse, another a teacher. Volodya Sukhorukov finished veterinary school and returned to the *kolkhoz*, rising to become its director. Their photographs and letters are also displayed in the little museum. Kolya Makarov, who as a boy cared for the horses, wrote: "I've lived in many places in our motherland, and now live in Chirchik, in Uzbekistan. But I'll never forget our countryside, our park, our gardens, which we planted with our own hands, our Oka, where we sunbathed and swam. Wherever I've been, I close my eyes, and I see our beloved children's home."

"When we first came here, they were children of the war—tough, wounded kids," Alexandra Nikitichna recalled. "They slept on straw mattresses, they shared everything, they worked hard. They lived as Communists, suffused with the Soviet spirit—'Thank you, Comrade Stalin!' "

But with time, Alexandra Nikitichna continued, the children changed: "We started getting degenerate kids, children of alcoholics, abandoned children, children taken from broken homes. We had boys who'd just grab girls, girls who went with soldiers. They'd run away, they stole in the village. You know, there were eighteen orphanages in the *oblast*. In the beginning, only one was for troubled children. In the end, there were only two for normal children. All the others were for the abnormal."

After Lev Vasilievich retired, a progression of directors came and went, mostly Party hacks who stole what they could before moving on. Complaints from the village intensified, and in 1977 the orphanage was closed down.

A fierce competition broke out for the property, which included the school, the linden park, and the forest down to the river. Lev Vasilievich was by then the local Party secretary, and he remembers all kinds of factories, institutes, and Party organizations coming around, each promising to build new housing, install new electric lines, or pave the road. The head of the Kaluga Turbine Works, Valentin Vladimirovich Priakhin, took a more direct tack: He met with the secretary of the *oblast* Party committee, plied him with vodka, and got him to sign an order. In those days, the *obkom* secretary was the god and tsar of an *oblast*. Thus the property of the old manor entered into the incarnation in which I found it, the "rest base" of the Kaluga Turbine Works.

As for the remainder of the old estate, at the end of the war it was still parceled out into several separate collective farms. Twelve surrounding villages were gradually consolidated into one *kolkhoz* of 3,728 hectares (9,212 acres), embracing all the old Sergiyevksoye lands. It was named after Alexander Suvorov, the great eighteenth-century Russian military commander. Like all agriculture in northern Russia, and like the Soviet state, the Suvorov *kolkhoz* soon began to decline.

Alexandra Nikitichna remembered the progression of *kolkhoz* directors. The first was Stepan Ivanovich Dervuk:

> He was a big man, and he drove around in a cart seeking out drunks. If he found them, he would chase them with a whip. "We have an agreement, brothers: First we work, then we have fun!" he'd bellow. But then he began tippling himself.
>
> Next was Andrei Pavlovich Shevchenko, his wife was Tamara Fyodorovna. Oh, he was a gypsy—tall, with curly hair. He liked the ladies; he liked to flirt and joke. He was here a long time. He built the House of Culture, the kindergarten, the memorial to the war dead, the paths. Then there was Sushchenko, and another, but they did nothing. Now the young people are leaving; they have no interest. They built a settlement for refugees, but they all intend to leave as soon as possible.

Alexandra Nikitichna pointed to various houses. "Look: Over there, Olya lives alone. There, their son is leaving for the army, and they're drunk all the time. Next is a drunk. In that listing house, she's a pensioner who makes moonshine. Next is Lyuda, who drinks. The next one is an eighty-seven-year-old woman. This whole settlement, there's no one young. Up there, there's a woman with many children. Her husband killed an old woman, beat her like an animal, he and his brother took her money. The brother got caught, but the husband took the money and disappeared."

"When I came here in 1950, there were five *kolkhozy* and good, strong authority," said Lev Vasilievich Savitsky. "Now there are twelve villages in the *kolkhoz*, and all but three are dying. These are interesting times," he added with disdain. "It could still all return to Stalinism."

Again and again I heard that litany of decline and degeneration. In my last talk with Alexei Lagutin before he died in April 1994, he told me how after the war he plowed 10 hectares by the river and blocked a stream for irrigation, and there planted tomatoes, cabbages, cucumbers, carrots, beets, and the sweetest watermelon of anyone. One of his cabbages reached 16 kilograms and was exhibited in Kaluga. So Shevchenko, the director, came and ordered him to stop—he was embarrassing the *kolkhoz*. "We live on the land, and we buy cabbage," Lagutin said, more in sadness than in anger.

Those were days when the director of the *kolkhoz*, Vladimir Pavlovich

Sukhorukov, still talked to me. Of 340 *kolkhozes* in the region, he said, smartly ticking off the figures, only 24 were showing any profit. His *kolkhoz* was among the poorest: of 280 families in Koltsovo, 150 were workers at the *kolkhoz* and 50 were pensioners he had to support.

"There were more than three hundred workers when I was a boy," he said. "Why the drop? Kids went to the city, and only those on pension stayed. In the five years I've been director, only three young people have stayed on."

In Ferzikovo, Alexei Pronin, the chairman of the regional *soviet*, picked up the refrain. "There were traditions, discipline, and now there's nothing. In Koltsovo everything is stolen—the feed, the supplies. We paved the road, built houses, brought in new people, good people, but there's no order.

"In the 1960s, the private sector fed the whole country. Then Khrushchev messed it all up. Before, you had all you could want. Then the politicians took the cattle away from the peasants, and now there's nothing."

15

First the Garage, Then Build Democracy

My family and I returned to Moscow for a second tour early in 1991, in time to witness the demise of the Soviet Union. When we had left in December 1986, Gorbachev's glasnost and perestroika were still tightly controlled Communist campaigns. When we returned, a revolution was underway. Taboos were being lifted in history, literature, and politics; the press was breaking free; Western computers, video machines, fast foods, and literature were flooding across the borders. Long-suppressed feelings of nationalism were erupting, often violently, in the Baltic republics, in Nagorno-Karabakh, Azerbaijan, Georgia, Tajikistan, Uzbekistan, Chechnya, and Moldova. The economy was on the verge of collapse: Basic foods were being rationed, the ruble was sinking, and a series of stopgap measures, like the "currency reform" intended to mop up illicit accumulations of cash, served only to antagonize further a frustrated populace. Siberian miners, once the epitome of the progressive proletariat, began to organize strikes.

Gorbachev, hailed at first as the incarnation of hope and reform, rapidly lost political control and popular support. Seeking to appease first the right, then the left, then the provinces, he was abandoned by them all. Only the West faithfully continued to chant "Gorby, Gorby!" and to adulate the man whom they credited with putting a peaceful end to the cold war. Massive demonstrations regularly filled Manezh Square, adjacent to the Kremlin—"democrats" demanding reform, old-guard Communists demanding a crackdown. Boris Yeltsin, the popular leader of the Russian Federation, relentlessly chipped away at Gorbachev's powers. In December 1990, just before we returned, Foreign Minister Eduard Shevardnadze, initially a close ally of Gorbachev, resigned with an emotional warning that a dictatorship was looming.

Crises and clashes followed in rapid succession. My first real sense that the tide was turning against the Communists came on March 28, 1991, when Gorbachev banned a pro-Yeltsin demonstration and called out troops to seal off the entire center of Moscow. It was a dress rehearsal of the end. The Yeltsinites defiantly rallied outside the cordon under a wet snow and marched around the Garden Ring Road to Mayakovsky Square, and the troops did nothing. After the institutionalized terror of the Communist system, when a whispered threat was enough to strike terror into a man's heart, the paralysis of these soggy and confused young recruits ringing the Kremlin was dramatic evidence that the old system was losing its grip.

Gorbachev played his last card that spring, reaching for an alliance with the increasingly assertive Soviet republics in a new Union Treaty. Hardline Communists, convinced that the new dispensation meant the end of the Soviet Union, tried to depose Gorbachev in the celebrated putsch of August 19, 1991. While Gorbachev was still on vacation in the Crimea, the desperate Party stalwarts ordered tanks into Moscow and declared their cabal, the State Committee for the State of Emergency, in charge. Gorbachev, a man with nerves of steel, defied the rebels from house arrest at his Crimean retreat, while Yeltsin defied them from atop a tank outside his headquarters in the "White House," the Russian Federation headquarters on the Moscow River. The public rallied, the troops balked, and within three days the coup dissipated.

Early in the morning of Wednesday, August 21, when people realized that the tanks were not coming, they began walking home from the White House as free men and women. It was a moment that no one who was there will ever forget. For five years before then, I had watched Communist regimes crumble across East Europe, and now the barricades were falling in Moscow itself, in the heart of the empire. Everyone knew that massive trials still lay ahead, that the dismemberment of the Soviet Union was also the start of vast and unpredictable movements. I wrote in the *New York Times* that weekend: "To have been at a nighttime march in Leipzig, to have witnessed the proclamation of a republic in Budapest, to have sensed the pride of those who faced guns in Timisoara, to have wandered among the barricades in Moscow, is to have known moments when doubts and differences are suspended and people come together in a singleminded quest. It may sound mawkish, but call it freedom."

To be sure, not everyone saw it that way, at least not in the village.

In that last autumn of Soviet rule, I went several times to Koltsovo, in quest of both my roots and a different perspective on the changes then underway. On one cold, slushy November day, I found a group of mechanics sitting around a kerosene heater in the garage. They were dressed in greasy quilted-cotton jackets and muddy boots, and puffed on the foul tobacco Russians call "makhorka," rolled in strips of newsprint. The garage itself was an unfinished structure of prefabricated concrete slabs ringed by the rusted remnants of combines and tractors. Some of the men were recent arrivals, refugees from ethnic strife in Uzbekistan, Azerbaijan, and the Crimea.

They all agreed that if they had owned the tractors, they would never have let them disintegrate in that way. Then why not take the government's offer of private land, I asked, and start their own farm?

"And where would we get anything?" asked Nikolai Sargayev, a 35-year-old resettler from Uzbekistan. "Who would give us a cow, hay, machinery, spare parts? We don't have the money to buy anything, anyway. Besides, most of us don't even know how to work the land any more. I'm a mechanic."

But the prices at the farmers' markets were soaring. You could soon earn enough to pay for the tractor and the fuel. The men sat sullenly drawing on their smoldering rolls of newsprint.

"I was at the market in Kaluga," suddenly declared the dispatcher, Nina Dobritskaya, shutting off a squawking two-way radio. "Two of those southerners, some kind of Asians, were selling pomegranates for a price I'm ashamed to repeat. Jackals, they're all jackals. They didn't even grow them. And in Moscow, I heard sausage is selling at a hundred and sixty rubles. We get two for our meat. Jackals!"

I persisted: But you can sell your meat for a hundred and sixty rubles, you can sell your goods to middlemen. (The ruble was then worth six to a dollar, and 700 rubles was a good monthly wage.)

Nobody answered. Out here a middleman was still a bandit, especially the swarthy men from the Caucasus or Central Asia who dominated the farmers' markets, and who had driven Nina Dobritskaya from her home in Azerbaijan. To sell what you did not produce yourself was still suspect; to exceed government-set prices was wrong. For decades they had been taught that personal gain was wrong, even criminal. Communism had taught them that each thing had an immutable value determined by the state, that reselling goods at a higher price was "speculation." Only two years earlier, anyone who picked up one of the potatoes left in the field after the harvester had passed could go to prison. If the harvester broke down, whole fields of potatoes were left to rot, and nobody dared touch them.

Now Moscow was suddenly preaching that high prices were the wave of the future, that middlemen were not speculators but *commersanty*. Private peddlers, like the thousands lining Moscow streets with the odd can of food or utensil to sell, had even been spotted behind the railroad station in Ferzikovo.

"No, never!" raged Lev Vasilievich Savitsky, the old Communist. "Don't ask me to become a peddler. I'd die of shame. I have a conscience still!"

"That's exactly the problem," said Sasha Trunin, one of the few advocates of reform in the village, in a whispered aside. "Those with a conscience won't sell. I could," he added with a grin, "but I'm too lazy."

Now warmed to the subject, the mechanics raged at the futility of it all, spitting on the cement floor and liberally sprinkling their speech with oaths. Even if

*Lev Vasilievich Savitsky, retired director of the former
Koltsovo orphanage, and Sasha Trunin outside
Savitsky's house.*

they did take the offer of a plot of land, where would they get seed and fuel and plastic sheets for the hothouse except from the same *kolkhoz* from which they had pilfered all their lives? Besides, the "democrats" were in power in Moscow now, but who knew how long they would last?

"It's a real mess here. Nothing but drinking. Nothing gets done," said Sargayev. "We're trying to bring natural gas out here. They give us a few pipes—in exchange for meat, of course. We lay them, then we wait. Maybe next week, maybe next month, we get some more pipe."

This was what it had come to, the Bolshevik dream of a regimented, mechanized agriculture, back to what Deilidovich had described 130 years earlier in his pessimistic study of Kaluga agriculture: "It is hard to find an enterprise where there is so much 'what if,' 'maybe,' or 'good enough' as in agriculture." The reporter for a local newspaper described driving by a barn where cows were bellowing because they had not been milked in days. A single milkmaid was leaving for the day. Where were the others? "I don't know, they didn't show up." And why wasn't she milking the poor cows? "I've finished my shift."

"I'd get out of here if there was somewhere to go," said Dobritskaya, now close to tears. "But where? Everywhere it's the same mud, the same manure. Maybe they have glasnost somewhere, maybe they have democracy, but not here. We're used to working under the old system—as it was, so it stays. What would happen if we went on strike? No, if this privatization comes, it'll have to come from above, not from below. That's how it's always been. You know what we say: Fish begin to stink from the head down."

The chairman of the *kolkhoz*, Sukhorukov, was 35 then. He had nothing against the privatization of land, he said, but he had more pressing concerns: he needed 100,000 rubles just to meet the payroll through spring. Besides, he asked, how do you go about dividing up a collective farm?

"We're trying to figure out how to assess the land and equipment so we can divide it up," he said. "But each field has a different value, we have fifty pensioners, some equipment is old. Economically, we're on our knees and naked. Today they announced that prices are being freed. But the prices they pay don't even cover our expenses, and if we don't pay our tax, they fine us ten thousand rubles."

An old woman, wrapped in shawls and shod in large felt boots, shuffled into his office to complain that the *kolkhoz* had failed to deliver some promised hay. Sukhorukov made a note and promised to take care of the matter. He sat silently for a while, looking at the woman slowly making her way out. "We're simply not ready. These people are just too afraid to leave the collective. We work badly, we live poorly, we lose money. But at least we still have the collective."

I felt no temptation to remonstrate. On the road home, the last red rays of the sun were lighting the broken belfry, and Sukhorukov's parting words hung in the air, a sad echo of the ancient village tenet: "At least we still have the collective."

In November 1991, I wrote the first of several articles about Koltsovo/ Sergiyevskoye for the *Times*. The story had unexpected repercussions. I was interviewed on television, on radio, and in newspapers; Phil Donahue and Vladimir Posner, a Russian journalist who had grown up in Brooklyn and was a popular television interviewer, made the story a topic on one of their television talk shows in Russia. A month after my article appeared, on December 20, 1991, *Izvestia* ran a full-page article under the headline "SERGE GOES TO THE LANDS OF HIS GRANDFATHER," with the subhead: "The Russian Village through the Eyes of an American, and of Our Correspondent." Their correspondent was Arnold Pushkar, who went to Koltsovo and did some digging, though he never talked to me.

Under glasnost, *Izvestia* had evolved from mouthpiece of the Soviet government into the most influential independent voice in Russia, and the contrast between this article and the *Trud* article of 1985 was striking. I was still "Syerzh," but this time I was the hero of the piece, not the villain, and Pushkar's own view of the *kolkhoz* and its denizens, especially the unfortunate Chairman Sukhorukov, was far more damning than mine. Even his nostalgia for a heavily romanticized past went far beyond anything I allowed myself.

> Now, all that remains of the old gentry nest are the ruins of the bell tower, the built-over school, and a barn. I imagine the tears that welled up in Serge's eyes looking on the skeleton of the bell tower, whose great silver bell, cast with the money of the parishioners, spread its clear sound for many miles.

I liked the bit about the tears. Six years ago, *Trud* had gushed with sarcasm over Syerzh's "powerful nostalgia"; now *Izvestia* was sympathizing with his imagined tears. Pushkar went on to summarize the *Times* story and to recount the history and legends of General Kar, the Osorgins, and the advent of Communism. Then he delivered his own bitter indictment of Soviet rule:

> So began the era of the great destruction of what Russians—nobles, peasants, merchants, and craftsmen—had created over our thousand-year his-

tory. In the village, the executor of the revolutionary slogan—"Steal! Destroy!"—turned out to be the drunk Prokhor Fomichev. One after another, he knocked down and demolished the buildings of the estate. He died as he lived—freezing on his own stove. Not even the brick foundations of the cast-iron fence around the manor were left intact. Where is this fence? Where is the gold and silver of the church, the landowners, and the merchants? All squandered.

. . . Of course, all that Serge wrote about Koltsovo and the local Suvorov Kolkhoz, of whose twelve villages only three remain, is true. And there would be no need to follow in his footsteps, if it were not so sad. And so alarming for Moscow and its hours'-long lines for milk; for St. Petersburg, buying grain from Finland; for my beloved, cold Ekaterinburg, where as a university student I knew the pangs of hunger. If we did not see with Serge the closed circle around Koltsovo, and did not feel the need to find some exit, some hope.

Sentimentality aside, Pushkar had done his homework, and the picture he drew of the *kolkhoz* was devastating. Though it had at least ten times as many workers as a Western farm, he wrote, the *kolkhoz* produced one-seventh of the grain per acre produced in foggy England, and its average annual yield of 5,500 pounds of milk per cow was far below the average of 13,000 pounds in America. The usual scapegoats of the Soviet regime—climate and supply shortages—could not be blamed here, he continued. Right in the *kolkhoz*, Pushkar found a pensioner named Kuznetsov whose cow produced 11,000 pounds of milk, as did most other privately owned cows. And the *kolkhoz* had all the silage, beets, hay, and manure that it required. Again and again, Pushkar heard the common laments—that there aren't enough people, that they plow too late, that they plant too late, that the fertilizer is laid on too thick, or not at all. "And nobody's conscience is bothered by the fact that the state wrote off 5 million rubles in debt last year," he continued, "or that the *kolkhoz* already has 400,000 rubles in new debts and will have to take another loan to pay the wages."

Pushkar encountered the same resistance to privatization that I had:

While I was in the village council, two old women walked by. Demonstratively swearing, they shouted that they won't take land, and that if anyone does, they'll burn him out immediately. When I met with one of the mechanics, a graduate of the orphanage, A. Tsvetkov, 'San 'Sanych to his friends, and a collectivist from childhood, he put it succinctly: We don't want to stand out; we will work collectively, as Old Man Lenin directed.

Pushkar concluded with a flourish:

Serge's Mercedes flashed and disappeared in the distance, and we sit with the Koltsovo farm council with our heavy hearts. And yet the ice has begun to move. . . . While I was at the farm council some people came to apply for land. A retiring army warrant officer, Nikolai Nesterov, received 60 hectares. He'll work with his eldest son. The chairman put his stamp on the paper, and my soul felt lighter.

It was extraordinary stuff from a press that until so recently carried daily paeans to harvests and blasted any foreigner who dared to criticize. The article was reprinted in the Ferzikovo *Red Banner,* and I've yet to meet anyone in the village and its environs who was not keenly aware of it.

As a result of the publicity, dozens of people with links to Koltsovo, Osorgins, or Schmemanns sought me out to tell me their stories, to show me their photographs, and to read me their poems. A woman in her eighties called from St. Petersburg, asking if I knew of "the three Schmemann girls" with whom she had lived before the revolution (my father's first cousins—two were still living, in Paris and Munich). Nina Semyonova, going blind and approaching her end, wrote out her memories. Nadezhda and Antonina Likhachev, sisters who had studied at the Koltsovo teachers' institute in the 1920s, got in touch, and I spent many hours leafing through their albums and poems.

An old woman in Ferzikovo, Polina Ivanovna Kushpil, got in touch with me and begged me to come, and on my last visit to Koltsovo I stopped by her house. She used to read newspapers to her old, illiterate mother, she said, "and when I read her 'Dreamy Syerzh,' she figured it all out!" Polina Ivanovna said her mother had sung in the choir at Sergiyevskoye and often talked about the Osorgins. "She was helping Iokin at the mill when they were thrown out, and she remembered that when Mikhal Mikhalych and Elizaveta Nikolayevna passed by, the people ran out, and Mikhal Mikhalych said, 'Brothers, you won't rejoice over this.' Mama said they wept in three-part harmony."

The problem with all the publicity from the *Izvestia* article was that people assumed that I agreed with Pushkar, and I did not. He was obviously convinced that he was promoting reform and a return to core Russian values, but in fact he was only taking his place among the ideologues he purported to disdain. He charged that Marx had never seen a living *muzhik;* but Pushkar had, and when Sukhorukov, Tsvetkov, and the angry old women told him that they did not want private land, he haughtily dismissed them. I also found his denunciation of poor Sukhorukov unfair. The chairman was defending the *kolkhoz* not as a

Communist but as a man who had grown up there, who loved Koltsovo, who knew these people. The Soviet state took away their horses and plows, robbed them of initiative and youth, and made them dependent on the collective in their old age. Generation after generation of the strongest and most energetic peasants was taken away by collectivization, by war, or to labor in the virgin lands, the Donbass mines, and other "great projects" of Communism. And now those who remained—the pensioners, the refugees, and the drunks—were being told that it was all a terrible mistake, that they had to parcel out the land and abandon the one thing they cherished, security.

Nor could I share Pushkar's rosy view of the prerevolutionary past, when the villages purportedly fed Russia, men plied their skills in the cities, and women embroidered and danced. It reminded me of a quip of Steve Allen's: "You ain't what you used to be—but, then, you never were." These lands never fed Russia, and these villagers knew serfdom and injustice long before they met the Bolsheviks. And the grandfathers of these same Koltsovo *kolkhozniks* balked at buying up this same land when Mikhail Mikhailovich Osorgin offered it to them at bargain prices, for the same reason that 'San 'Sanych gave Pushkar: They didn't want to stand out.

The Soviet state stumbled on for four more months after the August putsch, until December 8, 1991, when Yeltsin joined with the leaders of Ukraine and Belorus to declare the Union of Soviet Socialist Republics finished. On December 25, Gorbachev resigned. Our children were home for Christmas, and they and my wife happened to be on Red Square when the red Soviet flag came down for the last time over the Kremlin and the white, blue, and red Russian flag rose in its stead. There was no ceremony, only the tolling of chimes from the Spassky Gate, cheers from a handful of surprised foreigners, and an angry tirade from a lone war veteran. My children noted the exact time, 7:32 p.m., and called me. That evening I wrote the obituary:

MOSCOW, December 25—The Soviet state, marked throughout its brief but tumultuous history by great achievement and terrible suffering, died today after a long and painful decline. It was 74 years old.

Conceived in utopian promise and born in the violent upheavals of the "Great October Revolution of 1917," the union heaved its last in the dreary darkness of late December 1991, stripped of ideology, dismembered, bankrupt and hungry—but awe-inspiring even in its fall. . . .

Reactions varied, depending on whether one listened to the ominous gunfire from Georgia or watched the dignified if bitter surrender of power by Gorbachev. Nobody really regretted his exit, but at least he had the dubious honor of being the first Soviet leader ever to leave office free, alive, and with a measure of dignity intact. There was no celebration. The taboos and chains were gone, but for the moment, so was the food. Long lines formed for staples that winter, some of which were rationed. The Soviet Union had given them pitifully little, but there was no guarantee that the strange-sounding Commonwealth of Independent States would do any better.

Measured against its own ambitions, the Union of Soviet Socialist Republics died a monumental failure. It had promised no less than the creation of a "new Soviet man," selflessly devoted to the common good, and ended up all but crushing the initiative and spirit of the people. It had proclaimed a new humanitarian ideology and in its name butchered 10 million of its own. It had envisioned a planned economy in which nothing was left to chance and created an elephantine bureaucracy that finally smothered it. It had promised peace and freedom, and created the world's most militarized and ruthless police state. It had promised a people's culture and created an anti-culture in which mediocrity was glorified and talent mercilessly suppressed.

In the end, promising a new life, it created a society that was unspeakably bleak—polluted, chronically short of everything, stripped of initiative and spirituality. While the bulk of the nation stood in line or guzzled rotgut vodka, the Communist elite raised corruption to new heights: the likes of Leonid Brezhnev and his cronies pinned endless medals on one another and surrounded themselves with fancy cars, vast hunting estates, armies of sycophants, and secret hospitals filled with the latest Western technology.

Yet the Soviet Union had also been an indisputable superpower, a state and a nation that achieved epic feats in science, warfare, culture. Perhaps all this was achieved despite Communism rather than because of it. Yet by some combination of coercion and inspiration, the system unleashed a potent national energy that made possible the rapid industrialization of the 1930s, the defeat of Nazi Germany in the 1940s, the launching of the first Sputnik in the 1950s, and the creation of a nuclear arsenal in the 1960s and 1970s. Even as the state collapsed, two cosmonauts circled the globe.

It is easy now, gazing over the ruins of the Soviet empire, to list the fatal illusions of the Marxist system. Yet the irresistible utopian dream fired generations of reformers, revolutionaries, and radicals here and abroad, helping to spread Soviet influence to the far corners of the globe. Until recently, rare was the third-world leader who did not espouse some variant or other of Marxist doctrine, who did not make regular pilgrimages to Moscow or join in the ritual denunciations of the "imperialists." It was a monumental failure, but it had been a grand dream, and an experiment on a scale the world had never known before.

It may seem the height of presumption that in 1917 Russia, a country then only at the dawn of industrialization and without a bourgeoisie or proletariat to speak of, should suddenly proclaim itself the creator of a radically new world order. But Russians have always had a weakness for the broad gesture. The greatest rulers, those who came to be known as "the Great" or "the Terrible," were those with the grandest schemes and the fewest scruples. A craving for grandeur seemed to come with the endless expanse, whether in epic novels like *War and Peace* or the claims to a "Holy Russia" and a "Third Jerusalem." Nothing happened small in the Soviet era, either. Twenty million died in the war, 10 million more in the Gulag, and pride of place was always given to grandiose construction projects—the world's biggest hydroelectric plant, at Bratsk; the world's biggest truck factory, Naberezhnye Chelny.

Many theories have been put forward to explain these appetites. There is the sheer expanse of a country that spans 11 time zones. There is the climate, which imposes a rhythm of long, inactive winters punctuated by brief summers of intense labor. I believe the key formative force was Russia's place astride two continents and two cultures, forever torn and forever fired by the clash of East and West. Russians have always divided themselves into "Westernizers" and "Slavophiles," and the death of the Soviet Union, like so much of Russian history, had everything to do with the struggle between the "Westernizing" democrats and free-marketeers and the "Slavophile" nationalists seeking identity in collective might.

The struggle continues, and always will. Viktor Erofeyev—the writer who had been expelled from the Writers' Union in 1979 along with my friend Zhenya Popov—once told me: "What remains after the Soviet Union is this Eurasian essence, this unique interplay of Europe and Asia, which will continue to amaze the world with its culture and totally unexpected actions. What was imported in Western Marxism will vanish. But Communism will not disappear, inasmuch as the spirit of collectivism is at the heart of this nation. The nation will always say 'we' rather than the Anglo-Saxon 'I.' "

Yet in that same Eurasian tradition, the government was always "they," whether it was the distant German bureaucrats of the tsars or the faceless Communist apparatchiks of the Kremlin. In the end, survival depended not on "them" but on what you could wrest from them and from that cold, hard earth. When the Communist regime began to crumble, there was something impressive, and even awesome, about the number of Russians—laborers, scientists, and composers alike—who spontaneously found a piece of land and began planting potatoes. Survival strategies shaped over centuries run deep.

The new Russia began its life in toil and suffering. On January 2, 1992, Yeltsin and his chief economic aide, Yegor Gaidar, a baby-faced economist in his thirties, boldly released the central lever of the Soviet command economy, freeing most prices to find their own levels. For better or worse, the action plunged Russia onto a turbulent new course. It will long be argued whether Gaidar was right or wrong, whether there was another way to wean Russia from its socialist ways, whether he went too far or not far enough, whether the crime, corruption, and conflict that came with the lifting of Soviet controls could have been avoided. The final verdict depends to a great degree on how it all plays out, and that will take some time.

Five years later, the debate still rages on. On a brief visit in early 1997, I found Moscow transformed: the massive Church of Christ the Savior, a replica of the church of the same name destroyed by Stalin in the 1930s, crowned a glittering city of restored buildings and brightly lit shops offering every conceiv-

able ware. But virtually every business, I was told, paid protection money to a crime syndicate, the reports of official corruption were legion, the military was in shambles, and the Duma was still more a rival for power to the president than a legislature. And beyond the confines of Moscow, with the exception of a few cities like St. Petersburg or Ekaterinburg, Russia remained backward and poor.

Yet I am convinced that a "third way" is always an illusion, and that the transformation of a Communist economy, whether Russian or East European, cannot be accomplished without dislocation and pain. In Russia's case, I also believe that by the time Gaidar was put in charge, there was little anyone could have done differently. It was too late for an orderly or controlled transition. It might have been possible years earlier, when Gorbachev and the Party were still in firm command. But if Gorbachev had been that radical, he would never have come to power in the first place. As late as March 1991, Gorbachev could still declare in Minsk, "I am not ashamed to say that I am a Communist and adhere to the Communist idea, and with this I will leave for the other world." And when several economists drafted a "Five-Hundred-Day Plan" for radical reform in the summer of 1991, he was unable to accept it. There were those who advocated a "Chinese option"—economic reform under ruthless political control. But by the time Yeltsin took charge, that would have required a crackdown more vicious than Tiananmen Square.

There was simply no painless way for a bankrupt and misdeveloped nation like Russia to emerge from the failed socialist experiment, and the challenge is to develop the new mentality and new institutions before the old habits of authoritarianism begin reasserting themselves. It is a race whose outcome is far from clear, as anyone who has been to Moscow in recent years has learned. Despite the crime, corruption, and governmental instability, new stores and new buildings have proliferated, hundreds of thousands of people have found employment in the new private sector, theaters are full, and for the first time in seven decades, the ruble is a real and stable currency. For every Russian who mutters the ancient Chinese curse, "May you live in a time of change," there are several who invoke the Russian proverb, "Blessed is he who has visited this world in its fateful moments."

Most of the people in my Koltsovo/Sergiyevskoye, alas, fell among the cursers. I had gone there about a month after prices were freed, when the Russian government was beginning to press collective and state farms to take charge of their own lands and fates.

It was deep winter. Wisps of wood smoke curled from the log houses sunk deep in snow, calves bellowed from a warm and pungent barn, and even the rusting equipment seemed less desolate half buried in snow. The reforms were the talk of the town. So was the *Izvestia* article, which suddenly thrust the isolated village into the harsh light of publicity. Under Communism, criticism in the press was invariably followed by "corrections," and many people were afraid that there would be repercussions.

Sukhorukov was furious. When I went to see him, he was guarded and cold. He clearly blamed me for the harsh criticism in *Izvestia*. It was the last time he agreed to see me.

Sukhorukov angrily ticked off the elements of what he described as "an unbearable situation." The "price liberalization" in force since the New Year had raised the price of milk sixfold and the price of meat eightfold, but the *kolkhoz*'s costs had soared tenfold, and on top of that, the government was introducing a 28 percent value-added tax. He needed 8 million rubles to finish building the garage, but all government subsidies had been halted, and the banks were demanding 25 percent interest for short-term loans. The *kolkhoz* had no money to pay wages, and would have none for months.

The problem was the same throughout the economy. Denied government credits and subsidies, state-owned enterprises simply accumulated debts among themselves. Millions of people were not paid for months but continued coming to work for lack of any alternative, and because their state employer was the only source they had for basic social and medical services. The total internal debt mushroomed from 39 billion rubles in January to 3.2 trillion rubles in mid-June, when Gaidar finally relented and started issuing credits again. It was the first of many retreats.

At the word "privatization," Sukhorukov drew a deep breath and cast a frustrated look out the window. But how do you divide up hillsides, forests, and fields? How do you divide thirty tractors among three hundred families, when the price of a new tractor has soared to 380,000 rubles? How do you explain to city people that only a third of the collective really understands or cares about the changes? And what do you do when the sowing season is approaching and every functioning pair of hands is critical?

In February, the *kolkhoz* held a general meeting to discuss Yeltsin's decree that all state and collective farms had to reform. I was not there, but Sasha Trunin attended and sent me a report.

The meeting opened with a speech by the chairman. Sukhorukov candidly described the dismal state of affairs; grain and milk production were pathetic despite decent weather in 1991, there was not a kopek in the bank, the *kolkhoz* had an old debt of 750,000 rubles and had just taken out another million at 25 percent interest. Sukhorukov declared that the only solution was to maintain the *kolkhoz* as is ("at least we still have the collective"). He urged the comrades to maintain unity against the new policies from Moscow, which were destroying the collective. To bolster his case, the chairman repeated a report passed from *kolkhoz* to *kolkhoz* that American farmers were coming to Russia to study the *kolkhoz* system and to adopt their advantages. In deference to the spirit of the times, he also insisted several times that he was not trying to predispose anyone in favor of the *kolkhoz*.

The chairman was followed by the specialists and foremen, who blamed rank-and-file *kolkhozniks* for plowing badly, for not washing the cows' udders before milking, for not taking good care of the equipment. For their part, the *kolkhozniks* complained that there were too many bosses and clerks who did nothing.

"Nobody had any proposals," Sasha wrote. "To quit the *kolkhoz* without someone's concrete support seemed at least as dangerous as staying in it, since none of them knew the first thing about marketing, and they were certain that they would never receive their share of the *kolkhoz* property without a crippling struggle. Besides, how can one work alone?"

Finally it came time to vote. Under Yeltsin's decree, they had three choices: divide the land and property among themselves and disband the *kolkhoz;* turn the farm into a shareholding company; or set up a collective enterprise, with each member owning a portion. The first choice was dismissed out of hand, and nobody understood the second, so they adopted the third, voting to change their name to Koltsovo Farmers' Agricultural Cooperative and to leave everything else more or less as is (two years later, all the signs and stationery still read "Suvorov Kolkhoz").

In the whole of Kaluga *oblast* 27 people took the offer of land. It was no surprise that most of them were not *kolkhozniks* or *sovkhozniks* but professional agronomists from the towns and cities who had a bit of initiative and capital.

The attempt at economic reform created an increasingly bitter chasm between Yeltsin and the Congress of People's Deputies, which had been elected by the Russian Federation when it was still part of the Soviet Union and was dominated by Communists of the old school. Its chairman was a pipe-smoking Chechen educator named Ruslan Khasbulatov, who began as Yeltsin's ally but rapidly developed a taste for power and turned against him.

By the first anniversary of Russia's emergence from the Soviet Union, both economic and political activity were virtually paralyzed by the power struggle between president and parliament. The last potential repository of order, the fledgling Constitutional Court, was swept up in the struggle when its chairman, Valery Zorkin, abandoned any pretense of judicial neutrality and plunged into the fray on Khasbulatov's side. Yeltsin tried to stay afloat by jettisoning Gaidar, and when that failed, he threatened martial law. The upshot was a referendum in the spring of 1992 on the presidency and the congress. It resolved nothing, but it was the first chance the country had to sound off.

Just before the referendum, I went back to my village to sample the mood. It was spring, the season of mud. It is impressive, Russian mud. Slithering in ankle-deep slime on what purports to be a street paved with concrete blocks, one can only feel sympathy for Napoleon floundering on the Smolensk road. In the nineteenth century, Turgenev, whose estate, Spasskoye-Lyutovinovo, was in a neighboring province, wrote of whole weeks when there could be no thought of travel.

I went to the dingy, four-room headquarters of the *kolkhoz* and began asking people how they intended to vote. Seventy-five-year-old Auntie Masha, there to pick up her pension, stomped her heavy stave and unexpectedly shouted for all to hear: "Me? I'm for Yeltsin, of course. You can't change them every few years. Look, just in my lifetime there's been Lenin, Stalin, Khrushchev, Brezhnev, and who's that other one? Let's give this one a chance!"

Three middle-aged accountants, all women who had received their comfortable positions through the old Communist Party, listened with patronizing smiles. "We need someone who will serve Russia, not Western interests or the mafia," said the chief accountant, with a sharp glance at me. "Wouldn't voters in Germany or America vote for what's best for their own country, and not someone else's?"

Outside, a clutch of men stood ankle-deep in the mud, sharing a bottle of cheap vodka and a smoke. "Yeltsin, *blyads,*" spat out a tractor operator, issuing the obscenity that means "whore" but is used indiscriminately to punctuate any drunken tirade. "What's he done for us, *blyads?* What do we have? The shop is empty, we barely saved the *kolkhoz,* this tractor costs five million now."

Most of the other men nodded in agreement. But the shop was even emptier before, I remonstrated, and the *kolkhoz* not only had these new tractors but also a nearly finished new garage. A tall man with leathery skin, one of a number of new settlers in Koltsovo who had been driven out of Uzbekistan or Azerbaijan, offered unexpected support.

Workers at the Koltsovo garage.

"Of course we still need Yeltsin," he said. "You want that Bolshevik manure back? You want them to tell you what to plant and what to say? At last something's moving, *blyads.*"

A group of young men wandered over, one with a single crucifix earring. "Only for Yeltsin," he declared, with evident disdain for the *kolkhozniks,* for their thick, blackened hands, their patched, oil-soaked quilted vests, and their cheap smokes. "I'm going into business, and as soon as possible." He was from Uzbekistan, he explained. He had fought in Afghanistan and had no intention of staying on the *kolkhoz* a minute longer than he had to.

"And you, Seryozha?" The men beckoned to a local youth walking by with a bucket of water. Seryozha studied the assembly calmly for several moments and then declared with a fervor that took everyone aback: "I'm going to vote for Yeltsin. The stench continues as long as the fish is rotting, as they say, and the others would only slow it down."

"Well, you won't get me to vote for Yeltsin," muttered the tractor driver. "Out with all of them, *blyads.*"

Sasha Trunin, my cultural interpreter in the village in which he was raised, described for me his own education in democracy in a wry essay he titled, in the Dostoevskian manner, "Confession of a Bewildered Voter."

Before the first elections, I had as much blind enthusiasm as everyone else who "sensed the waters moving." Experienced people, who knew the East and the West, convincingly said that the new Supreme Soviet will improve everything, that life will become freer and richer, and all that will be left for us to do is to work honestly and faithfully obey wise laws. Those of us who were far from the epicenter of the struggle earnestly studied the campaign platforms, biographies, and faces of the candidates, and in the end chose the youngest, handsomest, and most democratic deputy. Then we sat for hours in front of the television watching that unforgettable image with our tiny daughter, who pointed at the screen with her little finger and burbled, "deputies, deputies. . . ."

The face of the second elections was more defined and angry. We're talking here of the Russian *glubinka* [boondocks], 200 kilometers from Moscow, where I was working as a teacher in my native village. In politics, I am only prepared to fill the role of a rank-and-file voter, and this time, again, I was not looking for battle. Oh, I was prepared to voice my opinion if the opportunity offered itself, or, at most, to argue at the bus stop during the hour-long wait for a bus from Ferzikovo. But to consciously and actively come out on someone's side—God forbid. Yet it so happened that in elections to the *raion* council, a young teacher from our school decided to run against the chairman. Personally, this battle between an old Party worker and a young Komsomol activist did not excite me. But wherever I went, to the *kolkhoz* headquarters, to the club, to the village council, the same poster declared that we had but one candidate. My democratic conscience awakened, local pride came to life in my soul, I said something here, promised something there, wrote something to someone, and as a result I found myself her campaign manager.

. . . We held a meeting. Our adversaries had few arguments, but they were weighty: Construction of the road, the garage, and the gas line were not finished, and who would complete them, if not our man? The *kolkhoz* chairman even made a plaintive plea: "Elect our candidate now. Let's finish the construction, then you can elect whoever you want." On our side, we spoke of imminent changes, of new forces that will soon come to power, when fresh forces, like the young teacher, will be just what we need at the *raion* soviet. I tried to inject a bit of education, to convince those gathered there that democracy was not the same as anarchy, but rather a way of reaching agreement. But it was clear that no one bought this, so I concluded naively and earnestly: "Anyway, without democracy your new road will fall apart and the gas line will blow up."

The results were actually not so bad for us. About 40 people out of 300 voted for the teacher.

Next came a referendum about maintaining the Soviet Union intact, to which Yeltsin appended a referendum about creating the office of president, followed by elections for president. Trunin's education in democracy continued:

How did Yeltsin become the elected president? I mean, I was for him, but not loudly. When our kind neighbor expressed horror—"We'll elect him, and there'll be war!"—I answered modestly, "Oh, I don't know. . . ." And when my childhood friend, who worked in the *kolkhoz*, came by tortured by doubt and hangover and declared in horror, "Yeltsin will break up the *kolkhozy*," I half-heartedly advised him, "Take some land for yourself." He looked at me in disbelief. "What would I do with it?" When I listened to my city aunt—"Maybe he'll create a better life for us"—I confess I was embarrassed. I sympathized with another aunt, who issued a heavy sigh after she cast her ballot, saying, "Well, there it is, we've gone and voted for Yeltsin."

Who else? True, there were a few already then who voted for Zhirinovsky. "Why not? he's a cultured man, knows five languages. . . ."

The struggle between Yeltsin and the congress escalated to the verge of civil war, and after a round of violent clashes in the streets, the president ordered tanks to blast the White House—the same building that only 25 months earlier had figured as a bastion of the Yeltsinites and a symbol of resistance to the Communists. The clumsy assault lasted for most of the day, live on CNN, until the deputies surrendered and marched out of the bullet-scarred and burning White House.

Yeltsin called yet another election, this time for a hurriedly designed, two-chamber National Assembly, as well as a referendum on a new constitution. The turnout was moderate, and if the vote revealed anything, it was disenchantment. The biggest vote went to Communists and Vladimir Zhirinovsky, a demagogue whose tirades against ethnic minorities, Jews, the West, and anything else that came to hand played perfectly to the national mood of resentment. Yeltsin and his lieutenants lamely declared that what really counted was the vote on the constitution, which was declared to have gained the requisite 50 percent, though I'm certain it actually fell far short. When a member of the Election Commission raised public questions about the tally, Yeltsin promptly stripped him of his government dacha.

In Russian, "rule" is translated as *vlast,* which also means "power" and "authority." The terms have always been synonymous in Russia, and *vlast* has always devolved from top to bottom—from the all-powerful ruler down through the layers of courtiers, bureaucrats, or commissars to the *narod,* the people. But at its source, *vlast* is always one and indivisible, and to Russians, any attempt to dilute it is to create weakness and chaos. Russia's stab at a separation of powers between the president, the Congress of People's Deputies, and a Constitutional Court failed because the notion of a separation of powers is incompatible with the very concept of *vlast.* The West backed Yeltsin in his war with the congress because we believed he was the best hope for democracy; he attacked the congress because it challenged his *vlast.*

It was always my hope that Yeltsin would not consolidate power, and that this would compel the Russians finally to break their dependence on a "good tsar," on one central *vlast.* I had hoped that Russians might eventually build a thousand points of *vlast* and create a new rule from below. But the government's failure to create any order in the marketplace or in its own ranks only facilitated the rise of the notorious "mafias," vicious syndicates that divided all economic activity among themselves and enforced their order through gangland murders. At the same time, the ugly fiasco in Chechnya revealed Russia at its imperial worst. The "democrats," hailed as heroes when they battled Communism, came to be reviled as "so-called democrats" who would lead Russia to chaos and impotence. The Russians' euphoric embrace of the West in the first blush of independence turned to snarling resentment over the absence of anticipated aid, the Western condemnation of the Serbs in the Bosnian war, and especially moves to bring former Warsaw Pact countries into an expanded North Atlantic Treaty Organization. American palliative talk about a new "partnership for peace" failed to conceal from the Russians that the "civilized world" (their phrase) was not only reluctant to let Russia in but was holding it at arm's length.

Certainly the Western model had not taken hold, and there could be no denying the crime and corruption. But new stores and businesses were proliferating, the center of Moscow was restored and rebuilt from top to bottom, basic services continued uninterrupted, and after steadily dropping for three years, the ruble stabilized. And when elections were held again in the summer of 1996, Yeltsin, though ailing and weak, was still the choice over the Communists on the one hand and the right-wing demagogue Zhirinovsky on the other.

16

We're Still Alive

The time came to leave Russia.

We had lived there altogether more than ten years, from January 1980 through December 1985, and again from January 1991 through April 1995. In our first tour we caught the last heave of the cold war—the Afghan war, Reagan's "evil empire," the successive funerals of the old guard—and we witnessed the launch of perestroika. We returned in 1991 for the last gasp of the Soviet Union and watched the rise of a new Russia, with all its many hopes, illusions, intrigues, and failings. It was a remarkable stretch, made all the more so by an interlude of four years in Germany, during which the Wall literally came tumbling down. In the spring of 1994, I took a year off in Russia to work on this book. By the spring of 1995, it was time to move on to a new assignment.

I went to Sergiyevskoye for the last time on March 10, 1995. It was early spring, water was burbling and dripping everywhere, rooks were screaming from the treetops, the roads were turning to mud. The winter had been mild and the thaw early, so the Oka did not overflow its banks, as it had the year before, when it turned meadows into lakes and flooded low-lying villages.

The "rest base" stood empty most of the time now. With galloping inflation and the lifting of subsidies, a weekend there had become too expensive for ordinary workers of the Kaluga Turbine Works. But the maintenance men, cooks, and cleaning women stayed on. Though I had my own log house and could always stay there, I confess I preferred the old school, with its indoor toilets and steam radiators, and the linden park and bell tower right outside.

I rose shortly after dawn and went to the park. It was all very familiar now—the early-morning smell of wood smoke, distant barns, spring and frost, the crunch of the crust on the snow, the pale winter sky. I went to the site of the old manor house and followed its outlines in the mounds of overgrown masonry and the pits where cellars had been. Thick trees sprouted from the ruins—72 years had passed since the house burned down.

I pictured to myself what it must have been like a hundred years earlier. Across the courtyard, in the left wing, smoke was rising as the cook built his fires. The floorboards creaked as the stove tender plodded through the house in his felt boots, feeding frozen birch logs into the tiled Dutch stoves. Frost had formed on the windows of the children's room, where I stood, and eight-year-old Seryozha Osorgin was already up in his rumpled white nightgown, gazing spellbound at the black rooks leaping in the treetops. . . .

I wandered on toward the village. I passed the abandoned stable, the only one of the Osorgins' farm buildings to survive. Since my last visit it had been stripped of its ancient rafters, and whole walls of brick had been carted off. Along the road, three men, already drunk although it was not yet nine o'clock, were propping up a listing shed with old bricks. Where did you get the bricks? I asked. "The devil take it!" exclaimed one of them, fixing me with bloodshot eyes, "I don't even know anymore where we stole them."

Children were gathering at the two-story school, where nobody had bothered to take down the old portraits and a bust of Lenin. Sasha Trunin's wife, Sveta, taught there many years, and I had often dropped into the teachers' room for a chat with the Koltsovo intelligentsia. Theirs was a permanent struggle against a village world that always held intellectuals and their book learning in disdain. I once asked Sveta to put her feelings down on paper:

In the "cultural" center of the village, where the village council, the club, the store, and other important places are clustered, the school stands to the side, a bit out of place. Mental labor is not only secondary here, it simply does not figure in the same context as physical labor. To villagers, even to teachers, "work" is what they do in their garden plot. That's what they say after finishing their classes: "I'll sit a bit more, then I'll go home and work."

Some pupils in the senior class don't know how to spell their own names, largely because they don't care how they're spelled. They read by

The Koltsovo school, with Lenin still prominent.

syllables, apply to the Institute of International Relations, become milk-maids, curse the "smarties," and become drunks. Actually, many drink from early childhood. I'd enter a small, dark house to see why a ten-year-old is not coming to school. Heavy air, flies, the child's eyes reflect suffering. He's been smoking since five years of age, which was also when we first saw him drunk.

"Sasha, do you have your books?"

"We don't have any money for that," says the young mother, a milkmaid.

. . . And yet the majority of children like school. The teachers don't smell of silage. The children don't have to clean after the cattle, they can rest from work in the garden, they can add a dab of eye makeup. There's only one superfluous thing about school—learning. Superfluous for everyone: for the pupils, for the teachers, and for the director.

I went on to the house of my old friend Alexei Lagutin, just up the hill from mine, in the oldest part of the village. It was a year since he died, but his widow, Maria Egorovna, still cried when we talked of him. She had her niece staying with her, a 12-old girl named Oxanna. Oxanna's mother had gone down to Chechnya to find her son, a conscript who had been sent there with his army unit, and bring him home. Many mothers were doing that. After the first reports of the chaos and carnage there, women got on trains and buses and made their way to the war to find their boys. They no longer trusted the government and saw no reason why their sons should be killed in so meaningless and distant a conflict.

Maria Egorovna laid out a breakfast of steaming potatoes, thick bacon, pickled cucumbers, tomatoes, cabbage, eggs, sour cream, honey, and preserves, and brought me up to date. Her old horse was stolen one night, but these days it wasn't worth even notifying the police. Sukhorukov was just back from a hospital—bronchitis, they said, but he had always had bad lungs. People said he was handing out calves to the *raion* leaders and building himself a two-story house. The *kolkhoz* was in disarray, everybody was grabbing what they could, cows, tractors, fuel, silage.

I continued on to the garage. It was still unfinished, and rusted machinery still jutted from the mud and melting snow. Two huge water tanks lay on their side, just as they had the first time I came there, seven years earlier. I asked a passing woman what they were. She looked surprised and said she had never noticed them before. At the *kolkhoz* office, Zoya Pavlovna, the bookkeeper, was locking the door as I approached. When she recognized me, she quickly walked off. "How are things?" I called after her. "As you see them. Everybody's written us off, but we're still alive." "How do you do it?" "We live off credit, how else? Nothing's changed except the plaque on the wall." But even that was figurative, as the plaque still carried the old name, Suvorov Kolkhoz. "We sell some milk in Aleksin, we grow grain for the cows. Luckily, we bought some new machinery before the fall."

But I had been coming long enough to know that there were other layers of reality here. I knew, for example, that this same busty, flirtatious Zoya Pavlovna had left her husband that winter, and that he had hanged himself from a tree in the gully, and I knew that I could never bring myself to ask her why, nor would she ever tell me. His was not the only violent death that winter. Seryozha Likhachev, a tractor driver in his forties, got into a drunken brawl with his son and died a few days later of the blows. They had often fought before, so no one was surprised. Nobody saw any point in calling the police. These things happened.

I knew the story of Seryozha Likhachev. He was the son of Polina Stepanovna Likhachev, an albino woman who played a major role in the village during and after the war as the tough chairman of the local *soviet*. It was she who had organized the construction of the airfield during the war, and it was probably she, a committed Communist, who sent the drunk Prokhor Fomichev to dismantle the church, and then turned him in for "parasitism," for which he spent seven years in the Gulag. Sometime in the 1950s, Polina Stepanovna decided she wanted a child, so she went to the forester living alone in the woods and came back pregnant with Seryozha. People said she never had another man, and the forester never figured again in her life, or their son's. On growing up, Seryozha took to vodka and often beat his wife and son, until the son grew big enough to fight back, and killed him.

There are many such horrors below the placid surface. There was the woman who lived alone by the linden park with her many children. She had come to Koltsovo with her husband and family to escape some feud in the south. One day her husband went to a nearby town with his brother, robbed a woman, and beat her to death. The brother got caught, but the husband disappeared with the money. . . .

I went over to the dairy farm. Old Pyotr Isayevich Kuznetsov was there alone, getting salt for the cows to lick. He had retired fourteen years earlier, but there was no one else to do the work. "What's there to say? The cows are down from twelve hundred to eight hundred, everyone's stealing, they live by selling cows and getting loans from the government," he said, ticking off the points on his big leathery fingers. "We're back to Communist rule without Communist discipline. Before, you could complain to the *raion* and they came down with an investigation. You could write a letter. Now there's nobody to write to.

"Anyway, the young people are leaving. They have no interest in this. We built a settlement for refugees, but they all intend to leave as soon as possible. Who needs these cows?"

I wanted to talk over all these things with Sukhorukov. I knew that he had just returned from the hospital and that he was home, and I also knew he would not see me or talk to me anymore. I went anyway. I kept knocking until his wife came out. He was not there, she said, and no, he would not be there later, or tomorrow. No, she didn't know where he was, she said, standing firm in front of the door.

The doors to Koltsovo were closing to me once again. For a few years, the collapse of Communism had thrown Russia wide open, enabling me to find my Sergiyevskoye, to share the parlors and prayers of my ancestors, to glimpse the charm and squalor of Russia's heart, to catch the echoes of a native land. But I did not belong there. I was Russian enough to feel for these people, even to love them, but too foreign to tolerate their maddening fatalism and disorder. And they, who met me with open arms and shared with me their memories, they did not need me. Sukhorukov was convinced I had exposed him to the ridicule of the world; others never really understood why I kept coming back. In the beginning, I was an exotic visitor from a distant land and an even more distant past, but with time the novelty wore off, and I came to represent a past they did not want to be reminded of, and a hostile world that was seeking to undermine their fragile security and their collective with some alien concept of "democracy."

Many in the village pointed accusingly at the large house Sukhorukov was building for himself. I suspect he was simply following the pattern of so many other former Soviet managers and beginning to look out for himself. It was not so much greed as the loss of coordinates. Sukhorukov was already the third generation of Soviets raised on Communist ethics, which condemned all private enterprise as selfish and bad, declared collective farming the only legitimate agriculture, and held service to the paternalistic state as the highest duty. He could not simply jettison all that when a new government suddenly shifted direction and declared that private enterprise was good, socialism was bad, and all the achievements of the past, the *kolkhoz* included, were obsolete and wrong. Abandoned by the state he thought he was serving, stripped of the guidelines under which he was raised, Sukhorukov could think of nothing better to do than to take what he could for himself and try to keep the *kolkhoz* going. That was how many of these people understood "free enterprise."

Yet the same ability to function in conditions of chaos and corruption that made Russia so frustrating to foreigners and reformers was also its abiding strength. As Goryainovo, Karovo, Sergiyevskoye, or Koltsovo, this place had survived serfdom, reform, revolution, and war; these people had known despotic and benign *barins;* they had been stripped of religion by the Bolsheviks, then of Marxism by the democrats. Yet nobody was starving or freezing; as Zoya Pavlovna had put it, "Everybody's written us off, but we're still alive."

It was time to leave. Driving through Ferzikovo on my way home, I spotted Alexander Viktorovich Kandidov, the editor of the Ferzikovo *Vesti,* standing by the roadside in a worker's padded cotton jacket. His voluminous files and bottomless memory were an invaluable repository of information about the Communist era in Koltsovo, and he had been waiting by the roadside in the cold to say goodbye. He also wanted to show me a story in the latest edition of his newspaper. It was headlined "Second Birth" and signed by "V. Bulgakov, First Secretary of the Raion Committee of the Communist Party." It was the first such article in the paper since the collapse of the Soviet Union.

"There are few really devoted Communists left today in the *raion*, but they do exist," Bulgakov wrote:

Many in the old Party were casual members, who betrayed the idea of Lenin, of socialism. Riding a wave of populism, they broke that power, turning their consciences and minds 180 degrees. . . . Today it is not a secret that we are starting our work in difficult conditions. Of the 1,500-strong army of former members of the CPSU [Communist Party of the Soviet Union] in the *raion*, only 45 are left. But we are nonetheless filled with determination to carry on, to return the country to the path of socialism, to instill in the population true democracy and justice.

"See? They're coming back," said Kandidov with a sly wink. I smiled back, though I wasn't sure whether his wink was meant to mock the Communists or to imply that they had never really left, or something else entirely. It was a story with no end. It was also getting dark, and in winter the country roads were treacherous at night. I had to go. I hugged him warmly and drove off.

Sergiyevskoye/Koltsovo.

Afterword

In the fall of 1996, a year and a half after I left Russia, I received a letter from Alexandra Nikitichna. Sergiyevskoye was for sale.

"The fact of the matter is that the Kaluga Turbine Works is bankrupt," she wrote. "It is selling its rest homes, including the rest base in Koltsovo. It would be desirable to pass this hallowed place into good hands. Some 'new Russians' [the popular term for the flashy post-Communist millionaires] came and looked around. But they have but one goal, to resell the land and increase their capital."

Alexandra Nikitichna continued that Gennady Mikhailovich Steshin, the director of the home, had asked her to contact me. The "base" comprised seventy-two acres, including the old linden garden, the school, and the broken bell tower. The price was one million dollars.

I was amused that Steshin still held to the old Communist stereotype of Americans as people with millions stashed in their top hats. Of course I would have liked to emulate my ancestor and shout, "I buy it!," and thus give this story a neat conclusion. I loved the beauty of the place and had reveled in its echoes, and, like Alexandra Nikitichna, I hoped it would end up in good hands. But even if I had a million, my life was elsewhere.

On January 27, 1997, I went to Russia on a brief assignment, to cover Natan Sharansky's first visit to Moscow since his expulsion. I was struck by the changes that had taken place in Moscow: the rebuilt Church of Christ the Savior rivaled the Kremlin in majesty, the old center was brilliantly illuminated through the long winter night, glittering shops offered every conceivable ware. But the politics were still chaotic, and the economy was running on its own underground rules, which for most people meant paying protection money to racketeers and avoiding taxes.

Joined by two cousins and my daughter's fiancé, I drove to Koltsovo. Steshin had heard from Alexandra Nikitichna that we were coming, and he greeted us formally in his office in the old school, under a huge painting of Lenin reading

Pravda. A product of the once-mighty Soviet military-industrial complex, he had never taken the painting down, and with Communists resurgent in the Duma, there was no reason to do so now. "If it's no secret, what has brought you here?" he began, obviously hoping that we had come to buy the rest home. We had to disappoint him, but parted amicably.

Little had changed in the old place. The talk of the village was an incident at the New Year's Eve party in the club, during which two girls somehow obtained a .22 pistol and accidentally shot a cook from the rest base, Lyuba Solovieva. The shot was drowned out by the music and everyone presumed the victim was drunk, and by the time someone noticed she was wounded, she was already dead.

Sasha and Sveta Trunin had left Saratovo and had moved back into their old house, and he was teaching in Ferzikovo. We sat drinking tea and talking of all that had happened since we last met. The massive Russian stove spread a sleepy warmth in the log house, and through the frosty windows the low winter sun gilded the eternal Russian landscape of birches and snow. My grandfather's words came back to me: "You too, my children, and you, my grandchildren, you are not foreign, you have your rightful, personal place by my side, on that same dear Sergiyevskoye soil, which will nourish you and give you life, if only you do not turn away from it."

I had claimed my rightful place on this Sergiyevskoye soil, I thought, and it did not require a Soviet or a Russian deed.

Acknowledgments

One of the blessings of the changes that have taken place in Russia is that a reporter can openly thank his Russian sources. My first and greatest debt of gratitude is to the people from Koltsovo who opened their memories, their hearts, and their long-concealed folios of documents and letters. They all figure in the story by name, but I would like to use this space to express once again my sincere appreciation for their generosity, patience, and warm hospitality, to Alexandra Nikitichna Trunin, Alexander Vasilievich and Svetlana Mikhailovna Trunin, Alexander Viktorovich Kandidov, Lev Vasilievich and Tatiana Tikhonovna Savitsky, Irina Yakovlevna Denisova, Nadezhda Sergeyevna and Antonina Sergeyevna Likhachev, Filip Yakovlevich Golubkov, Viktor Pavlovich Sukhorukov, and Gennady Mikhailovich Steshin. I also would like to honor the memories of Alexei Andreyevich Lagutin and Nina Georgievna Semyonova.

While rummaging through archives in St. Petersburg, Moscow, Tula, and Kaluga, I was helped by many archivists who seemed delighted finally to share the knowledge that they had preserved for so long. I am especially indebted to Dmitry Nikolayevich and Irina Andreyevna Antonov of the Tula State Archive, and to Natalia Nikitichna Doronina, a teacher at the Kaluga Pedagogical Institute, who guided me through the Kaluga State Archives.

Many relatives in Moscow and in the West made letters, documents, and photographs available to me. In Moscow, Antonina Vladimirovna Kamarovsky, who as a girl took lessons from the Osorgins, opened suitcases full of old photographs and sketches, some of which are reproduced here. In Paris, Juliana Samarin, a granddaughter of Mikhail Mikhailovich Osorgin, showed me her many photo albums and folios of original drawings by Maria Osorgin, some of which appear on these pages, as well as photographs and documents. The Reverend Michel Ossorguine, the son of Georgy and Lina Osorgin, shared photographs and archives pertaining to a father he never met, and graciously let me use the silhouettes by Maria Osorgin.

An invaluable link to the past was supplied by Serge Troubetzkoy, of Sea Cliff, New York, a son of Grigory Nikolayevich Trubetskoi. Born in Moscow in 1906, Troubetzkoy has dedicated much of his prodigious energy and enthusiasm to recording family history. I learned much from his archives, but my deeper gratitude is for his incomparable memory and loving inspiration.

I am also indebted to Eugene and Helen Troubetzkoy, of Hastings-on-Hudson, New York, and my aunt, Sophia Ozerov, of New York City, for sharing with me their rich collections of family photographs. In particular, the Troubetzkoys provided many of the photographs that appear within these pages by Olga Nikolayevna Trubetskoi (1867–1947), Liza Osorgin's sister and a serious amateur photographer.

As I noted, this book grew out of a series of articles in the *New York Times*. I had often talked to colleagues about the village, and it was Joseph Lelyveld, then managing editor, and Bernard Gwertzman, then foreign editor, who encouraged me to write about Koltsovo, and gave the stories ample space and fine display. My deep thanks to them both, and to the other fine editors on the Foreign Desk. Shortly after the first story appeared, Jonathan Segal of Knopf wrote me urging me to turn the stories into a book. He has been patient and supportive ever since.

There is no formula to express what I owe my family. My late father remains my firmest guide. His rich knowledge of Russian culture and spirituality, his enthusiasm for America, his celebration of life, and his deep and joyous faith permeated our home. My mother has been an invaluable and steadfast support for us and our children in our many years abroad, and a constant inspiration through her energy and love. I came to appreciate much of the beauty of Sergiyevskoye through her eyes. My children, Anya, Sasha, and Natasha, all participated in the exploration of Koltsovo, and all carry within them a bit of Sergiyevskoye. My deepest gratitude is, of course, to my dear wife, Mania, who has been with me through all the many travails, discoveries, frustrations, and joys of this chronicle. This book is also hers.

Notes

Much of the material for this book comes from family memoirs and letters, and from various archives in Russia that became accessible after the collapse of the Soviet state.

The major sources for family history were the unpublished memoirs of my great-grandfather Mikhail Mikhailovich Osorgin and my grandfather Sergei Mikhailovich Osorgin.

Mikhail Mikhailovich Osorgin dictated his memoirs to his daughters during their last years in the Soviet Union. He left several drafts of the voluminous and incomplete manuscript—which he titled "What I Heard, What I Saw, and What I Did in the Course of My Life" (*Chto ya slyshal, chto ya videl i chto ya delal v techenii moei zhizni*)—in the Lenin Library in Moscow, along with other family papers, trusting (correctly) that they would be preserved. I read part of the memoir in the library—now the Russian State Library—but the bulk was laboriously transcribed from microfilm copies of Osorgin's handwritten draft by Juliana Samarin, a granddaughter now living in Paris.

Sergei Osorgin wrote his memoir "Bylye gody" (Years gone by) in New York, where he spent his last years, from 1952 to 1957. He gave copies to each of his four children.

Several members of the large Trubetskoi family published memoirs. Grigory Nikolayevich's *Gody smut i nadezhd: 1917–1919* (Years of Troubles and Hopes: 1917–1919) (Montreal: self-published, 1981) is the source of a very moving description of Sergiyevskoye. I drew on Sergei Evgenievich Trubetskoi's memoirs, *Minuvsheyehe* (The Past) (Paris: YMCA Press, 1989), for descriptions of life in Moscow in the last years of tsarist Russia.

Many letters and documents of the Osorgins' extended family in emigration have been gathered and compiled into privately bound collections by Serge Troubetzkoy of Sea Cliff, New York. The first volume of his "Chronicle of Family Correspondence" (1986) covers the years 1917–1930, the second (Labelle, Quebec, 1987) the years 1930–1945. Mr. Troubetzkoy also joined with two cousins, Pierre Troubetzkoy and Vladimir Tolstoy, in compiling a list of the descendants of Prince Nikolai Petrovich Trubetskoi—"Recueil généalogique et photographique de la descendance du prince Nicolas Pétrovich Troubetzkoy (1828–1900)" (Paris, 1984). An updated volume was printed in 1995.

A most unexpected trove of materials was revealed with the collapse of the Soviet state, when many documents that were presumed destroyed surfaced intact in various archives. A large collection of materials pertaining to the Trubetskois, collected by Olga Trubetskoi, had been stored in the Central State Archive of Literature and Art in Moscow. I also spent much time poring over many dusty and long-concealed folios in the Military Historical Archive in Moscow, the Central State Historical Archive in St. Petersburg, the Tula Historical Archive, and the State Archive in Kaluga.

The fall of Communism also enabled many Russians to publish memoirs that until then had circulated only among trusted relatives and friends. Those on which I drew for this book include Sergei Golitsyn's *Zapiski utselevshego* (Notes of a survivor) (Moscow: Orbita, 1990); Vladimir Trubetskoi's *Zapiski kirasira* (Notes of a cuirassier) (Moscow: Rossiya, 1991), and Oleg Volkov's *Vek nadezhd i krushenii* (Age of hopes and ruin) (Moscow: Sovietsky Pisatel, 1989).

For the Soviet period, as I have noted throughout the book, many people from Koltsovo (Sergiyevskoye) who heard of my interest generously shared their memories and materials. All the translations from Russian are mine.

Chapter 1: *A Corner of Russia*

PAGE

3 *a Russian village:* In Russian, the word for village, *derevnya*, is also the word for "countryside," and denotes the entire social, economic, and cultural life of rural Russia, where more than half the country's population was born, and where many Russians still consider their spiritual roots to be.

As an administrative unit, *derevnya* in tsarist Russia specifically denoted a small village. Even smaller settlements—often only one household—were variously called a *pochinok*, a *khutor*, or a *vyselok*. A more substantial village, usually with a church or a manor, was a *selo*. Several villages made up a *volost;* several *volosti* comprised an *uyezd* (roughly, a county); and the largest regional administrative unit was the *gubernia*, or province. The Soviets renamed the *gubernia* an *oblast*, the *uyezd* a *raion*, and the *volost* an *okrug*.

6 *my grandfather Sergei Osorgin:* In emigration, the Osorgins adopted the French transliteration of their name, Ossorguine. In the interest of consistency, simplicity, and clarity—and with apologies to my mother and other Ossorguines in the United States and France—I use the simpler English transliteration, Osorgin. I generally follow the same rule with other Russian names (e.g., Trubetskoi rather than Troubetzkoy), unless a spelling has become standard in the West (e.g., Tsar Nicholas II rather than Nikolai II). The name Kar also appears in Russian as Karr and Karov, and in English as Carr or Car. I use the most common Russian spelling, Kar.

10 *". . . which indeed was marvelous"*: kn. Gr. N. Trubetskoi, *Gody smut i nadezhd: 1917–1919* (Years of troubles and hopes: 1917–1919) (Montreal: Monastery Press, 1981), pp. 61–68.

10 *still the* barin: *Barin* was a common form of address among peasants to a landowner. The honorific is akin to "master" but a touch more familiar. Peasants also deferentially referred to their masters in the third person in indirect speech.

17 *one of his letters smuggled to the West:* The letter was written to Nikita Struve, editor of *Vestnik*, the quarterly journal of the Russian Student Christian Movement in Paris, on May 14, 1972. Excerpts were first published on August 9, 1972, in the Russian-language New York daily *Novoye Russkoye Slovo*.

21 *". . . failure is more typical of the human condition than heroism"*: Ian Buruma, *The Wages of Guilt: Memories of War in Germany and Japan* (New York: Farrar, Straus and Giroux, 1994), p. 6.

23 *". . . duplicity to triumph among themselves"*: Marquis de Custine, *Empire of the Czar: A Journey through Eternal Russia* (New York: Anchor Books, 1989), p. 233.

Chapter 2: *Dreamy Syerzh*

27 *fir trees at Christmas:* Though nominally an agency of the Foreign Ministry, the UPDK was obviously linked closely to the KGB. All of our Soviet help, from maids to translators, drivers, and even repairmen, were supplied by the UPDK. We knew that part of their job was to report on us, but that did not prevent me and many other correspondents from developing close working relations and even friendships with our Soviet employees, many of whom stayed on after the collapse of the Soviet Union. I'm convinced that they served us far better than they served the KGB and were genuinely happy to see the system collapse. I pity them the double role they were compelled to play by their paranoid system. I am also grateful for their help, and I cherish their friendship.

27 *the highway to Kaluga was closed:* The Soviets made Kaluga a mecca of their space program, because Konstantin Tsiolkovsky, an early theoretician of rocketry, was born and taught there. Seeking to demonstrate that space travel was entirely "made in the USSR," the Soviets built a huge space museum dedicated to Tsiolkovsky in Kaluga, to which schoolchildren were taken on mandatory pilgrimages and where cosmonauts deposited mementos of their space flights. After the Soviet state collapsed the museum fell on hard times; my wife and I visited it in 1994, and we were almost alone.

42–3 *All else is separate:* Unpublished poem by Alexander Trunin. Translated by Serge Schmemann.

Chapter 3: *Exotic Aliens and Serfs*

55 *many Scotsmen among them:* Some of the more illustrious descendants of Scottish expatriates include the hero of the Napoleonic wars Field Marshal Mikhail Barclay de Tolly; two of Peter the Great's closest comrades-in-arms, Yakov (James) Bruce and Patrick Gordon; a renowned palace architect of the eighteenth century, Charles Cameron; and the poet

Mikhail Lermontov, who was descended from one Captain George Learmont, a Scottish adventurer who entered Russian service in the early seventeenth century and claimed descent from Thomas of Erceldoune, a.k.a. Thomas the Rhymer.

55 *Catherine's husband, who had been overthrown and murdered in 1762:* Pushkin notes that there was a widespread belief at the time that the tsar survived the murder attempt, and Pugachev was already the fifth pretender to have come along. Even Catherine's son and heir had doubts about the fate of his father: On coming to the throne as Paul I, his first question to an aide was, "Is my father alive?"

57 *a modern guidebook to the region:* V. S. Zelenov, ed., *Turistskiye tropy Kaluzhskoi oblasti* (Tourist routes of the Kaluga oblast) (Tula: Prioksoye knizhnoye izdatelstvo, 1990), p. 96.

60 *historian named Ya. K. Grot:* Ya. K. Grot, *Materialy dlya istorii Pugachevskago bunta* (Materials for the history of the Pugachev rebellion) (St. Petersburg, 1862), p. 8.

63 *two separate and egregiously unequal worlds:* The people of Russia were divided into *sosloviye*, or estates, each with its specific privileges. The *dvorianstvo* was the highest. But unlike the landed gentry and aristocrats of Europe, the Russian *dvoriane* did not originate as a feudal caste. It was a service estate, descended either from subordinate princes or the military and civil servitors of Muscovite tsars. Under Peter I (the Great, 1672–1725), the hereditary *dvorianstvo* was expanded to include all civil and military officials who achieved a high rank in the state service or were awarded a major state distinction.

Peter also began granting titles. The only indigenous Russian title was *kniaz*, "prince," which was appended to the surnames of all families descended from Russian or Lithuanian princes. Peter the Great began conferring the European titles of count and baron, and these titles, like *kniaz*, were used by every member of the family. Russia also recognized the ranks and titles of all the nations in the empire, from Tatar descendants of Genghis Khan through Georgian princelings, Bessarabian landowners, German "Baltic barons" descended from the Teutonic Knights, and the many well-born but impoverished Europeans (like the Kars) who came to Russia to seek their fortune. The *dvorianstvo* had its own local and provincial assemblies and elected marshals, who maintained scrupulous genealogical and property records and served many local administrative functions.

63 *". . . legalized by chance":* Ivan Turgenev, "Nekotorye mysli o sovremennom znachenii russkogo dvorianstva" (Some thoughts on the contemporary significance of the Russian *dvorianstvo*) in *Sobraniye sochineniy* (Collected Works), vol. 11 (Moscow, 1983), pp. 284–85.

63 *". . . erased from history":* Yu. M. Lotman, *Besedy o russkoi kul'ture* (Discourses on Russian Culture) (St. Petersburg: Iskusstvo-SPB, 1994), p. 28.

64 *". . . an epoch of slavery":* Baron N. N. Wrangel, "Landowning Russia," in *Starye gody* (Years gone by), a bimonthly journal "for lovers of art and antiquity" published in St. Petersburg from 1907 to 1916. The editor was Pyotr Veiner, an art historian and bibliophile who remained active in the first Soviet years safeguarding art and antiquities, until he was arrested and executed in 1925.

65 *"Baron Brambeus and Rousseau":* Verse by Nikolai Gumilev. "Baron Brambeus" was the pseudonym of the popular writer Osip Senkovsky (1800–1858).

Chapter 4: *Cards and Madness*

68 *owner of the estate Avchurino:* Dmitry Poltoratsky's son Sergei Dmitrievich was well known in intellectual circles in his day as a friend of Pushkin, a witness to the French Revolution, and a bibliophile. He amassed a huge library at Avchurino, for which he built a four-story tower in Gothic style, and which he eventually donated to the Rumiantsev Museum in Moscow, whence it passed to the Lenin Library, now the Russian State Library. Poltoratsky was also a passionate card-player and lost a fortune. In the end, he was compelled to flee Russia to escape his debtors, and he died in Neuilly, France, in 1884. The old estate became the Avchurino Kolkhoz; the Gothic tower still stands.

70 *". . . he settled in Kaluga": Grandmother's Stories:* This is a collection of stories that a young member of the gentry heard from his grandmother, Elizaveta Yankova, a landowner's wife of no particular distinction save her memory, who lived from 1768 to 1861. The *Stories* are an invaluable record of Russian gentry life of the period, ranging from the gossip of court balls to epidemics and everyday life. The grandson, D. D. Blagovo, originally published the stories in a journal. Then, in 1885, he published them as a book. It was republished in 1989 as *Rasskazy babushki: iz vospominaniy piati pokoleniy. Zapisannye i sobrannye eyo vnukom D. Blagovo* (Grandmother's stories; from the memories of generations. Recorded and collected by her grandson D. Blagovo) (Leningrad: Nauka, 1989), p. 68.

73 *playing cards at the English Club:* Cards played a central part in the life of a Russian gentleman, far in excess of anything in Europe. The literature of the time is filled with the drama and imagery of card-playing—Pushkin's *The Queen of Spades* and Dostoevsky's *The Gambler* are but two of the better-known instances in which cards become a game of life, casting chance against fate. "What is our life? A game," declares Herman in *The Queen of Spades* before casting the card that holds the difference between total happiness and total ruin. Stakes were always high and often dramatic: In the early 1800s, Prince Alexander Nikolayevich Golitsyn lost his wife to Count Lev Kirillovich Razumovsky, a notorious Moscow reveler known as "Comte Léon," and by the cockeyed conventions of the time it was the poor woman who bore the brunt of social ostracism—at least until, at a ball, the gallant Tsar Alexander I publicly invited her to dance with him and addressed her as "Comtesse," thus conferring respectability on her new marriage. With time, the passion for games of chance spread beyond cards, and a grand duke losing vast fortunes in Monte Carlo or the reckless young officer playing Russian roulette became national stereotypes.

Chapter 5: *A Spiritual Cradle*

85 *house on Bolshaya Basmannaya:* The house no longer stands, but I have the address: "Parish of the Church of the Great Martyr Nikita in the Old-Basmannaya Sloboda, behind the Pokrovsky Gates, behind the earthen bulwark." Staraya Basmannaya was called Karl-Marx Street under the Communists, but has its old name back now.

86 *rigid codes of chivalry and honor:* Honor was a dead-serious and often complex matter in a caste descended from warriors, and nowhere more so than in the Imperial Guard regiments,

whose officers' mess was the final arbiter in matters of a gentleman's duty. One cousin of the Osorgins, Princess Agrafena ("Grusha") Obolensky, was courted by an officer named Panyutin, but she refused him in hopes of making a better match. After a year, she reconsidered and announced to Panyutin that she was now prepared to accept his offer of marriage. He, in the meantime, had gone south to Georgia, where he bestowed his attentions on a Georgian lady. Honor now required him to return to Grusha, since he had made her an offer of marriage, but that in turn so sullied the honor of the Georgian woman that her four brothers challenged him to consecutive duels. The officers of Panyutin's Hussar regiment convened to ponder the sticky dilemma and ruled that he must first marry Grusha and then defend his honor, thus in effect condemning Panyutin to death and Grusha to instant widowhood. The wedding was held in secrecy for fear of the enraged Georgians, and soon after, Panyutin was duly killed on the field of honor. Grusha Panyutin lived out her life a widow. It was evidently not easy. In a letter to her cousin, Olga Trubetskoi, in 1895, she wrote, "*La vertu m'ennuie plus que jamais*" ("Virtue bores me more than ever").

96   *name days:* In Russian tradition, the name day—the day on which the church celebrates the saint after whom you are named—is celebrated much as a birthday, with a party and gifts.

100   "*. . . warms the soul*": A. K. Larin, Preface to *Dmitry Ivanovich Malinin: Opyt istoricheskogo putevoditelia po Kaluge i glavneishim tsentram guberni* (1912) (Dmitry Ivanovich Malinin: Experience of a historical guide to Kaluga and the main centers of the province [1912]) (Kaluga: Zolotaya Alleya, 1992), p. 5.

Chapter 6: *Real Country People*

107   "*. . . to rise early*": Trubetskoi, *Years of Troubles and Hopes*, pp. 64–65.

108   *his sister Varya:* Varvara (Varya) Mikhailovna Osorgin (1859–1917) married Yakov (Yasha) Grigorievich Zhilinsky (1853–1918), a career military officer. General Zhilinsky was appointed head of the General Staff in 1911 and then governor general of Poland and commander of the northwestern front. He was held responsible for Russia's initial setbacks in East Prussia in World War I and was reassigned to the rear. In 1915 he was named Russia's representative to the Allied Council in Paris. Zhilinsky was shot by the Bolsheviks in the Crimea.

  Mikhail Osorgin writes of his sister that Varya was not particularly pretty but had a marvelous voice. She did not like the country and was always eager to get back to St. Petersburg. Mikhail Osorgin was never close to Varya.

109   *Rubinstein:* Anton Rubinstein (1829–1894) was a pianist and composer, and a cofounder of the St. Petersburg Conservatory. He and his brother, the pianist Nikolai Rubinstein, were friends of Prince Nikolai Petrovich Trubetskoi, Mikhail Mikhailovich Osorgin's father-in-law (see note to p. 110), and it was through Trubetskoi that Anton Rubinstein met Varya Osorgin.

109   "*. . . previous lethargy*": Dmitry Malinin, *Experience of a historical guide to Kaluga and the main centers of the province*, p. 52.

109   *made Kaluga eminently suitable as a place of "internal exile":* Among the more prominent pre-revolutionary exiles in Kaluga were Bishop Soltyk of Cracow in 1768, the last Crimean

khan in 1786, the Kirghiz Sultan Arigazi-Abdul-Aziz in 1823, and Queen Thekla Iraklievna of Georgia in 1835.

110 *Prince Nikolai Petrovich Trubetskoi:* The numerous Trubetskois played a major role in the life of the Osorgins, both in Russia and in emigration.

Prince Nikolai Petrovich Trubetskoi (1828–1900), vice governor of Kaluga from 1876 to 1885, had 13 children from two marriages. By his first wife, the wealthy Countess Lyubov Vasilievna Orlov-Denisov, he had three children, among them Pyotr (1854–1936), marshal of nobility in Moscow and my wife's great-grandfather. By his second wife, Sofia Alexeyvna Lopukhin, Nikolai Petrovich had 10 children, including Sergei (1862–1905), philosopher and rector of Moscow University; Evgeny (1863–1920), philosopher and professor at the universities of Kiev and Moscow; Antonina (1864–1901), who married Fyodor Samarin, a member of a celebrated family of Slavophiles and conservatives; Elizaveta (1865–1935), the wife of Mikhail Mikhailovich Osorgin; Olga (1867–1947), the family chronicler, whose voluminous archives are now in the Central State Archive of Literature and Art in Moscow; Grigory (1873–1930), whose memoirs are cited above; and Marina (1877–1924), who married Prince Nikolai Viktorovich Gagarin, and whose daughter Sonia married her cousin Sergei Osorgin (they were my grandparents).

Grigory Trubetskoi was especially close to the Osorgins. He served as ambassador to Serbia and deputy minister of Foreign Affairs before the revolution, and afterward became active in the political affairs of the volunteer (White) army in southern Russia, as its official first for religious affairs and later for finances. Thirteen years his senior, Mikhail Mikhailovich tutored Grigory as a boy and took a special liking to him, while Grigory felt at ease with the shy and patriarchal "Mishan." With time, Grigory and his kind, generous, matronly wife developed similar ties to the Osorgin children, and especially to the young Georgy. It was to his "Uncle Grishanchik" that Georgy wrote his most thoughtful and moving letters from a Soviet prison.

In emigration, the large villa in the Paris suburb of Clamart that Grigory had purchased with his father-in-law, Count Konstantin Chreptowicz-Butenev, served as a center for his entire extended family. There they built the small chapel at which Mikhail Mikhailovich Osorgin, after finally leaving Russia in 1931, was ordained a priest. The chapel, which was also my father's first parish, still stands.

123 *bouquets of pussy willows:* On Palm Sunday, Russians traditionally bring pussy willows to church as a substitute for palm fronds and a symbol of the impending renewal of life. The feast is accordingly known in Russian as "Pussy Willow Sunday"—Verbnoye Voskresenye.

Chapter 7: *A Leave-taking of Past Greatness*

130 *Grand Duke Konstantin Konstantinovich:* The grand duke (1850–1915) was a grandson of Nicholas I and an uncle twice removed of Nicholas II. He was the last Romanov to be buried in the cathedral of Sts. Peter and Paul in St. Petersburg before the revolution.

133 *Guards regiment:* One of the second Mikhail Mikhailovich's nephews, Vladimir Sergeyevich Trubetskoi, described in his memoirs the difficulty of choosing a regiment:

"It was spring, and I needed to quickly choose a regiment. But how was one to be guided in this? . . . I didn't understand then what was good and what was bad about a regiment. My mother was still in London, and I didn't know what to do. To me, it seemed important to choose a regiment that was stationed in a major city and had a good uniform. At the General Staff store on Prechistenka, I bought a color poster with the uniforms of all the Russian cavalry regiments. There were so many that the eyes ran wild. They were all beautiful, but I liked the Hussars best. (It's not for nothing that one of the aphorisms of Kuzma Prutkov says, 'If it's beauty that you seek, join the Hussars.')"

To Trubetskoi's mother it was self-evident that the military meant a regiment in the Life Guards: "The Guards gave a 'position in society.' They opened better prospects for a career. And above all, officers were chosen selectively and exclusively from the nobility." Of the Guards, moreover, Princess Trubetskoi recognized only the elite Chevalier Guards and the Preobrazhensky Life Guards regiment. Vladimir wanted to join the cavalry, but the Chevalier Guards was too expensive, and his mother feared that her irresponsible son would soon get into debt. Eventually, his uncle Mikhail Osorgin persuaded Vladimir to join the Blue Cuirassiers, formally Her Majesty's Cuirassier Life Guards regiment. (Vladimir Trubetskoi, *Zapiski kirasira* (Notes of a Cuirassier) (Moscow: Rossiya, 1991).

For valor in World War I, Vladimir Trubetskoi was awarded the St. George's Cross, Russia's highest military award. After the revolution, unlike most of his relatives, he stayed in the Soviet Union. He vanished in the Gulag in 1937 along with his eldest daughter. His wife died in prison in 1943, and their surviving eight children all suffered for their heritage.

133 *". . . famous people in Russian history"*: Yuri Lotman, *Discourses on Russian Culture*, pp. 42–43.

138 *Russians are notoriously given to conspiracy theories:* The reactionary "village writer" Vasily Belov once pounced on me at a dinner party in Moscow, demanding to know why "your President Clinton" directed operations at the Moscow "White House" on October 4, 1993, when President Yeltsin sent army tanks against the Congress of People's Deputies. To Belov, it was inconceivable that an operation like that, improvised only hours before it was launched and pathetic in execution, was not the product of some global intrigue.

141 *massive uprising of peasants:* Richard G. Robbins, Jr., *The Tsar's Viceroys: Russian Provincial Governors in the Last Years of the Empire* (Ithaca, N.Y.: Cornell University Press, 1987). Robbins cites these figures from P. N. Pershin, *Agrarnaia revoliutsiia v Rossii: Istoriko-ekonomicheskoye issledovanie* (The Agrarian Revolution in Russia: An Historico-Economic Inquiry), vol. 1 (Moscow, 1966).

152 *assailed the monarch directly:* The story is told by Roberta Thompson Manning in *The Crisis of the Old Order in Russia: Gentry and Government* (Princeton: Princeton University Press, 1982), p. 112.

Chapter 8: *"We Will Renounce the Old World"*

155 *one of the most splendid estates in Russia:* Bogoroditsk was built by Catherine the Great for her own use, and the estate eventually passed to an illegitimate son she had had by Grigory Orlov. She gave the child the name "Bobrinsky," from the Russian word for "beaver," be-

cause after his birth he was sent abroad in a beaver wrap. Count Vladimir Bobrinsky was his great-grandson.

156 *the only Osorgin to marry at Sergiyevskoye:* This intermarrying can be a bit unnerving, but it was not uncommon among the *dvoriane*. Far more questionable is my grandfather's marriage to his first cousin, which required a bishop's permission. The Church also had a rule against two brothers marrying two sisters (I don't know why). This rule led to a rather tense unauthorized wedding at Sergiyevskoye. The problem arose when two Trubetskoi half-brothers, Pyotr and Sergei, fell in love with two Obolensky sisters, Alexandra and Praskovia. Pyotr married first, unaware of his brother's ardor. After eight years of unfulfilled love, Sergei and Praskovia decided to marry in defiance of the Church. The second Mikhail Mikhailovich arranged for a quiet wedding in Sergiyevskoye officiated by an army chaplain from Kiev, assuming that this priest would not be aware of the problem. At the last minute the chaplain balked, but Mikhail Mikhailovich "convinced" him—at what cost we don't know—and the wedding went ahead.

161 *"black hundreds":* This was the term used for reactionary populist groups in the early twentieth century. Pro-absolutist and virulently anti-Semitic, their broad demands included improvements in the lives of workers and peasants.

162 *melodramatic but reasonably accurate report:* N. Dobrotvor, *Krovavoye poboishche v Tule. Gubernskaya komissiya po oznamenovaniyu 20-oi godovshchiny 1905 g.* (Bloody slaughter in Tula: Provincial commission on the establishment of the 20th anniversary of 1905) (Tula: Izdaniye Tulskogo Istparta, 1925).

168 *So ended Mikhail Mikhailovich's public-service career:* Sergei Osorgin writes in his memoirs that his father's principled opposition to the death penalty was the reason for his resignation. Under the martial law introduced in 1905, military tribunals could order executions (and did), but the sentence had to be endorsed by the governor. Sergei Osorgin writes that his father refused to do so and, after long discussions with the Interior minister, resigned.

Mikhail Mikhailovich makes no mention of this in his memoirs. I suspect that Sergei, recording his recollections many years after his father's death and having no access to his memoirs, confused Tula with his father's tenure in Grodno and Kharkov. In both of those provinces, Osorgin indeed had confrontations as a result of his opposition to the death penalty. Even if this was not the immediate reason for his leaving Tula, it surely would soon have become one. Under the new prime minister, Pyotr Stolypin, so many people were hanged by military tribunals that a noose came to be known as "Stolypin's necktie."

168 *Vice Governor Khvostov, who now became acting governor:* By now Khvostov openly sided with the reactionary right. He subsequently published letters he had written to his father, an influential senator in St. Petersburg, assailing Osorgin's handling of the October crisis. Among other things, he claimed that Osorgin had kept a carriage standing by so he could escape if things got hot, and that it was Osorgin who had ordered the police to protect his residence on the night of the shooting. Khvostov—smart, cunning, and ambitious—later served as governor in Vologda and in Nizhny Novgorod, and as a reactionary "black hundreds" delegate to the Duma. In September 1915, he was appointed Minister of the Interior, the thirteenth in Nicholas II's reign, but he was fired five months later, when the tsar discovered that he was among those plotting against Rasputin. Khvostov was executed by the Bolsheviks in 1918.

Chapter 9: *Soon It Will Be Ours*

176 *white mushrooms:* Though *belyi grib* translates as "white mushroom," it is actually the *boletus edulis,* also known as *cèpe* and *porcino.* The *masliata* that the children were allowed to pick is the *boletus lutens,* a more common and less prized variety.

180 *a gentry ball was still a grand ritual:* I am indebted for many details about Moscow social customs to the memoirs of Prince Sergei Evgenievich Trubetskoi (1890–1949), one of Sergei Osorgin's many cousins, with whose family he lived while a student in Moscow. They were about the same age, studied at Moscow University at about the same time, and married two sisters, their cousins Sonia and Marina Gagarin. (Kn. S. E. Trubetskoi, *Minuvsheye* (The Past) [Paris: YMCA Press, 1989], pp. 67–71.)

184 *Sergei had his first serious talk with Sonia on that stump:* In the fall of 1991, my uncle Michael Ossorguine, Sergei's oldest child, came to Russia and went with me to Sergiyevskoye. A massive stroke several years earlier had damaged some of his faculties, but not his artistic eye or his sense of humor. He kept looking for the stump, about which he said his father often talked; I was not aware of "the stump" at the time, but we found one that seemed appropriate, and Uncle Misha began to speak with dramatic intonations: "Now I will tell you the story of what happened here as I heard it from my parents. My father recalled dancing snowflakes . . . sparkling frost . . . her beauty . . . their love. My mother remembered his runny nose."

That fit with my memories of my grandparents: my grandfather romantic and cozy, with an antique pince-nez over a massive mustache redolent of sweet pipe tobacco; my grandmother practical, rather strict, unsentimental.

Chapter 10: *Hussars to Commissars*

191 *whose commander was Dmitry Alexandrovich Lopukhin:* In one of his first battles, Lopukhin watched through binoculars as his only son, Georgy, fell while charging the German trenches. An adjutant galloped up to report on the battle: "The trenches are taken, the Germans are in flight, one officer killed." "Who?" asked Lopukhin. "Cornet Lopukhin." The commander crossed himself, rode up to his slain son, silently made the sign of the cross over him, kissed him, and immediately returned to action. His officers said that thereafter he seemed to be looking for death, which he soon found: Three months later he was heavily wounded in the stomach and died in terrible agony in Warsaw.

199 *Nikolskoye-Gagarino:* The manor of Nikolskoye-Gagarino still stands, one of the most elegant of surviving rural manor houses. It was the first "closed area" my wife and I visited, soon after travel restrictions were lifted in September 1992. Turning off the main Riga highway, we drove right by a military base with a missile displayed outside the gates—probably one of the ABM bases ringing Moscow. On our return trip, a horrified policeman stopped us. He had never heard of the change of rules and refused to believe that foreigners were now allowed to go anywhere they wished. Glancing around, he leaned close to me and quietly

asked, "Are you aware of what's behind these trees?" "A missile base," I answered casually. He stood, stunned and obviously confused, then waved us on in resignation.

203 *landowners on all sides were being thrown out:* Among those evicted were the Princes Golitsyn from their Gorodnya estate. In February 1918 a group of fifty former farm laborers, Red Army soldiers, and Kaluga workers organized a commune in Gorodnya called Krasnyi Gorodok (Red City), taking 540 acres of the best land and most of the surviving horses, cattle, and equipment. *Pravda* reported in 1924 that "local *kulaks* waged a vicious campaign against the commune. They poisoned the communards and in every other way tried to damage the communal economy. Stacks of grain and hay were set on fire. The former owner of the estate also did not leave the communards without attention," *Pravda* continued. "He wrote them a letter from abroad: 'Bandits and thieves! Go ahead and steal without conscience my house, my property, my cattle. The devil take you. Only preserve my century-old linden park. On these lindens, planted by my ancestors, I will hang you, wretches, when I return.'"

204 *without even being given a chance to get dressed:* The unfortunate neighbor was E. D. Bylim-Kholosovsky, a liberal landowner who had rented rooms at his estate, Bogimovo, to Anton Chekhov for the summer of 1891, after the writer returned from Sakhalin. In a letter from Bogimovo, Chekhov described Bylim-Kholosovsky as "a young *barin* who affects a loose blouson and huge boots and is very absent-minded and liberal, and keeps as his bookkeeper a red-haired, toothless maiden named Amenaisa Yerastovna."

Of the estate, Chekhov wrote: "Huge house, outstanding park, unavoidable views at the sight of which for some reason I am compelled to say 'Ahhh,' a stream, a pond with hungry carp that love to get on a hook. Many sick, smell of iodine and walks in the evening. I work on my Sakhalin, and, during breaks, so as not to kill my family of hunger, I caress the Muse. . . ."

After Bylim-Kholosovsky was expelled, Bogimovo became a commune, then a *kolkhoz*, and just before World War II the house was converted to Psychiatric Hospital No. 4, which it remains today, with 250 patients and one doctor.

207 *made their way to France:* The eldest Osorgin daughter, Sofia, fled eastward from the revolution with her husband, Nikolai Lopukhin. After an arduous odyssey across Siberia and Manchuria to Harbin, in 1929 they boarded a Chinese freighter for the United States, and thence steamed to Paris to be reunited with their families.

Mikhail Osorgin—the third Mikhail Mikhailovich—served after the revolution on a Red Cross train, which he managed to transfer to the command of the White armies. In 1919, in Yalta, he married Countess Elena Muraviev, who was a nurse on the train. They left Russia with the evacuating White armies and eventually settled in Paris, where Osorgin helped to found the St. Serge Theological Institute. He remained at the institute (of which my father, Alexander Schmemann, was a graduate) as an instructor and choir director until his death in 1950.

Chapter 11: *The Classes Struggle and a Tractor Arrives*

214 *Kolchak:* Admiral Alexander Kolchak (1873?–1920) was the leader of anti-Bolshevik forces in Siberia in 1918–1919. He was finally defeated and captured in Irkutsk in 1919 and executed in 1920.

215 *62 tovarichestvos [associations]:* The state farms (*kolkhozy*), artels, and *tovarishchestvy* were all various organizations of collectivized land. State farms were directly run by the state. The *artel* was a farming cooperative, which came later to be known as a *sovkhoz*. The *tovarishchestvo* was a grouping of small landholdings whose owners worked collectively; *tovarishchestvy* were soon absorbed into *sovkhozy*.

217 *a history of vocational education in Kaluga:* V. D. Lagutin, *Kratkiye ocherki istorii narodnogo obrazovaniia Kaluzhskogo kraya* (A brief study of the history of public education in the Kaluga krai) (Kaluga, 1987), pp. 144–47

219 *the first man in space:* Yuri Gagarin was one of the biggest stars in the Soviet pantheon. One reason, of course, was that he symbolized the Soviet Union's early victory in the space race. The other was that the Soviet Union had precious few heroes: Most of the leaders after Lenin were disgraced and expunged from history, and few generals, writers, or scientists managed to stay sufficiently ideologically pure to be glorified by the state. Gagarin was perfect—a genuine hero with a beautiful smile, and he died in the crash of a fighter jet in 1968, seven years after his historic flight, before he could tarnish his image. But such canned legends never survived the streets: Stories were always circulating that Gagarin crashed his jet because he was drunk, or shooting moose, or had smuggled a woman on board.

222 *Evdokiya Timofeyevna Pokrovsky:* I met Evdokiya Pokrovsky through her son, Konstantin Konstantinovich Pokrovsky. For most of his life she had concealed from him his clerical roots, believing that it could endanger his career as a nuclear scientist. The truth came out when she read about me in a newspaper and told her son that his grandfather had come from the same village as mine. Pokrovsky tracked me down, and I read to him Mikhail Mikhailovich Osorgin's description of his grandfather, Ilya Pokrovsky, the last reader (subdeacon) in the church.

Chapter 12: *On the Path to Communism*

229 *". . . a new despotism":* Richard Pipes, *Russia under the Bolshevik Regime* (New York: Knopf, 1993), p. 493.

230 *Patriarch Tikhon:* After the collapse of the Soviet Union, Patriarch Tikhon was canonized as a saint of the Orthodox Church. His remains were discovered concealed under the floor of the Old Cathedral of the Donskoi Monastery, where his body lies.

232 *"red popes":* "Red popes" (*krasnye popy*) was a derogatory term for priests of the "Living Church," a breakaway branch of the Russian Orthodox Church which the Soviet regime recognized and patronized in an attempt to create disunity among believers.

244 *". . . unnatural, irregular perversions":* Lev Kopelev, *Ease My Sorrows*, translated by Antonina W. Bouis (New York: Random House, 1983), p. 244.

Chapter 13: *Seventeenth Versta*

246 *Peredelkino:* Many such elite suburbs sprouted around Moscow, as Russia's new masters evolved from egalitarian revolutionaries into a new class of pampered bosses. These compounds ranged from clusters of modest houses to spacious two-story wooden houses set on large wooded lots for senior commissars and honored servants of the state. Peredelkino was a large settlement, with several dozen large wooden houses and an imposing neoclassical House of Creativity, where esteemed writers could retreat to replenish their creative juices with sweet Crimean champagne. Most residents were there as a reward for placing their pens at the service of the state. What is remarkable is that several genuine writers also found their way to Peredelkino.

    The most famous was Boris Pasternak. His house in Peredelkino, where he endured the storm over the publication of *Doctor Zhivago*, and where he died in 1960, was turned by his heirs into an unofficial museum, which drew a steady stream of visitors and controversy. The house of the late Kornei Chukovsky, Russia's favorite children's writer, was also maintained as a museum, and it was there that Alexander Solzhenitsyn spent his last days waiting for arrest in 1972. Writers and poets who rose to prominence in the 1950s and 1960s—such as Anatoly Rybakov, Bella Akhmadulina, Yevgeny Yevtushenko, and Andrei Voznesensky—all had dachas in Peredelkino, and through the early 1980s these were among the few places where it was possible for foreigners to visit without any hassle. The charm and prestige of Peredelkino attracted a less savory element as well. Viktor Louis, a Soviet "journalist" celebrated as an "unofficial" channel of Kremlin information (and disinformation) for generations of Western correspondents, had a dacha nearby filled with antiques and icons, as well as a garage with several cars, including a Bentley and a vintage BMW. The old estate of the Barons Bode, adjacent to a lovely church whose gleaming cupolas could be seen from afar, was restored as the suburban residence of the Patriarchs of the Russian Orthodox Church.

    After the collapse of the Soviet Union, we learned of another, far more lavish estate, hidden farther in the woods behind high walls and unmarked gates. There the bosses of the Communist Youth League—few of them under fifty—had built themselves a vast compound of glistening marble and glittering chandeliers. The compound was typical of the tasteless extravagance found wherever the proletarian dictators congregated. We found it in 1992, when the Komsomol opened the restaurant to foreigners with dollars.

    The fate of the writers' colony, as of the Writers' Union and every other Soviet institution, is now up in the air. Already the ostentatious brick mansions of the new rich are sprouting on all sides. But at least the Pasternak and Chukovsky houses have been officially designated as museums.

246 *Maxim Gorky:* Gorky (real name Alexei Maximovich Peshkov) (1868–1936) was a writer who supported the Bolsheviks, though he opposed their seizure of power in 1917 and lived abroad in the 1920s. On his return, he became first president of the Union of Writers in 1932 and a prime formulator of the official Soviet literary doctrine, socialist realism. He died, or was killed, in 1936.

247 *the lives of the emigrants and their former homeland diverged:* When I was growing up, "Russia" and "Soviet Russia" were two different things. Our émigré Russia was something that existed in Paris, New York, and wherever else Russian émigrés managed to regroup and restart their lives, and we regarded the Soviets who occasionally ventured out much as other Westerners did, as exotic and a bit suspicious.

The emergence of an independent Russia after the collapse of the Soviet Union created a problem for many in the Russian diaspora. The new Russia had very little in common with their mythical homeland. Reactions varied. Some younger Russians with Western skills went to Russia to take advantage of the new opportunities there (at one point I counted 23 relatives in Russia, all doing quite well). Many older émigrés, by contrast, could not reconcile their émigré Russia with the real thing and reacted by simply ignoring it. The Russian Church Outside Russia, a conservative émigré church that for 70 years had maintained that it was the true successor to the prerevolutionary Russian Church, simply dismissed the Moscow Patriarch and the Russian Orthodox Church as illegitimate because of their links to Soviet regimes, and went on as if nothing had changed.

Similarly, relatives inside the Soviet Union found the émigré world increasingly alien. Andrei Trubetskoi, for example, unexpectedly found himself on the other side, among Western kin, when he was wounded during World War II and captured by the Germans. He felt out of place and longed to return to his homeland, however oppressive its regime. He looked with disdain on Russians who entered the service of the Germans in the belief that they were helping to liberate Russia from the Communists. Andrei had no sympathy for the Communists, who had killed his father and sister, but Soviet Russia was his country, which he had to help defend from the German invader.

Andrei Trubetskoi's story is one of the most extraordinary sagas I heard in the Soviet Union. He was born in 1920 as the son of a former imperial officer who stayed on after the revolution. The family was banished first to Zagorsk, north of Moscow, and then to Uzbekistan; his father, mother, and eldest sister (and many other relatives) perished in the purges and the Gulag. Andrei was drafted into the army in 1939 and was gravely wounded on the northwestern front in 1941. Left behind German lines, he was discovered in a POW hospital by another Trubetskoi, who had just been liberated from a Soviet prison. Because the Trubetskois are descended from the fourteenth-century Lithuanian ruler Gedimin (and probably because the Germans assumed that a Russian prince was by definition virulently anti-Soviet), the Germans let Andrei go. He spent several years with relatives in Poland, Austria, and Germany, but he felt strongly that his place was inside Russia, for better or for worse, so he joined the partisans in 1944 and fought his way back home. Despite heroic service with the partisans, he was arrested in 1949 and sentenced to ten years for treason. Released in 1955, he completed a doctorate in biology, directed a laboratory of cardiological studies, and raised a fine family of five.

We became close friends. Soon after my wife and I arrived in 1991, Andrei finally received from the KGB the death certificates of his father and eldest sister, and he learned that both were executed almost immediately after their arrest in Uzbekistan in 1937. The family was never told that, and had continued sending parcels for many years. We all gathered in the Church of St. Ilya in Moscow for the long-delayed funeral service, at which the death certificates, in Russian and Uzbek, with the cause of death listed as "shot," were placed where the bodies normally would have been. Andrei also received the KGB files on his mother: she had taken some refugees into her crowded home, and one of them promptly denounced her to the police to make more room in the apartment. As a "former person," and a princess at that, she had no defense. She soon died in prison, apparently of raw despair: the mug shot released by the KGB shows a face distorted by horror.

Andrei told me that of all the suffering he endured, the only experience he was unable to talk about for years was the interrogations by the KGB. The humiliation, the sheer injustice, was too overwhelming. But he and his wife prevailed.

She, too, was remarkable. Born Elena Golitsyn, she was a shy and modest architectural restorer who traveled across the Soviet Union to fulfill the promise she had made as he was being arrested—that she would find him wherever he was sent. She never doubted she would find Andrei; her only fear was that she would find him bowed and broken. When she finally spotted him, in a long line of *zeks* returning from the Kazakhstan quarry where he worked, her heart lifted with joy: he was walking tall and proud.

Now fate had brought us together. We were related through the Trubetskois: his grandfather, Sergei Nikolayevich Trubetskoi, the philosopher and rector of Moscow University, was my great-grandmother Liza Osorgin's brother. He wrote the play that brought my parents together, and had himself been married at Sergiyevskoye.

248 *Ilf and Petrov:* The pseudonyms of Ilya Fainzilberg (1897–1937) and Yevgeny Katayev (1903–1942), writers whose *The Twelve Chairs*, published in 1928, and *The Golden Calf*, 1931, satirized aspects of Soviet society.

249 *"... a firm belief in God":* Sergei Golitsyn, *Zapiski utselevshego* (Notes of a Survivor) (Moscow: Orbita, 1990), pp. 247–50.

249 *Menshevik:* Derived from the Russian for "minority," the Mensheviks were the non-Leninist, relatively moderate faction of the Social Democratic Labor Party. The Leninists came to be known as "Bolsheviks," from the word for "majority." The Mensheviks were suppressed after the 1917 Revolution.

250 *fledgling political police:* The Soviet secret police was known by a variety of names and acronyms from the time Felix Dzerzhinsky created the "Extraordinary Commission to Fight Counterrevolution and Sabotage" (Cheka) by a secret resolution of December 7, 1917. In 1922, it became the GPU (State Political Administration); in 1923, the OGPU (Consolidated State Political Administration); in 1943, the NKVD (People's Commissariat for Internal Affairs); in 1943, the NKGB (People's Commissariat for State Security); in 1946, the MGB (Ministry for State Security); in 1953, the MVD (Ministry of Internal Affairs); and after 1954, the KGB (Committee for State Security), which it remained until the Soviet Union collapsed. The current Russian successor is called the Federal Security Service.

252 *mining venture in Georgia:* In 1925, Harriman entered into a deal with the Soviet government to mine manganese in the republic of Georgia, with Elliott as his representative. Two years later, the travails of doing business with the Communists forced Harriman to liquidate the venture, and he concluded that Americans doing business in the Soviet Union were prey to "the grandest aggregation of corruption, incompetence, and utter brutality that the world

has seen for centuries." (Rudy Abramson, *Spanning the Century: The Life of W. Averell Harriman, 1891–1986* [New York, 1992], p. 163).

257 *X.B.:* These are the Cyrillic initials for the words "Christ is risen" in Russian (*Khristos voskrese*).

260 *Descent into Darkness:* Written between 1977 and 1979, the work was included in a collection of Volkov's writings published in 1989 on the occasion of his ninetieth birthday (Oleg Volkov, *Vek nadezhd i krushenii* [Age of Hopes and Ruin] [Moscow: Sovetsky Pisatel, 1989], pp. 6–434.).

263 "*. . . whose name I do not even know*": Interview with Jo Durden-Smith, published in the Moscow *Times*, December 4, 1993.

264 *a letter to a cousin:* The letter was to Serge Grigorievich Troubetzkoy, who included it in a collection of family letters that he published at his own expense (S. G. Troubetzkoy, ed., *Semeinaya pis'mennaya khronika s 1917g. do 1930g* [A Family Chronicle in Letters from 1917 to 1930] [Sea Cliff, N.Y.: self-published, 1986]).

265 *my mother, who was eight years old . . . :* My mother, Juliana Ossorguine (in the French spelling), was born on October 6, 1923, in Baden-Baden. Her parents were then living in a house owned by the Gagarins, Villa Menshikov. When she was three, the family moved to Clamart, outside Paris. Like many émigrés, her father, Sergei, tried many jobs but never resumed a career. My mother attended the College Ste. Marie in Neuilly and obtained her licencié ès lettres (B.A.) in classics at the Sorbonne. In New York, she taught French and Russian at the Chapin, Spence, and Brearley schools, and was headmistress of Spence from 1977 to 1981. She is now retired and lives in the New York suburb of Crestwood.

Chapter 14: *Thank You, Comrade Stalin*

278 *Birobidjan:* In 1937, Stalin proclaimed Birobidjan, a remote corner of the Khabarovsk territory in the Russian Far East, a "Jewish Autonomous Region." But few Jews ever settled there; in 1979 the 10,000 Jewish inhabitants composed only 5.4 percent of the region's population.

Chapter 16: *We're Still Alive*

306 "*evil empire*": I can't think of anything else said about the Communists by the West that created such a stir among them. They had answers for all the standard accusations—of human rights violations, of being militaristic, closed, and repressive ("What about your Negroes?" they would smugly retort). But "evil empire" was a qualitatively new charge, one they could not simply turn around, and it came from an American president they thought they could understand. The commissars in the Kremlin always preferred Republicans; Democrats like John F. Kennedy and Jimmy Carter were ideologues in the Soviets' eyes, stuck on human rights and grand gestures, while Republicans were like themselves—

conservative, businesslike, pragmatic. The last Republican in the White House before Reagan, Richard Nixon, had initiated détente, and their premier America-watcher, Georgy Arbatov, assured them that Reagan would follow suit. I'm convinced that the "evil empire" tag, followed in 1983 by the "Star Wars" initiative, was critical in undermining the old guard and helping to clear the way for Gorbachev.

Index

Credits

Grateful acknowledgment is made to the following for permission to use illustrations from their collections:

Eugene and Helen Troubetzkoy: Photographs by Princess Olga Trubetskoi on pages 46, 67, 87, 91, 108, 110, 115, 131, 140, 144, 174, 183

Antonina Kamarovsky: Photographs on pages ii, 252; drawing by Maria Osorgin on page 249

Sophie Ozerov: Photographs on pages 178, 192, 266

Juliana Samarine: Photographs on pages 8, 62, 72

Michael Ossorguine: Silhouettes by Maria Osorgin on pages 3, 26, 49, 66, 82, 102, 128, 153, 169, 190, 211, 229, 246, 267, 285, 306, 333; illustrations on 251, 253, 261

Alexander Kandidov: Illustrations on pages 161, 165, 272

Koltsovo Museum, Alexandra Trunin, director: Photographs on pages 216, 219, 226, 238

Trud: Illustration on page 29

Grateful acknowledgment is made to the following for permission to use their photographs:

Bill Swersey: Photographs on pages 5, 41, 308

Otto Pohl: Photographs on pages 219, 312

Mary Schmemann: Photograph on page 243

The photographs on pages 97, 274, 288, 296, and 301 are from the author's own collection.

A NOTE ON THE TYPE

Pierre Simon Fournier *le jeune,* who designed the type used in this book, was both an originator and a collector of types. His services to the art of printing were his design of letters, his creation of ornaments and initials, and his standardization of type sizes. His types are old style in character and sharply cut. In 1764 and 1766 he published his *Manuel typographique,* a treatise on the history of French types and printing, on type-founding in all its details, and on what many consider his most important contribution to typography—the measurement of type by the point system.

Composed by North Market Street Graphics, Lancaster, Pennsylvania
Printed and bound by Quebecor Printing, Martinsburg, West Virginia
Designed by Peter A. Andersen